www.wadsworth.com

www.wadsworth.com is the World Wide Web site for Thomson Wadsworth and is your direct source to dozens of online resources.

At *www.wadsworth.com* you can find out about supplements, demonstration software, and student resources. You can also send email to many of our authors and preview new publications and exciting new technologies.

www.wadsworth.com
Changing the way the world learns®

Navigating the
Research University

Navigating the Research University

A Guide for First-Year Students

Britt Andreatta

University of California, Santa Barbara

THOMSON
™
WADSWORTH

Australia • Canada • Mexico • Singapore • Spain • United Kingdom • United States

Navigating the Research University: A Guide for First-Year Students
Britt Andreatta, Ph.D.

Executive Manager: Carolyn Merrill
Technology Project Manager: Joe Gallagher
Advertising Project Manager: Linda Yip
Senior Project Manager, Editorial Production:
  Samantha Ross
Manufacturing Manager: Marcia Locke
Permissions Editor: Chelsea Junget
Production Service: Laura Horowitz,
  Hearthside Publishing Services

Photo Manager: Sheri Blaney
Cover Designer: Paula Goldstein
Cover Art: Calder, Alexander (1898-1976),
  © 2004 Estate of Alexander Calder/Artists
  Rights Society (ARS), New York. "Untitled,"
  1930. Oil on canvas, Private Collection.
  Photo: Art Resource, NY
Compositor: ATLIS Graphics
Text/Cover Printer: Malloy Incorporated

Thomson Higher Education
25 Thomson Place
Boston, MA 02210-1202
USA

Asia (including India)
Thomson Learning
5 Shenton Way
#01-01 UIC Building
Singapore 068808

Australia/New Zealand
Thomson Learning Australia
102 Dodds Street
Southbank, Victoria 3006
Australia

Canada
Thomson Nelson
1120 Birchmount Road
Toronto, Ontario M1K 5G4
Canada

UK/Europe/Middle East/Africa
Thomson Learning
High Holborn House
50-51 Bedford Road
London WC1R 4LR
United Kingdom

Library of Congress Control Number:
2005920674

ISBN 0-534-64419-8

Discussion of material in Chapters 5, 6, and 7 is based on findings from the "Your First College Year"
survey by the Higher Education Research Institute, and is used with permission.

SECTION I Academic Development

Section III Community Development

Chapter 9 Planning for the Future 322

Preface

The first year of college is an important time in a young adult's life. It is a time filled with transition as the student adjusts to the academic demands of higher education while simultaneously dealing with social and personal issues associated with young adulthood. This is true whether the student is attending a local community college, a private liberal arts institution, or a premiere research university. However, the experiences associated with each type of institution can by quite different. While many guides and texts exist that discuss the college experience, texts that explore and describe issues associated with undergraduate education at *a research university* have been nonexistent. Many instructors, like myself, have been forced to compile readers from a wide variety of sources, often with large gaps in specific content or perspective.

Additionally, the transition for many high school and transfer students to the academic rigor of a research institution can be difficult. While students are expected to adapt to their university's demands, few texts provide them with guidance in *how* to do so. Students often gain skills in academic inquiry via a slow progression through discipline-based courses with little understanding of how to accelerate or maximize their academic performance. While many fine texts exist that introduce students to "skills for college success," many of these are not appropriately targeted for the student at a research university with its unique academic focus. Furthermore, few texts do justice to the social and personal development students face, which can also be impacted by the unique nature of a research university.

Navigating the Research University: A Guide for First-Year Students seeks to address the issues stated above by providing first-year students with a comprehensive introduction to education at a research university. While orientation sessions and other first-year programs are designed to orient the student to the many aspects of university life, this text will help the student *navigate* the university on a daily basis. It is written primarily for the first-year student, both freshman and transfer and is suited for use in a variety of settings, including:

- Orientation programs
- Summer reading programs
- Introductory writing courses
- Freshman experience courses
- Freshman seminars
- Freshman interest groups, and
- Transfer preparation courses.

Families of first-year students might also find it helpful in understanding their student's experience. It has a broad scope and is applicable to most research institutions in the United States, yet will leave students and instructors the ability to make appropriate connections to their particular university. Utilizing my 15 years of experience as a faculty member and administrator, I hope to provide students with valuable information based on empirical research, student experiences, and the expertise of university staff and administrators.

Features

Each chapter of this text includes the following features:

- A narrative that includes definitions and explanations of the chapter's content
- "What This Means to You"—This feature discusses how the various topics mentioned in the chapter often materialize in the daily experience of the student.
- "Might I Suggest . . ."—In this feature, I offer my personal advice and suggestions for how students can make the most of their educational experience regarding the specific content.
- Student Stories—In this feature, current students share their advice and suggestions for success.
- Reflections for Writing—These questions for written reflection and critical thinking require students to focus on their experience at their particular institution.
- Exercises—Students can do these written or experiential activities to learn more about their particular institution and engage in critical thinking.

Acknowledgments

I would not have been able to write this book without the effort and support of many people. I wish to offer special thanks to the following wonderful friends and colleagues:

The Publishing Team

The amazing team of folks at Thomson Wadsworth who helped guide me at every step along the way. Bill Brisick, Sales Manager; Annie Mitchell, former Executive Manager for College Success; Carolyn Merrill, Executive Manager of College Success; Samantha Ross, Senior Production Project Manager; Chelsea Junget, Permissions Editor; Laura Horowitz, Project Manager, Hearthside Publishing Services; Barbara Willette, Copy Editor, Hearthside Publishing Services; Diane Geesey, Designer, Hearthside Publishing Services; ATLIS Graphics, Compositor.

The Chapter Contributors

Tania Israel, Jarrod Schwartz, John Mitchell, and Brandon Brod for your knowledge and expertise in diversity education—Chapter 7 would not exist without your help. Dr. Ian Kaminsky and Twilight Schroeder, for your help and guidance with Chapter 5. To my friends and colleagues who have helped me teach our freshman experience course over the years. This book is a compilation of your wisdom and experiences. Special thanks to Katya Armistead, Seth Avakian, Brandon Brod, Linda Croyle, Houston Dougherty, Suzanne Perkin, Don Lubach, Brian MacDonald, Otis Madison, Joe Mazares, Claudine Michel, Garrett Naiman, Joy Pehlke, Jack Rivas, Peter Russell, Lisa Slavid, and Chris Stanton (we miss you). Thanks also to Carolyn Buford, Debbie Fleming, Yonie Harris, Al Wyner, and Michael Young, for your support and guidance.

The Reviewers

Thanks also to the following reviewers. Your insights and recommendations helped me to strengthen this text.

Beverly Anderson, *University of Tennessee-Knoxville*
Kenneth Bartlett, *University of Toronto*
Glenn Blalock, *Texas A&M-Corpus Christi*
Anita Blowers, *University of North Carolina at Charlotte*
Kevin Corcoran, *University of Cincinnati*
Brian Corkery, *University of Iowa*
Robin Diana, *University of Rochester*
Dwight Fontenot, *University of Michigan*
William Holmes, *Lamar University*

Liese Hull, *University of Michigan*
Becky Jordan, *University of Kentucky*
Leslie Monaco, *Kent State University*
Denise Ohler, *Edinboro University of Pennsylvania*
Karla Thompson, *New Mexico State University at Carlsbad*
Nancy Taylor, *Radford University*
Sue Wasiolek, *Duke University*
Jodi Webb, *Bowling Green State University*

My Incredible Interns

Over the years, you have not only helped me do my job better but have also taught me so much about students and what they need from their faculty and administrators. I'm sure you'll see our conversations reflected in this text. Thanks for everything! Courtney Ross-Tait, Beth Van Dyke, Joy Phelke, KC Mmeje, Angeli Mancuso, Tricia Rascon, Manuel Silva, Maggie Stack, Elizabeth Ozar, Sara Aminzadeh, Veronica Del Castillo, Jenny Benda, Kassi Wiest, Miles Ashlock, Christine Lai, Nina Tringali, Nacho Ibarra, Michael Jackson, and Amalia Rothschild.

My Students

What would I have done without you? I am so honored for the time you have shared with me and the trust you gave me in supporting your success. I always look forward to your visits to my office and your emails. Thanks for sharing your journey with me and allowing me to learn and grow in the process. I wish to especially thank Brendan Burke, Sarah Davis, Nick Duggan, Shauna Graham, Tanya Grimes, Justin Harris, Dana Hanson, Sabrina Kwist, Justin Palmer, Heena Patel, Erin Pullin, LaTosha Traylor, Andrea Wells, and Adam Zettel.

My Family

First and foremost, I wish to thank Chris Sneathen, my partner and soulmate. Your love and support made this accomplishment possible for me. You are a blessing to me every day. To my children yet to be . . . this book is for you. To my mother, Georgene Burton, for being an awesome role model, and an eagle-eyed proofreader. I wouldn't be here without your love and support. To my father and step-mother, Mike and Barbara Ewing, for supporting me and this project in all the ways you have. Special thanks to my best friends and Santa Barbara family—Lisa Slavid, Tania Israel, Kyle Richards, Geoff Stevens, Henry Rosa, Monica Lenches, Jeanette Gardner, Cameron Nelson, John Mitchell, Garrett Naiman, Twilight Schroeder, Dave Robin, Angeli Mancuso, Teresa Fanucchi, Geoff Green, Pema Teeter, Cherie Carter-Scott, Lynn Stewart, Michael Pomije, and of course, Reverend Karen Weingard. You guys rock! And your love makes my life joyous.

Britt Andreatta

About the Author

Britt Andreatta, Ph.D., is currently the Director of First Year Programs and Leadership Education and a faculty member for the departments of Sociology and Education at the University of California at Santa Barbara. Her duties include coordinating and teaching UCSB's freshmen experience course (INT 20), coordinating programming and mentoring efforts for all 4,000 freshmen students, coordinating programming for parents of freshmen during summer orientation, coordinating UCSB's various leadership programs, serving as a diversity trainer, and teaching "University and Society" (Sociology 102) as well "Introduction to Leadership" (Education 173). She provides training on the nature of the first-year experience (for both freshmen and transfer students) to students, staff, and faculty both at UCSB and at other institutions.

Dr. Andreatta has an M.A. in Communication, and a Ph.D. in Education. Her dissertation, entitled "The Effects of Social and Academic Integration on the Retention of First Year University Students: A Quantitative and Qualitative Study," earned second place in the 1998 Hardee Dissertation of the Year Award. In 1999, she received UCSB's prestigious Getman Service to Students Award. In 2003, Dr. Andreatta won the award for Outstanding Experienced Professional by the American College Personnel Association (ACPA). And in 2005, students on her campus honored her with the Professor of the Year Award. She has also published an *Instructor's Manual for the Freshman Year Experience,* which is used in conjunction with *If Life Is a Game, These Are the Rules* by Dr. Cherie Carter-Scott at over 100 colleges and universities in the United States.

Dr. Andreatta has created several exciting programs for parents of first-year students. In 1994, she designed a workshop entitled "Your Student's First Year," that highlights the many issues that students face during their first year at college and provides family members with suggestions on how to support their student's success. In addition, she recently cocreated "Parents in Transition," (with Dr. Peter Russell and Dr. Jeanne Stanford) a workshop that focuses on the parent-student separation process and helps parents adjust to the changing relationship with their student. Both workshops have been adapted to over 150 colleges and universities in the United States, Canada, and Australia.

She lives with her partner, Chris Sneathen, in Santa Barbara along with their two cats (Misty and Tuscany), two chickens (Thelma and Louise), and a beta fish named TJ. In her spare time, she enjoys surfing, reading, yoga, singing in a band, hanging out with friends, and enjoying the many fine flavors of Ben & Jerry's ice cream. Learn more about her at www.brittandreatta.com.

Introduction

Why This Book

As the author, I am assuming that you currently are, or soon will be, attending a research university as either a freshman or a transfer student. I also attended a research university as an undergraduate, and I now work at one as both the Director of First Year Programs and a faculty member in two academic departments. In my experiences in working with students over the years, from freshmen to graduating seniors, it has become clear to me that many do not fully understand the nature of a research university and the degree to which it affects every aspect of their college experience. The qualities that are unique to a research university shape everything about your daily experience as a college student, including:

- Who teaches you
- The content of your courses
- The focus of your majors
- The resources available to you at your campus
- The expectations faculty have for your academic performance
- The quality of your classmates
- The nature of your social experiences
- Your career choices
- Your development as a future leader

In addition, college students in general face transition issues such as separating from their family, making choices involving alcohol and other drugs, living in a diverse community, getting involved, and developing leadership skills. The purpose of this book is to give you a clear understanding of what a research university is and to offer some suggestions about how you can successfully navigate your college experience. While orientation programs are designed to *orient* you to the various aspects of the institution you are attending, this book will serve as your travel guide, helping you to *navigate* the sometimes rocky and confusing environment.

In this book, I will explain many things that are often understood by the faculty and staff at a research university but that are rarely clearly communicated to, or comprehended by, students. Most new students do not understand how attending a research university really affects their daily lives. In response to this, I have created sidebars throughout each chapter called "What This Means to You" in which I will connect the information you have just read to more concrete examples of student experiences. In addition, I will provide you with some of my hints and suggestions for ways to succeed at a research university. These sidebars are called "Might I Suggest . . ." and will be things I often say to students who meet with me for assistance during their first year. You will also find advice from current students in a feature called "Student Stories." Finally, I will close each chapter with some reflections and exercises that will allow you to take the information from that chapter and personalize it to your experience at the university you attend.

I have organized this book into three areas of development: academic, personal, and community. Each focuses on a different, yet equally important, aspect of your university experience. It is important that you read Chapter 1 first, as it provides the information and background you will need to understand the remaining material. However, at that point, you can read the chapters in the order of importance or necessity to you, knowing that together, they will provide a complete guide to a successful university experience. The content of each chapter mirrors many aspects of education at a research university. Each topic will include current statistics from studies about college students as well as theories that illuminate important aspects of the college experience or student development. This book is interdisciplinary, in that it draws from a wide range of disciplines to form a more complete understanding of the research university experience of first-year students.

If your classes will be beginning soon, I recommend reading the "Quick Start Guide" starting on page 5. This will give you a quick overview of the various things you need to know to immediately navigate your campus and get you ready for the first week of classes.

Information for Students and Instructors

This book has been written to provide all first-year students, both freshmen and transfer students, with useful information for making the most of their experience at a research university. Freshmen and transfer students often have very different needs, so where appropriate, I have provided advice that is specific to each population. However, there are also many places of overlap between the experiences of freshmen and transfer students. In these areas, your own experience as a member of those populations will guide your interpretation of the material. Finally, this text is written to cover the broader themes and issues that are relevant to students at a research university. However, you will need to take this information and put it in the context of your specific university. In this way, you can customize the material to suit your specific needs.

A Word to Freshmen

If you have been admitted to a research university, it means that you have demonstrated a strong performance in high school, which indicates that you are prepared to *begin* a university-level education. Your admission is a reflection of your potential, but your choices as a university student will ultimately determine your performance and success. With this in mind, it is important to remember that this is not "high school, the sequel"—it is an entirely new level of education that you have not yet seen nor experienced. Your ability to successfully adjust to this new experience greatly depends on your willingness to let go of how you used to do things and enthusiastically embrace being a beginner again. Your first year in college will be somewhat similar to your first year in high school. There will be a new and unfamiliar environment, higher expectations for your performance, and also many students who are older and more experienced than you. This can be disconcerting after you have worked so hard to achieve so much success in your high school. You definitely bring many strengths to your university experience, and you were selected from thousands of other applicants because of the promise you have demonstrated. Feel good about your past accomplishments and also embrace the attitude of being a new learner again. You will eventually gain the skills and experience you need to master this environment as well. I hope this book will guide you in making the most of your university experience from your first day to your graduation ceremony.

A Word to Transfer Students

If you have been admitted to a research university, it means that you have demonstrated a strong performance in college (most likely a two-year community college), which indicates that you are prepared to *begin* a university-level education. Your admission does not guarantee that you will automatically be as successful as you were at your previous institution—it is an entirely new level of education that you have not yet seen or experienced (unless you were already attending a research university). You do have a distinct advantage over the freshmen, which is to say that you have a lot of experience with some aspects of higher education such as choosing classes, going to office hours, and writing a research paper. However, all of these aspects change as you transfer from your previous institution to a research university. In some cases, the changes are minor; others will bear no resemblance to your previous experiences. In addition, transfer students have much less time to adjust to the new environment than freshmen do, as you have to get going on your major and graduation requirements immediately.

The greatest error that transfer students make is to think, "I know how to do this already" and not seek the assistance they need or utilize the support that is offered, such as orientation, advising, and counseling. This choice can have a negative impact on both your academic and social transition to your new campus. You definitely bring many strengths to your university experience, and you were selected from hundreds of other applicants because of the promise you have demonstrated. Feel good about your past accomplishments and also embrace the attitude of being a new learner again. You will eventually gain the skills and experience you need to master this environment as well. I hope this book will guide you in making the most of your university experience from your first day to your graduation ceremony.

A Word to Instructors

I hope you will find this text useful for helping students navigate the research university environment. The order of the chapters mirrors how I teach my own course and the order in which I present the material. I have found that it is imperative to focus on the academic issues first, as students are expected to begin performing immediately at the university level. While students are certainly going through social and personal transition issues as well, I have found that discussions of these topics are more effective later in the term when students have built more trust and rapport with both their instructors and classmates.

However, I recognize that each campus is unique and that your students might best be served by a different order of material. For this reason, I have written each chapter to stand alone. While there may be references to prior or following chapters, knowledge of that content is not needed to comprehend the material presented in any one chapter. With that said, I do suggest assigning at least portions of Chapter 1 first, as it provides an overview of what research is and the mission of a research university.

The material I chose to present in each chapter represents my own search over the years for appropriate studies and theories that are both relevant to students and academically appropriate for a research university. However, there are certainly other theories and studies that would have worked as well. Feel free to augment this material with other, even contradictory, material as a way to customize it for the needs of your students and the values of your particular campus. Finally, this text is accompanied by an instructor's manual/test bank that features sample syllabi, discussion questions, classroom activities, exam questions, writing assignments, and recommended readings. I hope you find it useful in creating a dynamic and engaging academic course for your students.

As you use these materials, please know that I am eager to hear any suggestions you might have for future editions of this text or the instructor's manual/test bank. Please send any comments or suggestions you have to me via email at britt@brittandreatta.com.

Quick Start Guide

This Quick Start Guide is designed to help you navigate the first few days of attendance at your university. Below are typical issues or questions that new students need to address before the start of classes. Many of these issues are addressed in much more depth in subsequent chapters, but this guide will provide you with the essential information to get started.

Academic Issues

Advising, Registration, and Orientation

Before you can start attending classes, you need to select and enroll in classes for your first term. Most universities provide some kind of orientation program to present students with important information on academic requirements and the registration process. It is strongly recommended that both freshmen and transfer students have assistance in selecting courses their first term, as inappropriate choices can have negative consequences for both progress and performance. If you have not already attended such a program, contact your university to find out the options that are still available to you and attend one as soon as you can. Even if formal orientation programs have concluded, you can still arrange an individual appointment with an academic advisor in your college.

Finding Your Classes

Before the first day of classes, it is a good idea to walk around campus to find and confirm the location of each class. That way, you will not find yourself lost on campus or late for your classes. Often, locations and times of classes can change from what was published when you enrolled. Always double-check the times and locations using the most up-to-date information, such as an online schedule of classes or a recent printout of your confirmed schedule.

First Classes

The first day of classes will include full lectures, so come to class prepared to take notes and to stay the entire time. You will also receive a syllabus in each class that gives you valuable information. It will tell you the books and readers that are required for your class and also when assignments will be due. It's always a good idea to review all your syllabi together the first couple of days of the term. That way, if you discover that you will have four final exams on one day, you have time to drop or switch one of your classes before the deadline.

Adding and Dropping Classes

Your campus should have a publication that explains the process for adding and dropping classes, including the deadlines for doing so and any fees that are affiliated with the process. It's a good idea to write these dates in your planner so that you don't miss them. If you know that you need to adjust your schedule, be sure to do so right away. If you have any questions or concerns, see an advisor in your college as soon as you can. If you do not plan on completing a course, be sure you officially drop it from your schedule—lack of attendance does not guarantee that you will be dropped by the instructor.

Books and Readers

Your syllabus for each course will tell you the books and readers that you will need. It's a good idea to purchase these as soon as possible, as sometimes the supply runs out and students have to wait a week or so before new ones arrive. You will have a full reading schedule the first week, so it's important to get started right away. Books will be found in the campus bookstore and also at many on-line bookstores. Most bookstores have some kind of organizational system that allows you to look up a particular course and instructor to find the books assigned. You might have the choice to buy a new copy or a previously owned copy (which will be cheaper but will also have someone else's highlighting and notes). Used books can be problematic because you may end up with the wrong edition of the book or you might find that the previous owner's comments hinder your own learning process. You might find that your instructor also lists optional books. You will want to ask your instructor whether they are truly optional or whether there is an expectation that students will utilize these materials in some fashion. There is probably a short period of time in which books can be returned to the place of purchase. Be sure you pay attention to these deadlines if you decide to drop that course.

A reader is a compilation of articles and other readings that the instructor has put together in a packet or book. The syllabus will usually tell you where the reader can be purchased. Readers are usually *not* returnable once purchased, so make sure you plan to stay enrolled in the course before you buy the reader. Finally, ask your instructor whether or not you are expected to bring the books and readers to class. Unlike high school, most university classes do not require students to bring materials to each class. For this reason, you will find that very few campuses have lockers for students' things. Students typically carry the items they need for that day's classes in a backpack or tote bag.

Notebooks and Supplies

Very little guidance is provided to students regarding notebooks and other supplies. You might occasionally find a reference to a certain calculator that you need or a specific type of folder in which to submit papers, but those specifications are pretty rare. As a result, you really have the freedom to purchase the types of school supplies that best suit your needs. Some students prefer three-ring binders; others like spiral-bound notebooks. Some students like to keep the notes for all of their classes in one place; others like a separate notebook for each course. It's really up to you to discover the system that keeps you the most organized. As you learn more about your needs and skills, you might change your preferences over time.

Meeting Your Instructors

You will find in Chapter 1 that instructors can have many different titles. Not all instructors are professors, so calling an instructor by that title might be incorrect. Until your instructors clarify this for you, the best term for your primary instructor (the one leading the lectures) is "Doctor." Most of your primary instructors have Ph.D.s, so this title is the most accurate and respectful. You will also have secondary instructors who lead discussion sections or labs. These instructors are usually graduate students, so the appropriate title is "Mr." or "Ms." until you are told otherwise. Some instructors are comfortable with your using their first name, but do so only if they give you permission.

Paying Tuition

If you have not already paid your tuition for your first term, you will need to take care of this right away. You should have received some type of billing statement from the university regarding the payment deadline and forms of payment they will accept. Be sure you pay attention to this deadline, which can creep up on you quickly during the hectic first days of the term. Also, sometimes the deadline is at 12 noon rather than the end of the day. Missing the deadline may have some penalties, such as being dropped from your classes and/or having to pay a late fee. Sometime deadlines are adjusted for students who are receiving financial aid.

Receiving Financial Aid

If you are receiving financial aid, you would have received some information from your financial aid office regarding when and where you will receive these funds. Again, there may be deadlines you need to adhere to or documents you need to process. Review the materials and make sure you follow the instructions. Failing to do so can bring about penalties and may delay the disbursement of your funds.

Attending Convocation and Other Events

Your campus probably has organized a series of events and programs to welcome new students to campus. These should be published in some type of calendar or announcement that either was sent to you at home or is available once you arrive on campus. An important event to look for is an official induction ceremony, often called Convocation. Attendance at this event is usually mandatory and is a great way to learn some important information you need to know as a new student. Also, there may be mandatory meetings for your college or major department, and your attendance will be expected. Be sure you keep track of the dates and times of these events so that you don't miss them. There will also be many optional events that you might find it useful to attend, such as study skills workshops or orientations to the library. Read through the calendar of events and plan to attend as many as you can.

Social and Personal Issues

Moving to Campus

If you are moving to campus, you will want to make sure to allow yourself enough time to move in your belongings and get settled before classes begin. If you are moving into a university-owned residence hall or apartment, you will receive an informative packet about when to move in and what to bring. Read through this carefully and follow the instructions. This packet should also tell you about utilities that are included, how to receive mail and packages, and any meal services that are available to you, including where and when meals are served.

If you are moving into housing that is independent of the university, you probably signed a lease or contract of some kind that outlines important information that you should be familiar with. Most likely, you will need to arrange for basic utilities such as phone, electricity, gas, and cable. Contact your local utility companies to set up these services. Many require deposits, so you might want to discuss this with roommates. Finally, ask whether there are any student discounts or specials that are available to you.

Living with Roommates

If you will be living with others, it is important to establish some guidelines early on about how you will live together in a way that respects each person's preferences. It is a good idea to have a meeting in the first week that you live together to establish some groundrules that each person agrees to follow. That way, you won't have to worry about these issues later on or figure out how to confront someone if they are doing something that bothers you. Some typical issues to discuss are:

- How will shared bills be handled? Who will put the various utilities in his or her name? How will costs be split or shared? What happens if someone doesn't pay his or her share on time?
- How do people feel about sharing belongings, such as clothing, cars, and computers? Will food be shared or does each person have a separate supply? If so, how is that indicated? Can people borrow without asking?

- What kind of study environment does each person need? When and how much do they need to study? How will noise, such as music and TV, be addressed if someone needs quiet for studying?
- How do people feel about overnight guests? Do the others need to be notified in advance or asked for permission? Is there a limit to how many overnight guests a person can have in a term or a limit to the number of consecutive nights? Who will ensure that the guest adheres to the ground rules? When people share bedrooms, are there any special considerations needed for romantic or sexual relationships?
- How will cleaning duties be shared? How will people know what needs to be done, and by when? What if someone doesn't do his or her share? What happens if people have different comfort levels with messiness or cleanliness?
- How do people feel about hosting parties? Do others need to be notified in advance or asked for permission? What about buying and serving alcohol? If this violates campus or state laws, how does that affect everyone? Are there special considerations for minors? What about having or using other drugs in the living space?

These are only a few of the items to discuss but you will want to create a shared understanding of how you will live together. You might also want to establish periodic meetings to see if anything needs to be discussed or addressed. Your campus may also have some handouts or guidebooks on successful roommate relationships that would be helpful to utilize.

Bank Accounts

Conducting business is generally easier if you have an account with a bank that is local to your university's community. Many local businesses do not take out-of-town checks, and it is certainly easier to make deposits and withdrawals if there are branches or ATMs on or near campus. For this reason, many local banks offer student specials to start a checking account, and you might want to explore these options. If your family will be making deposits to your bank account, choose a bank that has a branch in your hometown. If your campus has a period of welcoming events, you might find that banks and other local utility companies are present on campus to facilitate signing up for their services.

Parking

If parking is not affiliated with your living arrangements, you will need to contact the university's parking office to find out options available to you. Some campuses have ample parking, and students are able to purchase parking permits easily. Other campuses with limited parking often have additional stipulations regarding eligibility for parking, such as how far from campus a person lives. In addition, campus parking may be zoned for different groups, such as students, staff, and faculty. Parking fees can range from free to very expensive. Look into the options that are available to you to decide whether having a car on campus is worth it to you.

Health Records

Most universities require new students to supply health records to the campus health center. You should have received information about this from your campus with instructions about where and when to send these files. In addition, many campuses now require that students show proof of certain immunizations, such as those for hepatitis B or meningitis, in order to stay enrolled. Be sure that you take care of these items before the stated deadlines. Also, if you have been under the care of a psychiatrist for mental health issues, it is important that these records also be included. The stresses of the first year of college can often affect mental health, so it's always a good idea to make sure your doctor is in communication with campus health officials in order to guarantee the best care for you.

Attending Events

In addition to academic events, your campus will probably host many social events to help students get to know each other as well as the campus. Some of these are designed for certain populations, such as students living in a residence hall or students pursuing a certain major; others are open to everyone. Some are educational in nature; others are purely social. Again, read through the calendar of events and take note of the ones that interest you. These special events are usually not repeated throughout the year, so take advantage of them while you can. These events can be a great way to help you meet new friends, become familiar with various opportunities and activities at your campus, and help you feel comfortable with the new environment.

Academic Development

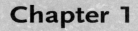

Chapter 1

Research and the Research University

If you are, or soon will be, attending a research university, it is important for you to grasp the nature of research in general to fully understand how this affects you as a student. The research mission affects every aspect of an undergraduate student's education, including what you learn in your classes, the majors from which you can choose, who teaches your classes and the quality of their teaching, the makeup of the student body, various opportunities that are or will be available to you, and your future options after college. Many students apply to research universities because of their prestige without really understanding the nature of the research mission.

This chapter will provide you with an overview of what research is, how faculty conduct research and share it with the world, the ways in which research affects almost every aspect of the university environment, and the various members of the campus community. Whether you are a freshman or a transfer student, this knowledge will provide you with an important base from which to understand the information presented in the remaining chapters as well as your own daily experiences as a university student.

The Purpose of Research

Research is the process of discovering and creating *new* knowledge—that which has not been known before. This is very different from teaching, which is the dissemination of known knowledge. Research is very important to human society because it has allowed us to develop almost every aspect of what surrounds you. From turning on a light switch, to the medicines you take, to eating microwave popcorn, to cell phones that take pictures, research has played a role in bringing these things to society.

Research also plays a role in making our society a better place by allowing us to understand how people function in the world and how they interact with and influence each other. You are surrounded by research every day. Pick up any magazine and you will find comments like these:

Researchers at the University of Florida have found a way to embed drugs within the inside surface of a contact lens. The enhanced contacts will be used to treat eye disease like glaucoma, which need small, steady doses of medication (*Men's Health,* August 2003).

"Adult notions of hypercompetition and overscheduling have created a culture of parenting that's more akin to produce development, and it's robbing families of time together," theorizes William Doherty, a University of Minnesota professor of marriage and family therapy, adding, "Frantic families equal fragile families." (*Time,* October 27, 2003).

New knowledge can come about in a variety of ways from happy accidents such as the one in which researchers at 3M created the nonsticky glue that makes Post-it notes so useful to following a hunch, as many inventors have done. Through a process of trial and error, Ben Franklin discovered electricity and the Wright brothers discovered how to fly. There is also the process of formal research, which is done in a detailed and very structured way to systematically search for new answers. For example, scientists systematically test various chemicals and the impact they have on cancer cells. This requires a steady and slow process of trying something new and recording the results, making an infinitesimally small adjustment, and then trying it again and recording the results. This process allows researchers to chart their progress and to recreate findings should they prove to be successful.

Research can happen in all kinds of places and can be done by all kinds of people. Some prominent places in which research is conducted are corporations as they work to develop "new and improved" products to sell, government offices and labs, private "think tanks," hospitals, and educational institutions of all kinds. While all of these places for research are important, this book will focus on research as it occurs in a university setting and how this affects the education of undergraduate students.

The Research Mission of a University

According to the Carnegie Foundation for the Advancement of Teaching, there are 3,941 institutions of higher education in the United States, ranging from two-year community colleges to Ivy League private universities. The Merriam-Webster OnLine Dictionary defines a college as "an independent institution of higher learning offering a course of general studies leading to a bachelor's degree." A university is defined as "an institution of higher learning providing facilities for teaching and research and authorized to grant academic degrees; specifically one made up of an undergraduate division which confers bachelor's degrees and a graduate division which comprises a graduate school and professional schools each of which may confer masters degrees and doctorates." As a result, a university may house several colleges and schools within it.

A research university is a university that has a research mission. This means that the *primary* goal of the institution is to bring together a group of the best minds in the world to do their research. These people, the faculty, are hired and promoted largely on the basis of their research skills—in other words, a primary focus of their jobs is to produce new knowledge and share it with the world through publications. This requires lots of time and incredible skill. In addition, these faculty members need to disseminate known knowledge in a process called teaching. Both aspects are important in a student's educational experience at a research university.

In the United States, the Carnegie Foundation for the Advancement of Teaching uses size, the amount of federal funding received, and the number of doctoral degrees awarded per year to classify all universities as public or private and "intensive" versus "extensive." To see the Carnegie Classification of Institutions of Higher Education or to find out how your university is classified, see Appendix A or visit the Carnegie Foundation's website at www.carnegiefoundation.org.

In addition to the Carnegie Foundation's classification system, research universities can distinguish themselves by becoming members of the prestigious Association of American Universities (AAU). According to the AAU's website, the AAU "is an organization of research universities devoted to maintaining a strong system of academic research and education." It consists of sixty U.S. universities and two Canadian universities. The AAU was founded in 1900 by a group of fourteen Ph.D.-granting universities in the United States to strengthen and standardize doctoral programs. Today, the primary purpose of the AAU is to provide a forum for the development and implementation of institutional and national policies that promote strong programs in academic research and scholarship as well as undergraduate, graduate, and professional education. A current listing of members in the Association of American Universities is available online at www.aau.edu and member institutions are indicated in Appendix A. If you look at your campus's website or promotional materials, you might find references to both of these organizations.

Who Conducts Research

Conducting research requires a set of specific and well-honed skills, as does flying a large commercial plane. Just as a pilot needs to go through extensive training and years of practice to become a qualified and excellent pilot, so does a researcher. Some of the specific skills and abilities that a person needs to excel at research include critical thinking, reading, analyzing, creative thinking, and writing, to name a few. In addition, researchers must be very knowledgeable about the area or topic they are researching. A person would need to know chemistry very well to research aspects of it, and another person would need to know history in order to conduct historical research.

Not all people are good at, or interested in, doing research—just as not all people want to fly planes. Research is a type of career that certain people are drawn to and must spend years of study to prepare for. Faculty who are hired to be researchers must have an advanced degree in their field. Types of advanced degrees include a Doctorate of Philosophy (Ph.D.), a Doctorate of Medicine (M.D.), a Doctorate of Education (Ed.D.), a Master's in Business Administration (M.B.A.), and a Juris Doctor (J.D.). These advanced degrees signify that after completing his or her undergraduate degree in college, the person chose to go on for more schooling to become an expert in a particular field. Many of these degrees require several years of graduate study; for example, a Ph.D. in Anthropology takes five to seven years to complete, and an M.D. requires four years of medical school followed by a residency program.

Most faculty members at research universities have a Ph.D. in a particular discipline, such as physics. A discipline is a field or area of study, such as history, biology, mathematics, literature, dramatic arts, sociology, electrical engineering, or music. A large part of the degree is learning and mastering the research skills that are required for that particular discipline as well as conducting an original research project. This research project must focus on a narrow topic within the larger discipline. This research project culminates in the person's doctoral dissertation, which is a sort of "final paper" exemplifying the person's research skills

Might I Suggest...

If you are like most freshmen, you probably didn't know what a research university was really about, nor are you particularly interested in a career as a researcher or a professor. That's OK! The best part about attending a research university is the research, so I strongly recommend getting involved in research during your college experience. Not to do so is kind of like going to the Hershey's Chocolate Factory and not trying the chocolate. Sure, there are other things to do, but you miss out on the whole point of the place. At a research university, you have the amazing opportunity to participate in research by working with faculty in their labs, classrooms, and even far away from the campus on research sites. Students at my campus have been involved with the following:

- Traveling to Tibet and recording the unwritten languages of mountain tribes
- Documenting and coding violence in television programs
- Photographing the annual fashion shows in Milan
- Testing how a new medicine affects the symptoms of drug addiction
- Deep-sea diving to document the mating patterns of a newly discovered fish
- Taking samples from the ice core in Antarctica

You could participate in groundbreaking research as an undergraduate student and even publish or present your work as a scholar. It's an opportunity not to be missed!

There are several ways to get involved in research. First, you can approach faculty members whose classes you enjoy and ask whether they have any positions open in their research projects. Second, you can visit the department to see whether there are any postings for jobs or positions. Finally, there might be an office on your campus that coordinates student involvement in research. Check with your college or major department to find out more about this. And don't be discouraged if you have to start out with less-than-glamorous work. Often, faculty members expect you to work a bit with them before they give you access to the truly cool stuff, so be patient.

and specialty. Every Ph.D. program around the globe requires doctoral students to do extensive study in their discipline and then to choose a very narrow area in which to focus their research.

Today's most famous theorists were once doctoral students and were required to follow this standard process. Let's look at an example. Dr. Stephen Hawking, the world-renowned physicist who, among other things, proposed the existence of black holes, attended the University College at Oxford University as an undergraduate, where he studied physics and graduated with a degree in Natural Science. He went on to earn his Ph.D. at Trinity Hall at Cambridge University, where he narrowed his interests to Cosmology, which is the study of the universe as a whole and the basic laws that govern it. After earning his Ph.D., he worked at Cambridge University. Dr. Hawking's research led to the groundbreaking work of combining the theory of general relativity with quantum theory, which is considered one of the great developments in science. Throughout his astonishing career, Dr. Hawking has published articles and books on a wide range of topics within his field. If you visit his website at www.hawking.org.uk, you will find a list of his 184 publications from 1965 to 2002.

Although not all research university faculty are as famous as Stephen Hawking, most have a similar history. They have all completed intense academic study and are motivated by a desire to learn that is so strong that they pursued it as a career. Many faculty members are also motivated by the desire to teach. You can find out more about your faculty's research history and publications by looking them up in your campus library's database or by visiting them in office hours and asking about their work.

The Academic Disciplines

There are literally hundreds of academic disciplines in the world, and it would not be very efficient or cost-effective for every campus to do research in every discipline. As a result, each college or university chooses to offer a certain set of disciplines in which students can earn a degree. You can discover the disciplines that exist at your institution by looking at the academic departments that are listed in the general catalog. Each department will indicate the particular disciplines that are offered.

If your institution has a biology department, this means that your university has a group of faculty who specialize in research in the field of biology and will offer one or more majors within the biological sciences. Within that field of biology, each faculty member will specialize in a very narrow subfield of that discipline. If you explore your general catalog, you will find that each major lists the areas of study that are available at your school.

For example, at the University of California at Santa Barbara, we offer six subfields of biology: molecular, cellular, developmental, ecological, evolutionary, and marine. This means that students here can find several faculty members who are nationally recognized for their work in each of these areas, as well as ample courses to choose from on these topics. Likewise, our department of communication specializes in three subfields: mass media, interpersonal communication, and organizational communication. The faculty that are here specialize in one of these major areas and are engaged in research and teaching classes on topics related to these areas. As a result, a student at this school could focus on one of these areas in his or her own choice of classes while completing a major in this field. There are obviously many more areas within this field, such as rhetoric and intercultural communication, which are not offered at this institution. However, you will find rhetoric programs at Purdue University, the University of Nebraska at Lincoln, The Ohio State University, Carnegie Mellon University, and many others. Programs in intercultural communication can be found at the Pennsylvania State University, Pepperdine University, the University of Wisconsin, and the University of Kansas, to name a few.

Essentially, a department consists of a group of faculty members who are experts in their subfields and who offer a set of courses that satisfy a bachelor's degree and often a master's or doctoral degree. Each university must decide which fields it will offer and then build a strong department by hiring faculty members who are renowned researchers in that field. It is generally better for a department to focus on a certain set of subfields and then bring in the best researchers it can to create breadth and depth within those few subfields than to try to offer a wider range of subfields.

It's important to remember that the primary mission of the institution is to conduct research, so these decisions are made from the perspective of carrying out that mission to the highest degree possible. Each institution makes informed choices about being very strong in certain areas, knowing that other areas will become the hallmark of another campus.

All of these various academic disciplines can be a bit unwieldy, so they are often clustered with similar disciplines that share general philosophies or practices. According to Compton and Tait (1992), these clusters can be defined in the following ways:

- The humanities are the academic disciplines that study human thought and experience through the written record of what people have thought, felt, or experienced in a variety of cultures. Subject areas include languages, literature, philosophy, history, and religion.
- The social sciences are the academic disciplines that study human beings and their behavior from a variety of perspectives: as individuals (psychology), within social groups (sociology, ethnic studies), within cultures (anthropology), within social structures (education), or even as economic and political entities (economics, political science, global studies).
- The arts are the academic disciplines that explore and represent human thought and behavior in creative works. Creating works of art is a way of both coming to understand and expressing ideas and feelings. Subject areas include studio art, dramatic art, film studies, dance, and music.
- Quantitative studies are the academic disciplines that create systems for describing the physical world or human behavior in abstract or mathematical terms. Subject areas include mathematics, statistics, and computer science.
- The physical and biological sciences are the academic disciplines that study the physical world, its inhabitants, and the symbolic relationships within.

Subject areas include biology, ecology, physics, geology, chemistry, and environmental studies.
- The engineering sciences are the academic disciplines that study how scientific knowledge can be applied to practical uses for society. Subject areas include civil, electrical, mechanical, computer, and chemical engineering.

Not all campuses organize their departments in these exact groupings, but the general categories are fairly accurate. These categories are not distinct, and aspects of our world can overlap several disciplines. For example, poverty is a topic

What This Means to You

One assumption that the faculty and administrators make is that students have "done their homework" in looking at what a school has to offer. We often assume that you looked at the various types of colleges and universities available to you and chose to attend a research university because you wanted this particular type of education. We also assume that you explored which majors were offered before you applied to various universities; if so, then you should find yourself at an institution that offers the kinds of fields you might want to major in. If you did not check this out before applying or if you were undecided at that time, you might discover that your institution does not offer what you want. If this is the case, you can consider choosing from the majors that are offered or transferring to a different institution that does offer what you are looking for. I discuss choosing a major in more depth in Chapter 3, but you can receive very helpful advice from academic and career advisors, as well as the faculty, at your campus. Many disciplines overlap, so you might be able to find a field comparable to the one you were hoping to study.

Some students are disappointed to find the research emphasis at a research university. They were hoping to find classes that prepared them for specific careers. While there are very few classes that do this, the majority of students graduate from research universities and go on to successful jobs and careers in nonresearch areas and many find the research background they gained helpful in their careers. The prestige of their degree does have value in the workplace even though the content of their courses might not have given them specific job skills. It is true that to be competitive in today's job market, many students need to gain important job skills while in college. The best way to do this is through internships. Internships provide students with preprofessional work opportunities in real companies and organizations in the surrounding community, on campus, and even in another city, state, or country. Some internships are paid and some are not, but all will provide valuable job training as well as a chance to "try on" a career before you commit to it. To learn more about internships, visit the office on your campus that provides career advising. It is never too early to secure an internship, and many career advisors recommend completing at least three before you graduate.

that can be explored and researched in all of these disciplines. An economist might explore the relationship between minimum wage jobs and the number of people living in poverty. A sociologist might research the relationship between the quality of a poorer community's public high school education and the college success of its graduates. A biologist might study the effects that inadequate nutrition has on bone density. An ethnomusicologist would be interested in the forms of music that have their roots in poorer communities. A mathematician might want to create a statistical model of how long it would take a family on welfare to rise above the poverty level on the basis of different salaries. As you can see, the possibilities are endless.

How Research Is Conducted

Discussing research in a general sense is a bit challenging to do because each discipline has a unique approach. There are sets of prescribed processes, called *methods,* that researchers can use to best address the topic they are exploring. For example, a biologist might be interested in what causes a healthy cell to become cancerous and multiply out of control. To learn more about that process, the researcher will need to work with cells and do a variety of tests that involve lab work, Petri dishes, microscopes, chemistry, and so on. A biologist could not ask the cells to fill out a survey about why they multiply. On the other hand, a sociologist who is interested in how the economy of a neighborhood is related to crime rates might not find it very useful to look at skin samples of criminals under the microscope. In this case, looking at police records and census data would be far more useful. The more creative disciplines such as music or art focus more on the creation or production of new works, so "research" in these fields is often focused on the work associated with writing an innovative composition or creating a specific sculpture. However, there are also subfields in these disciplines that might use more traditional research methods. For example, ethnomusicology is the study of how music relates to the expression of a specific culture, so a researcher in this field might analyze sound patterns of a certain regional genre

Might I Suggest...

Even though you might be taking classes in a wide variety of disciplines, there will be some connections among them. Students gain the most from their education when they can draw connections and see similarities among the various courses they are taking. Instead of approaching your history class as a separate entity unto itself, see how what you are learning in that history class might be relevant to your biology class or your language class. Look for the bigger picture and the interdisciplinary nature of things whenever you can. You might even find that this allows you to bring a unique and critical analysis to a course you are taking and ultimately improves your performance in that course.

or conduct surveys to ask people in a particular tribe about the ceremonial purpose of their songs.

Each field has its own way of conducting research, and there are certain methods of inquiry that are appropriate for getting answers to questions. One of the things you will learn during your university education is how these fields differ from each other and the various ways in which research is conducted in each field. Once you select a major, you will be introduced to the methods that are appropriate to the field you selected to study. In chemistry, you will learn how researchers precisely measure and control various experiments. In anthropology, you will be introduced to how researchers observe and document aspects of a culture without interfering with it. These introductions will allow you to better understand and evaluate the various material you will learn in your courses for a particular major. Should you choose to pursue research as a career, you will be taught research methods and procedures in much more depth in your graduate studies. It would be impossible to provide an overview here of all the disciplines because the list would take up the rest of this book! Suffice it to say that learning about research will make up a large portion of your education at a research institution. If you want to learn more, use your general catalog to see the types of research classes that are offered in various departments.

How Knowledge Is Shared

Referring back to the purpose of research as finding and creating new knowledge, it is important that once this knowledge is found, it can be shared with others. This sharing of knowledge is another primary aspect of the "job" of being a researcher. As a result, faculty must continually engage in writing and speaking about their research as a way to add what they have learned to the body of knowledge of their field. This is most often done in writing in the form of journal articles and books. The way most research is shared with other researchers is through something called a scholarly journal, which is a monthly or quarterly publication that features write-ups of the latest studies that have been done in a particular field. Each discipline has several of these journals, with each journal focusing on a certain aspect of that field. Most researchers subscribe to several of these journals to stay current on the latest findings, and the campus library subscribes to hundreds of journals so that they are accessible to faculty and students alike.

For example, in the field of education, some of the scholarly journals are the *Journal of Higher Education,* the *Journal of College Student Development, Higher Education Review,* and the *American Educational Research Journal.* Some journals for the field of marine science are the *Journal of Marine Biology and Ecology, Marine Ecology Progress Series, Ecological Monographs, Oecologia,* and *Marine Biology.* It is important for a researcher to stay up on the latest developments in his or her field, so reading journals is a big part of a researcher's job. Your faculty members will often be reading several books and journals simultaneously. The ability to read and comprehend copious amounts of material on a consistent basis is a trademark skill for the research profession. (See "What This Means to You" below.)

While your faculty are in the process of learning about others' research, they are engaging in their own research with the ultimate goal of also sharing it with their professional colleagues. The type of research that faculty members conduct varies greatly and is guided by their discipline. Some faculty members are conducting experimental studies of some kind while others are analyzing already existing material to create new connections and understandings. Once a researcher completes his or her work, it is time to write up that research in some form in order to share the new knowledge with others by having it published. Studies are generally shared in the form of a paper or journal article, while other research lends itself more to being a book chapter or an entire book. You will find that, in general, writing a series of journal articles is more affiliated with the sciences, whereas writing a book or book chapter is more affiliated with the humanities. Research also takes a lot of time. Depending on the field, it can take several months to years to initiate, plan, conduct, and complete a study. For this reason, most researchers are simultaneously working on several research projects, each in a different stage of completion. For example, Dr. Tania Israel, an associate professor in clinical psychology, is currently working on the following projects:

- Three studies in which she is preparing to collect data
- Four studies in which she is collecting and analyzing data
- Six manuscripts in preparation for submission to be published
- Three articles submitted for publication and awaiting reviews from editors
- Two proposals submitted for book chapters in other editor's books
- One book that she is coediting and providing feedback to the authors who are submitting chapters

What This Means to You

Ultimately, this affects your daily experience as a student in that your faculty members pass along expectations for this level of reading to you. We are used to reading large amounts of material, so faculty rarely think we are assigning "too much." When we put together our books and readers for your classes, we are truly assessing what we think you need to know—and for faculty, it's hard for us to eliminate material because so much of it seems relevant. In addition, we put together our courses independently of each other; we don't compare notes to see how much is being assigned in mathematics or art history. As a result, you could find yourself in a set of courses with heavy reading loads. The sooner you develop the skills needed to read and comprehend large amounts of material, the better off you will be. This and other important skills are discussed in Chapter 2.

This particular faculty member is engaged in several research and writing projects simultaneously; many of your faculty members will be just as busy working on one book rather than several articles. This workload is very typical, and it does not include the work of teaching several classes a year as well as holding office hours and serving on campus and nationwide committees. These responsibilities also take up a lot of time. It is common for most faculty to work fifty to sixty hours per week—more than is required for the average full-time job.

Scholarly Standards for Publication

It would be very chaotic if every person writing up research did so in his or her own unique way. It would be very difficult to review and analyze the work in any kind of consistent or fair manner. As a result, some professional standards have been created for academic writing that all researchers and scholarly publishers follow. One aspect of this standardization has to do with writing style, and there are several manuals and guides that faculty use; these are discussed in more detail in Chapter 2. Another aspect of this standardization has to do with format. There is no one standard format for books or book chapters; each project is different, and the format is created in consultations between the researcher, editor, and publisher. However, empirical studies *do* have a specific format with which they need to be written, and they are usually published as articles in scholarly journals.

Essentially, every article needs to include the following sections in the following order; since you will no doubt read hundreds of these journal articles before you graduate, it's important for you to understand them as well:

1. An *introduction* to the general topic being studied.
2. A review of all that is currently known about that topic—this is known as the *literature review* and is an overview of all (yes, all) relevant past research, most of which has been published in journals and books.
3. From the literature review comes a discussion of what makes this study different from that which has already been done—in other words, a justification of what makes it "new" knowledge and an answer to the question "Why should this study be done?"
4. A detailed list of specific research questions this study attempts to answer—this often includes educated guesses about what the researcher thinks will be found, which are called *hypotheses*.
5. A detailed description of how the study was conducted, or the *methods* that were used and how these were implemented—this includes the who, what, where, and when of the study.
6. An overview of how the data were analyzed (quantitatively or qualitatively) and what the *results* were with regards to the specific research questions—essentially, the researcher has to address whether the hypotheses were right or wrong and to what degree (often using statistical indicators).
7. A discussion of what the researcher thinks the results mean with regard to the hypotheses and the general topic—this is also known as the

discussion section and is essentially the author's interpretations of what the study indicates in the bigger picture of that topic or discipline.

8. A list of all literature that was reviewed or mentioned in the course of the study with all the information that another person would need to look up those references—this is called the *bibliography*.

9. Finally, throughout the paper, there may be relevant charts and graphs that illustrate aspects of the study or the results.

All of this has to be written in a formal way that is very objective and factual. The only place where the researcher's opinion is allowed is in the discussion section, and even there, that opinion must flow logically from the results of the study and the topic at hand. In addition, a researcher is held to the utmost ethical standard that everything written is true, is authentic, and represents the work of the person who wrote it.

Once the researcher has written up the study and has edited and proofread it numerous times to ensure that it is of the highest possible quality, the researcher submits the paper to a specific journal to be considered for publication. Other researchers in the same field review the article extensively and anonymously. The reviewers do not know the identity of the author, and the author does not know the identities of the reviewers. The reviewers evaluate the paper on the basis of the quality of research that was done, the extent to which it contributes new knowledge to the field, and the quality of the writing. The paper can be rejected or sent back to the researcher for revisions based on any of these issues. Eventually, if the researcher did a good study and has good writing skills, the paper will be published in the journal in the form of an article, thereby contributing to knowledge of that field. This whole process can take many months, and even years, from the date a study was completed to the date it is published. Books take even longer; getting a book published is often a multiyear process. If the submission is deemed to be poor in some way, it will be rejected for publication. At this point, the author has to correct the problems the reviewers identified in the article or book before it can be resubmitted for publication.

The Cutting Edge

Why all this is important for you to know is that it actually illustrates one of the main benefits of attending a research university. While researchers are conducting their research, writing their articles and books, and spending hours in the library, they often share their newly discovered knowledge with students in the classroom that same day—long before others will read about it. This is known as the *cutting edge,* and it refers to the fact that the new knowledge that is being discovered every moment at a research university is woven into the education of the students who are currently enrolled. You will hear information in your classes that will not even be published for at least three to four years and will not reach a textbook until later still.

Let's take this book as an example. Although it is more of a text or reference book than a research-related book, the publishing process is similar for most books. I am writing this sentence on October 10, 2003, while sitting in my home office in Santa Barbara, California. I began to work on this book last December (nine months ago) when I wrote a five-page proposal that gave an overview of the book and an outline of the various chapters. I gave this proposal to an editor at Thomson Wadsworth, who liked my idea. Before she could sign a contract with me, she needed to be sure that the book would be marketable, so she sent my proposal out to three anonymous reviewers, who generally agreed with her and provided me with some helpful feedback. That whole process took six months, and I signed a contract with Thomson on July 15, 2003.

Then I began writing. I have spent many hours writing, editing, researching, and rewriting the first three chapters (including this one). I am hoping to send off this particular chapter to my editor by early November. She will send it out for reviews to anonymous reviewers, who will critique it and offer suggestions. On the basis of their feedback, I will either have a lot of reworking to do or, I hope, only minor changes. While this chapter is being reviewed, I will be writing other ones, and each chapter I finish will be sent out for reviews that I will later need to incorporate. I am hoping that I will be done with the first draft by April 2004—that means all chapters will have been written and sent out for review. Once I receive all the reviews back from the chapters, I will have to make those suggested changes by August 2004. At that time, the entire book will be sent out to more reviewers, who will read the entire text and offer more suggestions. I will incorporate those changes by October 2004. Finally, the book will be entrusted to the good people at Wadsworth, who will edit it some more, lay out the book in a visually pleasing fashion, create a cover design, and send it to the printing press to be printed and bound. I hope to have an actual copy of this book in my hands by April 2005. If you are reading this, it means that the whole process worked and these words made their way from my computer in California in 2003 to your hands on today's date.

As I was writing this book, I shared all of these ideas with my students in my class lectures. That means that freshmen at my university began hearing about these ideas in the fall of 2002. Even if you are the first person to buy this book, you will be reading these words nearly three years later. So listen carefully in your lectures this week—you might hear something the world will not know for a few years. Pretty cool, huh?

Epistemology, Bloom's Hierarchy, and Critical Thinking

Epistemology is a word you'll often hear at a research university. It is the study of knowledge. In essence, it explores what knowledge is and is not and how people gain knowledge. The processes of discovering new knowledge, disseminating it to others, and learning it are all activities that occur at a research university on a daily basis. More specifically, there are certain levels that both faculty and students go through in gaining an understanding or knowledge of a certain topic. In 1956, Benjamin Bloom created a taxonomy, or hierarchy, of various levels of knowledge that was later revised by Lorin Anderson in 1990 (see Table 1.1). The first two levels focus on learning and memorizing the material as well as understanding it. The third level requires applying or using that knowledge. While these first three levels are often the hallmark of K–12 education, you will find that this is not the case at a research university. Remember, a research university places more emphasis on discovering new knowledge, which includes looking at things in new ways. As a result, the first three levels of Bloom's hierarchy serve as the background or base from which the new levels of knowledge are reached. The top three levels of analysis, synthesis, and evaluation are more directly related to the research process in that they require a person to take a set of known information and transform it in some way to create something that was not present before.

Table 1.1 highlights the levels of the hierarchy, provides an overview of the kinds of skills students would be asked to demonstrate for each level, and gives examples of question cues and student behaviors.

The top three levels of Bloom's hierarchy (analysis, evaluation, and synthesis) are all part of another concept called *critical thinking*. You will hear this term a lot at research universities because it is a primary goal of your faculty to teach you how to engage in critical thinking. Critical thinking is essentially the process of suspending your beliefs and authentically looking at other options. This is a crucial skill for researchers because the search for new knowledge must be committed to finding the "truth" and not just confirming what one already believes. The processes of analysis, synthesis, and evaluation require us to let go of the material as we know it and to become open to altering it through taking it apart, putting it together, or assessing it in some new way.

What This Means to You

You'll be expected to learn material at all levels of the hierarchy, and your faculty will design assignments to test your ability to do so. Many students often "understudy" in that they only memorize and understand the reading or lecture material, that is, they focus on only the first two levels. While this is important, it is really only the first step, and students should be studying to perform at the upper four levels as well. Students are often surprised to find that their exams require them not just to summarize the information they studied, but also to apply, analyze, synthesize, or evaluate it—and often all four! Students might also be asked to complete different assignments that measure their competency in all six levels. Successful students will utilize Table 1.1 as a study tool.

Table 1.1   Bloom's Hierarchy of Knowledge

Competence	Skills Demonstrated	Question Cues	Sample Behaviors
Knowledge (*Memorizing*)	Student remembers or recognizes information, ideas, and principles in the approximate form in which they were learned. • observation and recall of information • knowledge of dates, events, places • knowledge of major ideas • mastery of subject matter	Write, list, label, name, state, define, tell, show, describe, identify, recognize, quote, examine, tabulate, who, when, what, where, etc.	The student will define the six levels of Bloom's hierarchy of knowledge.
Comprehension (*Understanding*)	Student explains, comprehends, or interprets information based on prior learning. • understanding information • grasp meaning • translate knowledge into new context • interpret facts, compare, contrast • order, group, infer causes • predict consequences	Explain, illustrate, exemplify, predict, summarize, infer, paraphrase, interpret, contrast, associate, distinguish, estimate, differentiate, discuss, extend	The student will explain the purpose of Bloom's hierarchy of knowledge.
Application (*Using*)	Student selects, transfers, and uses data and principles to complete a problem or task with a minimum of direction. • use information • use methods, concepts, theories in new situations • solve problems using required skills or knowledge	Use, compute, solve, implement, demonstrate, apply, construct, calculate, complete, illustrate, examine, modify, relate, change, classify, experiment, discover	The student will write an instructional objective for each level of Bloom's hierarchy.

Category	Description	Verbs	Objective
Analysis (*Taking Apart*)	Student differentiates, classifies, and relates the assumptions, hypotheses, evidence, or structure of a statement or question. • seeing patterns • organization of parts • recognition of hidden meanings • identification of components	Analyze, compare, contrast, organize, order, categorize, separate, connect, authenticate, classify, arrange, divide, select, deconstruct	The student will compare and contrast the levels of analysis and synthesis.
Evaluation (*Judging*)	Student appraises, assesses, or critiques on a basis of specific standards and criteria or justifies a decision or course of action. • compare and discriminate between ideas • assess value of theories, presentations • make choices based on reasoned argument • verify value of evidence • recognize subjectivity	Judge, recommend, critique, justify, assess, decide, rank, grade, test, measure, convince, select, explain, support, discriminate, conclude, compare, summarize	The student will justify the effectiveness of writing educational objectives using Bloom's hierarchy.
Synthesis (*Putting Together*)	Student integrates and combines ideas to create a product, plan, or proposal that is new to him or her. • use old ideas to create new ones • generalize from given facts • relate knowledge from several areas • predict, draw conclusions	Create, design, invent, produce, hypothesize, develop, combine, integrate, modify, rearrange, construct, substitute, plan, compose, formulate, prepare, generalize, rewrite, what if?	The student will design a classification scheme for writing educational objectives that combine all six levels of Bloom's hierarchy.

Might I Suggest...

When you study, focus on applying the material you are learning to all six levels of Bloom's hierarchy. Study in such a way that you could answer the kinds of question cues listed in Table 1.1. Also, don't assume that topics will be presented one at a time; you might be expected to apply these levels to two or more topics simultaneously. For example, in an introductory sociology class, you might have started the class learning about the modern sociological theories, including symbolic interactionism, then later read information on the Civil Rights Movement of the 1960s and a few weeks later hear a lecture on the effects of globalization on today's world economy. A faculty member might ask you to analyze the Civil Rights Movement and the effects of globalization from the perspective of a symbolic interactionist. Clearly, this question would test your knowledge and comprehension of those three seemingly separate pieces of information, but it would also require you to apply the theory to these two situations and analyze them from that theoretical perspective. Needless to say, many new students could walk into this exam feeling completely prepared and yet walk out feeling blindsided. Be prepared—faculty can and do utilize the whole range of Bloom's hierarchy to assess your mastery of the material. If you can study accordingly, you will excel in your classes.

The Importance of Academic Integrity

Because the primary mission of the university, as well as that of each of your faculty members, is to create and discover new knowledge, you can probably understand that academic integrity is an absolutely essential element of the entire research process. The whole value of research would collapse if it could not stand on the notion that people do honest work and represent their research accurately and completely. One of the worst violations a researcher can commit is to manipulate or misrepresent his or her findings; this invalidates the entire search for the "truth." Faculty have been fired for this. With that said, academic integrity is a value that is woven deeply into every element of your institution and is also expected of all students. You are expected to do your own work and stand by the quality of that work. Needless to say, cheating and plagiarism (using another's words or ideas without giving them credit) are serious violations of the essence of a research university. For this reason, it is important that you become very familiar with your campus's definitions and regulations regarding cheating and plagiarism. You will most likely find that these issues are very different from, and treated far more seriously than, what you experienced in high school. In fact, a typical high school book report would be considered plagiarism at most universities because it summarizes the words of another without giving appropriate credit.

Typical forms of cheating include a student's copying answers from a classmate on an exam, bringing and using unapproved notes and resources to the exam, having another person take the exam in his or her place, changing answers on an already graded exam and resubmitting it for credit, and stealing exam materials from department offices. Typical forms of plagiarism include using material from any source (e.g., books, lectures, the Internet) without giving the proper credit, purchasing a paper from the Internet or another source, turning in another student's work (even if it is several years old), using your own work from one class in another (you need permission from both instructors to do so), and stealing another student's work and turning it in. Even if you do not engage in cheating or plagiarism directly, you can be held responsible for aiding in another student's academic dishonesty.

When an instructor suspects a student of cheating or plagiarism, several actions can be taken. At some universities, instructors have the power to determine that student's grade on that particular assignment or even in the entire course without consulting anyone. The student would have to retake the course in the future to change the grade. All universities have some office or governing body that deals with cases of academic dishonesty; it might be called something like the Office of Judicial Affairs or the Committee on Student Conduct that oversees

What This Means to You

Be forewarned that the consequences for cheating and plagiarism are usually quite severe. At my campus, a first-time infraction typically results in a two-quarter suspension after a hearing. This means that the student must move out of the residence hall, lose financial aid, drop out of classes, and stop attending for the length of the punishment. With such steep consequences, it is important that you know what your campus's policies are. They are most likely published in a printed version and online, and a simple search at your campus' website will likely yield them. However, you can always speak to your instructors or academic advisors if you have any questions.

In addition, if you participate in the process of another student's cheating, either intentionally or not, you can be held accountable. You have to be very careful in how you share your work with other students. For example, if you let another student see your paper, it is up to you to make sure that he or she does not use it to cheat. For this reason, it is important to be clear with your peers how, and to what extent, they can utilize any materials you are sharing with them. In addition, it is your responsibility to keep your hard copies and computer files secure. If you let a friend use your computer and he copies your paper and turns it in, you can both be accused of academic dishonesty. Hopefully, your "friend" will be honest and tell the dean or conduct committee that you are not at fault, but if he doesn't, it will be your word against his, and the university might find you both responsible if they cannot discover the truth.

Justin's Story

My freshman year was totally ruined because I was accused of cheating. Halfway through the year, I got called in to my History professor's office. He told me that my paper was almost identical to another student's in the class. I was shocked because I had worked really hard on that paper and I had written it by myself. Apparently, the other student told him the same thing, so he had to accuse both of us of cheating because he didn't know who was lying. The class had 700 students in it, and I didn't even know the other guy! We were both sent to the Office of Judicial Affairs, where we were assigned a hearing, which didn't occur until over a month later. In the meantime, I still had to go to all my classes, including History, and try to focus, but I was a stress case, so it was hard. The hearing was really scary because there were twelve people in the room, and I had to try to prove my innocence. It turns out that he lived in my hall and kind of knew my roommate. He had asked to use my roommate's computer one night when I was out. My roommate was working on another assignment, so he let the guy use mine. The guy found my paper, and he copied it. I guess he just rearranged the paragraphs and turned it in. Luckily, my roommate was able to testify on my behalf because the other guy kept swearing that I stole his paper! I was found innocent, and he was suspended. But the whole thing was really stressful and made that whole quarter hell. Since then, I put a password on my computer, and no one is allowed to use it that I don't personally know. Even then, I have another password on my homework files.

the enforcement of campus regulations and issues punishments to those who violate them. In some cases, faculty have the option to turn the student over to this agency, and in some cases, faculty are required to do so. This agency usually engages in a judicial process in which all evidence is presented to an impartial group of people, usually comprising faculty, staff, and students, who hear the case and render a decision. If found innocent, the student is let go without penalty. However, if found guilty, the student faces serious consequences that can include suspension from the university for a term or two, or even expulsion. In addition, a guilty finding forces the creation of a conduct record for that student that must exist for five to seven years. All universities are required to divulge if a student has a conduct record, and this can damage a student's future admission to other institutions and many jobs.

Members of the University Community

The campus community is made up of many, many individuals. There are undergraduate students, graduate students, faculty, staff, and administrators as well as people from the local community in which the campus is located. Each of these groups plays some integral role in the daily functioning of the university and is part of what is known as *the community of scholars*. As we have discussed, the role of the faculty is primarily to conduct research. In addition, faculty are charged with teaching both graduate students and undergraduate students as a way to prepare future researchers as well as to provide the courses needed to satisfy graduation requirements. Staff and administrators play pivotal roles in ensuring that every aspect of the university runs smoothly and efficiently. In addition, people who live near the university often interact with and/or are affected by the university community in a variety of ways. Each of these groups has different responsibilities, needs, goals, and ways of working. As a result, it is important for you to learn more about these different communities and how they affect your daily experience as an undergraduate student.

Undergraduate Students

The part of the community of scholars of which you are a member is the undergraduate student body. This ranges from freshmen to graduating seniors—any student who is currently enrolled in a bachelor's degree program. In addition, you will find yourself a member of the freshman or transfer class or the "Class of [fill in graduation year here]." On some campuses, class identity is quite strong, and you will find yourself identified by your group and familiar with many people in your class. On larger campuses, this is much harder to do. At the University of Georgia, there are over 25,000 undergraduate students and a freshman class of 5,000 students, and the only time the freshmen are seen as a group is during the first week of school at Convocation, the official induction ceremony. Since not all students graduate in exactly four years, the entire freshman class is usually not together at commencement four years later. At larger research universities, most students know a smaller group of students whom they met in their residence hall, at their job, through a club or organization, in classes for their major, through a sport or hobby, or by some other similar avenue.

The role that undergraduates play in the community of scholars is to be both a consumer of knowledge and as a producer of knowledge. As you take classes, your instructors will teach you information about that particular topic, and you will be asked to learn this material and demonstrate your mastery of it through exams, papers, and other assignments. The quality of your work will be assessed and reflected in the grade you earn. As you take introductory courses in a variety of disciplines, most often done to fulfill general education requirements, you will also be exposed to some elements of that particular discipline. This process helps students to learn more about both their interest in, and talent for, a particular discipline.

Once you select a major, you will begin to receive more specific training in how to conduct research for that particular discipline. This is where you also begin to be a producer of knowledge, as many of your assignments in these and other major classes will require you to write research papers and conduct mini research projects. If you show academic promise in your major, you might be invited to conduct a senior research project or to be involved in a faculty member's research project. You can also seek out these opportunities on your own by inquiring with the department or speaking to faculty members whom you have gotten to know.

Many undergraduate students serve in vital roles in large research projects and can even publish an article before they have received their bachelor's degree. If you aspire to continue on to graduate school, these are excellent opportunities to participate in, as they give you a chance to build your research resume early. Participating in research as an undergraduate definitely gives you an edge when applying to graduate schools.

In addition to their academic work, undergraduate students contribute to the campus community in the form of community service. Many students join clubs and organizations that serve the larger campus in some way, or they participate in student government or serve on an important campus committee that is trying to improve an aspect of the campus. This involvement is just as important in your overall education as your courses, so be sure to participate. These options are covered in more depth in Chapter 8.

Graduate Students

Most research universities have both graduate and undergraduate students. Graduate students applied for, and were admitted to, an advanced degree program (usually master's or doctorate) in a specific discipline at your campus. That means that, just like you, they have courses to take and papers to write in order to graduate. Depending on the program they are in, they will be graduate students for one to three years if they are pursuing a master's degree or four to seven years if they are pursuing a doctoral degree. You might not always recognize graduate students when you see them because many graduate students pursue their advanced degree right after finishing their bachelor's degree, so they are close in age to undergraduates.

Graduate students play some key roles in the workings of a research university. First, they are researchers-in-training. In their courses, they are learning the theories and research methods that are used in their disciplines (usually in much greater depth than that which is presented to undergraduate students). They must also become producers of knowledge by engaging in the type of research that is common in their discipline. Before they can graduate, they must produce original research under the close scrutiny of the faculty in their department. All of this can happen without undergraduates ever seeing it, as graduate students often work closely with faculty in small groups and seminars.

The most likely place where you will encounter graduate students is in your classes, as they often serve as teaching assistants, or TAs. TAs work with faculty members to help provide courses to undergraduate students—and frankly, the university could not run without them. They usually are responsible for running discussion sections, teaching additional material in those sections, and grading some, if not most, of your work. All of these duties are done under the close

> ## Might I Suggest...
>
> Get to know your TAs and other graduate students on your campus. They were all very successful as undergraduate students, and they probably have some useful pointers for you. Graduate students can assist you with the assignment they might be grading, provide advice on how to balance academics with a social life, and give you useful strategies for various academic skills, and they are usually in the know about the best coffeehouses in town. Take advantage of this important resource.

supervision of the faculty member who is the instructor of record for a particular course. Serving as a TA usually provides the graduate student with two important resources: money for school (as these positions are paid) and valuable teaching experience as they prepare for their own careers as faculty members. While most TA positions are technically quarter- or half-time (i.e., ten to twenty hours per week), in reality they often require more time than that, as each TA leads two to three discussion sections per week in addition to attending all lectures and grading students' work.

In some cases, very advanced graduate students may be promoted to a teaching associate position and given a course of their own to teach as hands-on job training; that is, they would serve as the instructor of record and have primary responsibility for that course. Some might even hire and supervise TAs, depending on the size of the course. These advanced students usually have several years of their graduate program under their belt and are close to graduating and becoming an entry-level faculty member somewhere else. Some campuses utilize quite a few teaching associates to teach introductory-level undergraduate courses; other campuses pride themselves on having their highest-ranked professors teach these courses.

Faculty

There are different types of faculty members at a research university. A faculty member is any person who has a contract with the university to provide teaching, research, or both. These titles may vary slightly from institution to institution, but they are generally similar across universities in the United States and Canada. The length of the contract may also vary; some faculty members have temporary or short-term appointments while others have long-term or permanent contracts. This distinction between the lengths of the contract is very important and essentially creates two categories of faculty.

Long-Term Contracts

The first category of faculty is people with long-term contracts, and it includes those with "professor" titles. The professorial titles are the most prestigious faculty titles at a research university. These positions focus most on the person's research skills, although teaching is important as well. Because the primary job responsibility is research, the teaching loads for professors are lower than those of lecturers (described in the next section). At the University of California, this means four to five courses per year and may range from large undergraduate courses to graduate seminars with as few as three students enrolled. These positions are paid the highest of the faculty titles and have many levels for growth and promotion.

These positions are also known as *ladder-rank* faculty because they are "on the ladder" to tenure. Tenure, which is job security, is a very important concept because it is closely tied to the process of research and is the way in which academic freedom is guaranteed. Academic freedom ensures for every faculty member the right to research and teach what she or he wants without fear of retribution or punishment. This means that a researcher can actively pursue controversial or marginalized topics without fear of losing his or her job. For example, a political scientist could research and publish things that were critical of the state or federal government, or a biologist could explore an unpopular theory about AIDS transmission. Academic freedom is a core value of a research institution and is held in the same sacred way that freedom of speech is held in the United States. In fact, the concept of academic freedom was born following the McCarthy era when scholars were routinely harassed and persecuted for holding views that the government did not agree with. Academic freedom and the tenure that guarantees it were specifically designed to ensure that McCarthyism could never be repeated in the United States.

Tenure is job security, and it means that a person has a job for life and cannot be fired except under extreme circumstances. Tenure is based on a person's contributions in four main areas:

1. Research, usually assessed by examining the quality and quantity of scholarly contributions (such as publications or creative works)
2. Teaching, usually assessed primarily by examining teaching evaluations from students
3. Community service to the home campus, usually assessed by examining the amount of participation in campus programs, on campus committees, and so on
4. Professional service to the discipline, usually assessed by examining the amount and level of involvement in professional organizations

Every faculty member with the title of professor goes through a very comprehensive performance evaluation in which these four areas are assessed. This review involves faculty from the same department, other departments on the same campus, professional colleagues from around the world, and various administrators up the chain of command all the way to the president or chancellor.

By far the most heavily weighted factor at a research university is the faculty member's research skills, which are often determined by examining the quantity

---

What This Means to You

If you think about it, faculty members are people who liked school so much that we never left. Ponder that for a moment. We were perhaps the top students in our high schools, and we went on to become the top students in our undergraduate colleges. We then chose to pursue a Ph.D. or other advanced degree that requires several more years of schooling. Once we graduated, we intentionally chose a career that required hours of reading, writing, studying, and research. Generally, we are truly excited about learning and we find the material we research and teach to be fascinating. And we think our students do too. We often assume that you intentionally chose a research university because you want to become a researcher yourself and are interested in the material we have to teach. This assumption can create a disconnection between students and faculty because we believe that you have a passion for learning, just like us, when students often are focused more on getting a good grade or a good job after graduation. Nothing slights our academic passion more than to have a student seem uninterested or bored, or worse, only focused on finding out what is on the test. Those kinds of priorities, and the attitudes that accompany them, are like knives to the hearts of your faculty. Think carefully about how you interact with these passionate educators and what you convey about yourself with your words and actions.

---

and quality of the person's scholarly contributions, such as publications or creative works. It is generally believed that the quantity of contributions indicates that the person is a competent researcher who regularly contributes to the new knowledge of the field and is respected by colleagues around the world. Therefore, this person will be a valuable addition to a university and will help fulfill its research mission.

There are four levels within the ladder rank or professor titles.

Assistant Professors. These are faculty members who have a Ph.D. and have been hired by the university for a specified period of time, usually up to seven years. They do *not* have tenure and are given a period of time in which to earn it. They have usually just completed their Ph.D. at another university, and this is their first professional job as a faculty member. During this time period, assistant professors are trying to demonstrate their research and teaching skills—in other words, their usefulness to both their field and their institution. Assistant professors have up to seven years to produce a professional file that shows them to be worthy of tenure. This means that they are trying to publish enough articles, book chapters, or other research results to be reviewed favorably and be granted tenure by their colleagues. Needless to say, this is a big job because assistant professors are also expected to teach and demonstrate their teaching prowess. When assistant professors are granted tenure, they earn a permanent

A Word about Office Hours

All instructors are required to have weekly office hours, the minimum being about two hours a week. This means that the faculty member teaching the course, as well as each teaching assistant, needs to have office hours every week. The purpose of office hours is to be sure that students have regular and easy access to their instructors for the purpose of doing well in that particular class. However, each instructor is free to schedule the hours at his or her convenience, so there is no guarantee that the office hours will not conflict with your other classes, job, and so on. To address this, most faculty members are also available by appointment, which means that you can request a one-on-one meeting with your faculty or teaching assistant. You can do this either in person before or after class, by phone, or by email. However, it is important that you have your schedule handy or give your instructor some options that work in your schedule. Once you have made an appointment, it is imperative that you show up. Your faculty member has taken time out of her or his busy schedule to be available to you, so missing an appointment is very unwise.

Many students are intimidated by office hours because they are not sure what they are supposed to do during them. Generally, office hours are a time when you can do the following:

- Ask questions about the week's lectures or readings—either because you did not understand the material and would like it explained further or because you have new questions about what it means in the bigger picture.
- Ask questions about your academic skills and get some advice—to show your instructor your lecture notes or chapter outlines and see whether you are capturing the right material and to the level of detail she or he would expect.
- Ask questions about an upcoming exam or assignment—to make sure that you understood it correctly and/or are approaching it in the correct way. For papers, you might also be able to have your instructor read outlines or even completed drafts and give you feedback.
- Ask questions about your past performance in order to improve—to find out why you received a certain grade for the purpose of learning how you can better prepare for future exams or papers.
- Bring something to your instructor's attention such as an error on the syllabus or a test question that might have multiple interpretations.

position at that university. If tenure is not granted, then they are asked to leave the university, and the temporary contract is ended. In other words, they are fired. The phrase *publish or perish* refers to this process and is often the mantra of stressed young faculty who are trying to gain tenure. Some campuses tie together tenure and promotion to the next level of associate professor; others keep these two processes separate.

- Ask for an extension on an assignment—but be sure you have a good and documented excuse, and even then, your instructor is not obliged to accommodate you.
- Ask questions about the major or the academic discipline—to learn more about the bigger scope of the field.
- Ask questions about the faculty member's research—to learn more about his or her work or to find out whether there is an open student position on the project.
- Seek advice about future classes to take, graduate programs to apply for, and the like.
- Request a letter of recommendation for graduate school or a professional job.

Remember, you are attending a research university, where the faculty are charged with discovering new knowledge and, in general, are people who love to learn. With that said, there are definitely things that you should *not* do in office hours:

- Ask for copies of lecture notes. It is your job to take your own notes. If you were absent, you need to make arrangements with a fellow student to get a copy of his or her notes. It is okay to request copies of handouts, but it might be easier to ask the student from whom you are getting the notes to pick up a set for you.
- Ask questions that might be offensive to your instructor as a professional scholar—things like "Did I miss anything important?," "Will this be on the test?," or "Are we expected to know this stuff?" These questions indicate that you are trying to do the bare minimum and are not dedicated to your work.
- Go over an assignment with the instructor for the purpose of arguing about the feedback you received or making a statement like "But I always get A's on papers." Your faculty have years of experience teaching and grading, so they probably have a few things to teach you about performing at the university level. Trust that you have been assessed accurately and fairly, and seek to learn how you can do better next time. However, faculty do make mistakes occasionally (e.g., we might have added a score incorrectly or misgraded a question), and it is fine to point these things out to us—just be mindful of your tone.

Associate Professors. These faculty members are more advanced than assistant professors in the career of academia. At some universities, advancement to associate status comes with tenure, while at others, tenure is earned separately. Once tenure is earned, associate professors have job security for life, but the university's expectations that they continue to produce new knowledge also last for a lifetime, so associate professors by no means reduce their publishing goals. But they do probably feel less pressure and stress, since they cannot be fired and this frees up some of their time for involvement in university and professional service. What motivates associate professors to continue researching is their passion for learning and teaching. At some campuses, future promotions and salary increases may be based on their research skills and the quantity and quality of new contributions. There may be several minilevels of promotion within the associate professor title that can be granted after each performance review every few years, if the person's performance record was satisfactory.

Full Professors. These faculty members also have tenure but have now achieved the highest level possible within this career in academia. They have been promoted from associate professor and granted the esteemed title of full professor. Again, full professors are motivated because of their intellectual passion. At some campuses, future promotions and raises may depend on their production of research. Full professors tend to be older because of the length of time it takes to reach the status of full professor. They are also the highest-paid members of the faculty in relation to assistant and associate professors, but salaries vary greatly across disciplines. Once faculty members achieve full professor status, they might also take on more administrative duties at their campus by becoming the administrative leader, or chair, of their department or by serving as an academic dean. Outside of their campus, they might become a leading officer in a professional organization or become an editor of a scholarly journal. If a professor chooses to stop or slow his or her research production, the result is career stagnation. Although the person will continue to have job security for life, there is a cost in that colleagues might not view that person as highly as before, and this can lead to fewer opportunities within the department or campus.

Emeritus Professors. These faculty members have served as full professors for many years and have now retired. They no longer have an active contract, although some emeritus professors are asked to teach an occasional course in their specialty. They are still viewed as a member of the community of scholars and often are given great respect, as they have reached the pinnacle of their field in academia.

Short-Term Contracts

The second category of faculty is people with short-term contracts. This includes teaching assistants and teaching associates, who were described earlier, in the section about graduate students.

Lecturers. These are faculty members who have been hired on the basis of their teaching skills. As a result, they have the heaviest teaching loads and are expected to teach several courses per year. At the University of California, this is usually nine courses per year. These courses may be introductory courses for freshmen or advanced courses for seniors. Occasionally, lecturers might be asked to teach a course for graduate students. Lecturers' contracts tend to have a specific time limit after which the contract is ended, no matter how good the lecturer was at the job. For example, there might be a limit of six years or a certain number of terms. These faculty positions are paid less than the professor titles, even though many lecturers also hold a Ph.D.

Visiting Titles. These are faculty members who have a Ph.D. and have been invited to be part of the faculty for a specified, and usually short, period of time. The term *visiting* can be attached to both lecturer and professor titles; it indicates that although the person is working at this particular institution for a short period of time, she or he has a position at another institution elsewhere in the state, country, or world. The "visiting" title usually matches the title that the person holds at his or her home institution; for example, someone who is an associate professor at home will be a visiting associate professor at the new campus. Visiting faculty often are invited because they bring a perspective or background that is not found among the regular faculty at that particular campus. Visiting faculty often accept the invitation because they also gain something from working and researching in the new location, for example, access to some data that would be harder to gain while at their original campus or an opportunity to work with a different group of faculty or students. Clearly, this arrangement is often very beneficial to everyone involved.

Acting Titles. The term *acting* can also be used with all the faculty titles; it indicates that the person is in a temporary position with specified beginning and ending dates. It also might indicate that the person does not hold a similar title at his or her home institution or company but does have the appropriate academic qualifications. An "acting" title can also be used when a person is asked to fill an empty position temporarily, until a permanent replacement can be hired.

Staff and Administrators

While faculty and students represent the main producers and consumers of knowledge on a university campus, their daily lives would not be possible without the work of the hundreds of staff and administrators who work there as well. Many staff and administrators have chosen to work at research universities because they believe in the power of education and discovery. They work in ways that enable and facilitate the research and learning process of both faculty and students. Without their efforts, many important aspects of the university would fail or falter. It is impossible to provide an overview of all that staff and faculty do so let's focus on how many people are involved every time an instructor wants to offer a class—it is the work of several people to do the following:

- Request the specific classroom space on the day and time the instructor wants to teach
- Coordinate all the classroom requests and make assignments that accommodate hundreds of classes and faculty with specific requests

- Publish all the various classes in a document from which students choose their classes
- Order the books the instructor is assigning and make sure there are copies in the bookstore
- Provide the instructor with a list of the students who enrolled in the class
- Stock the copy room with paper, staples, and a copy machine that instructors can use (and help when the copy machine jams)
- Order the media support the instructor needs for the lectures
- Assist in the making of syllabi and other handouts, including exams
- Ensure that there is a place where the instructor can park and walk safely to and from class
- Ensure that the lights and heating work in the classroom
- Stock the classroom frequently with chalk and other relevant supplies
- Clean the classroom of discarded newspapers and coffee cups as well as arranging the chairs (students can assist with this one by cleaning up after themselves)
- Assist students in finding the instructor's office hours or leaving messages for him or her
- Ensure that the instructor's phone, computer, and email are always working
- Provide the instructor with documents on which she or he can report student grades
- Process those grades and post them to student records
- Read and calculate student evaluations of the course
- Process the instructor's paycheck every month

And that's just a small taste of what is needed from the faculty's perspective. Think about the list of things that need to be done to allow you to sign up and successfully complete your classes:

- Advise you on how to choose and register for classes
- Create documents that help you understand your choices and relevant deadlines
- Provide you with a list of the classes you enrolled in
- Ensure that you have access to computers and email that function
- Stock the library with books and journals for your use
- Stock the bookstore with materials you need for your classes
- Counsel you when you are going through a difficult time
- Medically treat you when you are sick
- Process the payment of your tuition bills
- Provide you with financial aid when needed
- Advocate for you if something goes wrong (e.g., family emergency, illness, sexual assault, etc.)

- Monitor your behavior to ensure you are following the rules and address it if you don't
- Talk to your family when they have questions
- Provide you with cocurricular activities such as campus events, clubs, and organizations
- Encourage your success

Staff and administrators are involved with every aspect of the operations of campus, so their work affects your experience every day. Obviously, these positions range from the person who mows the grass to a medical doctor who treats students in the health center. Because of this variety, it is hard to make concrete statements that represent all of these positions, but in general, tenure or job security is not something that is extended to staff and administrators at most research universities. It is also important to distinguish between staff and administrators.

Generally, administrators serve in leadership roles as the director or coordinator of a department or program, such as dean, provost, director, vice president, or chancellor. They must provide guidance and leadership to the staff who work under them in that particular department or program and to the department itself that they oversee. This includes setting goals and making sure they are met, overseeing the annual budget and making sure operations stay within it, hiring and supervising all staff, responding to unexpected crises, reacting to government or state mandates, and various other duties. In other words, they ensure that the program or department is functioning at its best and successfully doing the work with which it is charged. In addition, administrators usually have to answer to another administrator who is above them in the university's hierarchy.

In contrast, staff members are generally people who work in a department or program and report to the administrator who serves as the director or coordinator. Small departments might have just a couple of staff members who cover a range of duties, while large departments might have hundreds of staff members, each with a very specific role and set of duties. Larger departments often have organizational hierarchies so that not every person reports to the head administrator but maybe to a manager or assistant director instead.

It is important to note that staff members often work very hard and do not receive the same prestige or status that is awarded to the faculty at a research university. On some campuses and in some departments, staff are considered "second-class citizens" compared to faculty and experience daily frustrations that stem from that attitude, such as lower salaries, less favorable parking spots, cubicles instead of offices, and all kinds of other privileges that they experience in less quantity or quality than those provided to the faculty. Needless to say, this can create a negative environment that might or might not be visible to students. In general, any staff members with whom you interact will greatly appreciate being treated with respect and thanked for the service provided.

What This Means to You

It is important to be aware that you are part of something bigger than just your university. You have now become a member of these communities, both the campus and the local area, for the duration of your college experience. Your actions and choices *do* have an impact on those around you, and only you can choose whether these will be positive or negative. Your behavior as a member of these communities is an important part of your education, and it prepares you for your future roles as an employee, a neighbor, a parent, and a partner.

The Surrounding Community

Every campus is located in or near a community of some sort, whether it is a small rural town, a large city, or something in between. The presence of a university, along with its many members, has a very real impact on the surrounding community. Some of the ways in which the surrounding community is affected by a university are employment opportunities, housing costs and availability, parking costs and availability, student behavior, general safety, economic growth, availability of resources, and space planning and development. These impacts can be positive—for example, the availability of jobs with good benefits or resources such as an extensive library or lectures and performing arts events that are open to the public. And some of these impacts can be negative, such as local emergency rooms being clogged with alcohol-poisoning cases or the kind of pranks that students seem to participate in "for fun" that affect others' property or personal comfort.

Many communities are involved with the local university in the form of beneficial formal and informal partnerships. One example on our campus is the adoption of a local elementary school: We provide some additional funding to the school, and many of our students volunteer there as tutors. Sometimes faculty share their expertise with the local community. For example, a faculty member in our education department has done groundbreaking research on children with autism. She shares her work with local families by providing free consultations and treatment programs. Many local businesses have also created preprofessional internships in which our students can gain valuable work experience while still in college. These beneficial relationships go both ways and represent collaboration in its truest sense.

Chapter Summary

In this chapter, the following topics were discussed:

- The purpose of research
  - The research mission of a university
  - Who conducts research
  - The academic disciplines
  - How research is conducted

- How knowledge is shared
  - Scholarly standards for publication
  - The cutting edge

- Epistemology, Bloom's hierarchy, and critical thinking

- The importance of academic integrity

- Members of the university community
  - Undergraduate students
  - Graduate students
  - Faculty
  - Staff and administrators
  - The surrounding community

Reflections and Exercises

1. Interview a Faculty Member

Select a faculty member whom you would like to get to know better. You might want to select someone from a major you are interested in or whose class you particularly enjoy. Call or write the faculty member, asking for an appointment and explaining that the purpose is to interview a faculty member. Be sure you know when and where to meet and make sure you are on time. Introduce yourself and ask the following questions:

What is your educational background?

What was your first year like at your undergraduate college?

How did you choose your major as an undergraduate?

What is your favorite memory from your undergraduate experience? What is your least favorite?

How did you decide to become a faculty member?

What is your typical week like in terms of responsibilities?

Which classes do you teach?

How would you classify your teaching style?

What methods of teaching do you utilize?

What do you like most about your job? What do you like least?

How would you define a "good" undergraduate student? What qualities should she or he possess?

What annoys you the most about undergraduates at this university?

What do you enjoy the most about undergraduates at this university?

What advice would you have for me in terms of succeeding in college?

2. Critical Thinking at a University

Choose one discipline from each of the categories below, for a total of three. Write in your choices.

Hard/natural scientists (chemistry, physics, biology, etc.):

_____

Social scientists (sociology, communication, ethnic studies, etc.):

_____

Artists (music, art, dance, drama, etc.):

_____

Relying on the assumptions and methods of your chosen discipline (i.e., you must think like a chemist, musician, or sociologist), consider how you might research the question, "How do people learn?"

How might your chosen discipline approach answering this question?

Hard/Natural Scientists	Social Scientists	Artists

How might your chosen discipline test its assumptions/hypotheses about how people learn?

Hard/Natural Scientists	Social Scientists	Artists

Look over the three columns. What is shared by the different disciplines? What is different?

What are the advantages and disadvantages of relying on any one discipline?

How do similar disciplines inform and support the learning process? What are the challenges of working across disciplines?

How might you, as a student, incorporate ideas from various disciplines in your own learning?

What does this exercise have to do with critical thinking?

3. Applying Bloom's Hierarchy of Knowing

Using the first four sections of this chapter as the text, identify the author's main points as well as any underlying assumptions or justifications the author presents.

Main points:

Underlying assumptions or justifications:

What method did you utilize for identifying a main point of the section?

How might this inform your reading and note-taking skills?

Were you able to identify any of the author's underlying assumptions or justifications? How did you do so?

How did these affect the overall section? How might this inform your own writing?

Next, identify the aspects of the material that correlate with the six levels of Bloom's hierarchy (knowledge, comprehension, application, analysis, synthesis, and evaluation). In addition, design two or three exam questions that would test a student's mastery of the material for each level; consider creating a variety of question types, including multiple choice, true/false, matching, and essay questions.

	Text Content	Possible Exam Questions
Knowledge		
Comprehension		
Application		
Analysis		
Evaluation		
Synthesis		

How did you determine which features of the text illustrated each level of Bloom's hierarchy?

How might you utilize Bloom's hierarchy in studying and preparing for exams?

NOTE: Consider doing this exercise for other courses and showing your instructor the results. You can gain valuable feedback about whether you are creating exam questions that are similar to ones she or he might create to test you on the material.

4. Academic Integrity

Using your campus's website, student handbook, and general catalog, find your university's regulations on academic integrity and determine the following:

How are your university's regulations communicated to students?

Look up and write down the definition for plagiarism.

Which office oversees the judicial process? What is the process the university uses when a student is suspected of academic dishonesty?

Are the consequences stated? What are they? (If they are not stated, call the office to ask.)

How might you be able to ensure that your work always meets the highest standards of academic integrity?

What will you do if you discover that your friend is cheating in a class?

What strategies can you use to protect your own work from being misused by friends?

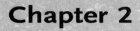

Chapter 2

Skills for
Academic Success

Now that you understand the overall concept of research and how it influences your experience as a student, let's shift our focus to the skills you will need to be successful at a research university. You will generally need three types of skills for academic success. The first type is skills that help you, a new university student, to manage your workload effectively and efficiently. The second type of skills helps you to perform successfully in your classes at a research university. Finally, you will need skills that are specific to research in your field of study or major. The first two types of skills are common to all students; the last type will vary depending on the discipline you choose to major in.

If you are a freshman, you will need to develop these skills as quickly as possible, as they are very different from the skills you used in high school. If you are a transfer student, you will need to increase and further hone skills you began to develop at your previous institution. You will find that although you are familiar with these skills, you will need to increase their pace, intensity, and overall quality to be competitive in the university environment. In this chapter, you will learn about the wide range of skills affiliated with student success at a research university. You will also gain some specific tips and strategies to increase your own academic success.

Workload Skills

Workload skills are very important and need to be mastered as quickly as possible, as they directly support your success from your first classes all the way through to graduation. Although you might have been very successful at managing your workload in high school or at a community college, you will find that the sheer quantity of work will increase dramatically at a university, as will the expectations for the quality of your performance. This means that a large part of your transition depends on how quickly you adjust.

Most likely, your campus has a department or program that offers workshops and training in many of the following workload skills. You will want to locate

Might I Suggest...

You might be tempted to think back on your previous successes in high school or community college and think, "I'm a great student." While it is true that you were a great student in that previous environment, it has yet to be determined how successful you will be at a research university. The bar has been raised in many ways, and the students who approach their academic work with that in mind will adjust more quickly and successfully than those who continue to approach their academics as they did before. Also, you will receive frequent feedback, in the form of exams and assignments, on how this transition is going for you. For example, if you receive your first university paper back and it has earned a C, you will succeed sooner if you are open to what that feedback tells you rather than saying things like, "But I have always earned A's on my papers." Your faculty are here to help you to adjust to this new environment, and there are many staff that will assist you as well. But you must be willing to seek out and utilize this assistance.

this program as soon as possible and sign up for as many workshops as you can. These trainers will provide you with valuable tips and suggestions for how to master these skills as they relate to your specific university. Many students make the mistake of thinking, "I already know how to do that." Even if you do, you will still walk away from each workshop with at least a couple of valuable new tips that you can begin using immediately. Ironically, many students, believing that it is the weaker students who use these services, avoid them because they feel confident in their own skills, but it is actually the A and B students who use these services the most, because they are seeking that extra edge to keep them at the top of their performance.

Assignment Management

For each of your classes, your faculty members will outline your assignments in the syllabus. By looking at the syllabus, you will be able to see how much reading should be completed before each lecture and when various assignments are due. Assignment management skills have to do with how well you are able to identify and complete these assignments by the date they are expected of you. This will require you to accurately record your assignments, assess the amount of time and effort they will take to complete and schedule your time appropriately, and then actually do the work at the time you allocated to do so. In addition, homework is rarely checked at a research university, so you need to ensure that you complete work on time and seek help if you are confused.

This might sound easy, but if you are taking four or five classes, you will need to compile all the reading and assignments for all of them in one location to truly see the workload for any one week. Once you see the overall picture of what you need to complete, you will need to allocate time for each course so that you can finish all the expected work on time. If you fall behind, you simply make the next week harder because you will have to complete the previous week's work in addition to that week's work. For example, you might have two chapters to read for your philosophy class and two more for your chemistry class. That might not sound like much, and you might be tempted to think, "I can do that later this

Might I Suggest...

Many students keep the syllabus for each class in a separate notebook and look at each one individually. I have found that this does not give the student an accurate picture of the amount of overall work represented in a week. I strongly recommend creating a weekly list or grid to see the overall workload you have per week. On the basis of your own work pace, estimate the number of hours each assignment will take. This will give you a more accurate picture of what needs to be accomplished in a week. Let's take a typical student schedule as an example (see Table 2.1). This student is enrolled in four classes, all with fairly common reading loads of fifty to seventy pages per week. Three of the classes have midterm exams, and one has a six-page paper—all of which will require some work in order to prepare. In addition, one class requires viewing a movie each week, and another requires listening to music. If the student were to just look at the list of assignments, she or he might feel that it's fairly manageable. However, if the student calculates the number of pages to be read and estimates an average reading pace of fifteen pages per hour, it becomes clear that there is fifteen to twenty hours per week in reading alone! Add to this the time to view the movie, take notes on the movie, listen to the CD, take notes on the CD, review lecture notes, and study the material already read, and this student has a very full schedule.

In addition, you will find that some of your assignments require quite a bit of preparation to complete. While the due date for the assignment will be on the syllabus, your instructors will rarely provide any structure for how and when to do the work required to complete it. For example, you might have a 10-page research paper due in the fifth week of the term. It is up to you to realize that to successfully complete this paper, you will need to select a topic, conduct extensive research in the library, analyze the results of your research, organize your results into a coherent argument, create an outline, write the first draft of the paper, proofread it and make corrections, proofread the second draft, make some more corrections, and, finally, submit the paper to your instructor. This could be hard to do well in just a few days, let alone starting the night before. A successful student will identify all the steps needed to complete an assignment and then create a timeline for accomplishing each step in a way that will eventually meet the deadline. It would be realistic to start this assignment three to four weeks before it was due, which means that you need to start it the second week of the term.

Table 2.1   Workload Grid

Class	Week 1	Week 2	Week 3	Week 4
Philosophy 4 (Intro to Ethics)	Chapters 1–2	Chapters 3 and 5	Chapters 7–8	Chapters 9–10 Midterm
Chemistry 1A (General Chemistry)	Chapters 1–2	Chapters 3–4	Chapters 5–6	Chapters 7–8 Midterm
Freshman Seminar 20 (Intro to the University)	Reader p. 1–62 View film	Reader p. 67–140 View film	Reader p. 141–212 View film Midterm	Reader p. 213–280 View film
Music 50 (World Music)	Book p. xvi–71 Listen to CD	Book p. 72–146 Listen to CD	Book p. 147–175 Listen to CD	Book p. 176–228 6-page paper due
Weekly total	233 pgs of reading = 15.5 hours 2 hours of film 1 hour of CD Work on paper	301 pgs = 20 hours 2 hours of film 1 hour of CD Work on paper	255 pgs = 17.5 hours 2 hours of film 1 hour of CD Studying for 3 exams Work on paper	302 pgs = 20 hours 2 hours of film 1 hour of CD Studying for 2 exams Work on paper

week—I have plenty of time," especially when more tempting activities are presented to you. However, if you were to see all of your assignments on one list and to account for the fact that most students read fifteen to twenty pages per hour on average, you might realize that those four chapters amount to more than what you'd imagined. It's typical that students are given 200 to 300 pages of reading a week, which translates to a lot of hours spent with books.

This process of assignment management is made all the more challenging because you will rarely be reminded that the work needs to be done; your instructors will simply expect you to do it. If you have questions, it is your responsibility to bring them up during class discussions or visit office hours for assistance. In addition, you might find that the reading is not reviewed during class time, so no one but you will really know if you actually completed your work. In other words, you will often be tempted to blow off your work, since there is no obvious or immediate accountability. However, remember that anything that was said during a lecture or read for the class is fair game on an exam, so it is entirely possible that you could be asked to read a book that is never mentioned in class yet will represent a significant portion of your exam. All this is to say that you will have a lot of work to do, and you are expected to do it all with no supervision. Assignment management has to do with how well you can identify and keep track of your workload in a way that ensures that you complete it each week.

Remember, there is probably a study skills program or department on your campus that can help you to develop your assignment management skills. But it is important for you to learn these as early in your academic career as possible, as they are directly correlated to your ability to perform at the level that you hope. In addition, you might wish to speak to your instructors about this in office hours. If you are having trouble managing the workload for a particular course, talk to your instructor about it and seek his or her advice. You will most likely receive some very useful strategies.

Time Management

Given the large amount of work you will be asked to do and the relatively little structure you will be provided for doing it, time management skills will become crucial to your success. The typical university student class schedule is very deceiving because it appears that you have a lot of free time every day. You might have a class at 9:00 A.M. and then not another one until 2:00 P.M. instead of being in class continuously from 8:00 A.M. to 3:00 P.M. as you were in high school. One of the biggest differences between high school and college is that the students' workload shifts from in-class time to out-of-class time. This is also true for transfer students in that research university classes probably meet less frequently and also expect more work to be accomplished in a shorter period of time than at your previous institution. It is commonly expected that students spend two to three hours on homework for every hour spent in class. This includes reading, reviewing and organizing lecture notes, working on a research paper, visiting faculty during office hours, doing homework problems, and studying for an exam. In addition, a lot of this work is not necessarily appealing or fun, so your motivation to dig into that chemistry book might not be very strong.

The ability to make yourself do work even when you are not in the mood is by far the single most important skill for your college success. You will need to assess your workload, schedule it in your day and week, and then get it done. This is what *managing your time* means: You will need to take advantage of that time after your 9:00 A.M. class ends and before your 2:00 P.M. class begins to get as much of your homework done as possible. In addition, you will need to be sure that you eat, exercise, sleep, and even play. To fit all these things in, you will need some method of scheduling your day. Most students find that a planner (either paper or electronic) is very useful. Once you write in the weekly commitments that have a set time (classes, meals, sleep, club meetings, etc.), you can then look at the open sections of your schedule and assign the various elements of that week's workload into those time periods. It is also important to be realistic. If it really takes you two hours to read a chapter, then don't schedule one hour for it. Put in two.

Time management is something that takes time and practice to master. You will definitely want to take any workshops on this topic that are available to you, and you will probably need to do so more than once. As your classes become

Might I Suggest...

I recommend using schedule grids to see your schedule accurately and to make the best use of your time for both academic and social purposes. You can easily create a blank master schedule on the computer and then update it each term with your current classes and commitments. This schedule should include basic activities for living, such as eating, sleeping, and exercising, as well as times for socializing and relaxing. Once you have your overall schedule set up, print out a copy of your master schedule for each week of the term. Then using the workload list you already created for your classes, schedule your homework into the blank spots on your schedule. Remember to include the various steps that lead up to the completion of an assignment. It is important to make this schedule realistic for you. If you are not a morning person, then don't plan to use those hours because you probably won't anyway.

Figure 2.1 shows an example of a schedule grid in which the student has efficiently scheduled her time. The student began with the fixed-time items (in gray) and then used the open times to schedule the week's workload that she has realistically estimated on the basis of her reading pace and abilities. This schedule represents the third week of the assignment workload in Table 2.1. The student also has realistically scheduled her social life for the weekends and time to just hang out and relax. At the end of this chapter, you will find a blank schedule that you can copy and utilize for your own scheduling, or you can create one using the table function of any word-processing software.

more intense and you add things like an internship or job and involvement in a campus club, you will need to fine-tune your skills even more. You can also find good resources in your campus bookstore and on the Internet. Time management is a lifelong skill that is always being adjusted depending on your current responsibilities. Even your faculty and your family are constantly working on their time management skills. In general, if you are attending a research university full-time, you should expect to spend approximately forty hours per week in class or on coursework. This is the equivalent of a full-time job! If you are spending less than that, you might find that you will not be earning the top grades or might even be in danger of doing poorly in your classes.

Assertive Communication

This skill is directly related to time management, and it is about the ability to say "no." All the best-laid plans can go awry when your roommate says, "Let's go out for a movie." You will find yourself having to choose between the fun of a movie with a friend and the dreariness of working on the English paper that's due in two days. Needless to say, most human beings would want to choose the movie, and you certainly can. But if you are choosing the movie or the computer game or the party every night, you will soon find your GPA far lower than it should be.

TIME	MON	TUES	WED	THURS	FRI	SAT	SUN
8–9	Breakfast	Breakfast	Breakfast	Breakfast	Breakfast	Sleep in	Sleep in
9–10	Phil 4	Listen CD	Phil 4	Library: Music paper	Phil 4	Sleep in	Sleep in
10–11	Study: Phil Chapt. 7–8	FS Disc.	Chem Chapt. 6	Library: Music paper	Music office hours	Brunch	Brunch
11–12	Study: Phil Chapt. 7–8	Lunch	Chem Chapt. 6	Lunch	Music office hours		
12–1	Lunch	Chem 1A	Lunch	Chem 1A	Lunch	Music paper	Music paper
1–2	FS p. 141–175	Chem 1A	Midterm prep	Chem 1A	Phil Disc.	Music paper	Music paper

Figure 2.1   Sample Student Schedule Grid

TIME	MON	TUES	WED	THURS	FRI	SAT	SUN
2–3	FS 20	Chem Chapt. 5	FS 20 MID-TERM	Paper outline	FS 20	Study for Phil midterm	
3–4	FS p. 175–212	Relax	Relax				IM Soccer
4–5	Music 50	Study for FS Midterm	Music 50	Chem Lab	Music 50	Study for Chem midterm	
5–6	Workout		Workout		Workout		
6–7	Dinner	Dinner	Dinner	Dinner	Dinner	Dinner	Dinner
7–8	Relax	FS Movie	Music p. 147–175	Paper outline			Study for midterms
8–9	Chem Chapt. 5			Watch TV			
9–10	Study for FS Midterm	Movie notes	Chem Chapt. 6		Socialize: Party at John's	Socialize: Girls' night at the movies	Music paper
10–11		Review lectures	Review lectures	Paper outline			
11–12	Sleep	Sleep	Sleep	Sleep			Sleep

Figure 2.1   (continued)

It is important to have fun in college, and balancing a good social life with a strong academic life should be one of your goals. Good time management allows a person to create a well-rounded life, but the truth is that most students find it difficult to say "no" to friends and family who tempt them with distracting activities when their work is not yet complete. As a result, first-year students say, "yes" far too often, and their GPA eventually suffers. Juniors and seniors are not necessarily smarter than freshmen, but they have usually mastered time management and the ability to say "no" in a way that supports their academic success. Some typical distractions that students need to thwart are as follows:

- Conversations with friends and roommates
- Hanging out and chatting with other students in casual settings (the residence hall, student center, local burger joint, etc.)
- Instant messaging on the computer
- Playing computer games
- Chatting on the phone
- Watching TV
- Going to campus events such as movies and workshops
- Partying

None of these is a problem in and of itself; the problem comes when an entire block of valuable study time is suddenly gone because one or more of these distractions successfully tempted the student. Although many students think, "Well, there's tomorrow," the likelihood is that the same distractions will arise tomorrow as well. It doesn't take too many nights like this before a student is dangerously behind in course work.

On rare occasions, first-year students study too much and do only coursework without letting themselves have any fun. This is equally unbalanced and also leads to negative consequences. While these students might have great GPAs, they might not be developing important social skills that are also a product of a good university education. In this case, the student might need to say "no" to studying, again keeping the forty hours per week in mind.

Reading Skills

The first aspect of reading skills is simply getting it all done! You will have hours of reading to do each week, so you will need to learn how to schedule it all in. You will find that you will be given an immense amount of reading to do

Might I Suggest...

At the beginning of the week, look over your schedule grid, making sure that all the assignments are covered. Determine how much free time you have in your schedule, and schedule it in as well. Allot yourself a certain number of hours when you will relax, chat, watch TV, play computer games, and so on—in other words, the number of times you will say "yes" to something tempting during that specific week. When an opportunity arises, assess whether this is the time you want to use one of your "yes's" or whether you want to save it for a more interesting activity. By approaching it this way, you will be making an active choice each time, rather than inadvertently giving away your important study time.

in your classes each week. In fact, it is not uncommon to cover the same amount of material in one term that it took a year to cover in high school or even community college. Each faculty member makes decisions about what material you need to be familiar with to truly understand the topics of the particular class that he or she is teaching. Faculty are generally not given any guidelines about how much reading we can assign, so you may find a wide range of workloads. Generally, however, you will find your workload to be much greater than it was in high school or community college. As I stated earlier, it is not uncommon to have 200 to 300 pages of reading to do *per week*. This might mean 80 pages in your sociology class, and then 70 in your environmental studies class, plus another 50 in your ethnomusicology class, and 70 more in your geology class. This is usually not light reading either. You might find yourself wading through material that is confusing or hard to understand, so it will probably take longer than if you were reading 500 pages of a novel for enjoyment.

The next important aspect is comprehension. It does no good to have completed your weekly reading if you really didn't understand it. You will need to buy a good dictionary and thesaurus or utilize the online versions, as you will often come across words of which you don't know the meanings. Look them up. You will also need to devise a method of identifying which part of the reading you understood and which part you have questions about. Your faculty will be able to assist you much better if you have specific questions rather than saying, "I didn't get it."

Finally, you will need to learn how to figure out what is important. Many students find themselves highlighting or underlining almost everything in the chapter because they cannot figure out what they need to focus on. The purpose of highlighting or underlining your reading is to identify the most important concepts so that you can focus on those during your exam review instead of rereading the entire text again. As a rule, it's best to read a chapter through once before you highlight anything. This allows you to assess the overall content of the chapter and see how the concepts are related. Once you have this overview, you can go back and highlight the important concepts. You want to avoid highlighting paragraphs of material; instead, focus on terms, phrases, and main points.

In addition, you will want to learn how to make notes in the margins. These margin notes should also help you to identify the important concepts but in your own words. Margin notes can also serve to identify where you have questions or opinions about the material. More important, margin notes are how you can assert your own views or responses to the author. You will find that critiquing what you are reading is an important part of critical thinking, so you should actively engage with the material in this way instead of just taking it in. You might also want to create your own written notes summarizing the main points of a chapter or article as a way to learn the material better and to use as a study guide.

The last aspect of reading strategies is that you can gain some insight into your faculty's expectations by examining the readings you have been assigned. As faculty members, we each get to choose our readings for the courses we teach, and we design our own syllabus. These choices we make tell you a lot about us— what we believe is important to know, our values, and our biases. Even for an introductory course, we have hundreds of topics to choose from and even more readings from which to select. If you examine your syllabus and reading list for these bigger clues, you will have a good idea what we are hoping to impart to you over the term and which topics we believe to be the most important. This can guide you about how best to structure your study time or which topics are certain to be on the exam.

When reading math and science texts, an additional skill is required. You will need to learn how and *when* to use certain formulas for solving problems. Most math and science texts are organized in a way that each chapter teaches you a new set of formulas related to various topics or concepts, and each chapter will have sample problems for you to practice using the formulas learned in that chapter (i.e., *how* to solve them). However, your exams will cover the material from several chapters, thus requiring you to know how to identify what formula or process the exam question requires you to use (i.e, *when* to use them). Most students find that while they understood each chapter and were able to successfully complete the problem sets, they may not have learned how to identify what, specifically, in the wording of the problem points to the use of one formula or process over another. Be sure that you read your math and science texts with this focus in mind.

Again, all of these skills can be learned, and you would be wise to seek out the study skills program on your campus, as they often offer workshops on reading strategies and text highlighting. Your instructor can also offer you some pointers. It would be fine to bring in your book or reader and show your instructor how you read it and the kinds of notes you took for the purpose of seeing whether she or he has some suggestions for improvement.

Taking Lecture Notes

This is a very important skill to develop because it will be the main tool you use to capture the material your instructors are teaching you. While a few faculty lecture from the book, most do not, which means that the lectures are on

What This Means to You

You will probably need to adjust your reading skills to gain the level of mastery of the material that is expected on exams and other assignments. This is hard to do at first, but you can go to office hours and get some pointers from your instructors about what their expectations are and whether your level of reading is preparing you to perform accordingly. Ultimately, your first exams and papers will provide you with feedback about your skills. Most first-year students, both freshmen and transfer students, find that they could have performed better on their first assignments. While this might be disappointing, it is important to look at what this feedback tells you about your reading skills. Go over your first assignments carefully for clues about how you can adjust your reading and other academic skills, and then create strategies to do so. Your instructors can often help you with this process and can provide other valuable insights.

Might I Suggest...

I strongly urge my students to first skim a chapter or article just to get the overall sense of the content. Then I encourage them to go back and do a more thorough read of the material, creating an outline of the chapter as they do so. Here, they pay attention to the natural cues the author has given the reader about how concepts are related. The placement of headings, subheadings, lists, and emphasized terms are clues to the student that usually aid in the creation of their outline and other study materials. I also encourage them to note questions they have as they are reading, which they later can bring up in discussion or office hours. I recommend that they use a highlighter only after this second reading and even then only to highlight the terms and concepts that are presented in that chapter. Finally, I suggest that students read the chapter one more time to move into a deeper level of really understanding the material and relating it to their prior readings and lectures. This is also where they can review their knowledge of the material to make sure they have considered it at all levels of Bloom's hierarchy as described in Chapter 1.

material you cannot get from any other source. Again, the sheer volume of information that can be conveyed in a typical lecture might surprise you. It is not uncommon to take eight pages of notes from one fifty-minute lecture. The first aspect of note taking is simply to write fast enough to keep up with your instructor. You will find that most of us speak far faster than you can write, so you will need to quickly develop a kind of shorthand with abbreviations and symbols. You can either develop your own or find more formal methods to adopt.

In addition, you will find that some faculty have very organized lectures with outlines, visual aids, and so on. You will come to greatly appreciate these instructors, as they often help you organize their comments into structured blocks of related material. They might even indicate which points are the most important. Unfortunately, you will also need to be prepared for instructors who just talk for an hour without any visual aids at all. They might be energetic and animated or speak in the quintessential monotone, boring voice, and you will need to turn their monologue into meaningful notes from which you can study. The most important thing to remember is that you will be held accountable for all the material the instructor presents, whether or not your note-taking skills are sufficient. For this reason, you will want to utilize a range of strategies for creating accurate and complete sets of lecture notes.

There are several useful methods that you can use for taking and organizing your notes. Some students use recording devices to capture the lecture and then replay it later to fill in their notes. Other students take a laptop computer to class and essentially transcribe the lecture, later going back and organizing the material a bit better. Some students work in pairs, utilizing the theory that two sets of eyes and ears (and fast writing hands!) are better than one.

There are books on this topic you can purchase, and again, your campus' academic skills program will most likely offer very useful workshops on this topic.

Take advantage of these as soon as you can. Some campuses also have note-taking services that allow you to buy a subscription to a course and receive a set of lecture notes taken by another student in the course. These services should be used only to *augment* your own notes, not as a substitute. Too many students are tempted to skip class or not take their own notes, and this has direct and negative consequences on their success. To combat this problem, some faculty have been known to instruct the note taker to leave out a portion of the lecture to give an advantage on the next exam to the students who attended lectures and took their own notes.

Sometimes, college students find it difficult to stay focused, or even awake, during lectures. This is especially true if the material is not interesting to the student or the instructor's lecture style is particularly unexciting. Some students respond to this challenge by reading the campus newspaper, text-messaging their friends, or allowing themselves to doze. This is not only rude to your instructor and fellow classmates, but also undermines your success, as you will be expected to know that lecture's content, regardless of how you feel about it. Use whatever methods you need to in order to be focused in class. Be sure you have gotten plenty of sleep the night before, sit near the front of the class, drink a double espresso, or whatever other methods work for you. You might even divide your tuition by the number of hours you are in class to discover how much you are paying to hear that lecture—it's usually more expensive than you thought. Also, it's important to realize that many instructors do not tolerate distractions during their lectures, so if you are talking, reading the paper, or sleeping, you might find yourself called out in front of the other students and perhaps even asked to leave.

Might I Suggest...

I recommend leaving plenty of space on your note paper as you take notes. Leave a wide left column and spaces between the material. This allows you plenty of room to add notes and comments later. It's a good idea to review your notes as soon as you can after the lecture has ended. While the material is still fresh in your mind, go back and fill in the details that you didn't have time to write down. Also, take a look at the information and see whether you can organize it into some main points or themes. Immediately note any sections that you know are incomplete or that you did not understand. You will want to address these as soon as you can, ideally before the next lecture, with either a fellow classmate or your instructor during office hours. It is always a good idea to pair up with another student in class to compare your lecture notes and assist each other in creating a complete and accurate set. Finally, go back to your syllabus and see whether there are any clues about the topics you were supposed to learn in that lecture or themes that related to previous ones. Your syllabus can sometimes serve as a master outline, thus placing this one lecture in context.

Academic Skills

This section highlights several important skills that every faculty member has developed over his or her career and will be expecting students to learn. These skills are directly related to how you will demonstrate your mastery of material through exams, papers, and other assignments, and ultimately, the quality of your performance in your classes.

Study Styles

The ability to study and study well is a skill. Every person studies differently and there is no one best way to study. However, each person has a style of studying that works best for him or her. It is important to learn about yourself and what helps you study in the most focused and efficient manner so that you can create it on demand. Here are some things to consider (answer these for yourself as you read them):

- What time of day is your focus the greatest? Morning, afternoon or evening?
- How many minutes or hours can you go without a break and be able to consistently focus?
- When you need a break, how many minutes or hours do you need before you can begin studying again and be focused?
- Do you prefer to sit at a desk, lie on the floor or a bed, or lounge on a couch or chair?
- Do you need silence when you study or do you prefer background noise like music or TV?
- What materials do you need around you when you study? (Things to consider: colored markers, notecards, blank paper, snacks, dictionary, and the like.)

All of these things make up your study style profile. After you discover these things about yourself, you need to intentionally design a study environment that maximizes your style. For example, if you need silence to study effectively, then you most likely will not be able to study in a residence hall; the library will be a better choice. If you study best lying on the floor with pillows and your MP3, then you will want to find a room, like a hall lounge, to set up in. If you are not sure where to find places that support your study needs, ask other students at your university or staff like academic advisors or resident assistants.

It's also important to maximize your study habits with regard to length of time you can focus. Some people can study for three hours and then only need a thirty-minute break before they can focus for another three hours. Another person will only be able to focus in one hour blocks and need at least an hour in between. Some students study best in the morning while others are night owls. You will want to design your days accordingly. Be sure to plan your studying when it will be the most effective for you.

Finally, don't forget that the best study habits can be undermined if you don't utilize assertive communication. If you know that you focus best between 7:00–10:00 P.M., then don't let your friends talk you into watching TV during that time. Or if you need silence and your roommate needs music, the two of you will need to find a solution that works for you both, for example, earphones and earplugs.

Preparing For and Taking Exams

In most institutions of education, exams are a primary way in which faculty assess their students' mastery of the material. It is our opportunity to "test" you to see whether you know the material well enough to have "passed" the subject—in other words, we can deem your performance good enough that you have satisfactorily completed a particular course. In addition, we use exams and other assignments to assess the overall quality of your work as it compares to that of

---

Might I Suggest...

When I make an exam, I go back to my lectures and reading material and start to see what material I could turn into fair questions. I look at the bigger themes, terms and definitions, broader concepts, and things that I made a point of emphasizing in my discussions with students. This list becomes the topics from which I will ask questions. Then I determine which types of questions I can make out of each topic. Things that appear in lists are perfect for multiple-choice questions, as are compare/contrast questions involving two related but very different concepts. Dates or titles can always be good for matching questions, as can term identifications. Then there are the basic "describe" or "define" short essay questions and the longer essay questions that are more complex and allow for greater analysis. It is very difficult to turn a simple term into an essay question, but it's easy to turn a description or analysis of a theory into one.

To ask a question, the creator of the exam needs to use language or phrasing that will let the test taker know what specific material is being tested. In other words, if I wanted to test you on Chickering's Seven Vectors of Student Development theory (you'll learn more about this in Chapter 6), I would somehow have to identify that in the question. Whether I ask a simple true/false question or an elaborate question, I will have to give you the clue of the author and the title so you know that I am asking about Chickering and not Tinto's Theory of Institutional Departure (also in Chapter 6). In other words, every question on every exam you take will have some identifying clues (e.g., author, title, time period, scientific grouping) to let you know what material the question is about. If you studied by associating information with its identifying clues, then these clues will help you to easily recognize what the question is about. However, if you studied the material

the other students in the course (if the class is graded on a curve) or to a set standard of performance (if it is not graded on a curve). This allows us to confidently assign a letter grade to your performance as a measure of your mastery.

Exams can come in many forms. There are *objective* exams that consist of questions with straightforward answers, usually demonstrating the knowledge or comprehension levels of Bloom's hierarchy. These often include multiple-choice, true/false, matching, and term identification questions, as well as mathematical or scientific problems that must be worked out. Then there are *subjective* exam questions, which involve the higher levels of Bloom's hierarchy: application, analysis, evaluation, and synthesis. These usually require writing of some kind and so are most likely essay exams. And of course, an exam can be in a combination of all of these formats.

Each faculty member chooses how and when to assess the students. Some faculty do not give exams at all; others give three midterms and a final. All of this will be outlined in your syllabus, including how much of your grade is accounted for by a specific exam. You will also want to find out whether the exam covers

without really associating it with its identifiers, then the clue and question might confuse you.

I strongly recommend that when you study, you always focus on associating the information with its identifying clues. That way, when I ask, "Which of the following is *not* one of Chickering's Vectors of Student Development?" and then I provide you with a list that is a mix of vectors from Chickering and concepts from Tinto's Theory, you know immediately which one is out of place. Otherwise, you might look at the list and recognize all of the terms and then get confused about which ones were Chickering and which ones were Tinto. Many students lose valuable points simply because the questions cues hurt them instead of helping them.

For the math, science, and engineering disciplines, you will be tested through exams that give you various problems to solve. These problems will cover all of the topics you have learned in class and can be in any order. They are designed to test your ability in three areas:

1. If you know what kind of problem you are being asked to solve (i.e., can you identify which formula or process you should use to solve this question—you may even get questions that require using more than one formula or process in combination with another)
2. If can you correctly use the appropriate formula or process
3. If you arrive at the correct answer to the problem

Be sure that you learn what, specifically, indicates what type of problem it is and what formula or process you would need to use. If you are not sure, visit your faculty member's office hours to find out before the exam date arrives.

a certain set of material or whether it is *cumulative,* meaning that everything in the course up to the exam day could potentially be on the exam. Talking with your instructors and reading your syllabus carefully will give you very good clues that will aid you in your exam preparation.

One way you can help yourself to prepare is to think like an instructor; in other words, imagine that you have to give an exam on the material and see what you would create for questions. Using Bloom's hierarchy, create questions in different formats (true/false, multiple-choice, matching, term identifications, essays) that test different levels of the hierarchy. Making exams is not rocket science, and you will probably identify many of the same questions your instructors do. These can serve as an excellent study guide for you. You might also look at your textbooks to see whether they have sample problems or questions at the end of the chapter or book. These can be good tools to use to test your knowledge and prepare yourself for the exam.

In addition, there are several strategies that can be used to help improve your performance on different kinds of exams. Most likely, the academic skills program on your campus offers workshops on these strategies, and students tell me that these workshops are quite helpful. There are also several books and Internet sites with useful suggestions. While these strategies can assist you immensely, they cannot make up for lack of preparation, so you will still need to put in the study time and know the information very well.

Finally, exams can be stressful and challenging assignments for students because there is pressure to do your best and many points hang on one to three hours of work. Some students experience performance or test anxiety; if you study hard and are confident walking into the exam and then find yourself freezing or blanking on the test, you might have test anxiety. There is usually a group of staff on campus that can help you with this; they will most likely be affiliated with either the academic skills program, student health, or counseling, as test anxiety is a stress-related issue. They will help you to assess your test performance and give you very useful strategies for performing better in these situations. However, if you find that your overall performance is severely hindered by test anxiety, you might want to seek out majors that utilize writing assignments instead of exams to assess students. You can also approach your faculty early in the term and request an alternate assessment format, but your condition would need to be well documented, and faculty are not obligated to accommodate you.

Following Instructions

Surprisingly, this is the skill that costs most first-year students more valuable points on exams and assignments than anything else. Bright students who are doing A work can earn a D or F on an assignment because they simply didn't follow the instructions carefully. Your faculty will give you pretty explicit instructions on assignments, and you can be assured that points are awarded or subtracted for each element of those instructions. It is in your best interest to read all instructions carefully and be sure you understand them.

These errors occur in two ways: The student either reads the question or assignment incorrectly or literally does not address a part of it, because she or he either forgot or did not think it was relevant. The first error can be addressed by simply slowing down. Especially on exams, take the time to read and reread the question and make sure that you really understand it. So many students glance at a question, see familiar terms, and say, "I know this one!" and quickly circle the answer that seems obvious, or they write down all that they remember about that topic. However, we are often asking you to take something that you learned in the class and apply it in new ways or to address the subtleties of that particular issue. We also often add the word "*not*" to a question. For example, a question might ask, "Which of the following statements exemplifies the tenets of the Transformational Style of Leadership?" but it could also ask, "Which of the following statements does not exemplify the tenets of the Transformational Style of Leadership?" The list of statements that follows is going to be pretty similar, and a student has to read the question accurately to be able to pick out the correct answer. If students do not read the question carefully, they could give the wrong answer even though they really studied the material and are sure they did well when they left the exam. These students are often shocked to get the exam back and learn that the answer was wrong and that it cost them points.

The second type of error has to do with lack of thoroughness; a student literally forgets to answer a part of a question or does not think it's necessary to do so, thereby automatically losing points attached to that particular piece. You would be surprised how many first-year students do this, especially in their first term or two. It seems that most students have to earn a few C's and D's that could have easily been A's before they slow down and start getting much more careful about following instructions. However, you can avoid this by just being very careful from the beginning.

When grading students' work, instructors can grade only what the students actually did on the assignment, not what they knew the students were capable of. On numerous occasions, faculty become frustrated when grading exams because we see the names of some of our best students on the exams that contain the most mistakes. Even though we know that they know the material, we absolutely have to grade what is in front of us.

Also, be sure to take your time and ask for guidance if you are confused. During an exam, never leave early. Always take the full amount of time given to you. If you finish early, use the extra time to go back and carefully review your work. Double-check your answers and make sure that you addressed all parts of the questions. You would be surprised how many students pass over a question, planning to come back to it, and then leave without ever doing so. On written exams, you can always insert an asterisk or an arrow and then add additional information in the margins or on the back of the page. If you are not in an exam situation, you have even more assistance available to you because you can meet with your instructor ahead of time to make sure that you thoroughly understand the assignment. You can probably even show your instructor a partial and/or completed draft to make sure that you are on the right track.

Dana's Story

To illustrate, let's look at Dana, who is a freshman at my campus. She is a very bright student who took her midterm exam in American History, which consisted of an essay question worth 70% of the exam and then identification of two terms worth 30% of the exam. The instructions for the essay portion read as follows:

Essay: Spend about 5 minutes outlining relevant material and arguments you will use, and then write an essay that takes a position supported by evidence. We will be looking for persuasive reasoning and accurate use of historical perspectives. Here are two statements about 18th-century colonial America. Evaluate each one, drawing on evidence from the textbook, lectures, and *The Unredeemed Captive*. Which one do you find more persuasive and why?

Historian A: "North American colonists had virtually nothing in common with each other prior to the revolution. The only exception was their shared tendency to define themselves against outsiders, such as Indians, French Catholics, and slaves. This pattern of exclusion set the precedent of a national identity and helped them unite against Britain."

Historian B: "North American colonists had a great deal in common with each other prior to the revolution. Religion, consumer culture, and political values united the colonies. Their exclusion of outsiders was simply a by-product of an already strong sense of American identity."

Dana had studied very hard for this exam, so she was surprised and disappointed to find that she had earned a B-minus, especially since she absolutely knew the material. She also wasn't sure what she had done wrong because there were only positive comments, such as "good point" and "well argued," written in the margins. She had also received the full 30% for the term identifications, so she knew that the problem was in the essay. The two of us sat down to take a look at

Critical Thinking

As you can see by the American History midterm example above, you will be expected to engage in analysis and critical thinking with regard to the material you learn in each class. As was stated in Chapter 1, your education will require you to demonstrate your mastery of the material at all levels of Bloom's hierarchy, and the assignments your faculty give to you help them assess how well you are performing at each level. But we don't necessarily separate those levels into

what had happened. As a faculty member, I took the question and underlined what I saw were specific instructions and cues that explained what she needed to do—things that most likely had points assigned to them.

Essay: Spend about 5 minutes <u>outlining</u> [since this is included in the instructions, there might be points assigned to it, so the student should make a brief outline somewhere on the page] relevant material and arguments you will use, and then write an essay that <u>takes a position</u> [you will need to form a specific argument] <u>supported by</u> evidence [and justify your argument with specific material from class]. We will be looking for <u>persuasive reasoning</u> [how convincing your argument and evidence are] and <u>accurate</u> [this is where the studying comes in—you'd better know your stuff] use of historical perspectives. Here are two statements about 18th century colonial America. <u>Evaluate each one</u> [you need to evaluate both historians equally)], drawing on evidence from the <u>textbook, lectures, and *The Unredeemed Captive*</u> [you need to use all three, or you might lose points]. <u>Which one do you find more persuasive and why?</u> [this is the actual question you are answering—the rest of this information is the process your instructor wants you to use to do so].

Dana immediately said, "That's it! That's my mistake!" She realized that she had written a great argument for historian A but had never evaluated historian B at all. Sure enough, that was the problem. The instructor had allotted a certain amount of points for each historian, and although Dana had essentially gotten a perfect score on everything she wrote on that exam, there was no way the instructor could give her the points for the part she did not do. I am sure that her instructor also was disappointed to give her a B-minus when Dana clearly knew the material, but there was no other option.

During that meeting, I told her there was a very simple thing she could do with every assignment she had in every class that would solve this problem. It is described in the following "Might I Suggest..." box.

distinct assignments. As you can see in the history midterm, the knowledge and comprehension levels were clearly tested in the term identifications but were also woven into the essay exam. The student had to demonstrate the knowledge and comprehension of the material through the use of the evidence she utilized in her argument. In addition, the application level was tested by giving her a new scenario—the two historians' views—and the analysis, synthesis, and evaluation levels were all tested in the strength of the argument she made about who was more persuasive and why.

> ## What This Means to You
>
> You must be prepared to demonstrate your knowledge of material in a broader range of ways than just memorizing it. If you study only to the level of comprehension, then you will find that you have a lot of additional work to do to take that information and apply, analyze, synthesize, and evaluate it on the exam or paper. You might be successful, but you will be thinking on your feet, so to speak. If you actively engage yourself with the course material and learn and study it at the various levels, then you will be much more prepared for the types of questions you will inevitably be given on the exam or paper assignment. This will give you a distinct advantage over the students who only memorized the material.

Analytical Argument Formation

Related to this issue of critical thinking and Bloom's hierarchy is the concept of forming an argument. Many of your assignments will require you to take a position of some kind on the material you learned and make a case, or argument, for that position. This is actually one of the most exciting parts of education—when you take the standard material and breathe life into it that is unique to you. Every student who took that American History midterm could have had a very different answer as to who was more persuasive and why. And each of those answers or arguments can be "right" as long as they are well thought-out and supported with accurate evidence. You will find argument formation to be the most common writing process you use in your experience at a research university. In fact, it is the same process that faculty utilize when writing up a research study or writing a book. They must form their own persuasive argument and support it with accurate evidence.

The ability to form and successfully support an analytical argument is a skill, and it is one that you can learn and improve with practice. In fact, it is one of the primary skills that we seek to train you in during the four years of your university education, as it is so central to the process of research. Creating an analytical argument requires several steps that involve analysis and assessment, hence the name. It is essentially an argument or a position that has been arrived at through a logical and objective process; it is *not* an opinion, the difference being that opinions can be formed through a wide range of thoughts and experiences that do not necessarily include objective analysis. It is absolutely possible for a person to hold an opinion for which he or she could not successfully create an analytical argument. The reason this process is so crucial is because research is the search for "truth" on some level, and since human beings have personal values, experiences, and worldviews, it is important that the process have logical objectivity to neutralize those subjective forces.

For students, there are many different formats in which they will be asked to create an analytical argument, from the essay exam question or the ten-page research paper to the oral presentation or lab report. Faculty also engage in this process for their research publications as do professionals in corporations who utilize it for proposals and other business documents. Regardless of the format, there is both a process by which an argument is created and a standard form in which it is presented.

Forming an Analytical Argument

The following steps for analytical argument formation occur in this order, although the depth of analysis will depend on the assignment and allotted time. An exam question will require this same process but at a much quicker pace and therefore in less depth, whereas a research paper will include all of these steps in more depth. The following is tailored to academic work.

Background Research and Analysis

1. Learning the information on that particular issue. This might require examining a wide range of types and number of sources.
2. Reviewing the information you have learned and assessing it through evaluation and analysis. The goal is to eliminate what is irrelevant or invalid while keeping the rest.

Developing the Argument

3. Discovering what the information suggests, such as overall themes that become evident or looking for connections that exist between the material.
4. Forming several initial arguments and reexamining the information to see how well these ideas are supported by the existing data, then eliminating arguments that cannot be supported or altering them to account for the discrepancies.
5. Narrowing the focus to the strongest argument and searching the information for the best and strongest pieces that support that argument.
6. Exploring which groupings of material and order of presentation make the most sense and are most compelling.

Creating the Final Argument

7. Writing the argument in some format, such as a report, a speech, or a paper (see following for more details).
8. Reviewing and editing the written argument several times to make it the most clear, persuasive, and supported argument possible. This stage might require altering and editing your original position in some way.
9. Presenting the argument to others in some format.

Presenting the Argument

The form in which an analytical argument is presented is focused primarily on walking the audience (i.e., the instructor grading the paper, the classmates hearing the presentation, the colleagues reviewing the study for publication, or the CEO reviewing the proposal) through the process by which the creator came to

> ### What This Means to You
>
> A large portion of your academic experience will require you to read the arguments of others, listen to the arguments of your faculty, and to produce your own arguments in your coursework. The sooner you become familiar with the analytical argument process and form, the easier it will be for you to perform at the standard your faculty expect of you. Again, your faculty are there to help you with this process, as are the academic skills programs on your campus. Utilize these resources as you learn and master this important skill.

the conclusion that he or she did. Ideally, if you have formed a strong argument that is supported with accurate evidence, your audience will be convinced. The general form for academic work has several parts to it and a logical order.

Introduction and Thesis

1. Thesis—this is the overall argument you are trying to make; it is essentially the endpoint you arrived at as a result of your analysis, and it is what you hope to prove in your argument.
2. First assertion that supports your thesis—this is the first point you need your audience to see to get to the final argument; its placement as first is based solely on your assessment of its need to be so.

Body of Evidence

3. Evidence that supports or proves your first assertion—this is the evidence and information that supports that assertion (data, quotes, events, dates, facts, etc.), again presented in the order that is most clear and compelling.
4. Second assertion that supports your thesis—this is the second point you need your audience to see in order to get to the final argument; its placement as second is based solely on your assessment of its need to be so.
5. Evidence that supports or proves second assertion—this is the evidence and information that supports that assertion (data, quotes, dates, facts, etc.), again presented in the order that is most clear and compelling.
6. Repeat this process until you have outlined all the evidence that led you to your argument.

Conclusion

7. Closing that connects all the assertions to come to the logical conclusion of the argument stated—this is where you tie all the pieces together for the audience, and it should match the original thesis.
8. Resources used—this often takes the form of a bibliography or references page that lists all the sources of the information and evidence you used in your argument.

Common Mistakes

There are several common mistakes that people, students and faculty alike, make on the delivery of their argument (which is usually the final product that others read or hear). The first is that they did not start early enough to engage in thorough analysis or to produce a quality product. The second mistake is that their analysis is faulty. No matter how persuasive a writer you are, if you base an argument on inaccurate evidence or faulty logic, the argument is invalid. Third, the thesis is often not clear or specific enough to give the audience an accurate picture. The audience has to clearly see the final outcome to see how the rest of all the pieces support it. In the case of student assignments, you are often given a specific question to answer, such as "Which historian do you find more persuasive and why?" The thesis is *the answer* to the question, for example, "This paper will show that Historian A was more persuasive because <u>fill in with the reasons you will be providing</u>." A thesis can be more than one sentence if it needs to be, but it needs to answer the question in the most clear and concise way. You'll notice that it is impossible to write a thesis before you have done all the relevant analysis steps.

Fourth, the author doesn't make clear connections between the material presented and the argument or thesis being proved. You want to walk the audience through your argument and how you see the connections to be related. You do not want to lay out the evidence that convinced you but then leave the reader to come up with his or her own interpretation. This often leaves the reader thinking, "So how does this relate?" or "Interesting, but I don't get it." It is the author's words that tie the connections between the evidence and assertions back

Might I Suggest...

It is essential to leave enough time to do all the steps that are required to form an analytical argument and then to present it. First-year students are especially prone to waiting until the last minute to begin an assignment, and they simply run out of time to perform the process completely or well. Students often sit down at the computer the night before a paper is due and attempt to write the paper as they are typing it. Needless to say, this method usually produces both a weak argument and poor presentation. As a result, they are not able to earn exemplary grades. In addition, if you begin the process early enough, you can utilize office hours to seek your instructor's assistance in looking at the various stages of your analysis as well as your final product. Students can bring their faculty what is initially B or C work and through a process of editing, reworking, and rewriting, bring that work up to an A level. If they had turned in their first effort, that initial poor grade would have been what they earned. Take advantage of this valuable assistance. Remember, however, that it is in your interest to bring your *best* effort to your instructor to review so that she or he can help you to take it to the next level of excellence.

to the thesis. Students often write arguments in which the material is laid out but it's missing those important connecting sentences that tell the reader how it is related.

Fifth, the order in which the reader is walked through the argument is confusing or unclear. There should be some sort of natural flow to the order of information presented that the reader can easily follow.

Finally, it is just poorly written or presented. The most wonderful argument can become completely unclear with poor sentence structure, incorrect grammar, and typographical errors; or in the case of an oral presentation, it can be poorly delivered. A successfully presented analytical argument is 50% due to the analysis process the author used and 50% due to a clear and concise presentation.

Writing

Over the course of your university experience, between essay exams, lab reports, papers, project proposals, and the like, you will write hundreds of pages of material. Faculty researchers are constantly writing journal articles, book chapters, and books, and the ability to write a lot and write well is essential to a successful research career. As a result, the length and complexity of your writing assignments will grow with each year, and your skills are expected to grow as well. Since you have been admitted to a research university, it is likely that you did well in high school or at a community college and might be used to getting A's on your papers. While you might have been a good writer compared to other students in your high school or community college classes, chances are that you are not a well-developed university writer . . . yet.

Writing well depends on successfully developing a series of related skills. The first are those of assignment management, time management, and following instructions, which were discussed earlier in this chapter. The quality of any written project is directly related to whether you understood what you were supposed to write, were able to break it down into the related steps to complete the project, and then were able to devote the necessary time and energy to complete the project by the deadline. Most students fail to master these items first, thus greatly hindering their ability to produce an excellent finished product. Good writing takes a lot of careful planning, time, and revising. If you do not leave yourself enough time to write and rewrite at least a couple of drafts, you will have greatly shortchanged the writing process.

Remember, your faculty are engaged in this process daily, and it is not uncommon for us to work on a writing project for months before we consider it good enough to submit for publication. Faculty commonly write multiple drafts to hone and rehone their words. Since we go to these great lengths every day with our own writing, we expect you to devote a lot of time and energy to your writing as well. It's important to realize that this business of writing is vital to the field of research, and you will be expected to be as committed to good writing as we are, which means taking it seriously and devoting a lot of time to doing it well.

Good writing greatly depends on your ability to say what you mean clearly and concisely. This has to do with word choice and sentence construction. Some of you might be well developed in this area, and some of you might need to really work on these skills early in your university career. This can be especially challenging if English is not your first language. You will want to construct sentences that say exactly what you were trying to convey and that are easy for the reader to understand. Remember, the reader sees only the words on the page—what you actually said—and not what you were "trying" to say. In addition, you will need to use correct grammar and spelling. You would be surprised how much your computer's automatic spelling and grammar check programs do *not* catch. Don't rely solely on these tools—you need to read and reread your own work.

In addition, there a wide range of writing genres that you may be asked to utilize. Over the course of your undergraduate education, you may be asked to write scientific lab reports, fiction or poetry, film critiques, research papers, and essays about literature. It would be challenging to cover each of these genres in this text and do them justice, especially since each faculty member has personal preferences when teaching this material. Your introductory writing classes will help you learn about these genres and will provide you with opportunities to improve your mastery of them. In addition, each course you take will provide you with guidance as to how to write for that particular class or discipline.

One resource that you might find helpful is from Purdue University. They have created a wonderful Internet resource called OWL (Online Writing Lab). You can find it at: http://owl.english.purdue.edu/handouts/general/index.html. It can provide you with an overview of each genre and also includes excellent guides for each stage of the writing process from the initial phases of planning through final editing and proofreading.

You will also need to adopt an academic style of writing. Academic writing has a certain serious and objective tone to it—it definitely is *not* a written translation of how we talk. There is a formality to the language that is central to academic writing, again to create the seriousness and objectivity that are crucial in research. Academic writing is also usually, but not always, written in the third person. However, you will want to look at the specific requirements of each of your writing assignments to ascertain what that particular instructor wants from you.

There are several fairly simple ways to learn academic writing. First, pay attention to the books and articles you read in your classes. Most of the articles will probably be from scholarly journals rather than popular media and will be written in the academic form. You will want to emulate this tone in your own writing. Second, you will have the opportunity to take writing courses at your university. Many freshmen have been good writers in high school, but they have not yet learned the various forms of academic writing. Transfer students often learn that some community college writing is not in the form that is most often used at a research university. These classes will be very beneficial to your writing success in all of your courses, so approach them earnestly. Third, the academic skills department on your campus most likely has workshops or writing labs that are designed to help you hone your academic writing skills. Take advantage of these as early and as often in your first year as possible. Fourth, there are many good books and reference guides on writing. Invest in one or two and consult them often. Writing is a skill that requires hours of practice and repetition.

What This Means to You

To give you an idea of how extensive the editing process can be, let me tell you about the chapter that you are now reading. When I originally wrote it, I outlined my thoughts on the content and then wrote that material. I then reread it and edited no fewer than eight drafts before I felt good about the quality of the content and the writing. Then this chapter was sent to several colleagues, who evaluated it in an anonymous review process. There were two rounds of reviewers, who provided feedback that I incorporated through three more revisions. Then it was sent to Laura Horowitz, a professional copyeditor at Hearthside Publishing Services, who gave me extensive feedback that I incorporated in the final draft. Then it was laid out by a typesetter and went through another round of two drafts before it was ready to go to print. This chapter was revised approximately fifteen times and read by no fewer than ten people before it was fit to be published. And after all that, I know that there are *still* typos to be found and sections that could be improved.

Now this is obviously a professional writing project, and a student would not be expected to go to such lengths for a paper. But I am sure you can appreciate that a faculty member might be frustrated at reading a paper that is obviously a student's first or second draft and is filled with awkward sentences, typos, and incomplete arguments. When we read that paper in a stack with thirty other papers, it's naturally not going to seem as strong as another one in which the student did three or four drafts before turning it in.

It is important to note that academic writing is very clear and concise. Some students attempt to make their writing seem more academic by using a lot of big words or complex phrasing. These techniques often hinder the reader's ability to follow the author's argument and actually decrease the quality of the writing instead of improving it. Avoid this temptation and instead focus on strengthening the support of your argument and simplifying your phrasing.

Each discipline standardizes its writing by adhering to policies and procedures that are set out in very detailed writing style manuals. These style manuals articulate everything from the size and placement of subheadings, to how many spaces should follow a colon, to the correct way to cite references. The purpose for this is to standardize the writing process for researchers, since they submit work for publications from all over the world. However, all the disciplines have not agreed on one style. For example, the American Psychological Association has created the *Publication Manual of the APA*, which is the reference guide for many of the social sciences and humanities, as is *The Chicago Manual of Style*. However, many of the sciences use the *Council of Biology's Scientific Style and Format*.

Early in your university experience, before you select a major, you might find that each course you take requires you to utilize the style format for the discipline in which that course is found. This can be a bit confusing for students and also expensive. For example, the *Publication Manual of the APA* is 472 pages and costs $22. Obviously, this is a good investment once you select a major that will utilize this format, but not before then. Luckily, there are some very good reference guides that give overviews of each of the style's main rules you would need to use when writing papers. You will find these in your campus bookstore. A good one is *Hodges' Harbrace Handbook* by Glenn, Miller, Webb, and Gray (2004).

One of the most important features of academic writing, and the main focus of each of the style manuals, is citations or references. Citations are used to give credit to any work (print, video, Internet, etc.) that was utilized in the writing of that argument and paper. Crediting another person's work is highly valued in the research environment, so it is done with utmost care and accuracy. Each of the style manuals lays out a specific format for citing the author, year, and source where it was published, whether it be print, video, Internet, or lecture. It is quite common for researchers to read a journal article and see a reference for another book or article that they would like to utilize themselves. Citations make it easier for the reader to look up those same sources for their own purposes. Citations or references also help to keep the research field honest, in that no one can claim another's work for his or her own. To use another's ideas or words without crediting them is plagiarism, which is one of the greatest violations in the field of research. As was mentioned in Chapter 1, academic dishonesty is taken very seriously in the world of academia, which means students will also be held to the same standards.

What This Means to You

Your work, especially your writing, will be intensely checked for plagiarism. Your faculty know the articles and books they have assigned as well as the lectures they have given. Believe me when I tell you that they will know if you paraphrased or quoted something—and if it is not accompanied by a correct citation, you can and probably will be accused of plagiarism. In addition, we have access to the Internet too and most likely have seen any sites that you find. If you utilize a website in any way, it needs to be cited as well. Finally, if you are tempted to "borrow" a paper from another student, even if he or she took the class several terms ago, don't be surprised if you get caught and accused of cheating. Some departments keep elaborate files of past work, and there are even computer programs departments use that will scan a paper and compare it to a huge database of previously submitted papers. This can also be done with papers purchased on the Internet. Remember that we are professional educators, and there is nothing you can do to "get by" that we haven't already seen before and probably have a system for detecting. The simple solution is to start your assignments early enough that you are not tempted to use these time- and effort-saving measures. If you find yourself behind and unprepared, it's better to earn a bad grade (which can be repeated and fixed) than to receive a bad conduct record and possibly a letter of expulsion.

Might I Suggest...

There are several things you can do to improve your writing. First and foremost, you must understand the assignment and have sufficient time to do the argument formation and writing process at a high level of quality. In addition, it can be helpful to work with another student for the purpose of editing each other's work. I strongly recommend doing this only *after* you have worked out your basic argument; otherwise, you run the risk of creating similar arguments, which might appear to be cheating if the papers are too alike. But once you have worked out your own argument, a partner can help you to see where connections are not clear, sentences are awkwardly worded, typographical and grammatical errors exist, and flaws in your logic undermine your thesis. To do this well, you must each put on your "editor hat" and approach the work of finding what's wrong with the paper and making suggestions for improvement. For this reason, it is important that you give each other permission to be honest and critical. Without that agreement in place, students often are too polite with each other and say, "Yeah, that seems good" when there were many things that could have been improved. You want your partner to be as tough on you as your instructor will be.

Once you have worked with a partner and have edited your paper several times, I recommend reading it out loud to yourself. I know this sounds silly, but it really works! When you read the paper silently to yourself, your brain fills in what you *meant* to write, not what you actually wrote. Reading out loud will help you to hear those sections that are incomplete or awkward in a way that you cannot access when you read silently. I use the very same technique for every writing project I do, including this book. As I have stated before, you can also have the instructor read your work and give you feedback. However, I recommend showing the instructor a draft that is as close to final as possible. You don't want to waste your time with an instructor catching typos and awkward sentences when you could have done that yourself or with your student partner.

Public Speaking

Public speaking is another form of communication that researchers use to disseminate the new knowledge they have discovered to others. Whether it is a presentation at a national convention, a keynote address at a government function, or a lecture to a group of students, faculty engage in public speaking all of the time. As a result, you will find yourself being asked to develop this skill as well. It is a known fact that most humans are very nervous about speaking in front of groups, and you might even see this in your faculty. There is no question that public speaking is scary for many people, but it is another skill that can be acquired and improved with time and practice. Most likely, you will engage in public speaking in the form of presentations to your class on a particular topic or

Might I Suggest...

There are lots of ways to improve your public speaking. The most obvious and best method is to practice. Put yourself in lots of situations in which you will need to speak in front of others, and you will invariably get better at it and less nervous about doing so. There might be some public speaking courses at your university; if so, enroll in them early in your college experience. Also, there are many campus jobs that require public speaking, such as student government or a peer advisor position in which you give presentations on topics such as academic advising or student health issues. Seek out these jobs because they will most likely provide you with training and the opportunities to improve. Finally, your campus probably has a public speaking club, such as Toastmasters or the Debate Team, which is designed to train and support students in gaining public speaking skills. Utilize one or all of these opportunities because public speaking skills will not only aid in your college success but also greatly assist you in finding a good career after graduation.

assignment. Remember that you will still need to have developed a strongly supported analytical argument that you essentially speak instead of write (or maybe both).

Public speaking can be enhanced through clear and illustrative visual aids. Whether you utilize posters, handouts, overheads, or a computer presentation, think about creating visual aids that will emphasize and clarify the main points of your presentation.

Information and Technology Skills

Many of the academic skills that are listed in this section, as well as the research skills mentioned in the next section, rely on a solid base of information and technology skills. Information skills are those related to using various resources to seek information. These resources include your campus library, databases and reference guides, scholarly journals, the Internet, and a host of print, auditory, and digital media. Technology skills, on the other hand, refer to your ability to use various technologies, such as computers, easily and efficiently. Most technology is computer based and covers a range of both hardware and software options.

Most first-year students know basic library and computing skills from their prior academic experiences. However, these will need to be expanded and sharpened for success at the university level. Your campus will have workshops and resources to assist you in developing both sets of skills. You are encouraged to utilize them as early in your university experience as possible, as many of your assignments will require these skills for successful completion. Your campus library will most likely have workshops and classes in information skills that are particular to the resources available to you. If not, utilize the library staff to guide you. In addition, your campus will probably have a computing facility that offers workshops in computing skills if you feel that you need to gain some instruction. It would support your academic success to become competent in word processing, working with databases, using the Internet, and creating presentations. Also, many majors will require you to learn certain software packages and will provide courses and labs for you to do so.

Research Skills

Research skills refer to the specific skills you need to conduct research within a specific discipline. As you learned in Chapter 1, each field of study has its own way of discovering and creating new knowledge. As you choose a major and take courses in that department, you will be taught the range of research skills that are most often used in your field of study. These will focus on various methods that are used to gather data (e.g., surveys, experiments, interviews, ethnography) as well as the ways to analyze data (e.g., statistical analysis, content analysis). You will have to take several courses on these topics and even utilize them in course projects to gain mastery. Obviously, it would be difficult to provide an overview of all the possibilities in each of the disciplines here. To learn more, consult the course offerings for your major department, and you will gain a sense of the possibilities. Although these courses might seem uninteresting or even very difficult, it is important to do as well as you can in them, since much of your upper division and advanced major work will rely on these particular skills. If you have the opportunity to participate in a faculty research project or conduct your own independent research (an excellent opportunity if you hope to go on to graduate school), you will utilize these research skills on a daily basis.

Being an outstanding student at a research university requires a mastery of all of the skills listed in this chapter. As a first-year student, you are not expected to have developed or honed them yet. In fact, a large part of your education in the first year will focus on helping you to develop these skill sets as you take courses. As you continue to pursue your degree, you will continue to master these skills. You can support your own success by evaluating your abilities for each skill and seeking ways to improve them. Your faculty can provide valuable guidance, as can more advanced students. Take advantage of any resources or services your campus provides and explore others that are available to you through books and websites. Remember that this is not only an investment in your college success but one that will serve you in your professional pursuits as well.

Chapter Summary

In this chapter, the following topics were discussed:

- Workload skills:
  - Assignment management
  - Time management
  - Assertive communication
  - Reading skills
  - Taking lecture notes

- Academic skills:
  - Study styles
  - Preparing for and taking exams
  - Following instructions
  - Critical thinking
  - Analytical argument formation
  - Writing
  - Public speaking
  - Information and technology skills

- Research skills

Reflections and Exercises

1. Seeking Support Services

Utilizing your campus website, student handbook, and general catalog, look up the following about academic support services at your university:

Type of Service	Name	Location	Website	Hours	Materials	Plan for Use
Study skills program						
Library						
Computing facilities or labs						
Writing skills program						
Public speaking options						

Once you have found this information, visit each of the services and pick up their handouts and materials. If possible, sign up for a workshop or a one-on-one advising session as soon as possible. Next, set a schedule for using the various services offered by each program as early in your first term as possible.

2. Estimating Your Use of Time

One of the best ways to use your more time efficiently is to first understand how you currently use time. For one week, keep a daily log of how you spend your time. Using the blank schedule at the end of the chapter as your log, record your activities in 15-minute increments, including when you wake and how long it takes you to eat, shower, get to classes, talk to friends, and so on. Be sure to keep the log with you so that you can record all those minutes between things. At the end of the week, take a look at how you used your time and answer the following questions:

How many hours did you spend in class?

How many hours did you spend studying and doing homework?

How many hours did you spend performing basic living functions such as eating, exercising, and sleeping?

How many hours did you spend socializing or having fun?

How many hours did you spend on a nonacademic commitment such as a job or sport?

How much time was taken up on nonplanned activities?

Looking over your schedule, do you think you used your time as efficiently as possible? Why or why not?

How could you use your time more efficiently?

Could you have combined some activities? Which ones?

Using a blank schedule grid, map out these activities more carefully by intentionally giving them a specific time. Certainly schedule in studying, but schedule in hanging out with friends and relaxing too. If you need more assistance, visit the counselors at your campus's academic skills program.

3. Margin Notes

Using this chapter as an example, go back and write notes in the margins. Take notes of themes, lists, terms, and your reactions to the comments. Note where you agree and disagree, are confused, or do not believe the premise. Also note where you see connections within the different parts of this chapter and to Chapter 1.

On the basis of these notes, are there questions that you can ask your instructor?

Which exam questions might you be asked from this material?

4. Catalog Quest (Part 1)

Using your university's general catalog, find the answers to these questions:

List the primary requirements for your major.

Look up three classes that are required for the major and determine the following: What is the number and title of each class? How many credits is each worth? Are there any prerequisites that you must complete before you can enroll in that class? Does the topic interest you?

Course Title	Number	Credits	Prerequisites to Be Fulfilled	Interesting?

Look at the classes on research skills (e.g., experimental designs, statistics, ethnography, interviews). Which ones are required for all students in that major?

Are there others that are optional?

What does this exercise tell you about this discipline?

Are you still interested in this major? Why or why not?

Schedule Grid

TIME	MON	TUES	WED	THURS	FRI	SAT	SUN
8–9							
9–10							
10–11							
11–12							
12–1							
1–2							
2–3							
3–4							
4–5							
5–6							
6–7							
7–8							
8–9							
9–10							
10–11							
11–12							

Visit http://success.wadsworth.com/andreatta/ to download a blank copy of the schedule grid and the assignment management sheet.

Chapter 3

Degrees, Classes, Majors, and Careers

As a college student, you should have as a primary goal the successful completion of all the requirements to earn your bachelor's degree. For the next two to four years, you will be taking classes, fulfilling requirements, and preparing for the next stage of your life after graduation. Whether you are a freshman or transfer student, this chapter will focus on information you need to know to make appropriate academic choices. You will learn about the building blocks of a liberal arts education, aspects of undergraduate courses, an overview of teaching and learning styles, the connection between majors and careers, and how the university is organized to support your university experience.

An Undergraduate Education

Bachelor's Degrees

An undergraduate education is designed to culminate in a baccalaureate or bachelor's degree on the fulfillment of a specified set of academic requirements. There are several types of bachelor's degrees: Bachelor of Arts (B.A.), Bachelor of Science (B.S.), Bachelor of Music (B.M.), and Bachelor of Fine Arts (B.F.A.). Generally, bachelor's degrees require approximately four years of enrollment in terms of credits and requirements. This translates to twelve quarters or eight semesters, assuming a nine-month enrollment period. This general estimate was established so that a bachelor's degree would represent a certain amount of undergraduate coursework regardless of the institution at which it was earned. Although there are certainly differences across degree programs in the world, they generally adhere to this level of workload. A variety of factors can affect a student's ability to finish in four years, including the availability of required classes, the timing of when the student declares a major, the transferability of coursework if the student transferred from one institution to another, whether the student passes the appropriate number of credits per term, and the impact of extenuating circumstances such as withdrawing for a quarter or participating in nonaffiliated programs for which credits do not transfer. In the United States, the average time it takes to earn a bachelor's degree is now five years, but many universities still maintain a four-year completion rate. You might want to ask what the "time to degree" is at your university and inquire about any programs or schedules that promote timely graduation.

All bachelor's degrees include the completion of an academic major, which is focused study in one discipline. Many universities offer the opportunity to minor in a second discipline or even to complete a double major in two disciplines. Students have even completed double majors with double minors, although this took them longer than four years and they had to have very specific reasons for doing so. These possibilities are specific to each campus, college, and major, so you will need to consult your general catalog to learn about the options that are available to you. In addition to the major requirements, most bachelor's degrees require the completion of some additional college- or university-wide requirements, such as minimum number of credits, courses in specified topics, a general education program, and even elective courses. You will find all graduation requirements for your university in the general catalog and other official documents. It is your responsibility to read and understand them.

As was stated in Chapter 1, your major will introduce you to an overview of that discipline and its research traditions. You might be surprised by how many possibilities exist within one discipline. For example, the American Sociological Association has identified over forty areas of interest within the field of sociology, including family; organizations; occupations; sex and gender; community and urban sociology; social psychology; race; class; culture; environment; technology; aging and life course; collective behavior; social behavior; racial and ethnic minorities; emotions; political sociology; methodology; sociology of education; sociology of law; theory; social psychology; peace and war; Marxist sociology; sociological practice; population; political economy of the world system; mental health; comparative historical sociology; political sociology; science, knowledge, and technology; sociology and computers; alcohol and drugs; children; rational choice; religion; international migration; mathematical sociology; sociology of sexualities; and history of sociology. An introductory course in sociology will touch on many of these topics, and other courses will focus on individual ones in depth.

At any one campus, students can take classes on several of the topics within sociology depending on the research specialties of the faculty at that particular campus (look to your general catalog to learn more about what is available to you). In general, introductory courses give students an overview of all that the discipline has to offer and its historical development, while more advanced classes focus in more depth on specific topics. At some universities, major courses make up the majority of a four-year education; at others, the major may represent as little as one third of the overall degree. The difference tends to stem from whether the student is in an academic program that features a liberal arts or technical education. Both can exist within the same university, although they are usually housed in different colleges or programs so that there is a clear distinction between students who are pursuing one versus another.

The Liberal Arts Education

A liberal arts education is based on the philosophy that it is important to gain a well-rounded education across many disciplines. A liberal arts education usually requires the student to complete courses from all the major discipline groupings: social science, fine arts, humanities, physical and biological sciences, and quantitative and engineering studies. This approach allows students to gain a broad understanding across a wide range of disciplines while gaining a more in-depth understanding of one discipline through their major requirements.

Universities most often provide students with a liberal arts education through a structured set of requirements in which a certain number of courses must be completed in each area as part of the degree. This is often known as a *general education*. When a degree program has a general education component, the overall degree still has the same workload as those without it, but now the overall credits are split between the liberal arts and major courses. In addition, some universities allot a certain number of units for elective courses. Some colleges offer intense and in-depth training in certain fields, most often in the technical and performing arts disciplines; these programs might require little or no study outside of the major. However, there are certainly other programs that offer these same majors combined with a liberal arts education.

As a result, an undergraduate education can look quite different at each university. Even within the same university system, such as the State University of New York, each campus might have different requirements. Table 3.1 lists the bachelor's degree requirements for four different research universities in the United States. You are invited to add the requirements for your university.

You can see that all of these universities provide a liberal arts education and do so through general course requirements, but each program is unique in its approach.

Academic Classes

Course Workload

The primary way that an undergraduate education is attained is through the successful completion of academic classes. *Successful* means that the student received the minimum grade required to earn the credits associated with that class—in other words, to satisfactorily "pass" the class. The criteria for "passing" depend on many things. At some universities, any grade above an F is passing; that is, a grade of D-minus would grant the student the credits for the course. In other programs, passing is only achieved at the C level, and sometimes higher. You will want to check your undergraduate general catalog to find out the policies for your university. In addition, you might find that your major has different criteria for specific courses or for your overall grade point average (GPA) in your major. For example, you might be expected to earn no less than a B average in premajor courses to be admitted to the full major.

Each course is assigned a certain number of credits, which is determined by the overall workload affiliated with the course. In general, a four-credit course will be more work than a two-credit course. However, it's not necessarily twice as much work. When a course is initially created, the faculty member who designs it determines what the course content will be, outlines a general syllabus, determines how much work the course will include, and assigns the appropriate number of credits. This course proposal must then go through an elaborate approval process that includes other faculty and administrators.

Over time, a given course is eventually taught by different faculty members in the department, each of whom can offer a completely different syllabus as long as the course still fulfills the general catalog description. This allows each faculty member to make the course his or her own; it also means that students might find a wide range of workloads and teaching styles associated with the very same course. This is why any course's credit load is just a rough estimate of the course's actual workload. To get a true estimate, students would need to see the actual syllabus of the course compiled by the faculty member who is teaching the course the term it will be taken.

At most universities, the general estimate is that one credit involves about two hours of work per week outside of class time. In other words, a typical four-credit class requires eight hours of work per week that students can expect to do in the form of reading, reviewing notes, working on assignments, studying, and so on. In addition, students have in-class time (such as lecture, discussion section, or lab time) for about another four hours per week, making the one course worth about twelve total hours of work for the student. For universities that are on the quarter system, classes are generally four credits, whereas semester courses are often three credits. Classes can come in a wide range of forms, ranging from as little as half a credit to as many as six, depending on the course, the department, and the university.

The purpose of each individual class is to teach a specific set of critical concepts and learning outcomes to students. As was stated before, the faculty member who creates a course determines what the set of information will be, and the description that you find in the general catalog will give you a general overview

What This Means to You

For all first-year students, some adjustment is necessary to get accustomed to the pace of the workload at your university. It usually takes students one to two terms to get a feel for the pace, workload, exam scheduling, and other differences from the previous institution. This can be especially challenging for transfer students who already have experience in the higher education environment. Transfer students can often be caught off guard by the higher level of intensity or the increased pace, especially if the university is on the quarter system. In addition, it takes time to get used to the feel of a 12-credit schedule or a 16-credit schedule.

Table 3.1   Sample of Graduation Requirements from Research Universities

University	Graduation Requirements
Brigham Young University	• Languages of Learning (math, writing, foreign language, music) • Liberal Arts Core (five different discipline areas: civilization, American heritage, biology, physical sciences, wellness) • Arts and Sciences Electives (three disciplines areas: natural sciences, social and behavioral sciences, arts and letters) • Religious Education (14 hours of religious study in ancient and modern scripture, and modern church history and doctrine in the Mormon/Latter Day Saints religion) • Major of 20 minimum semester units • Total of 120 semester units to graduate

Colorado State University	• All-University Core Curriculum that consists of the following four areas:
	  – First-year seminar
	  – Competencies in writing, foreign language, math, and logical/critical thinking
	  – Foundations and Perspectives (general education in seven different discipline areas: biological/physical sciences, arts/humanities, social/behavioral sciences, historical perspectives, global and cultural awareness, U.S. public values and institutions, and health and wellness)
	  – Depth and Integration (elements of the major that connect with the Core Curriculum and end with capstone course)
	• Major of 27 minimum semester units
	• Total of 120 semester units to graduate

University of Illinois at Chicago

- Basic Core Requirements (general education in six discipline areas: English composition, humanities, social sciences, natural sciences, cultural diversity, and foreign language)
- Major of 27 minimum semester units
- Total of 120 semester units to graduate

Massachusetts Institute of Technology

- General Institute Requirements—(total of 17 subjects in the following areas):
  - Science requirement (chemistry, physics, calculus, biology)
  - Restricted Electives in Science and Technology
  - Laboratory requirement (scientific methods)
  - Humanities, Arts and Social Sciences requirement
  - Communication Requirement (writing, public speaking)
- Major of required and elective courses (wide range of units)
- Unrestricted electives of 48 or more units
- Total of 180–198 units to graduate (beyond GIRs)

Fill in Your University Here . . .

of the topics in the course. However, the content of these topics and the way in which they are taught will be unique to each faculty member who teaches the course. In certain disciplines, such as math and the sciences, there is more consistency in the material, as it is fact-based, but each faculty member can still bring a very different teaching style and method to the material. However, in most of the other disciplines, there is much less consistency, as there can be different perspectives and interpretations of the topics. In the social sciences and humanities, it is not uncommon to have two offerings of the same course that bear little resemblance to each other. In addition, some disciplines seek to teach a range of theories or perspectives on the material. This can often be disconcerting to students who are used to being taught, and later tested on, the "right" answer.

Course Levels

Another aspect of academic classes is the level of student toward whom they are geared. Most introductory courses are geared toward first- and second-year students (i.e., freshmen and sophomores). Each campus denotes these differently. At the University of California at Santa Barbara (UCSB), introductory courses are called *lower-division courses* and are numbered 1 to 99, for example, Anthropology 5, Art History 87, or Interdisciplinary 20. You will want to read your general catalog to learn how these distinctions are indicated at your university. Generally, these introductory courses provide an overview of the course topics. For example, a history course might cover a long range of time, or a communications class might cover all of the major areas of communication theory, such as interpersonal, mass media, and organizational.

More advanced courses are geared toward third- and fourth-year students (i.e., juniors and seniors). These are called *upper-division courses* at UCSB and are numbered 100 to 199, for example, Sociology 102 and Education 173. More advanced classes tend to go into a narrower range of topics in more depth. For

What This Means to You

This seeming lack of consistency in course content can be a frustrating thing for many first-year students. The K–12 system often teaches students to look for the "right" answer so that they can do well on the exam. At a research university, we are much more focused on thinking critically about the concepts and looking at multiple perspectives rather than one view or one answer. In addition, each of us brings our own unique view to a course, so it is not uncommon for one faculty member to teach a class in a completely opposite way from that of another faculty member or even to present conflicting information within the same course. One skill that you will want to develop is to adjust quickly each term to each faculty member's way of teaching and expectations and then produce your work accordingly. This might mean that you have to utilize different strategies for each of your classes each term.

Table 3.2   Sample of Course Numbering Systems from Research Universities

University	Introductory Courses	Advanced Courses	Graduate Courses
University of Idaho	100–299	300–499	500–600
University of Hawaii, Manoa	100–299	300–499	600+
University of Illinois, Urbana-Champaign	100–199	200–399	400–499
Yale University	course numbers have no connection to level		
University of California, Santa Barbara	00–99	100–199	200–599
Fill in Your University Here . . .			

example, a history class might cover a very narrow specified period of time in more depth, such as the civil rights movement, or a communications class might focus on one specific form of communication, such as intergenerational communication. Graduate courses are offered at a more advanced level for students who are pursuing master's or doctoral degrees in that particular discipline. At UCSB, these are numbered 200–599. Generally, undergraduate students do not enroll in graduate courses except under very special circumstances by faculty request.

Table 3.2 illustrates how these differences are indicated at a few research universities. Again, check your general catalog to learn about yours.

Introductory courses in each discipline are usually open to all interested students, whether or not they are pursuing the major. In contrast, the research methods classes are usually taken only by those students who are earnestly pursuing the major and are often required before students can begin taking the major's more advanced classes. These classes prepare you for the more in-depth material that is found in the more advanced classes. You will also find that research is still the primary focus of the advanced classes, but the focus is more on what research tells us about that particular topic. For example, a course on the effects of television viewing on children will most likely involve reading and learning about various studies that have been done on this topic. Students are expected to engage in critical thinking to assess the validity of these studies and their relevance to understanding of the issue. In addition, more advanced classes may have students conduct a mini-research project of their own or participate in a university-sponsored research project.

What This Means to You

In general, more advanced students will be in the more advanced classes. These students have a good bit of experience as students at a research university, so their study skills are more developed than yours probably are, as are their critical thinking and writing skills as well as their ability to manage the university workload. In addition, transfer students might find that their first term is spent adjusting to the new workload and level of a research university, so they might have more things to focus on than their peers who began at the same university as freshmen. Many first-year students, especially freshmen, are eager to jump ahead to more advanced classes, but this is generally not a good idea. When students jump ahead too far or too fast, they often put themselves in danger of not doing well because they will be competing against students who have more experience with the material and/or more experience as university students. The result is that when the grade distributions are analyzed by class level, the more advanced and experienced students tend to hold the top of the grade curve while freshmen are often near the lower end. This obviously has negative impacts on the freshmen's GPA as well as their self-esteem. New students are strongly encouraged to enroll in appropriate classes and move through their classes at the pace and levels that their advisors recommend.

Teaching and Learning Styles

Some factors that greatly influence the experience a student has in an academic class are the instructor's personality, attitude, and teaching style. Some faculty members are lively lecturers who are energetic and passionate about the topic. Others are incredibly shy and are very uncomfortable when speaking to a large audience. Sadly, a few might even feel that teaching is a waste of valuable time that could be better spent on research. Students tend to most enjoy classes that are taught by faculty who enjoy teaching and are comfortable speaking to an audience. In addition to their personality and general enthusiasm about undergraduate education, each of your faculty members will also engage in different teaching styles.

Teaching Styles

Dr. Anthony Grasha (2004) determined that instructors generally use one of four teaching styles. He argues that instructors can use these styles in different combinations based on the needs of the classroom environment, including the students' learning styles and ability to handle the material, students' needs regarding the instructor's control of tasks, and the instructors' willingness to build relationships with their students. Each student tends to have a teaching style preference that makes some instructors a good match for one student while another student would not enjoy that instructor's classes as much. The four teaching styles are as follows.

Formal Authority Approach. Instructors focus on specific learning outcomes in terms of content and Bloom's hierarchy (see Chapter 1). The instructor teaches the content through lectures and other class activities. For example, the instructor would teach the history of the civil rights movement.

Demonstrator Approach. Instructors focus on students performing or demonstrating mastery of the content through a procedure. The instructor uses demonstrations and student participation to teach students how to do the particular process and then observes their capabilities. For example, the instructor would teach students how to write an analytical argument, and then students would be asked to research and write an argument on some aspect of the civil rights movement.

Facilitator Approach. Instructors focus on the learning process of the students. The development of learning skills is as important as the content, if not more so. Instructors utilize student-centered activities to teach students how to use the content to problem-solve in that discipline. For example, the instructor could ask students to research and design a model for bringing about change on a current social justice issue. Students might be required to use the civil rights movement in their learning and preparation.

Delegator Approach. Instructors focus on the personal growth of the students and use content to help students enhance their human potential. Often, delegators focus on social skills such as communication, value-based decision making, or effective citizenship. This style is the most dynamic and requires the instructor to know the students' capabilities intimately and adjust the learning environment accordingly. For example, an instructor might design an interactive weekend retreat to explore issues of racism and other oppression.

Indiana State University has created a very useful resource for instructors based on Dr. Grasha's work. It can be found online at their Center for Teaching and Learning (http://web.indstate.edu/ctl). You might want to review the information there to learn more about these teaching styles and strategies that instructors use in the classroom.

Learning Styles

Preference for teaching style is related to the student's learning style, which is the person's preferred or best mode for processing information. The student learns best when the information that is presented matches their preferred mode. Originally, research in this area indicated that students fell into one of three categories: visual learners (who learn best by reading or seeing information), auditory learners (who learn best by hearing information), and tactile or kinesthetic learners (who learn best by doing). Felder and Silverman (1988) more recently discovered that there are actually eight learning preferences, and students can utilize a combination of them as well.

Dr. Felder currently teaches at North Carolina State University. He and his colleague Dr. Solomon have created a very useful website for students that provides several specific strategies for students to utilize. It is found at http://www.ncsu.edu/felder-public/ILSdir/styles.htm. They also have created an online Learning Styles Questionnaire that students can use to assess their learning styles. This can be found at www.engr.ncsu.edu/learningstyles/ilsweb.html. Following is a brief description of the eight styles and learning strategies that are useful to that particular style.

Active Learning Style. These students prefer to learn by doing and also prefer working with others. Some learning strategies that work well for active learners are to work in groups, explain material to others, take notes while reading or listening to lectures, brainstorm potential exam questions, apply the material to their personal experience, and have hands-on experiences with the material.

Reflective Learning Style. These students prefer to learn by thinking about things and also prefer working alone. Some learning strategies that work well for reflective learners are to review the material, listen and read about material, think about possible exam questions, and build memory skills.

Sensing Learning Style. Students who prefer this style tend to be good at memorizing and want to learn concrete information such as facts and rules. Learning strategies include asking instructors for concrete examples, thinking about practical applications of the material, and seeking out hands-on experiences.

Intuitive Learning Style. Intuitive learners like to ponder concepts and innovate new possibilities. Useful learning strategies for this style are to have instructors help to connect the material to the bigger picture, link material to broader theories and concepts, and find meaning in facts, statistics, and the like.

Visual Learning Style. These students prefer information to be presented visually, through pictures, demonstrations, and models. Learning strategies include using color to organize material, highlighting information, drawing or diagramming concepts to see relationships, finding visual representations of the material, and using films and other visual media for learning.

Verbal Learning Style. Students who are verbal learners like to have material presented in words, either written or spoken. Some learning strategies that work well for verbal learners are outlining notes of what they have heard or read, writing summaries of material, discussing material with others, and asking questions of instructors.

Sequential Learning Style. Sequential learners like to learn information in a step-by-step process. Learning strategies include defining the steps to learn a task, organizing material in a sequential order, and outlining notes of lectures and readings in a systematic fashion.

Global Learning Style. These students prefer to see the big picture in order to learn the details of the material. These students are best served by reviewing their syllabus and skimming reading before going back to learn the details, relating what they learn to their personal experience and knowledge, and studying one topic in depth rather than many topics over a short period of time.

It's important to realize that students often utilize more than one style and can also develop other styles over time as they gain new skills and abilities. You might also find that specific disciplines are more likely to align with certain learning styles, which is why some students feel an immediate connection with a certain course or discipline. For example, sequential learners often enjoy the field of history.

Students learn best when their preferred learning style matches the instructor's teaching style because the instructor's methods automatically line up with the student's best mode of learning. Table 3.3 shows how these two models of teaching and learning styles intersect to form matches between the instructor and the student.

Table 3.3   Matrix Showing the Intersection of Teaching and Learning Styles

Learning Style	Teaching Style			
	Formal Authority Approach	Facilitator Approach	Demonstrator Approach	Delegator Approach
Active		X	X	X
Reflective	X			X
Sensing	X	X		
Intuitive		X	X	X
Visual			X	
Verbal	X			
Sequential		X	X	
Global			X	X

What This Means to You

Getting recommendations for courses from other students can be helpful in your own search for classes. However, remember that the accuracy of a recommendation depends on several things:

- *Who is teaching the course?* A course can be wonderful or horrible depending on the instructor's personality and teaching style. Find out whether your friend liked the instructor and what, specifically, your friend enjoyed. Find out whether that instructor will be teaching that course again or whether the instructor will be someone different. If it is not the same person, then your friend's recommendation will not give you much help.
- *What are your preferred learning and teaching styles?* It is often the alignment of the instructor's teaching style and the student's learning style that makes a course enjoyable for a student. You might find that you do not enjoy the exact same class that a friend does because of your preferences for teaching styles and differences in your own individual learning styles. You will want to find students who are similar to you to know that their recommendations would be relevant to you.
- *What does the syllabus include?* The course your friend took had a certain content and workload that affected the lectures, the readings, and the assignments. If your friend loves objective exams while you prefer papers, you might not assess the class in the same way. Also, unless you enroll with the exact same instructor, you might have an entirely different syllabus from your friend's. Be sure to ask about these details to ensure that you will get the same experience.

Might I Suggest...

If you don't like a class, ascertain what, specifically, you don't like about it. If it is the content, then future classes in that subject area might not interest you. However, if it is more due to the instructor, then you don't want to eliminate an entire discipline simply because of one person. Give the field another try, but do more research about the faculty member who is teaching a particular course. Also, once you find an instructor you like, take more of his or her classes. Most faculty know what they will be teaching for the next two or three terms—ask and you will be able to plan your schedule accordingly. In addition, if you like a particular teaching assistant, ask which courses and sections he or she will be assigned to next term and be sure to enroll in them.

While learning styles indicate the mode in which a student learns best, students cannot always control the form and method by which they are taught. As a result, they might need to translate the information they were taught into the form that works best for them. For example, if you are a visual learner and are in a class that is taught by an instructor who uses the Formal Authority style, you might have to take your lecture notes and find a way to create visual representations of the material. Although this will take additional time and effort on your part, it will assist you in mastering the material and equalize your learning with that of students in the class who are auditory learners.

There are many great books and resources on learning styles. Your campus might even offer workshops on these topics, which would be very useful to a first-year student. It's a good idea to assess your learning style as early in your college career as possible (see the Reflections and Exercises at the end of this chapter) so that it can guide your learning and studying strategies.

Enrolling in Your Courses

Selecting Your Courses

To ensure that you end up in classes that you enjoy, you will need to do some investigating. Students often wait until the class schedule is available and then scramble to pick classes when it's time to register. Often, choices are based on things like the time of day the class is offered, whether it meets on Fridays, or whether it is considered easy. That would be like driving up to the car lot and buying the car that's in the front row. While you will certainly find some enjoyable classes this way, you are essentially making a gamble, and you will probably end up with more classes that you do not enjoy than those that you do. In addition, you will find that there are not many "easy" classes at a top-rated research university, so this strategy will quickly prove fruitless. To learn more, you will need to be proactive and seek out information about classes. Read university publications, look at on-line resources, talk to and meet with advisors, and talk to other students.

Registering for Your Courses

Given all of the information above, it is important for students to be prepared and informed when selecting classes each term. The university community holds students responsible for their choices, so you are expected to take the actions necessary to make informed decisions. (This new level of responsibility is discussed in Chapter 4.) This includes reading official university documents and websites as well as seeking help when needed. It is *your* responsibility to read about the various requirements you need to fulfill, both for your major and for your overall degree. If you have questions or concerns, you will find that many advisors

Might I Suggest...

You have many, many classes to take during your undergraduate experience, and investing a little time and energy can greatly improve the chances that you will enjoy your classes. By following the steps below, you can greatly increase your chances of having the educational experience you desire:

1. Go through your university's general catalog and highlight any class that sounds interesting to you. Don't worry that it might not be in your major or that it is for more advanced students. If it sounds like something you would like to take, highlight it. If you have a general education program at your campus, I strongly recommend going through the same process for each requirement: Review the list of classes that fulfill each requirement and highlight *only* the classes that seem interesting to you. If there are not any choices, find out whether different faculty teach the course and what the differences are between them. Choose the one that best suits you.

2. When the class schedule becomes available for a term, look at what is being offered and compare it to your list of classes that interest you. If a class that you would really like is not offered, wait until it is. Choose another requirement for which something that interests you is available.

3. Check out the faculty member who is teaching the class. Ask friends whether they have had class with him or her. Find out more about what that student liked and disliked and compare it to your own preferences. Remember to inquire about learning and teaching styles. If the class schedule does not indicate who will be teaching the class, call the sponsoring department and ask; they should be able to tell you who will be teaching it. Some even publish

are available to help you. You will usually find them in your college's main office as well as your major department.

You are also responsible for making sure that you are fulfilling your requirements in a timely manner with the appropriate grades. Many students find that it is helpful to keep an ongoing record of the courses they have taken and the requirements that they have satisfied with those courses. Some colleges and majors will give you prepared checklists that you can use to keep track of your progress. At other campuses, you might be on your own for doing so. You might wish to create a chart or table that has an area for each term for all four years. Then pencil in various requirements at the time when you plan to take them. Once you take a course, write it in the correct place in pen and indicate the requirement(s) it fulfilled and the grade you earned. Periodically review your progress with an academic advisor and make adjustments as necessary.

In addition to degree requirements, your university will provide you with ample information about the process for registering for your classes. Your university has a well-developed system by which all students can select and enroll in academic classes. It is your responsibility to make sure that you understand the teaching evaluations of courses and make them available for students to review.

4. If you would like more information about a faculty member's teaching style, I recommend watching him or her in the classroom for a few minutes. You can tell a lot in a short period of time. To do this, you would need the class schedules for both next term and the current term. Find the name of the person who is teaching next term and then look that person up in the current schedule to see when she or he is currently teaching. It doesn't have to be for the same class; you're focusing only on the instructor's teaching abilities. Then visit the class for a few minutes and see for yourself whether that instructor's style meets your needs. Just be sure to stand or sit quietly in the back so as to not disturb the class.

5. If you want to know more about a specific course, you can contact the faculty member who will be teaching it and ask whether he or she has a copy of the syllabus you can look at. If not (some of us wait until the last minute to pull the syllabus together), you can see whether there is an old syllabus that might be available or even just ask a few questions about the content and workload. Just be sure that you phrase your request in an appropriate manner; for example, you might say, "I'm thinking of enrolling in your course, and I'd like to know more about the content, the assignments, and your teaching style." That will be received much better than "I'm checking out your course—I don't want anything too hard, so I'm wondering how much work your class will be."

process and how to engage in it at the appropriate times. There are usually specified times and deadlines with regard to registration, some of which might have serious consequences if they are missed. These consequences can include missing out on available classes because you did not utilize the time in which you were supposed to register, late fees or fines, and even being dropped from classes or blocked from registering in the future for failing to heed important deadlines.

Be sure that you read registration materials carefully and that you understand what you are supposed to do and by when. Most registration systems are set up according to seniority by credits, the most advanced students registering first and the students with the fewest credits registering last. Some groups might get priority registration no matter what their credit standing, such as honors students or athletes in their competitive season. If you have questions or need assistance, contact academic advisors in your major or college. This means being able to take advantage of regular business hours; you will find that most campus offices are not open in the late evenings or weekends when students might be registering. Be sure that you take care of these issues before 5:00 P.M. on Friday.

Once you have registered, keep a record and check it to make sure that it is accurate. If you need to make adjustments to your schedule, such as addressing a time conflict when one class overlaps another or adding or dropping a class, it is your responsibility to do so. Most registration systems include opportunities to make changes to your schedule, but again, these may have certain time frames or deadlines in which you need to function.

Once a deadline has passed to drop a course or pay a fee, you will most likely have to deal with the consequences. Most universities cannot be flexible with these deadlines because they are set up to be efficient and effective in dealing with many thousands of students. Over the years, many students will seek exceptions, and university administrators just cannot grant them all. Your university might have an appeal process for certain deadlines, but this will probably require a written petition and documentation of an extreme circumstance that prevented you from adhering to the process or deadline.

If you are unsuccessful in enrolling in a class that you need through the regular registration process, you might need to try more creative ways to get the course. First, continue to try to add the class through regular registration methods during the window of time assigned to you to add and drop courses. Over that time, students are continually adding and dropping classes, which means that spots are often opening up in full classes just to be snatched up again a few minutes later. The student who repeatedly tries to add the class will likely gain one of these open spots. Also, there might be certain deadlines that precipitate classes opening up. For example, your campus might drop students from their classes if they fail to meet the fee payment deadline. That means that on that day or the next, spaces open up in quite a few classes; again, the observant student will be able to utilize this opportunity.

If these methods fail you, then the next step is to contact the faculty member who is teaching the course and request to be added. If you are not sure how to contact him or her, call the academic department, which should be able to provide you with an email address. Most faculty have the ability to add or drop students, although they might or might not have reserved spaces to do so. Your note should say something like this:

Dr. <u>fill in name here</u>,

My name is Garrett Patel and I am a junior, sociology major. I am writing because I want to enroll in your <u>fill in title here</u> course next term. I have attempted to enroll in the class several times during registration, but I have not been able to gain a spot. I would appreciate it very much if you could add me to your class. If this is not possible, please put me on your waiting list for the course. Thank you so much for your time and assistance. Please call or email me so that I know what my status is regarding this course.

Sincerely,

Garrett Patel

<u>fill in phone and email info here</u>

Ideally, you will hear from the instructor within a few days. If not, write back in one week and send the same note. If the instructor adds you or puts you on the waiting list, write back to say "thank you" and then be sure that you are on time for the first class. If you are late, you could lose the spot you have gained.

Your final option is to "crash" the class. "Crashing" is a long-standing tradition on many university campuses, and it is the process by which students gain a spot in a class that is full. You essentially show up the first day and try to gain a spot, along with the other people who are trying to do the same. If you were successful in being added to the waiting list, then you should be one of the first people the instructor adds. If not, then the faculty member will most likely have a process by which he or she handles crashers, such as taking people in the order of their class standing (seniors first, juniors second, etc.), or on a first-come-first-served basis.

Some faculty deal with crashers right away; others wait until the end of class. Be prepared either way. Also, persistence pays off in crashing. The more class periods you attend, the better are your chances. If you really need or want a class, come to the first three or four sessions before giving up. You would be surprised how many students who are enrolled drop the class during the first week or fail

Might I Suggest...

Many first-year students have experienced serious problems because they missed important deadlines. To avoid this problem, I recommend that you transfer all important deadlines to your weekly planner or monthly calendar so that you decrease your chances of missing them. Write them in big, red letters on your planner or calendar. Also, be sure to note times as well as dates. For example, at my campus, the deadline for many items is at 4:00 P.M., when the Office of the Registrar closes. Although this time is adequately stated in all materials, many students write down only the date and are often very frustrated when they attempt to drop a class or pay their fees online after 4:00 P.M. only to find that the system has shut down or the office has closed. Also, there is often a flood of student activity at 3:00 P.M., and many students find that they cannot get online or call in to the phone system because of the heavy traffic. Avoid these hassles by planning ahead.

Also, do not make the mistake of thinking that because you stopped going to a class, you have been dropped from it. Many universities have a policy that only the student can drop a course from his or her schedule. At the end of the quarter, faculty find that there are a few names on their grade sheet of students who never came to class. Since these students have not completed any work, the instructor has no choice but to give them an F. While the student can usually fix this situation through an appeal, it would have been so much easier if the student had officially dropped the course by the deadline. Always be sure to drop any class you do not plan on attending.

A Word about Grievance Procedures

Every once in a while, things can go wrong at a university, and a student's rights or safety are compromised. Unfortunately, sometimes an instructor or staff member treats students unfairly or inappropriately. Examples can include minor situations that can cause problems for the students, such as an instructor grading an exam incorrectly or a staff member being rude to a student. In addition, more serious problems can occur, such as a faculty member who drastically changes the assignments or grading procedures during the term or who treats some students very differently from others in ways that negatively affect their ability to perform well in the class. Faculty or staff might even make offensive comments or sexually harass a student. There is generally a standard procedure that students should follow if they have experienced a problem in which their rights or safety have been violated.

In less serious situations, the general procedure to follow is to start with the person with whom you are having the problem and determine whether it is a communication issue. State what you are requesting in clear and polite terms. You would be surprised at how many situations can be resolved with simple and direct communication. If this does not bring the results you would like, then you can take the situation up to the next level at the university. For a staff member, you would make an appointment with his or her supervisor, usually the director of the program or department; for a faculty member, you would make an appointment with the chair of the department. It is usually a good idea to write down a summary of what has happened so far, including dates and specific comments. Also, state what you are requesting in terms of a solution. Be sure you arrive on time; a missed appointment will not make you look very credible. At this meeting, you might learn about campus policies or procedures that could influence the situation and any processes that exist, such as petitions or grievance forms that you can fill out and submit.

to show up. If a spot does open up, you will be in line to get it. And if one doesn't, the instructor might just add you anyway because of your perseverance. Of course, if you are attempting to crash a course, you want to demonstrate that you would make a positive contribution to the class, so be sure to arrive on time, pay attention, and participate in class discussions when appropriate.

The Connection Between Majors and Careers

Most students and their families rightfully believe that a person who earns a bachelor's degree has more employment opportunities than does a person who does not. In addition, the salary earnings over a person's lifetime can be far greater for a college graduate, with even more earnings possible with

If this meeting does not bring satisfaction, you have the option of continuing to the next level of the organization. For staff, it might be the director or the dean, or possibly the vice chancellor or vice president, who oversees the division in which that department is located. For faculty, it would be the dean or provost for the college in which the academic department is housed. Again, make an appointment and be on time. Bring written documentation and make your request clear. If this final level does not bring the results you were hoping for and you still feel strongly that you have been wronged, you can work with the office that addresses student concerns, often called the ombudsman office, the dean of students' office, or the office of student complaints and mediation. You also have the option of seeking legal counsel.

In serious situations such as sexual harassment or threats of violence, the student should immediately speak to someone who can help. If the situation is urgent or obviously illegal, call your local police. If not, you may be able to pursue various options at your campus. Most universities have staff and administrators who assist students with these kinds of problems and can also protect them from retribution. Often, there is a complaint officer or an ombudsperson who handles these situations, but if you are not sure, contact your dean of students' office. You would want to make an appointment with this person as soon as possible. It is usually very helpful when the student has created a written summary of what has happened so far. This person can talk to you about a range of options and assist you in resolving the situation. These can include removing you from the situation in a way that keeps your academic record in good standing to assisting you in filing a formal complaint and following a grievance process in which the offending party's behavior can be evaluated and possibly punished.

postgraduate degrees. With this in mind, many students and parents believe that the path to high-paying jobs begins with the selection of the major. However, this is *not* true for most careers. Most careers, including the "popular" ones, such as medicine or law, can be pursued with a variety of undergraduate majors. The careers that do require a specific major are the technical careers, such as engineering or nursing, in which a specific course of study is required to have the qualifications needed for most entry-level jobs. Students who wish to pursue these careers spend their undergraduate years in a focused and intense program of study.

One of the most common myths is that there is a strong relationship between college major and a specific career. This is simply not true. In almost every career field, you will find successful people who have a wide range of college majors, with the exception of careers that require a strong background in technical training, such as engineering. These means that most undergraduate students can choose from a whole host of majors from a wide range of disciplines and still pursue almost any career that interests them. With this said, it is important that

What This Means to You

Most students and their families have expectations that an undergraduate education serves as a form of vocational preparation—in other words, training for a specific job. This is true at some colleges, especially those that offer specific job training courses such as hotel management or journalism, but it is generally not true at research universities. However, degrees from research universities are considered prestigious because employers usually seek the critical thinking, analytical, and writing skills that they know are taught at a research university. Employers know that students will have learned the latest theories and information for a field and, better yet, will have the skills to stay abreast of future developments.

Since classes at a research university do not teach other specific career or job skills, many students choose to augment their degree with job preparation activities. All students can gain this applied knowledge and/or job skill training by utilizing research opportunities, holding several internships, and taking advantage of university workshops on important job skills such as public speaking, leadership, and computing. Consult with the career services office at your university for more information about what is offered on or near your campus. Regardless of the major, most students can build an impressive resume while in college by designing their own vocational preparation program.

Might I Suggest...

It is never too early to visit your campus career services office to gain information about the available opportunities as well as to learn more about careers that interest you. While your use of the career center will increase during your university years, it is important to start early, even if you have no idea what career you wish to pursue. Most career centers even have assessment tools that can help you to learn more about your preferences and talents, which can guide you in the selection of your future career. The career center can probably even connect you with alumni who are currently in the career you wish to pursue so that you can learn more about what it is really like and how to best prepare to enter that field. As you get older, the career center can help you to prepare your professional resume, can assist you with interview skills, and even may bring employers to the campus to conduct real job interviews. As with any office, there will be a range of people who can assist you. Once you find a person with whom you connect, be sure to schedule future appointments with him or her. Over time, this person can guide your undergraduate experience and career development in ways that are best suited to you. Don't forget that your faculty can also assist you with career exploration and planning.

students and their parents not let these myths dictate the students' choices for a major. It is truly a shame when students limit their focus to one or two majors without even trying a wide range of classes. High school students have never been exposed to most of the disciplines they will find at a research university, so how can they select a focused field of study without exploring their options? And how good can a choice be if it is based on misinformation or myths? The best way to seek advice about career planning is to visit the career services office at your university. The staff there can give you concrete information on the various paths that lead to certain careers, the salaries that various careers offer, and other important information. Most families are surprised to learn how open the options really are in considering majors.

Another common myth is that a student needs to major in biology if she or he wants to get into medical school. This is simply not true. While medical schools require the completion of a certain set of courses during the undergraduate education (known as *pre-med courses*), students can complete these while pursuing a whole range of nonscience majors. In fact, there are so many biology majors who apply to medical school that a student actually improves his or her chances of admission by being anything *but* a biology major! What medical schools look at most is the grades in the pre-med courses and the MCAT scores. If a student does well in these two areas and pursued a nonbiology major, his or her chances are actually greater because of the unique educational background that student would bring to the medical school. Of course, the student would need to have excelled in the chosen major and have a strong GPA. A similar myth is that a student needs to major in political science or government to be admitted to law school. Again, this is simply not true, and in fact, students with non–political science majors and strong LSAT scores will again be more competitive against the hundreds of applicants with political science degrees. It is also not true that you need to have an undergraduate degree in the same field in which you wish to pursue a master's or doctorate degree. Although this is true for some fields, namely, the sciences, most graduate programs accept students with a wide range of majors.

It is important to distinguish choosing a major from choosing a career. Choosing a major is about discovering what you love to *study*. This means finding out what you would enjoy reading and writing about for four years. Separately, choosing a career is about discovering the type of *work* you love to do. This involves learning what you would enjoy doing or engaging in for forty or more hours per week. Both decisions are very important but require different considerations for different times of your life, and therefore, should be approached separately.

Selecting Majors and Minors

One of the many good things about attending a research university is that a degree from one is usually highly regarded by employers and graduate schools. In general, research universities tend to be more selective in their admissions process, which means that they can attract the best and brightest students in addition to world-renowned faculty. Together, these things create a prestigious institution of higher education. This positively affects students' postgraduate options because the students will possess a nationally respected degree. Since the final degree is prestigious, this increases the students' ability to pursue a wide range of majors.

The best way to select a major is based on two criteria: interest and aptitude. First and foremost, the student should pick a major on the basis of his or her interests. It is very difficult to pursue four years of study and excel in classes that are not interesting to you. Lack of interest directly and negatively affects a student's focus and enthusiasm for a class, both of which are necessary to perform strongly. Aptitude is also a strong factor in determining an appropriate major. Unfortunately for first-year students, lack of university experience, appropriate workload management, and academic skills can influence their ability to perform well. Aptitude can be accurately assessed only when these other issues are handled—usually by the end of the first year. Only when these adjustments to university-level work have been made can a student truly know whether she or he is good in a subject. Generally, if a student is working very hard, using all of the university resources that are available, and is still doing poorly, then it is safe to assume that the student will probably not be strong in that particular discipline. Although students may still choose to pursue the discipline, they might find that they have to work far harder than their peers and still might not do quite

What This Means to You

How do you know whether a class or discipline interests you enough to consider it as a major? A discipline is a good bet for a major when the following are true for you on a regular basis:

- You find yourself looking forward to a class.
- You don't want to miss class.
- You find the reading enjoyable and intriguing.
- You enjoy doing the assignments.
- You highly recommend the class or discipline to others.

If you are not sure about what career opportunities might be available, go meet with a career or major advisor. You might just be surprised at how many opportunities there are even for majors that seem somewhat limited in terms of career potential. For example, many students and families assume that sociology majors are limited to careers in social work. This is simply not true. The American Sociological Society identifies a wide range of career opportunities for people with a degree in sociology, including jobs in business, social service, government, journalism, politics, public relations, public administration, law, education, medicine, criminal justice, social work, counseling, advertising, real estate, public health, environment, finance, investing, and writing.

Might I Suggest...

Remember, choosing a major is about discovering what you would like to study. Here are three simple ways to see if a major might be for you. One is to read about the major in your general catalog. There is usually a description of the discipline and the specific subfields that are offered at your campus. You also want to read the course descriptions, both introductory and more advanced. If you find lots of classes that sound interesting to you, then you might enjoy this major.

Second, visit the campus bookstore and peruse the shelves associated with that particular major. Look at the books that are assigned for different classes. Glance over the table of contents and skim a few pages. If they sound interesting to you and something you would like to read, then that is another clue that it might be worth exploring.

Finally, talk to more advanced students in the major. Find juniors and seniors and ask them about the classes and the overall major. Remember to account for personal differences like interests, aptitudes, and learning styles, but if you like what you hear, then it's another good sign that you should check out this major by taking a course or two and then deciding for yourself.

as well. When students find the perfect blend of interest and aptitude, they look forward to attending their classes and doing their homework, and they generally feel that it is easy to excel.

Needless to say, students who choose their major on the basis of interest and aptitude tend to do well in their major classes, and this opens many doors in the worlds of both graduate school and employment. They will often have a high GPA and can get strong letters of recommendation both of which are important for postgraduate opportunities.

Declaring Majors and Minors

Each university, and sometimes even each college within the same university, has its own process for declaring majors. Usually, the process involves some kind of formal paperwork so that the appropriate departments are notified and the student's choice of major can be tracked. Some majors are open to anyone, so any interested student can declare them. Other majors require a certain level of competency, so there may be auditions or certain minimum criteria that must be met in order to pursue them. You will want to read about these policies in your university's catalog or speak to an academic advisor to learn more. The timing of when to declare a major usually depends on three things: the university's policies, a student's ability to find something that she or he wants to major in, and the need to graduate within four years. Needless to say, these things will not always be in perfect alignment.

Early in a student's college experience, the urgency to declare a major depends on the complexity of major requirements. Students in the sciences usually need to get started early on their major coursework, since it involves so many year-long series of science courses. If they want to graduate within four years, they need to begin their major requirements the first term. While second-year students can certainly begin a science major, they will usually not be able to complete it within four years. However, this might be a fine trade-off if they truly want to pursue the sciences as a life-long career.

In addition, students in certain technical and arts majors may have been admitted to a particular college or program. Changing majors out of that general discipline might require a change of colleges or academic programs, and this may even involve an application process. For example, at the University of California at Santa Barbara, students are admitted directly into the College of Engineering, the College of Creative Studies, or the College of Letters and Science. Both the College of Engineering and the College of Creative Studies have extremely high standards for admission and offer a very focused education in a limited number of majors. If a student in the College of Letters and Science wanted to pursue one of those majors, she or he would have to apply for admission with no guarantee of acceptance. However, a student in one of those two colleges could easily switch to the College of Letters and Science, although the student would lose his or her place in the original college and could not switch back later.

While some majors and colleges have strict policies like those outlined above, many do not. There are many majors that can be finished within two years and so can be declared by the end of the sophomore year and the student will be able to finish the degree within four years. This type of timeline can allow a student to explore a wide range of options through general education and elective courses that lead to the selection of a major. You will want to find out about these policies and options at your university by consulting the catalog or an academic advisor.

In some cases, declaring a major on paper has little to do with the student's actual course selection and completion. In other words, the student can be registered as a history major and actually be taking courses to fulfill the anthropology major. This is especially true in the first or second year when students are fulfilling a wide range of requirements. Although this can occur for a period of time, students eventually want to declare the major they are actually pursuing. Declaring a major often provides many benefits, such as being able to register for classes that are designated for only declared majors, having priority over non-majors for classes, receiving relevant notices from the department, and qualifying for certain opportunities.

Some majors, usually the most popular or crowded ones, might have some type of screening process to handle the demand. There might be a set of courses that all students who are interested in that major must complete, and there might even be a minimum GPA that must be met. In such cases, the introductory classes are often difficult and very competitive, as the intention is to weed out the less serious or talented students. If you are interested in one of these majors, be sure you really focus on doing well by utilizing your resources (office hours, study groups, tutors, etc.). If you fail to meet the GPA requirement, you will not be allowed to pursue the major, and you will have to find another one.

Changing Majors

Changing a major depends on the complexity of the majors and the timing in which the change occurs. Changing a major is usually accomplished through filling out a form or an online process. Changing from one major to another will be affected by all of the issues stated above, and this can limit some possibilities. If done quite late, it certainly can affect whether the student will be able to graduate within four years. In fact, some campuses do not allow students to begin a more complex major if they seek to do so after the second year. This is because many research universities are committed to graduating their students in a timely manner in order to accommodate future incoming classes. For example, if a campus estimates that a student needs 180 quarter credits to graduate, the administration might put a unit cap at 200 units to ensure compliance. Once students exceed 200 units, their registration could be blocked, and they have to meet with an academic advisor to determine how they can quickly complete a bachelor's degree. Depending on the situation, the student's choices of major might be very limited in the interest of finishing a degree in a timely fashion.

Sarah's Story

I came to school this year without any idea about what I wanted to major in. I just started taking classes to fulfill the general educational requirements, hoping that I would get some ideas. My first quarter, I took classes in a variety of topics: history, classics, and philosophy. I enjoyed them all, but I really liked my classics class, so I took another one my second quarter, along with biology, art history, and geology. Again, my classics class stood out as the most interesting and enjoyable. That quarter, I was also enrolled in the freshman experience course. One of our lecturers was on finding a major, and the speaker talked about how important it is to find a passion, something you *love* to study. It hit me right there in class. I love to study classics! The reading is totally interesting to me, and I looked forward to every lecture. So I have declared the classics major and am really happy. It's a very small department so I already know most of the faculty, and I am doing a directed reading with one of my professors. Luckily, my parents have been really supportive of my choice. I am not sure yet what I will do for a career, but I have time to figure that out. There are actually lots of career possibilities for classics majors, and I can always expand my options with some internships, which I will be looking into next quarter.

Double Majors and Minors

Many universities offer students the option of pursuing double majors and/or minors. A double major usually means that the student completed the work for two complete majors, with little or no overlap. To do this, some programs require students to use their elective courses for the second major. Minors are less work than a full major but still provide a significant amount of contact with the discipline. Not all academic departments that offer majors offer a minor, so you will want to explore the options at your campus. In addition, you would want to speak with an academic advisor to ensure that you clearly understand the process for pursuing these options and how to do so without taking too long to graduate.

The options of double majors or minors are usually considered when a student is genuinely interested in more than one field of study. In addition, these options allow the student to put two fields of study together in preparation for

Might I Suggest...

When a student selects a major, it is often for reasons that have little to do with the actual major. They might believe that a certain major will lead to a certain career or will ensure a certain future earning level. As I have already stated, it is very important to explore these beliefs and expectations with career and academic advisors at your campus so that you can make accurate and informed choices. However, it will still be important that you actually *enjoy* the major that you finally choose. Some majors sound great when you read the catalog but are disappointing in reality. Or they might be great majors, but a student cannot seem to perform at a level that is competitive with his or her peers. The bottom line is: If you have tried the suggestions I have previously offered (in terms of choosing classes wisely and finding faculty you enjoy) and you are still not enjoying or doing well in the major, do *not* pursue it! The major is clearly not a good match based on the criteria of interests or aptitude, and you would be better served by finding another major. I have seen students stick with majors that they either did not enjoy or were not good at, and it was painful to watch. These students spent four years in drudgery, unmotivated to attend class, unenthusiastic about learning, and, inevitably, unimpressive to future graduate programs and employers because of their grades. I truly believe that every person has a passion, something that makes their heart sing and that they find interesting and exciting. It is important for you to find that for yourself. There are lots of great assessment tools that can point you in the right direction, but ultimately, you have to listen to yourself and what *you* find compelling. This might be very different from what your parents wish for you or from what is supported by others. Ultimately, it is *you* who sits in the desk every day and must spend this precious time of your life focusing your energy on your studies. It is imperative that you make selections on the basis of your preferences and passions.

unique careers. For example, one student decided to pair art history with business economics because he wanted to work in auction services that specialize in art. After working with a career advisor, he learned that this combination of classes would uniquely prepare him to pursue his passion. In this case, the student had done his research about his future career options with a professional career advisor at his campus and made appropriate academic choices. All students can increase their career marketability by doing similar explorations with academic and career advisors.

A double major of any field paired with a foreign language opens up opportunities for international work as well as domestic careers in areas in which there are multilingual communities or clients. Be sure to explore these options with a career advisor on your campus so that you choose wisely and are not following out-of-date or inaccurate information. It is through these options that students can maximize their education at a research university with savvy career preparation that will poise them for successful careers.

How a University Is Organized

Research universities tend to be larger campuses, which mean that they are a big structure organizationally. Most colleges and universities organize themselves into various categories and then have more departments and programs within those larger categories. These larger categories are often called divisions, and there may be as few as two or as many as ten. Each division represents a different function of the university and they may be combined differently on each campus. As you navigate your education, you will find that you will deal with many different offices across all of the divisions. The following is a brief description of some typical functions and/or divisions that you might encounter.

A lead administrator such as a vice president or vice chancellor runs each division. The primary head of your campus, either a president or chancellor, supervises all of these lead administrators. Within each division, there will be a variety of departments and programs, each one run by another administrator and supported with various staff members. A look at your campus's general catalog, central phone directory, or website will probably give you an overview of your campus's organizational structure. Although this might seem irrelevant to you, it will help you to know which department to visit for a particular issue and who is in charge. As a student, the academic, housing, and student affairs divisions will most likely directly affect you on your campus, so more details are offered on those three areas.

The Academic Division

The Academic Division is designed to provide the structure, policies, and services needed to assist students in successfully obtaining an academic degree. This aspect of your campus will have the largest and most direct impact on your university experience, since it is the part of campus that will eventually award you your bachelor's degree. Again, because of size, some organizational structure will be in place, and you will want to find out what it is like on your specific campus. You will probably find that your university has a few colleges that are different from each other in terms of the types of majors they offer. One might offer several degrees in the different engineering disciplines, while another might offer a liberal arts education with a wide range of majors, and there might even be a unique college offering graduate-level education for undergraduates with advanced talent in one of a few fields such as literature or computer science.

Even within the University of California system, there is a wide range, with each campus organizing itself differently. For example, at UC Santa Cruz, there are several colleges (Cowell, Crown, Merrill, Porter, Stevenson, Kresq, Oakes, Eight, Nine, and Ten); each creates a smaller learning environment for both faculty and students, some of whom live in the college's housing. At UCLA, all undergraduates are in the College of Letters and Science, while there are seven professional schools for graduate students. As you travel to other universities, the organizational possibilities are endless. For example, the University of Arizona has over 300 degree programs organized into twelve schools and eighteen colleges, whereas the University of Florida has seven schools and eighteen colleges ranging from the fine arts to business administration to education to nursing. A school is a subdivision of the college and may house one or more academic programs or disciplines.

Colleges

In general, a college seeks to award a range of bachelor's degrees in a variety of majors. The college typically has certain graduation requirements in addition to those you must satisfy for your major. As a result, the college usually maintains student records on these requirements and has staff members that provide academic advising about them. Typically, these staff members are familiar with all the majors and so can provide advice about the majors offered in the college as well as advice for undeclared students. Your college might also boast an honors program and can provide you with information about how to qualify for, and the benefits associated with, membership. Your college has certain policies and procedures for its students (e.g., withdrawals, repeated courses), and there are staff that oversee and administer these policies. Most likely, the college has some kind of committee or administrative structure that oversees all of the major departments to ensure that they are operating in a similar and fair fashion. For example, it is the college's job to make sure that all majors are roughly equivalent in terms of requirements and difficulty. A main administrator known as a provost or dean typically runs a college, and depending on the size, there may be several associate or assistant administrators in charge of various elements.

Academic Majors/Departments

An academic or major department is a collection of faculty in a certain discipline, such as education or chemistry. This collection of faculty are located together in a specific building where they have individual offices, a main office, a copy room, a conference room, and so on. They determine the requirements you will need to fulfill to obtain a bachelor's degree in that particular field, that is, your major. You can be sure that these major requirements will include the theoretical and/or research traditions of that particular discipline. In addition, you will begin to see the specific research specialties of that particular group of faculty reflected in the courses offered and even the subspecialties that might be offered to you. The faculty in the department range from lecturers to full professors and are active and respected researchers and educators in that particular discipline. Your major department might also offer advanced degrees and might have graduate programs for students to pursue a master's or doctoral degree in that same discipline. The faculty teach, advise, train, and mentor the graduate students.

An academic department is run by a department chair. The chair is a current faculty member who has taken on specific administrative duties of running the department for a specified period of time. Usually, chairs are full professors who have achieved tenure and are at the highest level of their career path. Being a chair takes a lot of time and energy, which decreases research productivity, so these positions rotate through the faculty of the department. Duties include overseeing faculty meetings, supervising faculty in terms of classroom conduct and performance, scheduling courses for each term and determining who will teach them, overseeing the performance evaluation process of any faculty member who is being reviewed, overseeing the graduate student selection process, overseeing funding and grants, producing various reports, and responding to any requests from the overseeing college or high-level administrators.

Enrollment and Academic Support Services

Besides colleges and major departments, you will discover a plethora of other departments, services, and programs that support you in being successful in your academics. Most of these entities provide a specific service to the campus and are usually run by an administrator or director and supported by staff. It is important to note that not all of these are housed within the academic division on every campus; some are found in the division of student affairs. Some examples include the following:

- *Academic skills center:* Provides general skill development in areas such as note taking and exam preparation, as well as one-on-one or group tutoring in particular disciplines.
- *Judicial affairs:* Provides education on the campus regulations for academic integrity and adjudicates cases in which regulations have been violated.
- *Library:* Provides the campus community with a constantly updated source of scholarly resources, both printed and electronic, for conducting research of all kinds.
- *Information systems:* Provides the campus with computing facilities, labs, and services that support research, education, and communication.
- *Admissions:* Provides the process for students to apply and be admitted to an undergraduate program at the university. This also includes evaluating the transferability of coursework completed at another institution.

- *Orientation:* Provides an overview of important campus issues and services, including academic advising, faculty expectations, services for families, housing options, and so on.
- *Registration:* Provides a system for course registration, maintains student records and transcripts, and processes grades and other academic actions such as withdrawals and incomplete grades.
- *Financial aid:* Provides assistance with applying for various forms of aid (need- and merit-based grants, scholarships, loans, and work-study) from federal, state, and private sources. Maintains records and disburses funds.
- *Education abroad programs:* Provides assistance with student enrollment at other universities in foreign countries including applications, funding, visas and passports, housing, orientation, and other services.
- *International students:* Provides assistance with a range of issues like finding housing, providing language training, and assisting with visas to international students who have traveled from abroad to attend the university.
- *Disabled students support:* Provides services such as note taking, sign language interpreters, and textbook reading for students with physical or learning disabilities, be they permanent or temporary in nature.

The Student Affairs Division

The Division of Student Affairs is designed to provide the support services needed to keep students healthy and functioning so that they can perform well academically. This division is home to many services and programs that directly support the success of students, both academically and personally. This division typically includes the personal counseling component, career advising, recreational activities, financial aid, cocurricular activities such as clubs and Greek life, and services for certain populations such as students of color, older students, and lesbian, gay, bisexual, and transgender students. These services can vary greatly at each campus, but most research universities provide some version of the following services:

- *Student health:* Provides various levels of medical care to the student population. May include dental and eye care as well as psychiatric services.
- *Counseling:* Provides professional counseling services for students who are dealing with personal issues that might be interfering with success at the university, such as dealing with homesickness or a painful breakup, managing depression and other mental illnesses, and developing better social skills, such as assertiveness and communication.
- *Dean of students:* Provides general assistance to students and their families with problem solving and emergencies. Also addresses student conduct and grievance issues and gives referrals when necessary.
- *Career advising:* Provides advising and mentoring in selecting potential careers, obtaining internships, and preparing for a job search in terms of resumes and interview skills.
- *Athletics and recreation:* Provides various recreation facilities (e.g., gyms, pools, ice rinks) for students to maintain or improve their physical strength.

They may also support student athletic teams from club and intramural sports to intercollegiate athletic teams.

- *Cocurricular activities:* Provides a wide range of clubs or organizations for students to participate in, from Greek life and student government to clubs and volunteer opportunities.
- *Educational opportunity program:* Provides support services to student populations that might be considered challenged or disadvantaged in some way (e.g., low-income students, first-generation immigrant students, or underrepresented minority students), compared to their peers.
- *Multicultural programs:* Provides education and entertainment across a wide range of cultures and backgrounds and may also provide support or involvement opportunities for students of various backgrounds.

The Housing Division

If your campus owns and runs residence halls or apartments that students live in, then it will most likely have a division that operates and maintains the living spaces, manages contracts, provides meal services, and so on. This division also hires and trains a staff of professionals and student members who live in the building(s) and oversee the daily functioning and safety of the living community. In addition, they provide mediation services and respond in emergencies. On many campuses, housing and student affairs are combined in the same division. Some typical services include the following:

- *Contracts and assignments:* Manages the applications for, and assignments to, university-owned housing units, as well as overseeing the legal contract process and subsequent payment of fees.
- *Food services:* Provides daily meal services that meet a wide range of nutritional and personal needs to hundreds of people per meal.
- *Residential life:* Provides professional and student staff support to residents to ensure a safe and healthy community. Duties include providing individual counseling, workshops and programs, and social events, as well as maintaining appropriate behavioral conduct.
- *Judicial affairs:* Provides education on the policies and regulations for residential living and adjudicates in cases where regulations have been violated.
- *Student government and leadership:* Provides opportunities for students to serve in a leadership role by participating in student resident government and programming.

Other Divisions

As a student, you might not have much contact with these remaining areas, but they are still central to the running of a research university. In addition, they represent a variety of potential careers that you might wish to explore and there may be opportunities for student employment or internships:

- *Research affairs:* This entity is responsible for overseeing all research that is conducted at the university. This includes making sure that all studies and experiments are held to impeccably high ethical standards and that all human and animal subjects' rights are protected. In addition, this office manages a vast amount of research funding, as all grant or contract applications and disbursement need to be maintained and monitored. This office may also address copyright and intellectual property issues in terms of determining how much of a faculty's work (research results, patents, publications, courses, etc.) belongs to the university versus the individual faculty member and how compensation for these is determined. A research university also often houses independent research units that operate outside of academic departments and are not involved with offering academic credit for a bachelor's degree.

- *Business affairs:* A university is a large business, and this division maintains the various contracts and purchases that the campus engages in. This includes insurance and liability for various campus activities as well as ensuring that all contracts are legal. It might pay the utility bills and negotiate discount prices with vendors on things like computers, office supplies, and furniture. You might also find any campuses businesses, such as the bookstore or dining establishments, based here, along with all the various departments that keep the physical aspect of the campus clean and functioning (groundskeepers, carpenters, electricians, etc.).

- *Budget and planning:* This division often focuses on managing the various funding streams that come into and go out of the university. It also is primarily responsible for managing future growth in terms of new buildings, and meeting local codes and county ordinances.

- *Human resources:* This area is responsible for the employment aspect of the university. It is where people apply for and get hired for all university jobs. In addition, this department manages the benefits (health insurance, dental plans, etc.) for all employees as well as any labor disputes and union contracts. They also provide mediation services, training and development, and sometimes, professional counseling.

- *Institutional advancement:* This division fosters positive relationships with the local community, government offices at the local, state, and federal levels, alumni, and potential donors. This area might also have a department that works on media relations as well as large public events such as convocation or commencement.

The Academic Senate and Faculty Committees

Every university is a large organization and operates in many ways like a large corporation or a small country. When decisions need to be made, it is often a complex process that involves many constituencies and many layers of the university. Because of the research mission, faculty members play a strong role in the running of the university. From admissions standards to budget cuts to parking to academic requirements, every major decision must involve the faculty in some way. At some universities, the faculty play an integral role in the governing of most aspects of the campus; at others, the faculty are involved only with academic matters. All tenured faculty are members of a governing entity, sometimes called the academic senate, academic council, or faculty board. Each campus has its own academic senate, and in larger state universities that have many campuses, an additional systemwide academic senate is composed of representatives from all the campuses. It is through the workings of the academic senate that most of major decisions that involve academic matters are made, and a university president or chancellor who tries to do so without faculty involvement will find himself or herself in the middle of a political uproar. On campuses where faculty play a major role in other aspects of campus governance, the academic senate is still the entity that is involved.

Since there may be several hundred faculty members on a campus, the academic senate can be quite large, and it would be inefficient to have the entire faculty debate and discuss each issue. As a result, the academic senate usually splits itself into several ongoing committees that meet regularly to discuss campus issues. For example, there might be a committee on general education requirements and another committee on tenure review. In addition, new, short-term committees may be created to address a specific issue such as hiring a new vice president or responding to a current situation such as a formal reaccreditation process. There may even be a committee on committees to determine who will serve on which committees and for how long. Faculty, as part of their professional duties, are required to serve on committees and provide community service to the institution throughout their career. As was stated before, this level of involvement is part of the tenure review process. Faculty often serve on several committees, addressing a wide range of issues over the course of their careers. Most committees strive to have faculty from a broad range of disciplines and professional experience, and there is usually a certain term limit for any particular appointment. A faculty member might also be appointed to be the chair of a particular committee, which means that she or he oversees the running of the group and ensures that its work gets accomplished.

Most of this faculty governance will be unseen to the student eye, as committee meetings occur in small conference rooms across campus. Most academic senate meetings are open, and students could attend them, but it would require calling the academic senate office to find out the place and time of the next meeting and having the time and interest to attend. However, student involvement is very much needed in the governance of the university, and a few spots are usually reserved on these committees for undergraduate or graduate student representatives.

The most obvious way in which students are affected by faculty governance is that the faculty are primarily responsible for setting the academic requirements for all degrees awarded, including unit requirements, general education, and so on. For these broader campuswide decisions, faculty committees composed of tenured faculty from across the various disciplines are convened to create, implement, review, and revise requirements, policies, and procedures. This process is usually hidden to students and requires not only the approval of the specific committee involved but also the approval of other, related committees, and finally, it must be voted on by the entire faculty population, that is, the academic senate.

Might I Suggest...

Students who are interested can contact their campus' academic senate office to learn more about which committees are in need of student participation. The student voice is very important in these meetings, and students often find themselves educating faculty on the "real" student experience. Needless to say, this can also be a very positive experience for students in that it provides them with professional training experience and also the chance to make a difference at their campus. In addition, it creates the strong possibility that several faculty would be willing to write a letter of recommendation for the student.

In addition, the faculty determines the requirements that are specific to each major, but this process is limited to the faculty in that particular department; the premise is that only psychology faculty, for example, would know best what a bachelor's degree in psychology should consist of. However, each major must be in alignment with the workload and difficulty of other majors at the same institution, so even department-specific requirements and policies will need to receive the approval of some college or campuswide committee.

Chapter Summary

In this chapter, the following topics were discussed:

- An undergraduate education:
  - Bachelor's degrees
  - The liberal arts education

- Academic classes:
  - Course workload
  - Course levels
  - Teaching and learning styles

- Enrolling in your courses:
  - Selecting your courses
  - Registering for your courses

- The connection between majors and careers:
  - Selecting majors and minors
  - Declaring majors and minors
  - Changing majors
  - Double majors and minors

- How a university is organized:
  - The academic division
  - The student affairs division
  - The housing division
  - Other divisions
  - The academic senate and faculty committees

Reflections and Exercises

1. Catalog Quest (Part 2)

Using your university's general catalog, find the answers to these questions.

List the different colleges and schools at your university:

In which college or school are you enrolled?

Where would you find your graduation/degree requirements listed (i.e., publications and websites)?

How many different majors are available to you?

Look up your major department (if you are undeclared, choose one that interests you).

Where is the office located?

What is the phone number?

What degrees are available? Circle all that apply: B.A.   B.S.   B.M.   B.F.A.

Does this department offer a minor?   Yes   No

A master's degree?   Yes   No

A doctorate/Ph.D. degree?   Yes   No

List one or two requirements for your major.

Look up one or two classes that are required for the major and list the following information: What is the number and title of each class? How many units is each worth? Are there any prerequisites that you must complete before you can enroll in that class?

Look up one or two faculty members in your department and write down the following: their names, their research interests, the courses they teach, and where they earned their Ph.D.

2. Assess Your Learning Style

It is important to assess your learning style early in your college career. If you cannot find a service on your campus that provides information on learning styles, you can take an on-line inventory at one of the following websites. The first one features Felder's styles mentioned in this chapter, but there are other models as well.

- http://www.engr.ncsu.edu/learningstyles/ilsweb.html
- http://members.shaw.ca/mdde615/lrnstyles.htm
- http://www.metamath.com/lsweb/dvclearn.htm
- http://www.strongware.com/lsi/htm
- http://www.chaminade.org/inspire/learnstl.htm

How did the assessment you took classify you as a learner?

Does that seem accurate to you? Why or why not?

What does this information tell you about yourself as a learner at a university?

Given your learning style(s), what strategies can you utilize to maximize your learning?

3. Take an Interest Inventory

There are several assessment tools that can be quite helpful in assisting a student in discovering potential majors and careers. The Myers-Briggs Type Indicator and the Holland Interest Inventory come to mind, as does the Strong Interest Inventory. Visit your campus career advising center and ask whether it offers these assessments or can recommend some others. If so, take them as early as you can and meet with advisors to discuss how the results might guide you in your choices. If these are not available, check on the Internet, as they can often be found on various websites such as these:

- www.discoveryourpersonality.com/index.html
- www.promisingfutures.com/allaccess/career_planning/interest_inventory/ interest_inventory.htm

How did the assessment you took classify you?

Does that seem accurate to you? Why or why not?

What does this information tell you about yourself as a college student? How might this relate to your choice of a major?

How might this information guide your future career choices?

4. Conduct an Information Interview

One of the best ways to learn about future careers is to ask the people who are currently in them. They can tell you so much about what the career is really like on a day-to-day basis. This can be accomplished by conducting what is known as an information interview. This interview can be anywhere from thirty minutes to an hour in length and can be conducted in person or over the phone. There are several ways to set up an information interview. One way is to ask family and friends for any contacts they might have for people who are currently in the career that interests you. This can be a great way to set up an information interview because your family member or friend might be willing to make the initial contact on your behalf. Another way is to look up individuals in the phone book or on the Internet and contact them directly. In this situation, you will need to explain that you are a university student who is interested in pursuing a career in their field and that you are requesting an appointment to ask them questions about their career. Some people might not be able to accommodate you, so you might have to contact several people. Once you have an appointment, ask the following questions:

Tell me what you do.

How did you get to this place in your career?

What advice would you give me, a college student, about things I can do to prepare for a career like yours?

Are there any opportunities for college students to work at your company? How might a student like me qualify for them?

Use the information you gain from the interview to guide your future choices. If you need some assistance, make an appointment with a career advisor on your campus and bring the results of your information interview(s).

Personal Development

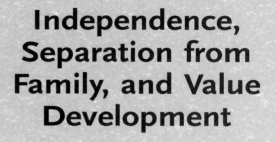

Chapter 4

Independence, Separation from Family, and Value Development

Going to college will have a significant impact on several aspects of a your life. In addition to the academic learning one might expect, you will go through a host of other changes as well. Students have myriad new experiences daily that shape the way they view the world as well as how they mature physically, emotionally, and socially. These changes occur as a result of their newly gained independence combined with exposure to a wide range of people and experiences that might be different from ones they have encountered in the past. Moving away from home and the family environment in which they have lived has a significant impact on students and their transition to fully mature adults. This chapter will explore various aspects of student independence, the process of separation from the family, and the impact this has on the student's value development as an adult.

It is important to note that in today's society, the term *family* can mean a lot of different things. Some students live with and were raised by their biological parents, while some lived in one or more families that included stepparents and stepsiblings. Some students were raised by other members of their biological family, such as uncles or grandparents, and some were raised by foster families or other caring people who were not related by blood. Some students might have left home at a young age and have been independent since their early teens, and some students might have children of their own. In this chapter, the term *family* refers to the person or people who physically raised you and/or had a significant impact on your development as a child.

Homesickness and Friendsickness

When students move away from home, they experience both the excitement of newfound independence and the loss of some of the comforts of home. New students experiences many exciting adventures every day with classes, activities, parties, and just being on their own. At the same time, they often miss their family and friends as well as the comforts of home, such as their room, the family pet, home-cooked meals, and their favorite hangouts. It is the balance between the excitement of the new and the loss of the old that determines when homesickness sets in. Homesickness occurs when the losses are more strongly felt than the excitement of the new. At some point, students begin to really miss certain elements of home and experience sadness and often tears. Homesickness is usually strongest during the first term, but the timing is unique to each student. Some students find the excitement of independence quite thrilling, and the new adventures and the fun keep the thoughts of home at bay for several weeks or even months. Other students find themselves wishing for home the very first night at school.

Regardless of when it happens, almost all students deal with homesickness at some point during their first year. However, not every student experiences homesickness in the same way. Some students notice that they are missing some elements of home, but these are mostly just passing thoughts during their very busy schedules. Other students can become almost debilitated with feelings of great sadness, find themselves feeling lost and alone, and thinking more and more of leaving school and returning home. Most students experience a bit of both—fleeting thoughts one day and then great sadness another, the latter usually after a particularly bad day in which they did not feel as good about college for some reason or another.

Homesickness is generally related to how well a student is feeling that he or she fits in at the campus, both academically and socially. Most university students came from environments in which they were quite successful; they were the

What This Means to You

You can expect to have good days and bad days at college, especially during your first year. The first term can be particularly challenging as you experience the daily discomfort of not knowing where things are or how to do things. Most humans feel uncomfortable in times of great change, and going off to college is one of those times. It can be just plain stressful even if it is also fun. The stress is greater for students who are used to being the smartest in their class or the leader of the club, as this period of transition affects their sense of self. If you have spent the past few years as a leader on your high school campus, it can be very challenging to your self-esteem to be in a different role. It is also likely that you will have days when you love college and are sure that you are at the right place and other days when you don't like college and want to leave. Do not be surprised by this; although it is disconcerting, it is quite normal. Give yourself time. It will take at least a term or two to truly find your way in this new environment. It will not happen within the first few weeks, so relax and don't expect that it will. Give yourself permission to be in transition and know that there are many staff and faculty who are available to help you find your way and your place in the university environment.

smartest students and were very involved and held leadership positions. While they can be these things again, this is often not the case the first term when they have yet to earn grades, join a club, or seek a leadership position. This can make high-achieving students feel a little lost and wish for a return to "the good old days" at home. Even if they are generally feeling successful, a bad grade on a midterm or an uncomfortable interaction with friends can make even the most independent student wish for some home comfort.

"Friendsickness" is an element of homesickness that has less to do with the student's home and family and more to do with the friendships the student has left behind. When most students leave for college, they have a group of friends whom they have known for years, if not their entire lives. These are strong bonds that come from hundreds of interactions over time in which the students have really gotten to know each other and understand each other on a deep level. Friendships like this take time to forge, so most college students will not develop such

Might I Suggest...

All students have good and bad days. What's important to pay attention to is the ratio of these days. If the good days are in the majority, even by just a little bit, then you are doing fine. Time will increase that percentage, as each day will bring more familiarity with your campus and opportunities to make new friends and get involved. If the percentages are equal or the bad days outnumber the good ones, I recommend two things. First, assess what's not working. Take some time to write a list of all the things that don't work for you. It's important not to edit but just to vent all the things that you don't like. Literally, write down everything—this list will become an important tool in changing your experience. Things to consider: How are your classes? Do you feel as academically prepared as your peers? Do you like your instructors? Have you made friends? Do you like your room? Does your computer work well? Have you found a study area that works for you? Do you like the general tone and atmosphere of your campus? Do you like your fellow students—are they people you can connect with? Do you enjoy the social scene, such as student parties and campus events? How is the weather? How are things with your family and friends back home? What activities do you miss the most? Do you like the activities the campus offers for student involvement? Are you involved in clubs or organizations?

Once you have written this list, make another. The next list would be "If you could wave a magic wand and make it all perfect, what would it look like?" Take this question seriously and really have fun with it. Let yourself fantasize and not worry about whether what you are wishing for is feasible or not. What would you change in each of the areas that don't work? Would you need certain resources that you don't have now? Would you need specific people, or types of people, around you? Is there something comforting that would help you to get through it? Keep focusing on what it would look like if it were *perfect*.

deep friendships immediately. While you will find some interesting acquaintances, it will take time to learn enough about each other to make these friendships feel similar to the ones you left at home. As a result, many college students find themselves experiencing friendsickness—wishing for time with a certain friend who always knew just the right thing to say or wanting to hang out with the group of friends who always had fun together. This is normal too, and again, patience is going to be useful in enduring friendsickness. But it's also important to keep those old connections strong. Utilize email, voicemail, snail mail, instant messaging, and any other available forms of communication to reach out to those friends when you need to. Although a phone conversation is not the same as hanging out in person, it can be a good substitute when times are tough.

Luckily, both homesickness and friendsickness diminish over time as you establish your new home away from home and make new friends in college. You can help to reduce homesickness and friendsickness by continuing to do what you

Now look at this list, and see which things you can actually accomplish. This is where you get realistic again and find out whether you can come up with some feasible solutions. You will probably see a few things right away that you can do to change your experience a bit. I recommend doing these as soon as you can. You will find that you feel more empowered because you have taken a step toward making your experience what you want it to be. Most often, these have to do with bringing home comforts to your campus environment. If you had favorite things in your room at home, have your family send them. If you used to run every day, find out where and when you can do that at your campus. If you really miss certain comfort foods, go out and buy them or ask your family to send you a care package. If you used to play with your cat every day, find out where there is a local animal shelter at which you can volunteer. There might be certain things that you cannot bring, but you will want to transplant as many of your important comforts as possible.

On your list, you will also see some areas that could be changed if you had the information or resources you needed to change them. For these items, I recommend making an appointment with an advisor or counselor who helps students with the adjustment to college. You might find these staff members affiliated with your first-year experience seminar or at the counseling center. You want someone who can help you with the bigger picture rather than just the specific area of academic advising. Show him or her your lists and share any insights you have gained from this exercise. Ask about the items you need information on; your counselor should be able to give you several recommendations or strategies that will help you.

You can use this process whenever you need to take stock of how things are going and what needs to change to make your experience better, not only in college but throughout your life.

can to increase your familiarity with your new campus and your fellow students. Take advantage of opportunities that exist for meeting people by attending social events (residence halls usually program many of these per term) and getting involved in campus clubs and organizations (you can read more about this in Chapter 8).

The Family Educational Rights and Privacy Act (FERPA)

Another aspect of your independence that you will notice right away is that the university will expect you to be solely responsible for your actions from the first minute you get to campus. While the university will certainly work with

Going Home for the Holidays

Returning home for the holidays can be a challenging experience for students with regard to homesickness. Sometimes trips home can make the homesickness worse, and sometimes they can make it better. You might even experience both at the same time!

While students are away from home, they often miss many aspects of their home life, but these get easier to live without over the weeks of the term. Breaks can bring quite a few wonderful experiences as you get to enjoy all the things you missed, such as your family's cooking, snuggling with your pets, watching TV with your siblings, and hanging out with your friends. While these experiences are enjoyable, they can sometimes make it harder to face having to live without them again, making the return to campus more difficult.

In some cases, absence really does make the heart grow fonder, and you'll have a new appreciation for things that weren't important before. For example, you might find that your "annoying" little brother is actually not so annoying when you don't live with him 24/7—in fact, he might actually be fun to hang out with. Once you discover more things that you appreciate, it can make it harder to leave them as well.

On the other hand, some things take on such significance while students are gone that it is hard for reality to live up to the expectations, and this can lead to disappointment. Sadly, this is often true with regard to friendships. Many students find that even just one term away can change the bond between people who grew up together. This change can be even more drastic if the friends at home did not move away from home to go to college because they are then more likely to still be doing the "same old thing." If this happens to you, try not to be frustrated. It is actually an indication of how much you have changed while at college. You will still be able to maintain solid friendships with some of your friends, though others might not stand the test of time, but inevitably, you will find new friends that you will grow to love just as much.

your family members, *you* are seen as the primary client. The university will give you a lot of freedom and responsibility and will expect you to handle it maturely. While this transition may be a bit shocking, it is important for you to adapt as quickly as possible. The reason the shift is so dramatic is that all colleges and universities are held to a certain law that does not affect high schools.

This important federal law impacts all college and university students in the United States. It is called the Family Educational Rights and Privacy Act (FERPA), and it was passed in 1974. This law states that the records of any currently enrolled student are private and cannot be discussed with, or released to, any person without the written permission of the student. The law was the result of many of the protests during the Vietnam War, when college-age students were being drafted to fight in the war. Many young adults felt that it was problematic that they were considered old enough to fight for their country, yet their grades were being sent home to their families. Many lawmakers and politicians agreed.

And of course, you get to confirm that some of the things that truly were annoying when you lived at home are still very annoying. These aspects often lead students to think, "I can't wait to go back to school so that I don't have to deal with this anymore," thereby making homesickness less of a problem.

Most likely, you will experience a combination of all of these possibilities. Although it can feel a little chaotic, know that all of your classmates are going through something similar at their homes, and you will have a lot to talk about when you get back to campus.

One of the ways in which you can make holiday breaks more enjoyable is to encourage better communication among your family members about expectations. Consider discussing the following questions as a family at the start of the break, as these are typical areas for miscommunication:

1. What expectations do you have about how house rules will be handled? Some things to consider are curfew, chores (laundry, cooking, etc.), and how people are to communicate.
2. What expectations do you have about personal freedom and independence? Students have a lot of independence at college and often expect this same level at home.
3. What expectations do you have about how much time the family will spend together? Are there certain days or events that are very important? What freedom will there be for each individual to schedule time with friends, with other family members, at work, and so on?
4. Is your family planning a vacation? Are all family members expected to participate? What choices do they have about their time during the vacation?

By discussing each person's expectations, potential conflicts and similarities can be discovered and addressed. Some negotiation might be required, but it will increase the chances of a great holiday for everyone.

The passing of this law significantly changed the relationship between institutions of higher education, the students who enrolled in them, and the families of those students. Before FERPA was passed, many institutions operated under a philosophy known as *in loco parentis,* which means "in place of the parent." This essentially meant that the staff and faculty at a university took on the role of parenting and watching out for the young adults, whose families had given over their care to the institution. Before passage of FERPA, institutions had many policies that facilitated in loco parentis, such as curfews in the residence halls, adult (i.e., professional staff) supervision in most areas of student life, and parental access to all student records, including grades, student health files, and counseling records. Essentially, the student was treated as if she or he was still a minor, and the university dealt with the family much in the same way as high schools do.

FERPA changed all of this. This law significantly altered many aspects of colleges and universities, changes that exist to this day. It is important to understand this because you and your family will be affected by FERPA on a regular basis, sometimes to your liking and sometimes not. Essentially, all student records are considered private and the sole property of the student. This includes admissions files, grades, student health records, counseling notes, billing statements, attendance information, and conduct records. The institution cannot share or discuss any of these with another person, not even a parent, unless the student gives written permission that identifies the piece of information she or he wishes to be shared and with whom. Without this written permission, the university would be breaking the law if it shared the information, and you will find that most university staff and faculty are rigorous in their adherence to legal codes.

FERPA also protects the family's information from the student. For example, most universities require that the parents submit their tax returns and other financial records, especially if the student is applying for financial aid. The family's information is also considered private and cannot be shared with anyone, including the student, without the written permission of the family members.

FERPA's Impact on Student Independence and Responsibility

FERPA was intended to acknowledge that a person who had gained admission to a college or university was treated as an adult (regardless of age) and capable of managing his or her university education. The focus shifted from the parents to the student as the primary client of the university and essentially limited the parents' ability to be involved with their student's university business. Of course, FERPA allowed students to make their own arrangements with regard to their family's involvement but still required the student to hold primary responsibility and be the person with whom the university interacts. This new level of responsibility also brought a new level of freedom. Students could make choices and decisions about their university education and personal lives without seeking the permission or approval of their family.

What This Means to You

Your family will not be told anything about your experiences at college. Unless you choose to tell them, they will not be informed of your grades, your student health records, your attendance, any counseling you seek, or even your conduct records. This information will be shared only with you. The positive side of this policy is that it gives you privacy and the ability to make your own choices without needing your family's approval or having to respond to their concerns. Many students find this very helpful, especially if they wish to pursue studies or activities that their family might not approve. The negative side is that you are ultimately responsible for ensuring your own success. Since your family will not know that you are skipping class or did poorly on a midterm, they will not be able to motivate you or help you do better unless you tell them and request their assistance.

It's also important to note that FERPA applies only to university records, not to public records, such as police records. Some universities are utilizing these public records and notifying the families of students who have been arrested for alcohol or drug offenses. The process is often called *parental notification* or something similar. You might want to find out whether your university has a similar process.

This means that students are granted the same rights and responsibilities as any other adult in society; in other words, they have the freedom to make choices every day about how to conduct their lives. Some choices might be influenced by laws and various penalties that exist for breaking them, such as stealing a bicycle or drinking when underage. Other choices will be influenced by other consequences that might be undesirable, for example, not paying rent or tuition on time. It is completely up to the adult to make an informed choice and to seek information or assistance if it is needed. There is no one who "makes" an adult make good choices or tattles on them when they don't.

FERPA ensures that every college student, regardless of their wishes and ability, will be treated as an adult who is capable of making appropriate choices. At most universities, this is accomplished as follows:

1. Universities give students information about relevant policies, procedures, rights, and responsibilities (usually in the form of official written guides such as college catalogs, student handbooks, and other material).
2. Universities expect students to read and understand the information they have been given, and students might be asked to sign a form stating that they have done so.
3. Universities assume that students are capable of making their own choices about all aspects of their university life, such as fulfilling academic requirements, following policies and conduct codes, paying tuition, and adhering to local laws.

4. Universities provide students with many support services and people who can help them if they need assistance, such as advisors, programs, and counselors.
5. Universities assume that students will understand the consequences of their choices.

Each student is individually responsible for making choices that influence the success of the university experience, academically, socially, and personally. This is a lot of responsibility, and there are many people who feel that 18-year-olds might not be ready for it, especially if they were not prepared in advance by their high schools and families. With the disappearance of the in loco parentis philosophy, universities addressed this issue by creating a whole new range of student services designed to provide a safety net of support for new students as they gain competence with adult life skills. While universities cannot and do not force students to seek help, even if they are in trouble, students will find that they are surrounded by talented and experienced professional advisors and counselors who are there to help them succeed. However, the student still needs to seek out this support by going to the services and asking for help.

While this new system of support services has definitely been successful over the years, many of today's college families are not as happy with FERPA as previous generations have been. The current generation of college students is generally closer to their families and more focused on academic achievement than their predecessors were (see Chapter 7 for a more in-depth discussion of generational differences). Many students *want* their family to conduct some of their university business for them, such as filling out forms or making calls to find out information. While the family member is essentially acting as a personal assistant to the student in these situations (i.e., doing some of the student's work for him or her), the university is not able to work with the family without violating this federal law. Even if the student provides written permission, it is usually required that this permission specify the exact piece of information for a short period of

Might I Suggest...

Ask for help! The staff and faculty are there to help you, and there is no penalty for asking for assistance. There is nothing you are going through, no matter how dramatic it seems to you, that they have not seen before. In addition, your records are private, so no one will have to know that you asked for support. Too many students suffer consequences that they didn't need to because they never said anything to anyone about a problem. The whole purpose of these support services, and the people who staff them, is to provide a bridge between the level of responsibility FERPA has given students and their ability to be successful. This is especially true for first-year students; although the law requires you to be responsible, universities know that students need help in this. Utilize the help. It is in your best interest to do so.

time; that is, a student cannot write a blanket permission that covers a whole range of interactions.

It is important to remember that this is a federal law that universities are forced to uphold. FERPA creates problems and inconveniences for staff and faculty as well. Sometimes, it would clearly be in the student's best interest to be able to work with his or her family, but the best the university can do is encourage the student to tell the family or to provide written permission so that the university can include them. You would be surprised at how many times students and/or parents are rude to university personnel simply for following this law. Please remember that they have no choice but to do so.

It is also true that many families are paying a majority of the bills for the student's education and feel that they should therefore have access to the student's information. Family members are especially interested in knowing their student's grades and whether or not the student is "in trouble." Although university staff can certainly appreciate this sentiment, it is not in accordance with the federal law. The student will be informed of any relevant consequences, and it is up to him or her to share this with the family. If you pay attention to the communication you receive from your university, you will notice that it is all addressed to you, the student, with very rare exceptions, which are addressed to "the parents of" the student (these are usually announcements for parent-related events or associations, not student business). This is because the student is the actual client of the university. All records are in the student's name, including billing statements, and only the student has access to them. While many students make

What This Means to You

You, the student, are ultimately responsible for conducting your university business. If you choose to have your family involved, then it is up to you to make sure that they follow through and meet deadlines as well. Lamenting that "my parents were supposed to do this but they forgot" will not change your responsibility. Also, if you choose to have some of your mail sent to your home address, you are still responsible for having received and read those communications. Most universities do *not* send out duplicate sets of information, so make sure your family knows to keep you apprised of any notices they receive so that you can take appropriate action. Often, the university informs students of important deadlines and information through the mail or the student's university email account; make sure you check often for these communications. Please know that there are often stiff consequences for missing deadlines, such as having to pay a late fee or even being dropped from all your classes or blocked from registering for the next term. While all of these situations can eventually be straightened out, it often costs you time, frustration, and money. In the case of being dropped from classes, you often cannot get back into the same ones and are forced to create a new, and less than optimal, schedule after everyone else has already registered.

arrangements with their family to pay their bills, the university sees this as a private arrangement between the student and his or her family. If the student were to become delinquent on a bill, it would eventually be turned over to a collection agency, and the student's credit would be affected, not anyone else's.

This means that family should not open their student's mail; in fact, it is illegal for any person to open mail that is not addressed to him or her. Most students have the option of having university communication mailed to an address that they specify. Students who do not live at home can choose to have mail sent to either their campus or their family's address. Students who live with their family could either have mail sent to their home address or establish their own post office box. Regardless of the arrangements the student makes, she or he is ultimately responsible for responding to any communication the university sends, including billing statements. Also, many universities now utilize university-sponsored email addresses to communicate with students. If your university provides you with an email account, be sure to activate it and check it regularly. It is your responsibility to read and respond to all official university communication, regardless of how it was sent. If you prefer to receive email at a personal account, arrange to forward your university email to that address.

Managing This Newfound Freedom and Independence

When young adults move away from home, their level of independence increases. The implementation of FERPA increases students' independence even when they live at home because its regulations force students to take more responsibility for their education. However, students who live at home might not have as much personal independence if their family still pays their bills, wakes them up in the morning, does their laundry, cooks their meals, and reminds them

John's Story

I learned the hard way not to have all my campus mail sent home. The college sent a letter to me at my parents' address with a warning that I needed to complete some paperwork by a certain deadline. Well, my mom held onto the letter thinking that she could just give it to me at Thanksgiving. I missed the deadline, and they blocked my registration! Not only did this cause me to miss out on all the good classes, but I couldn't register by the deadline, so then I had a $50 late fee. It was a mess.

After that, I had all the mail sent to my address at campus, even the bills. My parents pay my tuition, but now I have them deposit the money into my checking account, and I write the check for the tuition and turn it in on time. Not only can I make sure that I don't miss a deadline, but I now have a better appreciation for how much it costs them to send me to school. Even though I knew how much it cost before, there is nothing like writing that expensive check to make you really get it. I think it has made me take my education more seriously.

to do their homework. Many research universities are designed to be venues for full-time education, and very few students attend on a part-time basis. As a result, most research universities are residential in nature, with many students living on or near the campus in housing that is separate from their family's home. This means that most university students are experiencing a new level of personal independence in addition to the responsibility and freedom provided by FERPA.

The inevitable problem comes because many college students, especially freshmen, do not have the emotional maturity or experience to handle this level of responsibility and freedom. This is especially true if they come from a home or high school environment in which parents, teachers, and counselors took care of everything or were very involved in their student's choices. This can also be true for transfer students if they were living at home and have now moved out on their own. This new level of responsibility can represent a huge increase from what students previously experienced. Every day, students have the option to make choices with their academic, social and personal lives. Some examples include the following:

- Going to class . . . or not
- Seeking help on assignments . . . or not
- Being a considerate roommate . . . or not
- Drinking alcohol . . . or not
- Getting enough sleep . . . or not
- Paying bills on time . . . or not

This is quite different from high school, in which teachers and counselors would notify the family regarding most of these issues and the family could use their influence to alter their student's behavior. At a university, FERPA dictates that the only person who can be notified is the student. This is good news because it really treats students as the intelligent, capable young adults that they are. You will have the freedom to make your own choices and choose your own path. The university will honor *your* thoughts, feelings, and beliefs, not just those of your family. This is an exciting time, and this new freedom and responsibility bring you more opportunities than ever before to become the person you want to be, academically, socially, and personally.

However, there is a downside to this responsibility and freedom as well. As is mentioned in Chapter 2, some of these responsibilities are not necessarily fun or interesting, so the temptation to avoid them might be strong, especially if more pleasant options are available. The university sees the student as an adult and trusts him or her to make the right choices. A university education is a choice in our society—it is not required, as K–12 education is, so the university does not play any role in "making" students complete their responsibilities. The only role the university can, and does, play is to enact sanctions when policies are violated. For example, students need to maintain a certain level of academic performance and adhere to certain codes of conduct in order to remain enrolled. If the student chooses to not fulfill either of these, the university doesn't force compliance but rather terminates enrollment. This does not mean that there is no one to help you. In fact, more caring, professional staff and faculty will surround you than you have probably ever experienced before. The difference will be that they will be waiting for you to initiate contact if you need it. You might never get a call from an academic advisor, but the minute *you* choose to walk into the advising center, help will be enthusiastically provided.

The same is true for social and personal issues. Students will be able to find alcohol in most college environments, regardless of their age, and will have the option to choose when to drink, how much to drink, and with whom. A student could choose to party in a way that impedes his or her academic success or even physical health. Again, no one is going to stop a student from making these choices, but someone might step in to impose sanctions for policy violations, such as a citation for a minor in possession of alcohol or an eviction from a living environment, such as a residence hall, in which alcohol is not allowed. Students will find that ample information is provided on campuses about laws and policies as they relate to alcohol as well as social events and activities that do not include alcohol. Students are trusted to choose and face the consequences of their choice.

FERPA absolutely prohibits the release of any information about the student's academic work, including attendance, academic performance, and grades. This is to protect the rights of the students, especially students who truly do not want others to know these things. The fact that a student is attending a research university plays a role here as well. Research universities are often prestigious and

What This Means to You

Your ability to succeed or fail at the university is in *your* hands. You are considered an intelligent and capable adult and will be treated as such. You will find that a lot of people are available to help you but that no one will "make" you be successful. If you choose to skip all your classes, no one is going to call you and remind you that you need to go to class. It is assumed that you know that already and are making your own informed choices. Teachers and counselors do not call students in for a meeting about missed classes—but don't think that this lack of communication means you are getting away with anything. Your absences are noted each day and will figure into your final grade. If you fail your classes, the university will notify you on your transcript, and you might get a letter from the dean reminding you that you must earn a certain GPA to maintain your enrollment. Likewise, if you want to excel in your classes, you have the choice to go to office hours, seek extra assistance with assignments, and sign up for study skills workshops.

You are absolutely 100% in control of what you make of your education. If you spend your time trying to get by with the least amount of work or the most amount of partying, you will be able to do so, although your grades might not be what you had hoped. Likewise, if you want to excel, you will be able to create an intellectually stimulating and engaging education. The latter is much more enjoyable and rewarding in the long run and the real reason a person should attend a research university.

hold students to a high academic standard. It is assumed that students are intelligent and able to manage the level and complexity of being an adult in a university environment. With that said, most faculty would be frustrated, if not appalled, if a family member called them to discuss their son or daughter unless it was an extreme situation. In cases in which the student is incapacitated and unable to take care of business, for example, if a student had a serious accident or illness, then it would be acceptable for a member of the family to call for the purpose of notifying a staff or faculty member and getting information about relevant policies and procedures for withdrawals or incomplete grades. However, the staff or faculty member still could not release any information about the student to the family without the written permission of the student.

You would be surprised at the kinds of calls faculty members get from families. At one university, a mother called a history professor to inform him that her daughter, who was enrolled in his class, did not understand the paper assignment he had given and wanted him to explain it to the mother so that she could help her daughter with it. Needless to say, the professor told the mother that the student should come to his office hours and talk to him directly about the assignment. At another campus, a grandfather called a math professor to say that he was worried that his granddaughter was missing her early morning math class. He wanted to know whether there was a service that could wake her up and make sure she got to class! He also wanted the professor to call him and let him know if his granddaughter kept missing class. The math professor informed the man that she could not share any information about his granddaughter's attendance and that it was up to her to come or not.

Bloom's Stages of Parent/Adolescent Separation

When a young adult goes off to college and leaves home for the first time, the family goes through a transition, and all members learn new ways of interacting without being in constant contact. In addition, the student's new levels of freedom and responsibility add complexity to the process. Each member of the family has different feelings about the separation process, some positive and some negative, and each person has different ways of handling it. This is especially true when the student is eager for new freedom and the family is not ready to let go. Often, parents and students have tense or uncomfortable interactions as this happens.

One researcher found this process of parent/adolescent separation fascinating and decided to study what happens as parents and their young adults go through it. In 1980, M.V. Bloom studied several families as they went through this process, and he identified five stages. Bloom's model is very useful in helping both students and parents better understand this process. In fact, parents at some universities attend a workshop on this process as part of summer orientation, and students learn about it in first-year experience courses and seminars.

Bloom argues that there are five distinct stages of the parent/adolescent separation process: ambivalence, cognitive separation, emotional separation, values clarification, and new relationship. Each stage is characterized by different kinds of behaviors by both the student and the parent. The stages are linear, so a person generally moves from one stage to the next as he or she moves through the letting-go process, but each person in the family can be at a different stage, which definitely adds to the complexity of family dynamics and interactions. It is the lack of synchronicity in these stages that creates the most challenges in family dynamics. Finally, the timing of this process is unique to each family and to each child within the same family. Some families have gone through many of these stages in junior high and high school; others are just beginning on the first day of university classes. Please note that Bloom's research focused on families consisting of biological parents and children, but the stages can apply to any family in which one or more adults raised a child for a significant amount of time.

Stage 1: Ambivalence

This stage is characterized by all members of the family transitioning from parent-child to adult-adult relational patterns. This means that the parents have to be willing to move from telling their son or daughter what to do to advising or coaching when asked. This also means that students have to take more responsibility for their life and choices and cannot ask their parents to do everything for them. On both sides, there is a lot of vacillation between authority and autonomy as parents and young adults negotiate this new relationship. Often, these are messy and tense interactions because every family member wants a different level of authority or independence in a certain situation and family members most likely do not all want the same things at the same times. In addition, people are often resistant to change at this stage, especially parents, who might not be ready to let go yet.

Parents often handle their discomfort by working with rules. They say things like "You can do this" and "You cannot do that" as a way to maintain control, especially if they are not present to enforce the student's behavior. They might also make financial or emotional support conditional on certain behaviors or choices by the student. For example, they might say, "We'll only pay for college if you major in engineering" or "We won't pay for rent if you live with your boyfriend."

Students usually vacillate between acting young and wanting to be treated like an adult. They might say things like "I'm an adult now, and I should get to make my own decisions," followed by asking the parent to do their laundry. Students seem to want to be childlike when they choose (and thus be parented) and yet be adultlike shortly thereafter. These mixed signals confuse parents. Students can help in this stage by consistently acting like an adult. If they continually demonstrate their ability to act and behave like an adult, it helps parents to see, and therefore treat, their student in new ways.

Stage 2: Cognitive Separation

This stage is characterized by focusing on the intellectual aspects of the separation process. In other words, it is talked about in very logical and unemotional terms. The student or young adult is more likely to be in this stage and exhibit the unemotional aspects of it, although some parents, especially fathers, can be in this stage too. Since the parents are most often in the next stage, which is characterized by lots of emotions and sadness about the separation, the student often does not relate and focuses on the "logic" of moving away from home. Students can also become annoyed by their parents' emotions and tend to view them as over-reacting. The physical act of separation (i.e., moving out) helps the adolescent to define himself or herself as separate from his or her parents, so it is often met with excitement. In addition, young adults begin to define their separateness from their parents by being different in some way and accentuating those differences—for example, style of dress, music preferences, political ideology, or spiritual expression.

Parents in this stage are likely to discuss the student's leaving in very businesslike ways. The focus will be on how many bags to pack and what time the family should leave to make it to campus. There is little acknowledgment that this is more than a weekend getaway. With students, the focus is more on all the fun and exciting adventures that college will bring, with little or no acknowledgment that they are moving away from home. Students also don't see "what the big deal is" because they view their departure as temporary, since they will home for the Thanksgiving and winter breaks in just a few weeks.

Stage 3: Emotional Separation

This stage is characterized by the emotions of the separation and often the more negative emotions of sadness, loss, nostalgia, frustration, and uncertainty. Parents are more likely to experience this stage first, usually beginning a few weeks before the student leaves for college. The student typically does not reach this stage until well into the first term—it is essentially the homesickness that was described at the beginning of this chapter. It often takes students a period of time for the excitement of independence to wear off before they experience the stage of emotional separation. It is the fact that parents and students are not in synch in going through these stages that causes the most challenges to family dynamics.

This stage is often much more keenly experienced by the parents because they see their student's moving away as a marker that their role as a parent is ending and that their young adult has grown up. This can be disconcerting, since being a parent has been a major portion of their identity for the past eighteen to twenty years. If the parents have not thought about, or have not begun planning for, the next stage of their own lives, then this time can be very uncomfortable because every letter from the college and every bag that is packed is another reminder. Another issue that can complicate this stage is the parents' relationship. If they have not maintained their relationship as a couple, they might not know how to relate to each other outside of their roles as parents. When the last child is leaving home, this becomes even more evident. In this situation, parents might cling to their role as parents, which can infringe on the student's independence.

In addition, some parents experience some level of guilt as they reflect on their role as a parent and realize that they could have done certain things differently and perhaps better. They also often question whether they have "done enough" to prepare their child for the next stage of his or her life. Some parents are tempted to cram in last-minute parenting and find themselves giving lots of advice and reminders about making good choices and being safe. They might be taking lots of pictures of the student and acting as though they might not see the student for a very long time. Both students and parents are managing new levels of closeness and distance—though not necessarily smoothly.

Parents in this stage are often experiencing a range of emotions. Parents realize that this is the beginning of when their son or daughter becomes an adult and will not return to live at home in the same way again. This is often a result of reflecting on their own separation from their families when they were younger. They might be incredibly nostalgic and say things like "This will be our last Fourth of July together as a family." In addition, they might be experiencing feelings about their own age and stage of life as they realize that they are "old enough to have a child in college." Family members who are still in the cognitive separation stage are often very annoyed by the emotionality and clinginess of the parents who are in the emotional separation stage. Students can help in this stage by realizing that this is a big transition for their parents that might be uncomfortable or even scary. Although parents are excited for their son or daughter, their emotions about their own personal transition will also be coming up.

Stage 4: Values Clarification

This stage is characterized by the process the student engages in while developing new values. The student's peers exert strong influence, and parents often see their son or daughter veer away from long-held family values while testing them and exploring others. This process is described in more detail in the next section. Eventually, the student blends parental and personal values together in new ways, and the parents learn new ways to parent that allow for the student's new values.

Note that Bloom's work did not acknowledge that not all families easily embrace their child's development. If the parents are unable or unwilling to accommodate their student's values, some families can experience a split and estrangement at this stage. Parents who attempt to exert too much control in this phase (e.g., "It's my way or the highway") can cause the student to disengage from the family in serious and often long-term ways.

Stage 5: New Relationship

This stage is characterized by a new a positive relationship that is cocreated by the young adult and the parents. Separateness is balanced with connection and often families feel closer than ever before. The student has increased investment in relationships outside of the family (e.g., friends, coworkers, and romantic partners), and the family learns to accept that. Parents learn to provide support and guidance instead of control, and as they do so, students are more willing to seek support and guidance. Students gain a much better appreciation for their parents in this stage and often seek the input and wisdom that they intentionally ignored in previous stages.

Although students and parents will see these stages more distinctly the first year, the process is by no means over. Members of the family can move backward in the stages when a new issue or stressful situation arises. In fact, the stages often correlate with the values development and clarification process (described later in this chapter), so when the son or daughter makes a choice that concerns the parent, the family often responds by going back to stage one and working their way back through the stages again. This process is very noticeable during the college years simply because the college environment provides ample opportunities for the separation and values clarification stages, especially when values and experimentation collide. However, all young adults go through this process with their families whether they go to college or not. Depending on the individual family and the pace at which they progress through the stages, some will be in stage 5 during the first year, while others won't get there for years. The fifth stage will eventually become more and more common and is the hallmark of a healthy family when the young adult has become a full adult.

Understanding these stages can be quite useful for both students and family members. Each person not only can understand his or her own process but also can have a greater understanding of, and therefore empathy for, the experiences of other members of the family. This model can help the family to assess which stage each member might be in and provide some insight about how the process looks as a whole and some issues or behaviors that might be encountered along the way.

What This Means to You

You have probably already experienced some of these stages in the past few years. You and your family will have ups and downs in your relationship as you negotiate this new landscape. There will be days when you feel very close to your family and you miss them incredibly, and then there might be days when they annoy you and you want to be away from them. This is normal. The good news is that it gets better with time as each member of the family transitions through the five stages. In addition to understanding your own family's dynamics with regard to your separation and independence, this model can give you insight into the experiences of your peers. Your roommate and friends will be at various stages as well. You might want to share this chapter with them to help them understand what they are going through.

Might I Suggest...

Your family loves you and wants the best for you. They worry a lot about your happiness and safety when you are away. Some families aren't sure how to manage their student's independence, and they call too much; other families don't want to bother their student, so they call too little. You can help by giving your family some guidelines about how often, and when, you would like to hear from them. It also means a lot to your family when you call them too. They want you to miss them as much as they are missing you.

One thing that students often do is call their family when they are upset about something. Being able to vent, and even cry, to someone who loves you can be the perfect thing after a bad day. However, it's important to remember that after you hang up, your family will keep thinking about the conversation and worry about you. It is a good idea to give your family a balanced view of your life at college; if you call only when you are upset, they might think that you are miserable all the time. It hurts them that you are upset, and their parental instincts kick in—it is natural for them to want to protect you, especially if you say things like "I hate it here, and I want to come home." While this might be true in the moment, they won't know that you were feeling great a few hours later unless you tell them. Be sure to call them on the days that you love school and are happy that you came.

If your family tends to be a bit more involved in your life than you would prefer, you might want to monitor how much you say to them and when. If calling when you are upset only prompts them to tell you what to do and you don't want this, you might need to find other people to vent to when you are upset. Students often unknowingly give their family the impression that they cannot handle aspects of college life (because they call home upset about various things) and then are surprised that their family treats them as though they cannot handle college.

The Development and Clarification of a Student's Values

College will change you. In addition to providing you with a degree, it will provide you with a plethora of information and experiences that will shape who you are, what you believe, and what you value. This is supposed to happen, as it is part of the transition from being a young adult to a full adult. While exciting, this transition can be a bit bumpy at times, especially when family members are not supportive of some of your choices. All of this freedom and responsibility allows students to make their own choices, some that yield positive results and some that yield negative ones. Each choice brings an opportunity for the student to learn and grow. This also begins a process that many students and families do not expect: value development and clarification. Experiences with freedom and responsibility inevitably lead to maturation and value development in young adults, which can cause changes in relationships with family and friends. Students most often notice this during their first winter break when they spend a significant amount of time with family and friends back home. All of a sudden, they realize that they have slightly different views and beliefs from those of their family and peers. In addition, families often want to influence the experiences the student has at college. Many families believe that the student still needs their guidance, and many families attempt to influence their student's choices in everything from grades and majors to careers and romantic partners. This next section discusses the ways in which young adults form new values and the ways in which their families might react to their choices.

Value development and clarification make up an important part of any human's maturation process and occur throughout a person's life. However, psychologists and student development theorists have identified a period in a young adult's life known as the coming-of-age years, which coincide roughly with the ages of 17 to 23 years old. This is a time when young adults, who have been raised with their family's values, begin to discover new values as they interact with other people. Over time, they eventually test and clarify the values of their family and develop a set of their own values. This process can be accelerated by experiences that put a person into contact with a wide variety of people who hold different values. There are many experiences that provide this, such as traveling abroad or living away from home, near people who are different from those in the person's home community. A university campus is such a place, so value development is a process that most college students experience. Ultimately, the young adult creates his or her own unique set of values that are a blend of the family's values and some new ones that are meaningful to him or her.

Every generation goes through this process, yet it can create tension between a young adult and his or her family. It probably created tension between your parents and their parents and between your grandparents and their parents. This will most likely occur between you and your family, so you will find this information useful. There are essentially two processes that occur when a student leaves home: the separation process between the young adult and the parents (mentioned earlier in this chapter) and the value development and clarification process (described next). These two processes are integrally intertwined yet really are very different. You will be affected by these processes, which will, in turn, affect your relationships with family and friends.

The Values Formation Process in Children

During a child's formative years (ages 8 to 13), several influential forces shape a child's values and behaviors, the most influential being immediate family members such as parents and grandparents—usually people who have regular contact with the child. Other forces of influence are teachers and others in the school environment, the home community that includes neighbors and family friends, areas of membership such as a church or athletic group, the child's peers such as friends and schoolmates, the media to the extent that the child is exposed to its messages, and of course the child's personal experiences. All of these forces teach the child a set of beliefs and values that identify what is "right" and "wrong," what is "good" and "bad," and so on. Some of these messages may be explicit, such as a person saying, "In this family, we always clean up after our meals" or "Don't ever talk back to your elders." Explicit messages are usually conveyed verbally and are pretty clear. Some messages are implicit and are often communicated through nonverbal cues; for example, a father might look upset when a student earns anything less than an A, or an aunt might always clutch her purse more tightly when an unknown man walks past. Teachers and the media also contribute to a child's development with both explicit and implicit messages. One obvious example is how teachers treat students with regards to their intelligence. Over time, a child begins to view himself or herself as smart, average, or dumb depending on the messages the child received in the school environment. Another example relates to how attractive a person feels. All people in developed countries pick up messages about what "attractive" means through popular media such as television and magazines. Most humans compare themselves to a standard of attractiveness that is pretty narrowly defined by models and actors.

Over time, a child learns to incorporate all these messages to create a set of beliefs, behaviors, and values that guide his or her understanding of the world in both conscious and unconscious ways. This system of beliefs and values can be thought of as an onion with several layers (see Figure 4.1). The innermost layers represent those values that are deeply held and therefore not easily affected or changed. These are the values that people have pretty strong feelings about, for example, abortion or the death penalty. Values on the outside of the onion are lightly held and do not elicit strong feelings; as a result, they are often easily affected and changed with new information or experiences. An example might be which fast-food chain is believed to have the best burger. Values in the middle layers generally can also be affected, but it will take more information and more

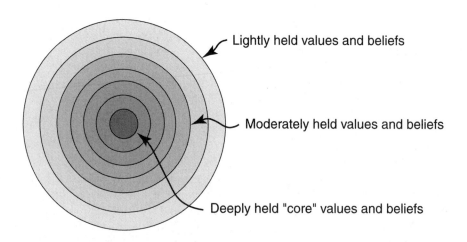

Lightly held values and beliefs

Moderately held values and beliefs

Deeply held "core" values and beliefs

Figure 4.1   Diagram of the Value Onion

experiences for these values to be affected. People usually have some feelings about these values but not to the extent that arises with deeply held values.

This onion is built over time by influential forces in the child's life as well as personal experiences that the child has as she or he grows up. By the time a child becomes a young adult, the value onion is well developed, and values are situated at the various levels in the onion.

The Role of Values in the Family System

Parents seek to raise their children in the best way possible with the goal of ensuring that their child outlives them. Most parents absolutely want their child to grow up to be a healthy and happy adult who lives a long time. Parents have developed their own values over time and through experiences, both positive and negative, and seek to pass this on to their children. They have developed these values through their own personal experiences, and as parents, it is their role to help shape and protect the development of their child. Even in abusive homes where parents are physically or emotionally cruel to their children, these parents would still argue that they are "doing their best" and often can't control what they say or do because of alcohol or drug abuse, mental health problems, or psychological wounds. The intent of the media is not always so positive; the media are usually involved in selling products of some kind, and that requires convincing people that they need the product. One way to do this is to make people feel that their life would be better (e.g., they would be prettier, happier, more popular, or richer) if they purchased a certain product or experience. While many would argue that this is heart of capitalism, it can't be ignored that young adults

---

What This Means to You

Your family already has encouraged you to follow certain paths that they believe are best for you and will continue to do so. They have already raised you with their beliefs and values about what is good, right, and true in the world. The experiences of college will provide you with many opportunities to make your own choices and to test and clarify the things you have been taught. As you explore and find your own way, you might experience tension with your family, especially if they feel strongly about a choice you are making that is not what they wish for you. This is a challenging time, but it is one that all adults must go through. If you are having tensions in your family, seek the support of counselors at your university. They have been trained in the issues that are specific to college-age students and can be quite helpful in assisting you with negotiating a new relationship with your family. Again, all of your records are private, so this person is there to be a sounding board to help you work through this transition, and what you say will not be discussed with your family. Counseling is also usually free or very low in cost, which is not true of similar counseling services outside of the university environment.

are also influenced by these messages and can have their self-image and self-esteem directly affected by media influences.

Although the family generally means well, sometimes families attach their desire for their child's healthy and happy life to a certain path, such as a specific career. Somehow "I want Sabrina to have a happy life, which means being able to support herself financially" becomes "Sabrina needs to become an engineer because those are the best-paying jobs." This can happen with a variety of things: which college to attend, which major to declare, which career to pursue, and which person to date. The value is positive, but the way in which it is expressed can be limiting to the student's freedom. When the daughter calls home to announce that she wants to be an art studio major, the family is probably upset and might try to influence the choice, simply because they have associated engineering with her health and happiness. Interactions such as these occur regularly, and college students might find themselves a bit stunned at their family's reactions to their exciting news about majors, romantic partners, or school activities. This is especially problematic when the family has narrowed the "right" path to a relatively small number of options that they feel very strongly about.

The Values Clarification Process in Young Adults

When a student goes off to college, she or he already has developed a sense of values through the influential forces mentioned previously, the most important being the immediate family. Leaving the family of origin and other influential forces *begins* the value clarification process. This is important because the value clarification process hinges on exposure to new values that invariably force an evaluation of those that the person previously held. This process is complex and is not necessarily completed by the time a person graduates or turns 23, but several of the stages have usually occurred by then. Over the years, I have observed students moving through seven distinct stages of the value clarification process. These are most often affiliated with individual values that are of medium to high importance—in other words, in the middle to deepest levels of the value onion. A person will go through these stages for each value separately and can be in multiple stages at the same time, each for a different value.

1. *Separation:* This first stage is the mere act of leaving the family of origin and other influential groups in terms of constant contact and influence. For example, when a student moves into a residence hall, the family no longer sees the student on a daily basis and is not there to comment on, or influence, the student's daily choices. The student probably also left friends and teachers behind, and while contact might be maintained, it is not the primary influence in the student's life. The physical moving and living in another location is the key to this stage, whether it is 5 miles or 5,000 miles away.

2. *Exposure:* This second stage occurs when a person is exposed to many people who hold values and beliefs, some which may be similar and some of which may be different. This can range from little things such as how

to cook spaghetti (do you put the noodles in the pot whole or break them in half?) to larger values such as political ideology or controversial issues such as abortion or gay rights. Exposure has to do with simply seeing and hearing other people's beliefs and values. This can occur for university students in the classroom, at a club meeting, in their faculty's office hours, or hanging out with peers. Research university campuses are especially rich with daily opportunities for exposure to different perspectives, beliefs, and values as the campus community is engaging in research and critical thinking.

3. *Clarification:* Once a person is exposed to another value or belief, this stage has to do with what the person does with that exposure. There are two possibilities.

   a. Confirmation: If the value that is expressed is the same as or similar to the one the student holds, then the interaction likely confirms the student's original value. This can occur on the conscious or unconscious level. A student might think, "I knew I was right about that. I'm glad that she knows this too." Or the student might feel a subtle level of comfort with the other person or the experience. When values are similar, this aspect of clarification is not very noticeable or obvious because it fits with the student's original way of seeing the world. When confirmation occurs, the next stage, "response to dissonance," is skipped.

   b. Dissonance: When a student is exposed to a value that is very different, the experience is often noticeable because it is uncomfortable on some level—in essence, it conflicts with the student's original value. This is because it challenges the student's original view in some way and creates what psychologists call *dissonance*. The strength of the dissonance is usually correlated with the importance of the value or the depth to which is it held. When dissonance occurs, the person moves into dealing with that dissonance in some way.

4. *Response to dissonance:* This stage represents how a person deals with the dissonance of having a value not confirmed, or even directly challenged, by a person or experience. This situation has to be resolved, at least psychologically, in some way. There are two options:

   a. Invalidation: One response is to invalidate the source of the challenge or conflict in some way, thereby eliminating the dissonance. This occurs when a student is judgmental and seeks to find something wrong with the source. For example, a student might invalidate the information ("He's just wrong. He doesn't know what he is talking about."). Or the student might invalidate the person ("She's weird if she thinks that. No normal person would."). It is usually easier to invalidate the person if she or he is a stranger or if she or he is the first one to challenge the value. It is harder to invalidate the person if she or he is liked and/or respected. If the student chooses to invalidate, then the process stops here, and the student's original value remains intact.

   b. Accommodation: The other response is to accommodate the new value in some way. This usually occurs under three conditions: The value is not tightly held, so it is fairly easy to alter; the person who is challenging the value is respected or trusted; or there have been previous challenges to the value, and this one achieves some critical mass in the mind of the student. There are two options for accommodation:

i. The first option requires the student to allow for more than one belief to be correct. This allows the student to hold onto his or her original value without invalidating the other. It usually sounds something like "Everyone is entitled to his or her opinion" or "That's not true for me, but I can see that it might be true for them." Essentially, the student allows for pluralistic views, when there can be more than one right or correct possibility.

ii. The other option is for the student to question his or her own original value and assess its validity in the light of the new information. The student might seek to alter some aspect of the value by creating conditions under which it is true or not, or the student might determine that the original value is invalid.

5. *Initial choice to integrate or not:* This stage occurs when students alter their original value in some way. They might alter some portion of their original value to include the new value, or they might completely adopt the new value in place of the original. Again, this depends on how deeply the value is held and the source of the dissonance.

6. *Family response:* This stage involves how the family responds to the student's shifting values. The response is usually related to how tightly held the value is in the family system. Those that are tightly held will elicit a quicker and stronger response than those that are not. The family is usually the source of the original value system and have raised the student to see it as the "good/right/true" way. They will generally not be in agreement that the value should be shifted. Their response will also depend on how much the family perceives the shift to be a threat to their child's overall health, happiness, and safety. If the threat is perceived to be strong, so will be the response. Families can and do utilize a wide range of responses, both verbal and nonverbal, to attempt to control the student's process. When possible, the family can attempt to invalidate the source of the new information or experience. If this is not successful, they might use more coercive tactics to influence the student as a way to exert control. When the student was living at home, the family had more options for asserting this control through sanctions, punishments, and even nonverbal disapproval that often affected a student's choices. With the student's increased freedom and independence, the family loses access to the old methods and sometimes uses more dramatic responses than ever before. Depending on the situation, responses can cover a wide range, including showing support, saying nothing, stating displeasure but acknowledging the student's right to choose, expressing that the student should feel guilt, reinforcing the value through religious or other culturally relevant information, yelling, threatening to discontinue support, and disowning the student from the family. This

response might be brief and quickly expressed, or it might be continually reinforced until the student acquiesces. Needless to say, this response can be quite upsetting to the student.

7. *Final choice to integrate or not:* This stage represents the choice a student still has after hearing or experiencing his or her family's response. Depending on the circumstances, the family might be able to influence the student back to the original value. In situations in which the student truly has returned to the previous value, everything returns to normal in the family dynamics until the next time a value is challenged. In situations in which the student does not want to return to the original value, she or he will have to find ways to keep the family either uninformed or misinformed about the choice or will have to face whatever consequences the family may be willing to administer. In this case, the student often seeks support from other people in his or her life as a way to balance the disconnection felt with the family.

This process occurs over and over for different values throughout a son or daughter's lifetime, although it is most pronounced in the first few years after the young adult moves away from the family. Also, each family has its own ways of going through these stages, and it won't be the same even for children within the same family. The process never really ends, as the values clarification process, and the family's response to it, lasts a lifetime. Ask any older adult, and he or she can tell you the issues that still create tension in their family and how they

What This Means to You

You and your family will also go through this process. You might not notice it at first, or even for a couple of years, but at some point, you will realize that your values are changing and are now somewhat different from your family's. Some of you will find that your families will be very encouraging of this process and will support your growth and development no matter what it looks like. Others of you will have families who try very hard to shape your values or keep them from changing too much but who will eventually come around, and you will find a peaceful relationship. Sadly, some of you will experience dramatic tensions and even estrangement from your family, especially if you veer drastically from deeply held family or cultural values.

Interestingly, there is a cycle to this whole process. Your adult family members went through this process with the family who raised them, and if you have children, you will go through it with them. You will eventually find friends and a romantic partner who share your beliefs and values. If you have children, you will find yourself imparting your values to them and probably feeling that you are doing a better job than your family did. And one day, your children will leave home and begin to test and question all that you taught them. That is the beauty and irony of it all!

Might I Suggest...

As you come up against these points of disagreement, you will find that you have opportunities to assert your views and make requests of your family; a relationship between adults is a two-way street, and some things might need to be negotiated. These conversations might not be easy, but it is your responsibility to guide your family in understanding what you want and how you want to interact with them. There are a few things you can do in these situations.

It's always a good idea to *really listen* to your family. Listen to what they are saying and find out whether you can hear the fears or concerns that underlie the comments they are making. If so, you can begin to address those issues directly. For example, if they want you to major in a certain field, they might be saying things like "It's important that you have a good salary and can support your family." The underlying fear is that you might end up in a low-paying job, struggling every month to make ends meet, and might not be able to have the kinds of things they wish for you, such as a home, a car, and vacations. Once you identity the fear, go do some homework. Find out about the salaries in the career you wish to pursue. The more information you can give your family that addresses their specific fear, the more likely they will be to change their perspective.

Another thing you can do is to ask your family to talk about their past. There is probably some aspect of their young adulthood that was important to them for which they did not find support from their family. It might have been whether, or where, they could go to college, a travel opportunity, a career path, or a romantic partner.

deal with them. Typical issues that tend to be the most problematic for families include the following:

- The job or career of the son or daughter
- The sexual orientation of the son or daughter
- The ethnic expression or identification of the son or daughter
- The political ideology and affiliations of the son or daughter
- The spiritual expression of the son or daughter
- The people the son or daughter dates
- The person with whom the son or daughter forms a romantic partnership
- The "risks" the son or daughter takes in terms of activities, traveling, places to live, and so on (The greater the danger as perceived by the family, the bigger the concern is and the more control the family is likely to try to impose.)
- How the son or daughter plans for big events such as weddings or holidays
- How the son or daughter raises his or her own children

It is important for every family to establish ways in which they will handle these issues and others that will arise as the young adult becomes a fully mature adult.

Ask them more about it—why it was so important to them, what it meant, and how their life might have been different. Really listen to what they are saying because their words will give you clues to how best to connect with them. Then, at a separate time (do not do this next step in the same conversation), talk to them about what you want and tie it back to their own experience. This has to be very genuine and also for an issue that is very important to you; if you use this method with something of low importance, it will appear manipulative.

If your family is reacting very strongly in a negative direction, give them some time to cool off. You will not get very far if they are upset, and things could escalate when they don't need to. If they are threatening actions such as not paying for college, you will have to assess whether you want to accept these consequences or not. In some situations, it will be absolutely worth it because the issue at hand is core to who you are, but sometimes, it's not worth it. Only you can decide.

Finally, you can always give up on that one issue and accept your family's wishes. You might choose to pursue the major or career that they wish or not date the person they dislike. However, while this solution brings immediate peace, it does not help you and your family go through the rest of the stages of separation and value clarification. The process gets arrested until the next issue, which might include where you should live or with whom you should fall in love. At some point, you and your family will need to negotiate a new relationship that allows you to pursue your own path. This is an essential step in your development as an adult.

Chapter Summary

In this chapter, the following topics were discussed:

- Homesickness and friendsickness
- The Family Educational Rights and Privacy Act (FERPA)
  - FERPA's impact on student independence and responsibility
  - Managing this newfound freedom and independence
- Bloom's stages of parent/adolescent separation
  - Stage 1: Ambivalence
  - Stage 2: Cognitive separation

- Stage 3: Emotional separation
- Stage 4: Values clarification
- Stage 5: New relationship

- The development and clarification of a student's values
  - The values formation process in children
  - The role of values in the family system
  - The values clarification process in young adults

Reflections and Exercises

1. Interview a Parent

This is best done with another student's parent rather than your own (preferably a parent whose child is the first or last to leave home). The purpose of this activity is to learn more about the parents' experience of their son or daughter going off to college, which might give you insight into your own family. Note: If your biological family did not raise you, you might want to find another student who has a circumstance similar to yours. Although university staff cannot release the names of students to you, you could ask an advisor or counselor whether they would be willing to pass along a note from you to students she or he knows who have a similar background, explaining what you want to do. Once you have found someone to interview, set an appointment of about thirty minutes and ask the following questions:

How do you feel about your son/daughter going off to college?

How does this affect you as a parent? What will change for you?

How does this affect you as a person, separate from your role as a parent?

What is the biggest challenge you will face in the coming months?

What is the biggest excitement you will face in the coming months?

What concerns do you have for your son/daughter?

How will you address those with him/her?

If you were to give me advice about how to understand my own parents, what would you tell me?

After you complete the interview, reflect on what you learned about this parent's experience. How might it be the same and different from your parents'?

You might want to share this interview with your own parents and ask them the same questions. This can lead to really great conversations about this important time in all of your lives.

2. Your Family and Bloom's Stages

Read over Bloom's stages and try to assess which stage you and each of your adult family members (e.g., parents, stepparents, guardians) are in. Then have them read about Bloom and find out what they think about the model. Ask each person to share what fears or concerns she or he has about the separation process and what things she or he is excited about or looking forward to. On the basis of these responses, talk about what each of you needs from each other in the different stages and how you can best deal with conflict when it arises.

3. Assess Your Value Onion

First, draw several concentric circles to represent an onion. You can either make one onion to represent different values or make a separate onion for each of the areas of education, work, and family.

1. Thinking back to what your family has told you and showed you through their actions, what do you think are their values regarding education? You might want to address issues such as the following:

   What is the purpose of an education?

   What criteria are important to look for in a college?

   Are there certain majors that are more valuable than others? Which ones and what makes them so?

   What part, if any, does "having fun" play in your education? Make a list.

   Then mark on the list which values you hold as well and place them on the onion to indicate whether this is a deep, medium, or lightly held value.

2. Next, do this process again for values about work.

   What criteria are important to look for in a job?

   Are certain lines of work more valuable or prestigious than others? Which ones and what makes them so?

   What part, if any, does happiness play at work?

3. Finally, do this process for the values about family.

   What criteria are important to look for in a romantic partner?

   Are there certain types of partners who are more valued than others? Which ones and what makes them so?

   What about interracial or same-gender relationships?

   What parts do happiness and commitment play in your relationships?

How is conflict addressed?

What does this exercise tell you about yourself?

Can you see any values that are deeply held by your family but are not as important to you?

Which values of your family do you think you will shift or change as you form your own?

How do you anticipate that your family will respond to these changes in your values? How might you address their responses or reactions?

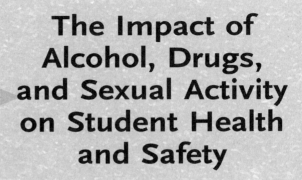

Chapter 5

The Impact of Alcohol, Drugs, and Sexual Activity on Student Health and Safety

As is discussed in Chapter 4, college students are given a lot of freedom and responsibility, which allows them to make their own choices about many things. This freedom also includes choices about alcohol, drugs, and sexual activity. It is common for young adults to experiment in all three of these areas, even though this experimentation might put their health or safety at risk, or be against the law. This experimentation seems to expand when young adults move away from home, as they no longer have some of the limitations that were placed on them by their family. As a result, most college campuses are greatly affected by their students' choices with regard to alcohol, drugs, and sex because of the potentially dangerous legal and health consequences of making poor choices. While individuals make these choices, the impact of these choices often spills over beyond the one person to affect others around him or her as well as the local environment. This chapter will focus on student freedom, alcohol and other drug use among college students and some of its consequences, sexual activity among college students, and many useful tips and suggestions regarding these topics.

The Tension Between Student Freedom and Student Choices

An inherent tension exists on college campuses between allowing young adults the freedom and responsibility guaranteed by the Family Educational Rights and Privacy Act (FERPA), managing student behavior and conduct as it relates to laws and campus policies, and, finally, keeping students safe and healthy. These three things might not be in alignment, as the student might want to engage in behaviors that break the law and/or are potentially dangerous—for example, underage drinking or having unprotected sex. Students' families often have expectations that the university will guide and protect their student from making inappropriate choices, much as they tried to do when he or she was living at home. Although parents did have the choice of calling the police if they found their child smoking pot, most did not and instead attempted to manage their child's behavior through other methods such as curfews and various punishments.

While a child's behavior can be guided, it is virtually impossible to force adults to make good and/or lawful choices. Even our society acknowledges this through its legal system. All adults in our society have the freedom to choose whether or not to abide by the law. Sure, there are consequences for not doing so, but first the person must be caught in violation of the law and then sent through a legal process that determines the person's guilt and any relevant sanctions.

Obviously, parents do not want their young adults engaging in behaviors that might endanger their health and safety, even if they are technically adults. The parents have spent eighteen years keeping their child alive and safe, and it can be very difficult to let that go. When parents send their son or daughter off to college, they want him or her to be alive in four years, and this isn't always the case. Every year, parents get calls from the police or campus officials with sad news about their son or daughter. A few get calls that their son or daughter is in jail for a serious crime. Many more get calls that their son or daughter is seriously injured and might not ever be the same. And some receive the devastating news that their son or daughter has died. The tragic part is that almost all of these situations involve alcohol and/or drugs and could have been prevented. These stories are in the media all over the country, and they heighten parents' concerns about their own child's safety. Parents tend to put a lot of pressure on the university to keep their student safe and healthy.

Separate from the pressure of parents, there is a general national concern for the health and well-being of young people. Many national studies are done each year that explore various elements that endanger youth. For example, the Centers for Disease Control conducted a large study in 1995 called the National College Health Risk Behavior Survey (NCHRBS). This survey involved 4,609 undergraduate college students from public and private colleges and universities (both two- and four-year) across the United States. The results are considered representative of undergraduate college students nationwide aged 18 years or older. The questionnaire focused on "health risk behaviors that contribute to the leading causes of death, illness, and social problems among young adults in the United States, including:

- Tobacco use
- Unhealthy dietary behaviors
- Inadequate physical activity
- Alcohol and other drug use
- Sexual behaviors that may result in HIV infection, other sexually transmitted diseases, and unintended pregnancies
- Behaviors that may result in unintentional injuries (such as motor vehicle crashes) and violence including suicide."

The results of this study and many others like it are sent to college administrators and faculty and are featured in many higher education publications. This results in increased awareness of these issues and a more focused commitment on the part of administrators and faculty to address them.

As a result of all of these pressures, most university administrators and faculty find themselves managing rather complex situations. They cannot force young adults to make good and/or lawful choices, but they can and do create policies and rules and enforce penalties for breaking those rules. The kinds of penalties that universities can apply are limited to what they control: enrollment,

What This Means to You

No matter which university or college you attend, you will probably notice two things. One will be the alcohol and drug use habits of your peers. Especially if you are living in a residence hall or an area that has a high concentration of college students, you will be in the position to witness and experience their choices involving alcohol and other drug use and the subsequent consequences of their choices, as well as your own. Most college students have consumed alcohol and other drugs in high school, but their use becomes much more prevalent in the college environment, in which hundreds or thousands of young adults are living together. If your campus has a reputation as a "party school," drugs and alcohol will probably be even more noticeable, since many students who like to use them will have chosen to attend that particular campus *because* of its reputation.

The second thing you will notice is that the campus administration will focus quite a bit on students' use of alcohol and other drugs. This conversation might even begin during orientation and will certainly be featured in policies for campus-owned living communities such as residence halls and apartments. You will be informed of the various consequences for violating campus policies along with both local and state laws. You will also see many educational programs on the effects of alcohol and other drug use as well as campus-sponsored social programs that are scheduled on Friday and Saturday nights as a way to offer alternatives to the party scene. Finally, you will witness some of the enforcement of these policies and laws. However, not every student is caught, so you will also see students get away with breaking rules and laws because campus administrators and police cannot be everywhere. In addition, even when a student is caught and prosecuted through either campus or legal methods, most of that students' peers never hear about the final outcome. This is because a student's conduct and/or legal records are private. I have seen students tell their friends that they didn't get in trouble when I *know* that they were written up, have gone through a judicial process, and are in the process of being expelled from either the residence hall or the campus.

As a result, you will need to find your own way with regard to alcohol and other drugs. Substances of all kinds will be readily available to you, regardless of your age and the institution you attend, and you will be faced with making choices that will ultimately affect your academic success, as well as your physical and emotional health. In addition, the people around you *will* affect your college experience, especially because of their choices to use alcohol and other drugs. Part of your success will depend on your ability to navigate these situations and to advocate for yourself.

education, and access to university property. University penalties are likely to be fines, mandatory educational programs, eviction from university property, and expulsion from the university. The local, state, and federal legal systems also have jurisdiction in any university environment and may be involved in prosecuting a young adult for his or her choices in addition to, or separate from, any process in which university may be engaging.

Finally, students have expectations too. While students want to be alive and healthy at the end of their college experience, they also want to have fun, and, according to many young adults, fun often involves alcohol, drugs, and sex. Students have a different impression of what is dangerous and when it is dangerous, and these impressions might not match those of their parents, the university, and the legal system. As in high school, when young adults found creative ways around their curfews and their family's rules, they are just as creative in college. Students who *want* to drink and/or take drugs will find a way to do so, despite policies and laws. And the students who do *not* want to do these things will still find themselves affected by the students who do. This is also true for sexual activity. Sexuality is a healthy part of any adult's life, and although sex is not illegal between consenting adults, students want to make choices involving this issue. Those choices affect other students around them and may also be of concern to the student's family, who might have different expectations for their sexual behavior. Even in the best of circumstances of a loving and committed relationship, students still need to worry about sexually transmitted infections and pregnancy.

Alcohol Use among College Students

There are many reasons that colleges and universities put so much emphasis on the alcohol consumption and drug use of students. The goal is always to decrease these behaviors and increase student safety. The primary reason is that the health and safety of its students are every campus administration's goal. Many campus presidents, chancellors, and deans have suffered the pain and anguish of talking to a parent whose son or daughter will never come home again. This is always much more tragic when the incident could have been prevented. No dean wants to make that call, and yet almost every dean has had to make many of these calls during his or her career.

Another reason campus administrators are concerned is that the institution's reputation is important because it influences the overall value of the degree and reflects on both the faculty and administration. A reputation as a party school can harm an institution's abilities to recruit the top, most serious student and faculty scholars. This in turn can negatively affect funding and other financial support, such as donors' monetary gifts and grants. Finally, a poor reputation can decrease the value of the degrees the institution confers, which harms every student who graduates from that campus.

With that said, there is probably no campus in North America where the discussion of alcohol and other drug use is not prevalent. Even a simple search on the Internet will yield hundreds of sites dedicated to the issue of decreasing college students' consumption of alcohol and other drugs. Most campuses have policies that attempt to control the availability and consumption of alcohol and drugs, and there are methods of enforcement for these policies. In addition, many attempts are made to compete with the lure of alcohol and drugs, so campuses dedicate a lot of money and energy to offering other tempting events, such as concerts, dances, and movies, to compete with weekend parties.

Why all this hoopla? When you talk to the average college student, many perceive their campus's efforts as an attempt to crack down on fun and believe that the administration overreacts to typical student partying. The difference lies in what the two groups see on a daily basis. A student might drink every weekend and attend many parties and not see, or recognize, any negative consequences of his or her behavior. The student might have good grades and suffer only the occasional hangover. In fact, this is especially true at research universities, where the top students are admitted. Students often *can* party frequently and still maintain excellent grades, a combination that many students use as the primary indicator that they are "doing fine."

On the other hand, the administration sees the bigger picture. They hear the reports every weekend of how many students went to the local emergency room for alcohol poisoning, how many students were victims of an alcohol-related crime, how many students had to drop out of school because of alcohol and drug problems, and how many students were victims of sexual assault in which alcohol or drugs were involved. Below you will find some national statistics about college students and consumption of alcohol and other drugs. These, as well as the local statistics for your campus, are always in the minds of administrators and faculty.

Current Data on Alcohol Use among College Students

Alcohol is the most commonly used and prevalent drug on college campuses. Although the legal drinking age in the United States is 21 years, many college and high school students gain access to alcohol and drink while underage. The problem is not low or moderate use of alcohol—having a beer with pizza after a big exam would not yield any negative health effects (although there might be some for violating underage drinking laws or campus policies).

The most problematic type of drinking is called high-risk or binge drinking, which is defined as five or more drinks at a sitting for men and four or more drinks at a sitting for women. High-risk or binge drinking—in other words, drinking a large amount of alcohol in a short amount of time—is what is most closely correlated with the negative effects of alcohol use, where use becomes abuse. According to the National Institute on Alcohol Abuse and Alcoholism (NIAAA), out of every five college students, two (or 40%) have engaged in binge drinking in the past two weeks, two more (another 40%) drank but not to excess, and one (20%) did not drink alcohol at all. The concern is that when students drink, they tend to do so in excess, the kind of drinking that is the most potentially dangerous or lethal to self and others (i.e., high risk). In 1997, the

College Alcohol Study found that students who binge drink two to three times per week (22% of college students) consumed a median of 14.5 drinks per week, which amounted to 68% of all the alcohol consumed by college students.

Nationally, 83% of college students indicate that they have consumed alcohol in the previous year. Of those students, 69% drank in the previous 30 days, and 22% indicate that they drink three or more times per week; these data come from the CORE Survey done in 2003 with 93,679 college students at over 197 institutions.

Negative Consequences of Alcohol Use among College Students

The problem is not the use of alcohol and drugs per se. If students drank and were able to be healthy, happy, and safe, there would not be such a focus on alcohol and other drug use. The fact is that use of alcohol and other drugs consistently leads to negative consequences for the student and for the college student population as a whole. While any individual college student might not see evidence of all of these problems, every campus administrator and faculty member does, as do many families of college students. The students in the 2003 CORE Survey reported problematic experiences from their alcohol and other drug use as shown in Table 5.1.

Most college students *do* see these negative consequences over time—if not for themselves, then for their friends, roommates, or romantic partners. Each term, I ask the students in my class whether they know someone who has a problem with alcohol or drugs. Almost all of the hands are raised. That's because, over time, the negative effects of alcohol and other drug use catch up to the students who use these substances frequently. While the students might get by for a few weekends without seeing or experiencing any problems, they will inevitably experience many of the problems listed in Table 5.1.

In fact, the NIAAA states that "Excessive drinking among college students is associated with a variety of negative consequences that include fatal and nonfatal injuries; alcohol poisoning; blackouts; academic failure; violence including rape and assault; unintended pregnancy; sexually transmitted diseases including HIV/AIDS; property damage; and vocational and criminal consequences that could jeopardize future job prospects."

The CORE Survey discovered a direct link between excessive drinking and academic performance. The following relationship was discovered between the number of drinks per week and grade point average:

- A's = 3.6 drinks per week
- B's = 5.5 drinks per week
- C's = 7.6 drinks per week
- D's = 10.6 drinks per week

Here are some other disturbing statistics:

- 1,400 college students between the ages of 18 and 24 die each year from alcohol-related unintentional injuries, including motor vehicle crashes.

Table 5.1   Percentages of Students Who Experience Negative Consequences for Alcohol Use

Percentage	Experience
60%	Had a hangover
49%	Got nauseated or vomited
36%	Done something I later regretted
33%	Driven a car while under the influence
30%	Missed a class
29%	Got into an argument or fight
28%	Had a memory loss (i.e., blacked out)
28%	Been criticized by someone I know
21%	Performed poorly on a test or important project
13%	Been hurt or injured
13%	Been in trouble with police, residence hall staff, or other college authorities
12%	Been taken advantage of sexually
11%	Thought I might have a drinking or other drug problem
7.4%	Damaged property (e.g., pulled fire alarms, vandalized)
6%	Tried unsuccessfully to stop using
5.1%	Taken advantage of another person sexually
5%	Seriously thought about suicide
1.4%	Been arrested for DWI/DUI
1.4%	Tried to commit suicide

- Each year, more than 600,000 students between the ages of 18 and 24 are assaulted by another student who has been drinking.
- Each year, alcohol is involved in 500,000 unintentional injuries of college students.
- Annually, alcohol is involved in 70,000 cases of sexual assault and acquaintance rape of college students.
- Alcohol use is associated with high-risk sexual behavior. Students who drink excessively are two to three times more likely to have had multiple sex partners in the past month than are those who drink responsibly.

- As many as 70% of college students admit to having engaged in sexual activity primarily as a result of being under the influence of alcohol or to having had sex they wouldn't have had if they had been sober.
- At least one out of five college students (20%) abandons safer sex practices when drunk, even if they do protect themselves when they are sober.

Connected to these statistics is a new concept known as *secondhand effects*—in much the way that secondhand smoke can be damaging to a nonsmoker's health, drinkers, especially binge drinkers, can negatively affect others around them who are not drinking to excess. For example, 61% of non-binge-drinking students who live on campus have had their study or sleep disturbed by someone else's drinking. In addition, 50% of these students have had to "babysit" another student who had drunk too much at least once during the past year. These secondhand effects can range from the annoying, such as noise, vomit, and litter, to the damaging, such as vandalism and property damage, to the truly dangerous, such as physically or sexually assaulting other students or causing accidents that kill people. Alcohol is involved in approximately 50% of all fatal traffic crashes among 18- to 24-year-olds—crashes in which someone, not necessarily the driver, dies. Many college students have been killed in fatal crashes involving alcohol; sometimes they were the intoxicated driver, and sometimes they were the sober passenger, other driver, or pedestrian.

Separate from all of these serious consequences of alcohol use, alcohol contributes to people just doing dumb things—things that hurt their friends and their community. It is no secret that alcohol impairs judgment; people become more likely to say and do things they would not normally do when sober. This includes making hurtful comments to friends, roommates, and romantic partners, things that often cannot be fixed the next day with a simple apology. Students who are under the influence also can say and do racist and sexist things that harm the overall campus community. This can change the whole feeling of safety that students of color and women have on a college campus, one that lasts long past the weekend. Students who are under the influence also often say and do homophobic things that they would not normally do when sober, again creating a sense of danger for an entire segment of the campus community.

Your college experience *will* be affected by drug and alcohol use. Either you will experience the direct effects of your own drinking or you will experience the secondhand effects of others'. You can mitigate the negative effects of alcohol and other drug use by your own choices of behavior, selecting the people you hang out and live with and the activities in which you participate. Although your university will do its best to address these issues, it is ultimately your responsibility to take care of yourself and protect your own health and safety.

In addition, students may develop alcoholism. Even students who are from families with no known alcoholism can become alcoholics. Students often don't identify alcoholism because they "only drink on the weekends," but alcoholism is focused on what happens to the person *when* she or he drinks, not how often or on what days. An alcoholic is a person who is dependent on or addicted to alcohol. This dependence can be psychological, physical, or both. This is differentiated from "problem drinking," in which there is no dependence. However,

How to Help a Friend

Here are some useful tips adapted from the University of Miami's PIER 21 Program entitled "Helping Family or Friends with Substance Abuse Problems:"

- Realize the negative effect that alcohol or other drug use is having on the person and that he or she needs to change some behavior. Be confident that your involvement is the right and caring thing to do.
- Don't do it alone. Talk with someone else, preferably a counselor, about the best way to approach the situation.
- Talk with your friend when he or she is sober. Make sure the your friend sees what you see and knows how you have been affected as well.
- Be prepared for negative responses, excuses, and even criticisms of your own behavior. Stay calm and don't take anything personally. Keep the conversation centered on your friend and how substances are affecting him or her.
- If your friend responds negatively, try again after the next instance of abusive behavior. Repeat after each incident, and be consistent with your message.
- If your friend responds positively, work with him or her to develop a plan for change. Suggest an appointment with the advisors at the student health center and offer to come with your friend.
- If your friend's drinking habits do not change, set some limits for yourself and remove yourself from situations that upset or potentially harm you. Ultimately, your friend needs to make his or her own decisions—only that person can be responsible for his or her actions.
- Find support for yourself and get attention for your needs. This is a tough thing to go through, but you do not need to do it alone. There are many resources available to help you through this. Take advantage of them.

the problem drinker is any person whose drinking causes a problem, whether academically, medically, legally, psychologically, or in relationships with people such as family or friends.

The following are indications that someone is experiencing problem drinking:

- *High tolerance:* The ability to consume large quantities of alcohol or other drugs and not show the effects
- *Blackouts:* A temporary loss of memory in which the individual was awake and functioning but later cannot remember anything about a given period of time
- *Negative consequences:* The person experiences them as a result of alcohol or other drug use (e.g. DUI) and continues to use in the same way
- *Denial:* The person does not believe or admit that use is causing problems
- *Avoidance:* The person does not like to talk about his or her use

If you or another person has any of these indicators, you might want to speak with a professional at your campus student health service, preferably someone who is trained in counseling on alcohol and other drug issues. This person can work with you, either to help you prepare to talk to your friend or to help you make changes in your own behavior.

Drinking Responsibly

The point is not to avoid partying but rather to party safely and responsibly. Partying is an important part of the social scene on college campuses, and the most successful students find a way to enjoy the scene with low to moderate alcohol use. To do this, it helps to understand exactly how alcohol works in the system and what causes the good and bad feelings associated with drinking. The following websites have some very useful information and are designed for college students:

- www.factsontap.org (this site is free to all users)
- www.mystudentbody.com (this site requires the campus to pay a licensing fee)
- www.b4udrink.org (this site requires the campus to pay a licensing fee)

Most people understand the concept of blood alcohol content (BAC)—a measure of how much alcohol is in the bloodstream; it is what is measured in determining whether a person is legally intoxicated. Police officers can measure BAC through devices such as Breathalyzers, but the most accurate measure is made by taking a sample of a person's blood and having it tested. In addition to its usefulness for law enforcement officers, the BAC is a great tool for college students. Understanding how your body is responding at different levels of intoxication can help you to make good choices about how much and how fast to drink.

First, let's look at some quick facts about alcohol. Katie Budke, a Health Educator at the University of Iowa, has the following to say:

Alcohol (ethanol) is a powerful, mind-altering chemical, no matter what form it is in—beer, wine, or liquor. Because alcohol consumption is so common in our culture, we often forget that it is a drug that the body treats as a toxin—a poison. It is a depressant that is absorbed into the bloodstream through your stomach and intestinal lining (remember, it is not digested like food) and is transmitted to all parts of the body. When alcohol reaches the brain, it affects the control centers resulting in poor judgment, slower reflexes, blurred vision, and problems with coordination. Your liver processes alcohol out of your system at an average rate of about 1.5 ounces of 80 proof alcohol an hour. Nothing you can do will speed this process up . . . not exercising, vomiting, or drinking 3 shots of espresso. Drinking faster than your body can process alcohol causes intoxication (literally alcohol poisoning).

So how do you figure out your BAC? Having your blood drawn and tested is the most accurate way, but obviously, people aren't going to do that in the middle of a party. The Breathalyzers that the police use aren't usually readily available either. There are now some handy strips that you can purchase that you put on your tongue to get a quick reading of your BAC. While not totally accurate, they can be a good guide and are easy to carry with you, so you can use them during parties.

Another useful tool is some of the BAC calculators that are available on the Internet. You enter in your gender, weight, number of drinks, and time in which they were consumed, and it gives you an estimate of your BAC (just type "BAC" into any Internet search engine, and it will return links to hundreds of sites). Some of them even allow you to input the exact type of drink you had (e.g., light beer, gin and tonic) and the type of glass you drank out of to give you the most accurate results. Obviously, students would probably not take a break from a party to go online to calculate their BAC, but using these charts *before* going to a party can help a student to determine how fast they will reach certain levels and to plan their consumption pace accordingly. These online calculators are based on weight charts that have been created to estimate BAC. Table 5.2 gives some charts adapted from the "Party Smart" website at the University of Connecticut (www.partysmart.uconn.edu/bac.html).

For example, a woman who weighs 120 pounds could see that having two drinks in an hour would give her an estimated BAC of .08%. She would most

Table 5.2 Alcohol Impairment Charts for Women and Men

ALCOHOL IMPAIRMENT CHART FOR <u>WOMEN</u>										
	APPROXIMATE BLOOD ALCOHOL PERCENTAGE									
N	Body Weight in Pounds									
E **V**	Drinks	90	100	120	140	160	180	200	220	240	
E **R**	0	.00	.00	.00	.00	.00	.00	.00	.00	.00	Only Safe Driving Limit
	1	.05	.05	.04	.03	.03	.03	.02	.02	.02	Impairment Begins
D	2	.10	.09	.08	.07	.06	.05	.05	.04	.04	Driving Skills Affected
R	3	.15	.14	.11	.10	.09	.08	.07	.06	.06	
I **N** **K**	4	.20	.18	.15	.13	.11	.10	.09	.08	.08	Possible Criminal Penalties
	5	.25	.23	.19	.18	.14	.13	.11	.10	.09	
&	6	.30	.27	.23	.19	.17	.15	.14	.12	.11	Legally Intoxicated
D	7	.36	.32	.27	.23	.20	.18	.16	.14	.13	Criminal Penalties
R **I**	8	.40	.36	.30	.26	.23	.20	.18	.17	.15	
V	9	.45	.41	.34	.29	.26	.23	.20	.19	.17	Serious Illness or Death
E	10	.51	.45	.38	.32	.28	.25	.23	.21	.19	
Subtract .01% for each 40 minutes of drinking.										
One drink = 1.25 oz. of 80 proof liquor, 12 oz. of beer, or 5 oz. of table wine.										
Deaths have been documented at BAC levels of .35–.50+										

(Continued)

Table 5.2   (continued)

	ALCOHOL IMPAIRMENT CHART FOR <u>MEN</u>									
	APPROXIMATE BLOOD ALCOHOL PERCENTAGE									
N E V	**Body Weight in Pounds**									
	Drinks	100	120	140	160	180	200	220	240	
E R	0	.00	.00	.00	.00	.00	.00	.00	.00	Only Safe Driving Limit
	1	.04	.03	.03	.02	.02	.02	.02	.02	Impairment Begins
D	2	.08	.06	.05	.05	.04	.04	.03	.03	Driving Skills Affected
R I	3	.11	.09	.08	.07	.06	.06	.05	.05	
N K	4	.15	.12	.11	.09	.08	.08	.07	.06	Possible Criminal Penalties
	5	.19	.16	.13	.12	.11	.09	.09	.08	Legally Intoxicated
&	6	.23	.19	.16	.14	.13	.11	.10	.09	
D	7	.26	.22	.19	.16	.15	.13	.12	.11	Criminal Penalties
R	8	.30	.25	.21	.19	.17	.15	.14	.13	
I	9	.34	.28	.24	.21	.19	.17	.15	.14	Serious Illness or Death
V E	10	.38	.31	.27	.23	.21	.19	.17	.16	
	Subtract .01% for each 40 minutes of drinking.									
	One drink = 1.25 oz. of 80 proof liquor, 12 oz. of beer, or 5 oz. of table wine.									
	Deaths have been documented at BAC levels of .35–.50+									

likely be breaking the law if she drove at this level, but she might even be violating public intoxication laws if she went out in public (these laws vary by state, so check with your local police). You'll also notice that the chart is slightly different for men; a man who weight 120 pounds could drink three drinks in an hour before reaching the legal intoxication level. This is because men have an enzyme in their stomachs that causes them to metabolize alcohol differently than women (Frezza et al., 1990). Pound for pound, men can metabolize more alcohol per hour than women, so men have a natural advantage in drinking competitions between men and women.

It's important to remember that charts like these are just a general guideline based on the assumption that a person metabolizes one drink per hour. The truth is that every person metabolizes alcohol differently, which is why you can have two people who weigh the same and drink the same number of drinks, but one person is much more affected by the alcohol. Every person has a different tolerance to alcohol, and there is no chart that can factor that in, so use these charts only as a rough guideline.

What happens to your body at the different BAC levels? A useful resource is available at www.factsontap.org along with a lot of really great information about alcohol and students. Compare these descriptions taken from that website to the previous BAC charts to get a sense of how many drinks per hour each level represents:

- *.02%–.03%:* You feel mildly relaxed and maybe a little lightheaded. Your inhibitions are slightly loosened, and whatever mood you were in before you started drinking may be mildly intensified.
- *.05%–.06%:* You feel warm and relaxed. If you're the shy type when you're sober, you lose your feelings of shyness. Your behavior may become exaggerated, making you talk louder or faster or act bolder than usual. Emotions are intensified, so your good moods are better and your bad moods are worse. You may also feel a mild sense of euphoria.
- *.08%–.09%:* You believe you're functioning better than you actually are. At this level, you may start to slur your speech. Your sense of balance is probably off, and your motor skills are starting to become impaired. Your ability to see and hear clearly is diminished. Your judgment is being affected, so it's difficult for you to decide whether or not to continue drinking. Your ability to evaluate sexual situations is impaired. Students may jokingly refer to this state of mind as beer goggles, but this BAC can have serious repercussions. See the information on "Sex and Alcohol: A Risky Relationship" (http://www.factsontap.org/riskyrel/Riskyrel.htm) for how to protect yourself.
- *.10%–.12%:* At this level, you feel euphoric, but you lack coordination and balance. Your motor skills are markedly impaired, as are your judgment and memory. You probably don't remember how many drinks you've had. Your emotions are exaggerated, and some people become loud, aggressive, or belligerent. If you're a guy, you may have trouble getting an erection when your BAC is this high.
- *.14%–.17%:* Your euphoric feelings may give way to unpleasant feelings. You have difficulty talking, walking, or even standing. Your judgment and perception are severely impaired. You may become more aggressive, and there is an increased risk of accidentally injuring yourself or others. This is the point when you may experience a blackout.
- *.20%:* You feel confused, dazed, or otherwise disoriented. You need help to stand up or walk. If you hurt yourself at this point, you probably won't realize it because you won't feel pain. If you are aware you've injured yourself, chances are you won't do anything about it. At this point you may experience nausea and/or start vomiting (keep in mind that for some people, a lower blood alcohol level than .20% may cause vomiting). Your gag reflex is impaired, so you could choke if you do throw up. Since blackouts are likely at this level, you may not remember any of this.
- *.25%:* All mental, physical, and sensory functions are severely impaired. You're emotionally numb. There's an increased risk of asphyxiation from choking on vomit and of seriously injuring yourself by falling or other accidents.

- *.30%:* You're in a stupor. You have little comprehension of where you are. You may suddenly pass out (i.e., lose consciousness) at this point and be difficult to awaken, but don't kid yourself, passing out can also occur at lower BACs. With an alarming BAC like .30%, your body will be deciding to pass out for you. In February 1996, an 18-year-old student died of alcohol poisoning with a BAC of .31% after attending two parties the night before.
- *.35%:* This blood alcohol level also happens to be the level of surgical anesthesia. You may stop breathing at this point. In February 1996, a second student, age 20, died of alcohol poisoning with a BAC of .34% after drinking six beers and twelve shots in two hours.
- *.40%:* You are probably in a coma. The nerve centers controlling your heartbeat and respiration are slowing down. It's a miracle if you're not dead. In April 1994, a 21-year-old student died of alcohol poisoning with a BAC of .40% after a party.

If people drank slowly and achieved each of these BAC levels one by one, they most likely would not keep elevating their BAC once they got to some of the pretty yucky feelings. However, when people drink a lot of alcohol in a short period of time, they can shoot up through several of these levels very quickly and may arrive at a higher level before they realize how drunk they are. Unfortunately, once alcohol is in the bloodstream, it cannot be quickly dispersed. Most college students end up with dangerously high BACs through activities such as beer bongs, shot competitions, and slides, and are in physical danger before they realize it. Unfortunately, by that time, judgment is impaired, and students sometimes continue to drink, increasing their risk of alcohol poisoning and death.

What Is a Drink?

One thing that is important for college students to know is what one drink really is. Most students have heard the information that one drink is 1.25 ounces of 80 proof liquor, 12 ounces of beer, or 5 ounces of table wine. But what does that really mean? Most students don't carry accurate measuring cups with them, and most college logo shot glasses are far larger than 1.25 ounces. It obviously will depend on the size of cup you use to serve alcohol—a 24-ounce cup filled to the brim with beer is two drinks, not one. Yet most students will call that one beer. To give you an idea of how much difference cup size can make, look at the comparison in Figure 5.1. All measurements were made using the typical red plastic cup (shown actual size) found at most grocery stores and warehouse stores. The cup reads "16/18 oz.," which means 18 ounces if filled to the rim or 16 ounces if filled to just 1/4 inch below the rim. We'll use the 16-ounce level, or 1/4 inch below the rim.

Symptoms of Alcohol Poisoning

Every year, many college students die from alcohol poisoning. Often, their friends didn't want to get them into trouble and believed that they would just "sleep it off." Alcohol poisoning is just like any other type of poisoning in that the body is being saturated with chemicals that can slow down or stop its basic survival functions. However, alcohol poisoning can usually be treated successfully

If filled with beer,
it would equal 1.3 drinks.

If filled with wine,
it would equal 3.2 drinks.

If filled with margaritas,
it would equal 7 drinks.*

If filled with Long Island iced tea,
it would equal over 10 drinks.*

*Traditional recipes, no ice.

Figure 5.1   Number of Drinks in a 16- to 18-Ounce Plastic Cup

if the person is given medical care soon enough. Don't take any chances with your friends; if you notice the symptoms listed in Table 5.3, call 911 immediately because the person is exhibiting indicators that he or she is being poisoned and needs medical help to recover.

Table 5.3   Symptoms of Alcohol Poisoning

Symptoms	What to Do
• Person cannot be awakened • Cold, clammy, or bluish skin • Slow or irregular breathing • Vomiting while unconscious • Shortness of breath, unconsciousness	• Call 911 immediately! Do not wait—these symptoms indicate that the person is in trouble. • Turn the victim on his or her side to prevent choking on his or her own vomit. • Continuously check on the victim until medical personnel arrive. If breathing stops, administer CPR.

A Note about Date Rape Drugs

There are several drugs that rapists can use to facilitate their crime, including Rohypnol and GHB. These drugs are odorless and colorless so can be easily slipped into the intended victim's drink without him or her knowing. There are three phases to how these drugs work that facilitate sexual assault. The first phase is that the drug makes the person feel ill to the point that she or he would want to leave the party. The person usually heads for home not realizing that that they have been drugged. The next phase happens very quickly, usually before the person can get home. The drug affects the person's ability to move and speak so that they appear extremely drunk and unable to take care of themselves. The rapist has usually followed the victim and is waiting for this phase to step in and "assist" the victim. Onlookers usually do not perceive that anything is wrong. The drug continues to affect the person's motor skills and leaves the victim essentially unable to move or speak for several hours but conscious of what is happening to them. It is during this stage that the rapist harms the victim. The last stage of the drug affects memory so that the next day, the victim has no real clear memories of the perpetrator or incident, and therefore cannot help police apprehend the suspect.

There are several things that students can do to prevent being a victim of this crime. The first is to assume that rapists come in all forms, including young adults who look like students. Some rapists intentionally focus on college towns because of the open parties that occur where alcohol is served and easy to drug. Just because someone is at your friend's party does not mean that your friend knows this person or that she or he is not a potential threat. As a result, *always* pour your own drinks and keep them with you at all times. If you have to set your drink down, get a new one. Also, crowded parties can make it easy for someone to reach over and pour drugs in a drink, even while you are holding it so be attentive to your surroundings. If you feel ill, immediately suspect that you may have been drugged. Do not leave the party but instead find people whom you know and trust to help you. You want to find a safe space before the next stage of the drug sets in, where you appear very drunk and become unable to communicate. Students can help each other by never letting a friend leave a party alone or leaving them behind. If you witness a scenario where a very drunk person appears to be being helped by an individual, don't assume that everything is OK. The best way to thwart this crime is to go up and insist on helping as well—that way you can ensure that the person is really escorted home and left in the care of friends.

Finally, realize that police officers in college towns are looking out for this exact scenario. If they see a very drunk person being helped by another (especially a drunk woman being helped by a man), they will most likely approach and ask the drunk person some questions. They are trying to ascertain if this a potential assault in progress. If the drunk person is not able to communicate clearly or does not seem to really know the person with them, the police may take the drunk person into custody in order to protect him or her. Unfortunately, they cannot really take the drunk person home because then she or he would still be vulnerable to others and the police could be held liable for anything that happened. As a result, it's really best to go out as a group of friends who look out for each other and keep each other from harm.

The Biphasic Response to Alcohol

If you go back and look at the list of what happens to your body at different BAC levels, you'll notice that the first two levels have more of the "positive" feelings—the ones that feel good and the reason most people choose to drink. The rest of the levels have more and more negative feelings, ending with dangerous and lethal consequences. This illustrates what is known as the biphasic response to alcohol (Marlatt, 1999). Researchers have found that the enjoyable part of alcohol consumption comes in the first couple of drinks as your BAC rises to .055—that seems to be the peak at which a person most enjoys the stimulant effects of alcohol that create the "good" feeling or the "buzz" (the first phase). After that point of .055, people start to experience the negative effects of alcohol as it begins to act as a depressant on the system (the second phase). As the BAC climbs higher beyond .055, the feelings get more and more "bad," and the dangers increase as well. We all know this, but we also live in a culture that believes that if a little of something is good, then more will be better. This is just not true for alcohol. While you might think that if you feel good after drinking three beers, you will feel even better after ten, in fact you won't. The truth is that once you reach the BAC level of .055, it's all downhill from there. Furthermore, if someone develops a high tolerance for alcohol, the euphoric feeling, or "buzz," is not as intense. The person often drinks more, not realizing that he or she is just moving more quickly into the depressant or dysphoric phase. Figure 5.2 illustrates this model.

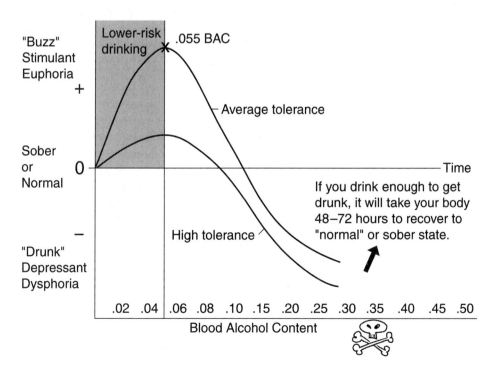

Figure 5.2   Biphasic Response to Alcohol Consumption

Stephanie's Advice

My name is Stephanie, and I'm a senior. My tip is that all students who choose to drink should learn how to "ride the buzz." Let me explain. As a college student myself, I have had great times with my friends. We have gone to some really fun parties in college, and we often drink. One of the lessons I learned early on was I later discovered to be the biphasic model. Although I didn't particularly care about its scientific explanation, I definitely knew that after I drank some alcohol, I would get that giddy, giggly feeling that was pretty enjoyable. We called that the "buzz," and it was the feeling you were going for. What became clear was that, if you didn't pay attention, you could kill the buzz by either drinking too little or drinking too much once you were feeling it. If you drank too little and the buzz started to fade, it was easy to increase it again, but if you drank too much, you soon found yourself not caring and drinking more and more until you got sick, blacked out, or both. Needless to say, those nights developed into horrible and messy mornings, which were dangerous too. Not only did we blow past the buzz (and therefore not really enjoy the effects of the alcohol we had purchased), but we also increased our chances of bad things happening to us.

My friends and I started to learn that it required some practice and skill to "ride the buzz"—the phrase we coined for finding that perfect balance of drinking at just the right pace to keep the buzz going before going over the top—it almost felt like surfing! Riding the buzz is an important skill that students who choose to drink should master. It's not about ingesting large amounts of alcohol quickly—beer bongs and shots are the fastest way to blow past the buzz because your body goes through the "good zone" too quickly and into the zone of poor judgment and negative effects. It's about finding a way to stay near .055 BAC over a long period of time. Here are some other pointers for learning how to "ride the buzz":

In addition to intentionally using the biphasic response to alcohol to your advantage, there are some other good tips for drinking responsibly, which can make a big difference in decreasing the chances that you will experience negative consequences of alcohol consumption. The most important is for you to choose to drink for positive reasons, not to escape from problems—when you do that, you still wake up to your problems, but now you have new ones too. If you are drinking to reduce stress or to try to forget, it is best to tackle this problem straight on; there are many positive ways to decrease your problems without adding new ones associated with alcohol. Make an appointment with a counselor at your campus to start working on the heart of the problem. Another important tip is to believe that alcohol is a complement to an activity, not the primary focus. Here are some other useful tips from the University of Miami's PIER 21 Program:

- *DO* set a limit for yourself before going out and having drinks. You should know, according to your body type and tolerance, how much alcohol you can safely have.

- Keep your tolerance low! It is possible to increase your tolerance by regularly drinking large amounts of alcohol . . . but why? You just make it harder and more expensive to reach the buzz. The buzz feels the same whether you get there on two beers or twelve, so you might as well be cost effective about it—and you'll save money for pizza later!
- Once you start to feel the buzz, ride it! This is where you want to start monitoring your feelings and drink at the pace to stay in the good zone. It usually means slowing down a little. You want to milk all of the good feelings out of the current buzz before you drink more; otherwise, you are wasting the good feelings that your first drinks brought you. When you start to feel it fade a little, drink a bit more but not as much as it took to get to the buzz in the first place (since your BAC is already elevated, you'll probably just need a little). If you want to have a drink in your hand, alternate between alcoholic and non-alcoholic beverages. Besides, people won't bug you if you have a drink in your hand—a plain cola looks just like rum and cola, and water looks like vodka.
- Don't compare your buzz to others'. Everyone has a different reaction to alcohol, so it's important to focus on when *your* buzz begins. It might only take you half a beer to feel it, while your friend might need four. If you try to match your friend beer for beer, you are going to fly past the buzz zone and end up having a much yuckier morning than your friend will be having.
- Toward the end of the evening, let your buzz start to fade. If you get good at riding the buzz, you will know exactly when to stop drinking to be in good shape the next morning.

It's the perfect solution—all of the fun of partying without any of the mess!

- *DON'T* go out with people who make you feel uncomfortable about not drinking. The people worth hanging out with are the ones who will respect you and your choices.
- *DO* be careful at bars, clubs, or parties where "Ladies Drink Free"—women are generally affected more quickly by alcohol than men, and an intoxicated person may be targeted for sexual assault.
- *DON'T* guzzle, play drinking games, or use devices to consume more quickly (e.g., beer bongs, funnels, shot slides, tubes, double shot glasses, etc.). Your body can only safely process 0.5 ounces of alcohol (about half the amount in an average drink) an hour. So, have one drink/hour and alternate with non-alcoholic drinks.
- *DO* take a break from drinking. Show yourself and your friends that you don't need alcohol to go out and have a good time. If you can't do that, then that is an indication that you may have a problem with alcohol.
- *DO* eat *before* and during drinking alcohol—it will slow down the absorption rate of the alcohol into your bloodstream. However, eating *after* you drink will not change anything—once alcohol is in your bloodstream, nothing can reduce the rate of absorption.

A Word for Students Who Do Not Drink

If you are one of the 20% of college students who do not drink at all, regardless of your age, then you might find the following information helpful. If your campus is known for its social scene, you might find it a bit challenging at first because it is most likely that many of your peers chose your campus because of its reputation. There might be a big emphasis on partying, and it might seem that there is nothing to do outside of the party scene. That is not true, but it can look that way, especially as most of your first-year peers will be eager to participate in the scene at the beginning of the term. (It's important to note that this generally wears off over the term as people get tired of the party scene, especially its negative effects.) Going with your friends is certainly an option, but you might find yourself "babysitting" the others who drink too much or always being the designated driver.

- Remember that it is becoming more and more acceptable for students to not drink.
- Choosing not to drink doesn't mean that you have to sit home alone on a weekend. You can still party and have a good time while sober.
- Choose an understanding group of friends—friends who either don't drink themselves or will support your choice to not drink even though they might choose to.
- Participate in campus activities and social events that don't focus on alcohol. While the student party scene might revolve around drinking, there are many other fun activities and events to participate in that don't. Check your campus newspaper and fliers posted around campus to find out more.
- Attend parties with nondrinking friends as a support system.
- Drink water, soda, and the like at events where alcohol is served. If you are not sure whether nonalcoholic options will be provided, bring your own. Remember, it's still important to watch your drink even if it is nonalcoholic. Predatory drugs work in sodas too.

- *DON'T* go to places where you will be bored if you're not drinking or where you will be uneasy without a drink in your hand.
- *DO* talk to your friends before going out to discuss what to do if: (1) someone is drinking too much, (2) someone gets drunk and starts hooking up with someone they probably wouldn't want to, (3) someone wants to leave but the others want to stay out. Prepare yourself and your friends to take care of each other and to support each other in making responsible choices.
- *DON'T* leave your drinks unattended, let someone else get your drink for you, or drink from a punch bowl—predatory drugs are out there!! They are colorless, odorless, and will leave you completely vulnerable to be taken advantage of. You are not always in a "safe place" with "safe people." Get your own drink, watch it being made, and keep it with you where you can see it at all times.

- *DO* get involved when you see someone else putting him/herself in danger. Alcohol poisoning, accidents, sexual assaults, drug overdoses, and drunk driving deaths are all real! Better to have someone ask you why you tried to keep them from having a good time, then to have his/her parents or the police ask you why you let them leave the party drunk. Care enough to get involved and do the right thing. Wouldn't you want someone to do that for you?

Campus Policies and Resources

As was stated earlier in this chapter, universities have felt compelled to respond to these issues for the health of the students. In fact the U.S. Surgeon General says, "Binge drinking is the most serious public health problem on American college campuses today." The U.S. Senate and House of Representatives have already passed resolutions calling for national action to address college binge drinking. Many universities are doing so and utilizing a wide range of methods to combat the problem of excessive alcohol and drug use among students. According to the Higher Education Center for Alcohol and Other Drug Prevention, these efforts focus on five primary prevention strategies:

- *Education:* Through academic classes, workshops, and programs in university-owned living environments
- *Early intervention:* By providing counseling and support to students who are experiencing problems with alcohol and other drug use
- *Environment:* Addressing the campus and community climate around alcohol and other drug use as well as availability
- *Enforcement:* Through campus policies and local and state law enforcement
- *Evaluation:* Frequently assessing the alcohol and other drug use of college students as well as the effectiveness of these prevention strategies, making adjustments as needed

Campus policies and local and state laws are a primary way in which student behavior is controlled. If you are living in a university-owned building, there will most likely be policies regarding whether or not alcohol may be on the premises (regardless of the residents' ages) as well as policies that discourage large parties—policies about the number of people that can be in a room, noise regulations, and the like. Even if a living environment consists of students who are over 21 years of age, you will still find policies that govern the presence of alcohol in the public areas. Housing staff often have the job of enforcing the policies in living environments, and these may be connected to campus judicial processes.

Local and state laws also play a role and go through the state legal system; laws against minors in possession of alcohol, public intoxication, and driving under the influence (DUI) are frequently used to attempt to keep students safe. Law enforcement agencies also utilize other, related laws to control alcohol and other drug use, such as laws against open alcohol containers in public, urination in public, noise ordinances, and regulations against large gatherings of people. Students can even be cited for biking under the influence (BUI), which carries the same penalties as a DUI. Many students don't know that they can be held liable for purchasing alcohol for others or serving alcohol to others, especially minors. Many college students over the age of 21 have found themselves in jail and held accountable for the injuries or deaths of partygoers who got the alcohol or drugs at their party. In a new trend across North America, called *parental notification,* universities use public police records (to avoid violating FERPA) to discover which enrolled students have been cited for an alcohol- or drug-related issue. These records are then shared with the parents of those students. Many campuses that have adopted this process have experienced a decrease in alcohol-related behavior among their students.

With all of this focus on enforcement, there is an even stronger focus on education and early intervention. Most campuses have professional staff that provide education on alcohol and other drug issues, as well as counselors who can help students who are experiencing addiction and other problems of alcohol and other drug use. In addition, police officers often hold information sessions to educate students early on about various laws and ordinances that might affect their choices and behaviors (you can also look up laws and penalties on state government websites). Even orientation programs include discussions on college student drinking and the various ways in which the campus is addressing these issues. In an attempt to compete with alcohol-centered parties, campuses often spend thousands of dollars—and in some cases hundreds of thousands—each year on hosting concerts, dances, and other events to provide alcohol-free alternatives to their students.

Might I Suggest...

You will find many resources available at your university related to alcohol and other drugs. Regardless of the climate of your campus and the choices of your peers, you will be able to find the types of experiences you desire and make the social scene work for you. Use the tips provided on previous pages to increase your chances of fun and decrease your chances of negative consequences. The most important tip to remember is to go with friends and make a pact to look out for each other. Don't leave friends unattended no matter what. Also, take advantage of the various programs and activities your campus offers. There are some really fun things to do on the weekends that don't revolve around alcohol and drugs. This might require you to break away from the group mentality of always going to the party scene. But just because your friends might not be interested in going to that concert or attending the Twister competition doesn't mean that there will not be lots of people there. If you can't find anyone to go with you, call the campus escort service and go anyway. You will probably get to meet lots of new people, students who share some of your interests and who have also chosen to forgo the party scene for the night.

Other Drug Use among College Students

While alcohol is by far the most prominent drug on college campuses, students also use a whole host of other illegal drugs. The second most common drug is marijuana, but every drug can be found if students wish to do so. Campuses are also struggling with a rise in inappropriate use of prescription drugs. Students often see these as "safer," since they are made by pharmaceutical companies and prescribed by medical doctors. However, prescription drugs can be dangerous and cause negative consequences, especially when not appropriately monitored by a physician. In addition, they can still qualify as illegal, depending on how they were acquired.

Current Data on Drug Use among College Students

Table 5.4 shows the current national statistics for other drug use, from the CORE Survey done in 2003 with 93,679 college students at over 197 institutions. It shows annual, monthly, and heavy use.

The National Institute on Drug Abuse has a very informative website that gives the latest statistics on use, forms, and effects of the most prominent drugs; check it out at www.nida.nih.gov. Although there is not the same wealth of information on the drug use of college students, there is still much to be learned by looking at national trends and common effects.

Table 5.4 Prevalence of Usage for Various Drugs

Substance	Annual Prevalence	30-day Prevalence	3 Times per Week or More
Marijuana	32%	19%	7.2%
Cocaine	3.7%	1.6%	0.2%
Amphetamines	6.8%	3.0%	1.6%
Designer drugs	3.3%	1.1%	0.1%
Hallucinogens	7.4%	2.6%	0.2%
Sedatives	2.7%	1.3%	0.3%
Opiates	1.3%	0.6%	0.2%
Inhalants	2.7%	1.0%	0.2%
Steroids	0.7%	0.5%	0.4%
Other drugs	2.1%	0.9%	0.3%
Tobacco	45%	35%	24%

Effects of Commonly Used Drugs

The following information is from NIDA and www.erowid.org on the five kinds of drugs (after alcohol) most used by college students (according to the 2003 CORE Survey).

Marijuana

- People use marijuana to get the following effects: increased relaxation, mood lift, increased awareness of senses, pleasant muscle sensations, relief for medical symptoms of pain and nausea, and increased appetite.
- Students who smoke marijuana get lower grades, are less likely to graduate, score significantly lower on standardized tests, and have reduced intellectual skills (such as registering, organizing, and using information) compared to their nonusing peers.
- Of all the drug-related visits to hospital emergency rooms, those involving marijuana experienced a 15% increase from 96,426 in 1995 to 110,512 in 2002.
- Marijuana quadruples a user's risk of heart attack in the first hour after use because of its effects on blood pressure, heart rate, and reduced ability of the blood to carry oxygen.
- Marijuana smoke contains 50–70% more carcinogenic hydrocarbons than tobacco smoke, leading to cancers of the lung, respiratory tract, and mouth.
- Marijuana is known to contribute to depression, anxiety, and personality disturbances in users.

Hallucinogens

- People use hallucinogens to experience the following effects: increase in energy, creative thinking, awareness and appreciation of music, awareness of senses, mood lift, closed- and open-eye visuals, and "profound life-changing spiritual experiences."
- Fifty-one percent of high school seniors report that it would be "fairly easy" or "very easy" for them to get LSD if they wanted it.
- The effects of LSD are unpredictable and are usually first felt about thirty to ninety minutes after ingestion and can last up to twelve hours. Users may experience extreme and/or simultaneous mood swings as well as delusions and visual hallucinations.
- Some users experience severe, terrifying thoughts and feelings; fear of losing control; fear of insanity and death; and despair. Fatal accidents have occurred during states of LSD intoxication.
- LSD users may manifest relatively long-lasting psychoses, such as schizophrenia and severe depression.

Amphetamines and Methamphetamines

- People use amphetamines and methamphetamines to experience the following effects: increased energy and alertness, decreased need for sleep, feelings of euphoria, increased sexuality, decreased appetite, and weight loss.

- In 1997, 4.4% of high school seniors had used crystal meth at least once in their lifetimes, an increase from 2.7% in 1990.
- Methamphetamine causes increased heart rate and blood pressure and can cause irreversible damage to blood vessels in the brain, producing strokes. It also causes respiratory problems, irregular heartbeat, and extreme anorexia.
- Over time, methamphetamine appears to cause reduced levels of dopamine (a neurotransmitter), resulting in symptoms like those of Parkinson's disease, a severe neurological disorder.

Designer Drugs Such as MDMA or Ecstasy, Rohypnol or Roofies, and GHB

- People use Ecstasy to experience the following effects: extreme mood lift; increased willingness to communicate; feelings of comfort, belonging, and closeness to others; feelings of love, empathy, and forgiveness; the urge to hug and kiss people; increased awareness of senses (sensations are bright and intense); "profound life-changing spiritual experiences"; and dissolution of neurotically based fears.
- Ecstasy is a psychoactive drug with amphetamine and hallucinogen qualities. In high doses, it interferes with the body's ability to regulate temperature, leading to dehydration and hyperthermia, which have caused liver, kidney, and heart failure in users.
- Ecstasy changes brain function, affecting cognitive tasks and memory. It can do long-term damage to serotonin neurons (a study using primates showed that only four days of exposure to Ecstasy created damage that was still evident six to seven years later).
- Ecstasy users often experience symptoms of depression for several days after its use.
- In 1995, only 421 people reported Ecstasy use during visits to hospital emergency rooms; by 2002, this had increased almost ten times—to 4,026.
- People use GHB and Rohypnol ("roofies") to experience the following effects: effects similar to those of alcohol but longer-lasting, mild relaxation, increased sociability, and decreased motor skills.
- GHB and Rohypnol depress the central nervous system and have both been used as "date rape drugs" because they are odorless, colorless, and undetectable when put in beverages. In the right amounts, they cause the victim to quickly feel ill and seek to leave the social setting, where they become unable to move and essentially helpless. In addition, memory is affected, so victims often have no memory of their attackers.
- GHB and Rohypnol are also taken recreationally because they create feelings of euphoria. Both can become lethal when mixed with alcohol and/or other depressants.
- In 1995, only 145 people reported GHB use during visits to hospital emergency rooms; this increased dramatically to 3,330 in 2002.

Cocaine and Crack

- People use cocaine to experience the following effects: increased alertness and energy, elevation of mood, a mild to high degree of euphoria, increased athletic performance, decreased fatigue, clearer thinking, and increased concentration.

- Cocaine and crack are the same drug in different forms (crack is the cheaper, more potent version most often used by lower-income people, although the legal penalties for its use are nearly ten times higher). Cocaine is a very addictive drug that stimulates the central nervous system, and one use of crack can be habit-forming.
- Ten percent of high school seniors have used cocaine, and 45% of twelfth graders say that they could get cocaine "fairly easily" or "very easily" if they wanted it.
- Cocaine and crack create a euphoric high, but its intensity and duration depend on the form of ingestion. The faster the absorption, the more intense but shorter the high. Users report feelings of restlessness, irritability, and anxiety.

What This Means to You

If you choose to use drugs, it is important that you understand the effects they have on your body. While the sensations might feel enjoyable, they can actually be affiliated with short- and long-term damage. (There are many useful and informative websites on the Internet that will give you accurate information about drugs and their effects.) It is also important to control, to the extent that you can, the quality and quantity of any substances you use, as these can greatly affect your body's response. Drug dealers often cut drugs with other substances (such as baby powder or even rat poison) to make a bigger profit. People have gotten very sick and even died from other substances that were in the drugs they were taking.

You will also want to assess how much, and in what ways, your drug use is affecting your ability to be successful academically, socially, and personally. Ultimately, only you can weigh the pros and cons of your use and make choices to stop or continue use. If you have questions about drugs or your own use or are concerned about your health, remember that the services of the student health office may be very valuable to you. Because of FERPA, if you seek confidential medical advice and personal counseling for alcohol and drug issues, your family will not be informed.

If you do not use drugs, you might still witness others' use or be affected by their use. You can always choose to find other nonusing students to socialize with, but if you are living with someone, the chances are greater that his or her drug use will affect you. You might need to talk to your friend and/or roommate to request certain limitations on drug use in your presence or your shared space. You have a right to enjoy your space just as much as another person. If these negotiations do not go well, you might also seek the assistance of housing staff or a campus mediator, or you might wish to find other housing arrangements.

> ## Might I Suggest...
>
> While drugs can certainly produce a positive-feeling experience, there is no doubt that they have negative short- and long-term effects on health. Even marijuana, which was long believed to have no serious consequences, is proving to have several dangerous long-term effects. As a student at a research university, you are very intelligent, and I encourage you to utilize your critical thinking skills in this area. While your drug use might have developed in response to peer pressure or a desire to rebel against your family, it ultimately will most affect you and your future. Get the facts. The website www.erowid.org is very comprehensive, as is the website www.drugabuse.gov. Go meet with an emergency room doctor, talk to counselors in your student health center, take classes on the subject, and utilize opportunities to talk with long-time users. All of this information will help you in making safer and smarter choices even if you choose to continue using drugs.

- Rates of cocaine use by college students have varied between 2.0% of all students in 1994 to 4.8% in 2000.
- Adults 18 to 25 years of age currently have the highest percentage of cocaine use of any age group.
- High doses or prolonged use can trigger paranoia as well as depression. Users can develop ulcerations of the mucous membranes in the nose. Users can die suddenly and unpredictably from cardiac arrest, seizures, and respiratory arrest. Consuming alcohol during use increases the risk of sudden death.

Sexual Activity among College Students

After all this discussion of alcohol and other drug use, it might seem odd to move on to the discussion of sexual activity. After all, sex is not an illegal activity and is part of most healthy adult relationships. While that is certainly true, the inclusion of sex in this chapter on health and safety focuses more on the fact that while sexual activity should be fun, healthy, and consensual, it often isn't, especially when students are consuming alcohol and other drugs. Consensual sexual activity can pose a health risk when people do not take precautions against sexually transmitted infections and diseases. Separate from that, many college students want to avoid pregnancy. Finally, sex that is not consensual, meaning that someone was assaulted or raped, is definitely of great concern, as the victims of these crimes often suffer emotional damage in addition to the physical damage that can affect their entire life and certainly their college experience.

Administrators on university campuses have long been concerned about the sexual activity and health of their students. Several decades ago, before the passage of FERPA, the concern arose out of a desire to enforce the societal moral codes about sexual activity—more accurately, that there shouldn't be any until marriage. Many of the in loco parentis policies and procedures focused on keeping the men and women separated and monitoring their evening activities. Students had curfews, and living environments were always single-sex with an "adult" living nearby to ensure compliance. It was typical to have policies by which students' doors had to be left open 45 degrees so that staff members could see what was happening inside, and some colleges were infamous for their "one foot on the floor" rule when students of opposite sexes were in a dorm room. Some campuses even had policies whereby a staff member would put matchbooks in the doors after the official curfew time to ensure that students were not sneaking out after hours. Students could be expelled for "fraternizing with the opposite sex" and pregnancy would "ruin" a young girl's life unless she was "lucky" enough to persuade the father to marry her.

All of this changed with FERPA and the nearly simultaneous shift in societal values about sexual behavior. FERPA allowed a student's room to become his or her private living space, and it removed responsibility from the university to monitor its students' sexual behaviors. While many living environments still maintained single-sex status, the removal of curfews and other policies allowed students to do what they wanted with whomever they wanted as long as they were not disturbing their peers. It's important to note that many sectarian schools still have policies in place to regulate social, and potentially sexual, interactions between students. Sectarian schools are private and can maintain policies and procedures that would not be legally viable in public institutions. In addition, sectarian schools focus on religious teachings and trainings and attempt to make the campus environment conducive to the spiritual teachings of the particular religion on which the school is based.

Although universities have moved away from trying to prevent sexual encounters between students, there is still a strong concern about students' sexual practices. This concern stems from the health risks that have been identified since the sexual revolution of the 1970s, such as more dangerous and incurable sexually transmitted infections and diseases (STIs and STDs) including HIV and AIDS. In addition, the awareness of sexual assault, especially acquaintance sexual assault, has increased dramatically in the past three decades and is a major concern on campuses nationwide. Given that many social and therefore sexual encounters between students now involve alcohol, the connection between excessive drinking and negative sexual experiences is also a serious concern.

Current Data on Sexual Activity and Its Negative Consequences among College Students

As was mentioned earlier, the Centers for Disease Control conducted a large study in 1995 called the National College Health Risk Behavior Survey (NCHRBS), which involved 4,609 undergraduate college students across the United States. Results from this survey that are relevant to this topic include the following:

- 86.1% had sexual intercourse (oral, vaginal, or anal) during their lifetime
- 68.2% had sexual intercourse in the three months prior to the survey
  - 29.6% of this group reported that they or their partner had used a condom always or most of the time (over two thirds did not)
  - 79.8% of this group had used some form of contraception the last time they had sexual intercourse (and 20.2% did not)
- 62.4% had sexual intercourse in the thirty days prior to the survey
  - 27.9% of this group reported that they or their partner had used a condom always or most of the time (and 72.1% did not)
  - 16.6% of this group had used some form of contraception the last time they had sexual intercourse (and 83.4% did not)
- 35.1% had been pregnant or had gotten someone pregnant
- 38.8% had ever had their blood tested for HIV (meaning that 61.2% have not)

Clearly, many of these statistics indicate that college students are not practicing the most basic of safer sex practices. Obviously abstinence is the only true safe method, while using a barrier method, such as a condom, during sexual intercourse can greatly reduce your risk. This lack of protection increases the risk of developing sexually transmitted infections and diseases, including HIV/AIDS. Some other alarming statistics include the following:

- It is estimated that eight million young adults under the age of 25 are infected with STDs.
- According to the National Clearing House for Alcohol and Drug Information, 60% of college women who acquire an STI, such as HIV or genital herpes, were under the influence of alcohol at the time they had intercourse.
- In 1999, HIV was the fifth leading cause of death for Americans between the ages of 25 and 44.
- It is estimated that people under 25 years of age represent at least half of all new HIV infections in the United States, most of whom are infected sexually.
- One third of people living with HIV are aware of their status and in treatment, one third are aware but not in treatment, and one third are not aware nor have been treated.

Combine this with the data above about the number of college students who are engaging in unprotected sex and the previous information about alcohol's effect on safer sex practices, and you have a dangerous situation on college campuses.

This information is scary enough when it relates to adults who are having consensual sex, but it becomes even more terrifying for students who are raped or sexually assaulted. According to the NCHRBS, 13.1% of college students reported having been forced to have sexual intercourse against their will during their lifetime. It is estimated that 22% of all women (almost one out of four) and 2% of all men will be the victims of a forced sexual act sometime during their life. Some of these sexual assaults may occur prior to college and some may occur later in life, but data indicate that the years of 16 to 24 are the most "rape-endangered" years in a person's life—and these are ages when college attendance is likely.

On most university campuses, the problem is not strangers attacking and sexually assaulting students, although this certainly does happen. In college communities, the problem is acquaintance assault, or "date rape," which occurs when a person is assaulted by someone he or she has had prior contact with, such as a friend, a hallmate, or someone the person had previously met at a party. Nearly 90% of acquaintance sexual assaults involve alcohol, which indicates that one or both parties had their judgment and physical abilities impaired in some way. More often than not, these cases begin with consensual kissing and making out. At some point, one person decides that the situation has gone as far as she or he is comfortable with. What ensues after that might range from subtle pressure from the other person to unending harassment to physical force. When the situation ends in a sexual encounter that one person did not want to happen, this is the legal definition of sexual assault; if physical penetration occurred, it is rape. It doesn't matter what the person who was assaulted was wearing, how many sexual partners she or he had previously, or how much she or he had to drink—if the person said "no" and it was not listened to, then it was sexual assault or rape. It is important to note that both men and women can be victims of sexual assault and rape. The assailant can be someone of the same sex or the opposite sex. Although the majority of reported sexual assaults occur with a man assaulting a woman, the other scenarios can and do occur on college campuses each year.

It is important to distinguish sexual assault from "regretted sex." Most adults experience regretted sex sometime in their life. Regretted sex occurs when, after you chose to engage in a sexual encounter, you later wish that you hadn't. "Later" can be the next hour, the next day, the next week, or even months or years later. Although a person might later wish that she or he had not done something, the fact that the person chose this action earlier means that it was not sexual assault or rape because it was consensual at the time it occurred. Obviously, regretted sex is not a pleasant experience either, and it is also often influenced by alcohol and other drugs. Students who are under the influence of some substance often make choices that they would not normally make when fully sober.

How to Help a Friend Who Has Been Sexually Assaulted

If someone you care about has been raped or sexually assaulted, you might be upset and confused about how to best support her or him. Here are some suggestions, adapted from the University of Colorado at Boulder and Pennsylvania State University, that you might find helpful:

- *Be clear that the rape or assault is not the survivor's fault:* Because the survivor might be questioning whether she or he is to blame for the sexual assault, assure the survivor that it is not her or his fault. If alcohol, drugs, or other circumstances were involved in the rape, the survivor might wish to consider the role of such risk factors in her or his life at a later point in the recovery process. Regardless of the circumstances, nobody deserves to be sexually assaulted, and the survivor is not to blame.

- *Listen:* One of the most important ways to support the survivor is to listen without judging her or him. Feeling able to tell her or his own story without pressure or fear of condemnation will help the survivor to process the experience of the sexual assault.
- *Believe the survivor:* Feeling that she or he is believed by family and friends is essential for a rape survivor's recovery. This person has to overcome many obstacles to be able to speak out about what has happened. Allow the survivor to know that you are open to hearing about her or his feelings and experiences. Although it might be painful for you to hear about what happened, letting the survivor know that you are willing to enter those difficult places with her or him is important.
- *Reassure the survivor:* The fact that she or he survived the attack means that she or he acted appropriately under the circumstances. Survivors often wonder whether they could have better resisted the sexual assault.
- *Encourage the survivor to get support:* In addition to offering your own caring, encourage the survivor to reach out to others. You can help to find someone with whom she or he can talk. Community rape crisis centers have sexual assault/rape counselors, as do many university campuses. These counselors have expertise in the survival and recovery process and can greatly assist a survivor in her or his recovery. Similarly, you might have many feelings about the rape or assault. Consider getting support for yourself, too. You will need to take care of yourself to be supportive of the survivor.
- *Respect decisions:* Remember that a survivor needs to make her or his own decisions as a step in regaining control and overcoming feelings of helplessness. Even if you wish to protect her or him, honor the survivor's wishes and decisions.
- *Resist seeing the survivor as a victim:* Continue to see the person as a strong, courageous individual who is reclaiming her or his own life.
- *Respect the process:* If you feel frustrated that the survivor is taking "too long" to recover emotionally, it is important to realize that everyone needs to process a traumatic experience at her or his own pace. You might want to suggest possible resources to the survivor, such as victim advocacy or counseling services, but do not pressure.
- *Recognize individuality:* Remember that each survivor of sexual assault responds uniquely to the assault, just as the recovery process is different for each individual.
- *Educate yourself about sexual assault/rape and the healing process:* If you have a basic idea of what the survivor has experienced, it will help you be supportive. Talking with other survivors and supporters of survivors and/or utilizing services designed to help survivors will help you to gain knowledge. It is also important to educate yourself about the rape and sexual assault laws in your state.

- *Take care of yourself:* A sexual assault can significantly affect the survivor physically, mentally, and emotionally; as a cosurvivor, you may experience some of these symptoms as well. Knowing what kinds of reactions to expect from the survivor, as well as from yourself and other cosurvivors, will help you better cope with the aftereffects of a sexual assault. Reactions can include, but are not limited to, sleep disturbances, substance abuse, eating disorders, difficulty concentrating, startle reactions, anxiety, depression, emotional numbness, shame, anger, and feelings of helplessness.

As a cosurvivor, you might also need support in coping with a loved-one's sexual assault. Taking advantage of counseling and victim advocacy services not only will help you personally, but also will help you support the survivor more effectively.

What to Do If You Are Sexually Assaulted

This information was adapted from Cornell University (www.gannett. cornell.edu/CARE/help.html):

- *Take care of yourself:* Remember that what has happened to you is not your fault. You are not to blame for what took place before or during the incident. No matter what you did or how you behaved, you did not deserve to have your rights or body violated. The assailant is completely responsible for what happened. And you have a right to get the care and attention you need to heal from the experience.
- *Tell someone what happened:* Talk to a friend or trusted confidant or call your local rape crisis center; there is usually a free and confidential 24-hour hotline that is staffed by counselors who are knowledgeable about the needs of rape survivors, who can lend support, and who will offer to accompany you to get the help you may need. Many university campuses also have counselors who help students who have experienced sexual assault.
- *Get medical care:* As soon as you can, get medical care from the student health center, the hospital, or a private physician. You will benefit from being examined for physical injury and disease. You might need to discuss options for pregnancy prevention. A medical report can also be useful if you decide to press charges against the person who assaulted you. Do not bathe, shower, douche, or change clothes before the medical exam.
- *You might want to report the incident:* It is your decision whether to report the attack. Your can notify the campus police or the local or state police. Filing an informational report does not obligate you to press charges. Should you choose to press charges later, a report will significantly increase the possibility of successful prosecution. You might want to talk to a rape counselor or a law enforcement officer about reporting procedures and options. Your campus office of judicial affairs or dean of students office can consult with you about violations that occur on campus property or between enrolled students. If the perpetrator is a member of the campus community, there might be campus judicial actions that can be taken.

- *Get support:* After the initial process of talking to advisors and getting medical care, you will want to get some more long-term support. Survivors often need the support of a counselor who is trained in working with sexual assault issues to recover both physically and emotionally from the attack. It is not uncommon for sexual assault survivors to experience any or all of the following symptoms: emotional shock, denial, nightmares, sleeplessness, intrusive memories or thoughts about the assault, inability to work or make decisions, impaired relationships, guilt, despair, depression, fear, anxiety, self blame, and anger. You will also want to surround yourself with friends and family who are supportive in your healing process.

Campus Policies

Unlike the situation with alcohol and other drugs, there are very few campus policies that govern consensual sex between adults, with the exception of sectarian schools. There might be policies in university-owned living environments about overnight guests and noise or actions that disturb roommates, but even those do not directly address sexual contact. Students are largely on their own to make good choices about when, with whom, and in what ways they engage in sexual encounters with others.

Some campuses have sought to decrease the incidents of acquaintance sexual assault by instituting recommendations for clear consent, meaning that people must give clear and verbal consent to each act of intimacy before it is initiated. For example, a student would need to ask, "May I kiss you?" and receive a clear "Yes" before moving ahead. Some argue that if a person is drunk, then consent cannot really be given since she or he is under the influence so the partner should not move ahead even if a "yes" has been given. While cumbersome, clear consent is useful in raising awareness about the importance of consent, especially when alcohol is involved, but its value has been strongly debated on college campuses across the country.

You will want to pay attention to any campus policies or discussions of these topics as they might influence your choices and experiences.

Resources for Healthy Relationships

Because of health education in K–12 schools in North America, most students are fairly informed about the basics of sexual intercourse, safer sex practices, and pregnancy. But this is not true of all students—you would be surprised by how many students don't know a lot of very important information. Just listen to an episode of the radio show "Love Line," and you'll discover that there are many people having sex without knowing basic information or safer sex techniques.

With that said, it is each student's responsibility to ensure his or her own sexual safety and pleasure. Unlike high schools, where the topic of sexuality often requires parental permission to discuss, university environments can and do have many open and confidential forums and resources to help students have safe and healthy sexual lives if they so choose. Obviously, some students will have personal or religious values that guide their choices around premarital sex, birth control, and the like, so their college years may be about practicing abstinence. Others will engage in sexual activity throughout their college experience and beyond. Universities want to support the range of students' needs so you will find information and resources available for both sexually active and abstinent student populations. In addition, universities are aware that students have a wide range of sexual orientations and can provide information that is relevant to heterosexual, bisexual, lesbian/gay, and transgender students (this is discussed more in Chapter 7). Your campus health center is a good place to look for information about sexual health, sexuality, and relationships.

Regardless of when and how you choose to become sexually active—as part of a long-term committed relationship or as a casual "hook up" one weekend—you will find that your relationships will be enhanced by three factors. The first is self-awareness, which is the extent to which you know yourself, both emotionally and physically. Emotionally, you will want to know your values around sex, intimacy, and relationships. What assumptions do you have about each one? How are they related to each other, if at all? What kinds of experiences have you had in the past? Both positive and negative experiences shape our beliefs about sex, intimacy and relationships. Understanding your values will allow you to communicate them clearly to a partner, which will increase the likelihood that your values will be honored.

Physically, you will want to learn about your body and its sexual response. The sexual response is a human function, just like digestion or sleep. Knowing how your body functions sexually is just as important as understanding what foods are nutritious and promote healthy digestion. This information is very useful in helping you know how to protect yourself from unwanted pregnancies and sexually transmitted infections. In addition, it can help you have a more enjoyable and satisfying sexual life, whether it be within a marriage or a casual encounter. Learning what you find pleasurable and what enhances your excitement is a personal exploration but it's really no different than learning about what foods you like and which ones you are allergic to. Knowing your preferences will allow you to be able to communicate them clearly to another person, thus increasing your chances that they will be honored.

This exploration leads to the second important factor: communication. All relationships, whether they involve intimacy or not, require communication. This is true for professional work relationships, parent-child relationships, roommate relationships, and so on. When a relationship includes emotional intimacy, sexual intimacy, or both, the need for good communications skills is increased. You will need to be able to tell your partner what you value, what you need, and what you want. Likewise, you will need to listen to your partner share his or her values, needs, and wants. With regard to sexual intimacy, communication can become far more challenging because of the difficulty people have discussing this topic. People may have discomfort with their own sexuality; even if they are comfortable, they may not feel comfortable with sexual terms and vocabulary and this can hinder good communication. Finally, sexual intimacy is an intensely personal topic and it requires vulnerability since the fear of rejection can be strong. This makes sexual communication one of the most challenging areas in relationships.

As couples communicate their individual values, needs, and wants, it is rare that they have complete alignment in all areas. Most likely, they have some differences that need to be addressed. This brings us to the third factor: negotiation. This requires the couple to find ways to negotiate a solution that both can be happy with. Some couples move into a competitive mode, where one person will get his or her way and the other person loses. This exacerbates their differences and eventually causes resentment over time and can breed mistrust and dislike. Others find ways to support and encourage their partner while still speaking up for what they want. If they work together to find a solution that works for both parties, then their differences can actually strengthen their relationship. This is especially true for sexual intimacy. Most likely, each person enjoys different things and is excited or bothered by different aspects of sexual activity. Finding the common ground is the basis for a healthy sexual relationship.

Self-awareness, communication, and negotiation are skills that you will want to learn and enhance for the betterment of all your relationships. There are many campus resources that will help you develop these skills. Simply attending university courses and living in a diverse campus community will build them and you will find workshops on these topics offered by your campus counseling center and leadership program. When you choose to become emotionally and/or sexually intimate with another person, you will want to strengthen these skills even more. Some of the campus resources that are likely to be available to you include the following:

- Academic courses on human sexuality, relationships, communication, and other related topics
- Sexual health education programs that offer workshops and other educational presentations
- Doctors and nurses who work at student health and can address sexual health questions
- Health educators who can meet with you and provide counseling/advising on a variety of topics including relationships, communication, and intimacy
- Counselors and advisors who work with the lesbian/gay/bisexual/transgender populations
- Rape prevention education and sexual assault counselors
- Books and Internet sites that address these topics. Be sure to check out "Go Ask Alice" sponsored by Columbia University at www.goaskalice.columbia.edu, and Teen Wire at www.teenwire.com.

Chapter Summary

In this chapter, the following topics were discussed:

- The tension between student freedom and student choices

- Alcohol use among college students
  - Current data on alcohol use among college students
  - Negative consequences of alcohol use among college students
  - Drinking responsibly
  - What is a drink?
  - Symptoms of alcohol poisoning
  - A note about date rape drugs
  - The biphasic response to alcohol
  - Campus policies and resources

- Other drug use among college students
  - Current data on drug use among college students
  - Effects of commonly used drugs

- Sexual activity among college students
  - Current data on sexual activity and its negative consequences among college students
  - How to help a friend who has been sexually assaulted
  - What to do if you are sexually assaulted
  - Campus policies and resources
  - Resources for healthy relationships

Reflections and Exercises

1. Learn about Local Laws

Find out about the local and state policies in your area. The website at www.epi.umn.edu/alcohol/pdf/Chrtbook.pdf contains a report called *Alcohol Policies in the United States: Highlights from the 50 States*. It's a quick way to look up your state, but be sure to check your state's government websites to find the most current information. Also, any police officer can tell you the current local, state, and federal laws and ordinances that might pertain to you, and police officers are usually quite helpful in answering any questions you might have. Following are some questions to consider:

What is the legal age for drinking?

What are the penalties for a minor in possession of alcohol?

What is the legal level of intoxication?

What are the penalties for a minor who is legally intoxicated?

What are the regulations and penalties for Driving While Intoxicated (DWI) and Driving Under the Influence (DUI)?

Are there different penalties for minors? Or for people on a bicycle or other form of transportation?

What are the penalties for open containers of alcohol in public?

What are the penalties for being intoxicated in public?

What are the penalties for urinating in public?

What are the legal penalties for possession of marijuana? Designer drugs? Hallucinogens? Cocaine?

Are there different penalties for minors in possession of these drugs?

Are there any other local laws or ordinances that students tend to violate? What are the penalties?

2. Ride-Along

Most police and paramedic services allow people from the general public to go on a ride-along. You usually accompany a police car or an ambulance on a typical shift and are right in the middle of the action for any incidents to which they respond. This can be quite an eye-opening and educational experience, especially if you do a ride-along in a college community on a Friday or Saturday night. Contact your local police and paramedic agencies to learn how to participate in this experience. When you participate, consider the following questions:

What did you witness during your ride-along?

How many of the incidents involved college students?

How did the officers or paramedics treat the people they encountered? How were they treated in return?

What did you learn from this experience?

How might you share what you learned with your friends and other students?

3. Interview ER Personnel

No one sees the effects of alcohol and drug use more than emergency room (ER) doctors and nurses near college campuses. In fact, all of their weekends are busy with saving the lives of college students who have been affected by alcohol and other drugs, through either their own use or that of others. In this exercise, you will learn more about the kinds of things that ER personnel see by interviewing a doctor or nurse who works in the emergency room nearest to your campus. First, call the hospital during regular business hours and explain that you are doing this assignment. Ask what the best procedure would be for scheduling thirty minutes of time with an ER doctor or nurse. If there are many students doing this assignment, it might be best to go as a group and do it together so as not to overburden the ER staff. Sit down with the staff member and ask the following questions:

Describe the kinds of cases you see on a typical weekend shift.

What kinds of short- and long-term effects do you see alcohol having on your patients?

What kinds of short- and long-term effects do you see different drugs having on your patients?

What advice would you give college students about drugs and alcohol?

Is there anything else you would like us to know?

Are there ways in which students can volunteer at this hospital?

4. Responsible Drinking Plan

If you are concerned about the drinking habits of a friend or you would like to learn more about creating a plan for responsible drinking for yourself, take action to do so. If your campus has alcohol and other drug counselors, make an appointment and check out their programs and services. You can also go to this great website sponsored by the NIAAA and follow the instructions to create your own drinking reduction plan: http://www.collegedrinkingprevention.gov/facts/cutdrinking.aspx

Chapter 6

The First-Year Student Experience

Being a first-year student is a unique experience because of all the various transition issues that are discussed in this book. It is also a very important time because the choices that are made in the first year often determine the level of success the student can achieve both while in college and after graduation. An enormous amount of personal growth and development occurs in college (as discussed in Chapter 4) that shapes a person's entire life. The purpose of this chapter is to help you understand the major themes affiliated with the first-year experience, for both freshmen and transfer students at a research university. Many students find it helpful to understand their own experience within the context of other first-year students' experiences. This chapter will provide you with the bigger picture of the first-year experience, first through student development theories and then through national statistics, so that you can see how your experiences compare to those of other students. You will see the many common themes and issues of first-year students across North America, which have served as the guide for writing this book.

Theories of College Student Development

The experiences of college students have been researched for decades. Many scholars have looked at a variety of issues, such as what benefits a college education brings, how and in what ways students develop and mature in college, which kinds of college experiences tend to be positive and which tend to be negative, and what leads to a person dropping out or leaving college, to name a few. Many of the staff and administrators at your campus have gone to graduate school to learn more about these issues. They may have completed a master's or doctoral degree in which they focused on higher education or student development, which is why they hold the positions that they do.

Many theories have emerged over the years that illuminate various aspects of the college experience. Each of them contributes to an overall understanding of a student's experience in college. Three in particular are very useful in exploring the first-year experience: Chickering's Seven Vectors of College Student Development, Perry's Nine Positions of Cognitive Development, and Tinto's Model of Institutional Departure. These three theories, in combination, provide a well-rounded understanding of the general college experience. Below is a brief summary of these theories. A few more theories that focus on particular student populations are introduced in Chapter 7.

Chickering's Seven Vectors of College Student Development

Arthur Chickering researched college students at a variety of schools in the Northeast. On the basis of this research, he proposed a theory that outlines seven different areas, or vectors, in which students develop (Chickering and Reisser, 1993). Although the theory is not linear (i.e., Vector 3 does not necessarily come after Vector 2), Chickering found that students develop simultaneously in the first four vectors and that sufficient development is needed in the fifth vector to be able to develop in the last two.

Vector 1: Developing Competence

This vector focuses on developing skills or competence in three areas. The first is intellectual skills, such as critical thinking and writing and the repertoire of skills found in Bloom's hierarchy, described in Chapter 1. The second is interpersonal skills, which focus on a person's ability to get along with others, and include listening, cooperating, and communicating clearly as well as responding to the needs of others and being able to help a relationship grow. Finally, manual and physical skills are a measure of basic health and fitness and include athletic and artistic achievements as well as self-discipline.

Vector 2: Managing Emotions

Chickering argues that this vector first focuses on a student experiencing and being able to acknowledge his or her feelings. Once this has been accomplished, the student can look for ways to express (not suppress) those feelings in healthy ways. Chickering would argue that a student who is angry should not suppress that emotion but rather should explore what the anger is about and then find healthy and appropriate ways to express it, such as going for a run or talking to friends. This vector also focuses on becoming comfortable with a whole range of emotions, even those that cause some level of discomfort such as boredom or nervousness and that the person needs to be able to manage the impulse of instant gratification. This directly relates to saying "no" to distracting temptations as discussed in Chapter 2 and choices made around alcohol and other drugs in Chapter 5.

Vector 3: Moving Through Autonomy to Interdependence

While students focus a lot on the independence and freedom of college, this vector is really about moving through that to another stage of *inter*dependence, that is, realizing that your words and actions have an impact on those around you just as their words and actions have an impact on you. There are both emotional independence, which is a freedom from the need for continual reassurance or approval, and instrumental independence, or the ability to solve problems in a self-directed way.

Vector 4: Developing Mature Interpersonal Relationships

This is a more advanced level than the interpersonal skills achieved in the first vector. There are two aspects here: the tolerance and appreciation of differences, which become relevant when one interacts with those who are different, and the person's capacity for intimacy in relationships, such as the extent to which the person trusts or opens up to others. Relationships become an interdependence between equals and therefore have more depth than previous relationships.

Note: Chickering argues that one cannot truly succeed at Vector 5 (establishing identity) without significant development in Vectors 1 through 4. He also states that the last two vectors are dependent on success in Vector 5.

Vector 5: Establishing Identity

This vector focuses on the person's self-concept and self-esteem with regard to several aspects of his or her identity. Development here reflects acceptance of and comfort with a variety of issues, including body and appearance; gender and sexual orientation; sense of self in social, historical, and cultural contexts (i.e., understanding the experiences of cultural groups, such as ethnic or religious, to whom you belong); self-concept through roles and life-style; sense of self in light of feedback from valued others; overall self-esteem and ability to accept aspects of one's self; and overall personal stability. All of these require some amount of self-exploration and reflection and depend on the competencies that are developed in the first four vectors.

Vector 6: Developing Purpose

Ironically, this vector actually comes later in a student's development and can be achieved only after the identity has been appropriately established. However, this is often the first priority for most students and their parents: the idea of choosing a major and a future career. Chickering states that developing purpose focuses on three areas: vocational plans (which stem from finding a passion), personal interests, and future commitments for family and other significant relationships. Balancing these three might require compromises.

Vector 7: Developing Integrity

This last vector reflects the person's overall alignment with his or her values and subsequent behaviors. There are three stages, which occur in the following order: (1) humanizing values, or a shift from rigid beliefs to balancing one's own self-interest with the interests of others, (2) personalizing values, or being able to affirm personal values and beliefs while respecting others', and (3) developing congruence, which means that values and behaviors match (i.e., "walking your talk").

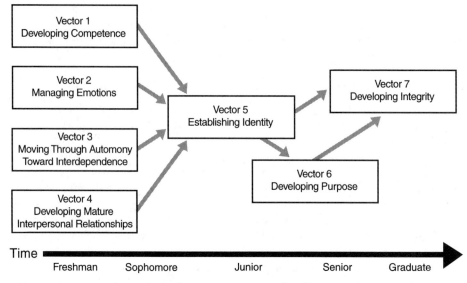

Figure 6.1 Timeline of Chickering's Vectors of College Student Development

It is important to realize that development in these vectors occurs over several years and not only in the first year. Although all students are different, the general time frame shown in Figure 6.1 is applicable to most students.

Freshmen would be working on the first four vectors during their first and second years at a research university; transfer students would most likely be addressing issues of identity during their first year.

What This Means to You

You can be attentive to your own development and actively focus on developing maximally in all areas. Understanding Chickering's model will help you to be more aware of how your college experiences are shaping your development, and you can even guide your own development. Your university will have resources, services, and opportunities aligned with each of the vectors. This will allow you to assess how you are doing in each one and then actively seek out support or assistance to work on the areas that you feel need more development. For example, if you know that you are *not* comfortable with your body image, one of the primary areas of Vector 5, you can focus some time and energy in that area. Campus advisors would be able to point you to the resources and opportunities that might help you, such as personal counselors (to assist you in accepting your body), nutritionists (to help you make good choices amid a plethora of junk food), and activities such as intramural sports or the recreation center (to assist you in exercising and caring for your body in a healthy way). There are even specialists who can assist with eating disorders and other issues that plague both male and female college students.

Might I Suggest...

I recommend that once per year, you read through Chickering's vectors and rate yourself on a scale of 1–10 (1 being "not at all" and 10 being "maximized") for how developed you feel in each of the vectors and subvectors. Don't worry if your numbers are lower in your first year or two—they are supposed to be. After doing the assessment, pick a few vectors to intentionally work on and seek the experiences and services that will help you do so. Each year, reassess, set new goals, and seek out new opportunities. This process will guarantee that you will make the most of your college experience. It will also give you something concrete to use in your graduate school applications and job interviews in terms of reflecting on your college experience.

Perry's Nine Positions of Cognitive Development

William Perry (1970, 1981) explored a completely different side of college students: that of cognitive development. Essentially, Perry researched in detail the intellectual competence development that Chickering identifies in Vector 1. Perry looked at how people learn and make sense out of information that is presented to them. Unlike Chickering's vectors, Perry's nine positions of cognitive development are linear, and you must complete one to move on to the next. Each of Perry's nine positions has unique attributes, but for the purpose of this chapter, it is better to look at them in three clusters. Students start off wanting to believe that information is very concrete and that experts know the "truth." Perry identified how students move from that belief to one that acknowledges multiple perspectives as well as multiple truths. This requires students to shift, both in what is believed to be "truth" and in what experts know and can teach you.

Dualism

This cluster contains the first three positions, which Perry named Duality, Multiplicity Pre-Legitimate, and Multiplicity Subordinate. At the beginning of this cluster, students see the world dualistically, meaning that everything can be sorted into dichotomous categories such as good/bad, right/wrong, and better/worse. Authorities are believed to know the "truth" and are always correct, so learning is about gaining the truth from the experts. A student might start off thinking, "Authorities know the truth, and I can learn the right answers." As students move through the first three positions, they start to realize that the "right" answer is not always easy to determine because all authorities do not always agree with one another. At first, a student might discount an authority figure if she or he does not seem to know the "right" answer. However, as students have more of these experiences, they begin to adjust their perception of what "truth" means and the role of authority figures. Students might complete this cluster thinking, "Experts know the 'truth,' but different experts might have different perspectives. I can learn the right answer for this particular situation."

Relativism Discovered

This cluster contains the next three positions, called Multiplicity Correlate or Relativism Subordinate, Relativism Correlate (Competing or Diffuse), and Commitment Foreseen. In these three stages, a student is making sense out of increased complexity of information and responds by swinging away from dualism to the other extreme of total relativism, that is, thinking that *everything* is relative. Students believe that they might have to choose from several experts' opinions and that there is no one "truth" because there are so many variables. The student is now reluctant to evaluate concepts as right/wrong or correct/incorrect because that does not allow for relativism and are in fact wary of authority figures who do. A student might think, "All knowledge is really contextual, so nobody really knows the 'truth,' and all possibilities are acceptable."

Commitment to Relativism

The final three positions of Perry's model are called Initial Commitment, Orientation in Implications of Commitment, and Developing Commitment(s). These stages see the student moving back from relativism to a middle ground that allows for commitment to certain views or beliefs as correct or true within a certain context. The student sees that people have to make choices based on what they know or find new information that is relevant to the current situation. While the "truth" is essentially impossible to learn, a person can make choices based on what is right for him or her in this context while allowing others the right to have different views. In essence, evaluation of concepts as right/wrong or correct/

What This Means to You

Most K–12 education is aligned with the dualism cluster—students are expected to learn the correct answers from their teachers. At research universities, the focus on the discovery of new knowledge and on thinking critically is more aligned with the last cluster. The college curriculum in general is designed to help students develop along Perry's positions. You will naturally become more relativistic over the course of your four years in college, but it can be a bit challenging at first. Most first-year students experience frustration in their classes because they have been used to thinking and studying in a dualistic way. This has earned them good grades in the past and is the system they know, so it is what many students cling to at the beginning of college. Freshman and sophomore students in particular expect the faculty to know the "right" answers and communicate them clearly so that the students can learn the information for exams. Your adjustment to university-level work will be smoother if you can accept that college will ask you to utilize new and different ways of thinking. If you keep Perry's model in mind, it will help you to shift your thinking and study skills to match those that your faculty expect of you. You will most likely be expected to process material in more relativistic ways than you have in the past.

incorrect becomes appropriate as long as it occurs with a certain context and is not indiscriminately applied as was done in the dichotomous phases. A student might think, "I know what my values are, and I think this is what is right for me. However, it is OK if someone else has different values and makes different choices."

Tinto's Model of Institutional Departure

Many universities are worried about a concept called *retention,* which refers to the number of college students who are retained, that is, who continue their education at the same institution through to graduation. This is also known as *persistence.* Universities want to have high retention or persistence rates because they indicate that the school is doing a good job of meeting its students' needs. In the 1970s, it became clear that large numbers of freshmen did not return for their second year and were leaving the institution or departing from higher education. Some of these students continued their college studies elsewhere, but many were dropping out of college. This became a source of national concern, and many campuses began focusing on ways to improve the freshman year experience. In fact, if you are reading this book in affiliation with some campus course or program for first-year students, it was most likely developed out of this national concern.

In the 1970s, Vincent Tinto began to research this issue and explored the things that affect a student's decision to stay in or leave college (i.e., drop out). His research led to the development of a model that describes the factors that affect and influence a student's ultimate decision to depart. Tinto has revised this model over the years, and his current model (1993) is a longitudinal look at the influences of the student's background characteristics, intentions and commitments, external commitments, the external community, and institutional experiences involving persistence. According to Tinto, students arrive at an institution with a certain set of background characteristics, such as family background, skills and abilities, and previous education, in addition to their individual intentions, goals, and institutional commitments. Through a variety of campus experiences over time, both formal and informal, students can become integrated into the academic and social systems of the college. In addition, the student's external commitments and the external community, namely, family and friends, affect the student.

There are many causes of withdrawal and/or dismissal from the college environment. First are individual characteristics, such as the student's skills and abilities. There are also the student's intentions (or goals) and commitments (or motivation/effort)—the goal of earning a college degree and the commitment to doing the work needed to accomplish this goal. This also relates to the desire the student has to attend and graduate from a particular institution. Second, the model focuses on the experiences a student has at an institution, as Tinto believes that they are the most important in terms of influencing a student's decision to stay or leave.

Tinto claims that there are four main categories of experiences that lead to leaving: adjustment, difficulty, incongruence, and isolation. Adjustment refers to

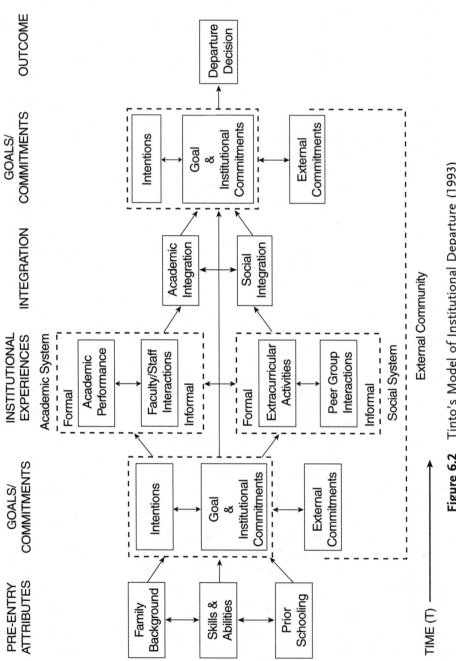

Figure 6.2 Tinto's Model of Institutional Departure (1993)

the time when the student is becoming familiar and comfortable with the new environment. Problems with adjustment usually arise from either the student's inability to separate from his or her previous community or the challenges imposed by the new and often tougher demands of the college environment (both academic and social). Difficulty refers to the academic standards of the institution and the student's ability to meet them. This is where students from poorer schools can find themselves unable to compete with their more privileged peers and unable to perform at satisfactory levels. Incongruence occurs when the student's needs and interests generally do not match those of the campus, because she or he either does not wish to be in college or is at the "wrong" institution for a variety of reasons, such as academic major, location, or other criteria of importance to the student. Finally, isolation refers to the lack of connections and interactions with other members of the campus community. Tinto states that when students are unable to become integrated into both the intellectual and social communities of the college environment, these students leave the institution.

The academic system of the university environment consists of the student's academic performance and his or her interactions with faculty, whereas the social system is formed by cocurricular activities and the student's interactions with his or her peers. Tinto acknowledges that the systems are interconnected and can affect each other: Students might not feel equally comfortable in both systems, and the student's social life can undermine or support his/her academic experience and vice versa. Full integration into both systems is not required for

What This Means to You

Just as with Chickering's vectors, understanding Tinto's model can give you insight into your own experience. This model suggests that your feelings about college will fluctuate many times throughout the year and will depend on the kinds of experiences you are having academically and socially. If those experiences become more negative than positive, you might begin to feel that you don't belong or don't want to stay. Just knowing that there will be good and bad days, days that you love your campus and days that you don't, can help you get through them. It's also important to look at what, specifically, is contributing to the bad days so that you can address those issues and actively seek to improve your own integration and persistence. You might have to actively seek out resources and experiences that will increase your integration. For example, academically, a student could visit office hours to interact with faculty, meet with an academic advisor, and use services that help increase study skills. Socially, a student could attend various campus events, join a campus club, and meet with a counselor. It's important to get help if you are struggling. There are many staff and faculty who are trained in student transition issues and can help you assess what's not working, help you to develop a plan, and support you in achieving it. These folks are paid to help you, so take advantage of their assistance.

persistence, but students usually need to meet minimum academic criteria to stay enrolled, such as a minimum GPA or number of credits completed.

The model includes elements of external forces and communities. Forces outside of the campus, including family, home community, state and national organizations, natural disasters, and work commitments, play a role in the decisions of students who depart from college. When the demands from these external sources are greater than those of the academic and social systems, the student can be pulled away from college attendance.

Most important, Tinto's model focuses on the importance of the student's perception of his or her own integration. Tinto emphasizes that it is the level of academic and social integration that students *perceive themselves* to have achieved through their experiences that largely affects their decision to continue or leave. Any campus counselor can share accounts about students who appear to be

Might I Suggest...

I recommend assessing yourself in each of the areas of Tinto's model so that you know which areas might need your attention. Take some time to answer the following questions.

- Do you feel that your prior schooling prepared you well for success at the campus you are attending?
- Do you have strong commitments to earning a college degree and to your current university in particular?
- What kinds of experiences are you having (formal and informal) in the academic system and social system? How are these going?
- Do you feel that you belong academically? Socially?
- Do your family and home community support your attendance at this campus?
- Are there commitments that draw you away from focusing on your academic and social experiences?

When you identify an area that could be improved, actively work on it. You can contribute to your own success by working to increase your own integration. Your campus will have many advisors and services available to help you do so—use them! Seek out any and all opportunities that will improve your integration.

I have used Tinto's model in my own research on college students. One thing that my data suggest is that the social integration is *more* important to students than their academic integration is (as long as they are able to stay enrolled) in their overall feelings of wanting to stay at a particular campus. Therefore, I recommend making sure that you spend some time and energy getting connected to several social networks at your campus. Living environments are good places to start, but you will also want to join at least one club and form study groups with fellow classmates. If you are having a hard time finding students with whom you connect, meet with an advisor or counselor as soon as you can. This person should be able to help you identify some potential student communities and opportunities for you to explore.

popular yet feel isolated and alone and therefore are prime candidates for withdrawal. It is clear that it is *only* the students' perception that matters in the ultimate evaluation of his or her integration.

As a result, Tinto states that programs and experiences that increase students' perceptions of both academic and social integration are likely to increase student retention as well. Tinto's model has had a large impact on college campuses around North America. Many have taken his model to heart and intentionally attempt to affect a student's integration process by providing programs, courses, counseling, and support so that students feel more integrated, both academically and socially.

Overview of Common Themes in the First-Year Student Experience

The U.S. Department of Education oversees many aspects of education in this country. This department's National Center for Education Statistics (NCES) houses a plethora of useful reports and current statistics, which can be accessed at http://nces.ed.gov. According to the NCES, approximately 13.5 million students are enrolled in degree-granting undergraduate institutions, 7.5 million of them attending a four-year institution and the remaining 6 million attending a two-year institution in 2003. Each year, approximately 1.5 million people enter higher education as first-time, full-time students—the "freshman" student. The NCES did a study over six years (1995–2001) tracking students' college attendance. One third of the students had transferred at some point in their college career; 42% of students at two-year colleges had transferred compared to 23% of students at four-year colleges. Interestingly, by the late 1990s, only 28% of adults in the United States had completed four years of college. Many students who begin college do not finish, and many more high school graduates do not attend college at all.

There are two primary sets of data that will be used in this section to highlight common themes in the first year. One is from another survey conducted by the Higher Education Research Institute. In 2002, the institute conducted a national study of college freshmen asking them about their experiences during their first year of college. Called Your First College Year (YFCY), the survey sampled 24,824 first-time, full-time students at 105 four-year institutions in the United States. For example, results of this study indicate that 80.4% of students were satisfied or very satisfied with their overall college experience.

A second source of data is my doctoral study done on the academic and social integration of freshman students. This study utilized both surveys and in-depth interviews, and all quotes in the following section are from real students who spoke in depth about their experiences. The following lists of issues represent a compilation of both of these studies as well as general trends noticed in recent research and common themes discussed at national conferences and on higher education online discussion groups.

Some of these issues affect both freshmen and transfer students; while others are more likely to be associated with only freshmen. There is an additional set of issues that are unique to the transfer population. Table 6.1 provides an

Table 6.1   Overview of First-Year Experiences Correlated by Student Development Theory

(Theories are indicated with a C for Chickering, P for Perry, and T for Tinto.)

Rate yourself on a scale of 1 (not affecting me at all) to 5 (seriously affecting my success).

Specific Issues	Relevant Theories	Rating 1-5
Academic Issues		
Reputation of campus	T	
Previous preparation	C, P, T	
Pace of the academic term	T	
Academic success skills	C, P, T	
Academic performance	C, P, T	
Intellectual self-confidence	C, T	
Academic dishonesty	C, T	
Contact with faculty	C, T	
Approachability of faculty	C, T	
Use of office hours	T	
Experiences with specific departments	P, T	
Use of academic services	T	
Majors and programs offered	T	
Level of students	T	
Level of competitiveness	C, T	

Social Issues	
Living situation	C, T
Social/friend networks	C, T
Activities offered	C, T
Impact of working and other commitments	C, T
Party/social scene	C, T
Impact of athletic involvement	C, T
Being in the minority	C, T
General Campus Environment	
Physical environment	T
Emotional environment	T
Distance from home	C, T
Personal Issues	
Family separation process	C, T
First-generation status	C, P, T
Personal crises	C, T
Mental health	C, T
Money and credit management	C, T
Burnout	C, T
Issues Unique to Transfer Students	
Academic differences between institutions	P, T
Transferability of previous work	T
Transferability of GPA	T
Progress in major	T
Nontraditional/reentry students	C, T
Social networks	C, T

overall summary of the general categories (academic, social, general campus environment, and personal) and the specific issues listed within each. In addition, there is an indication of which student development theory is relevant, and there is a place for you to rate how much that issue is affecting you.

Academic Issues

Within the academic experience, there are several factors that can affect the overall nature of a student's experience. Depending on the university and the student, each of these factors can contribute to either a positive or a negative experience. Following is a brief summary of some of the most commonly mentioned issues and the things that contributed to, or detracted from, students' academic and social integration.

Reputation of Campus

Students refer most often to either the academic reputation of the school or the social or "party" reputation. Whether this affects a student positively or negatively has to do with how well the student feels matched to the reputation. For example, a student who is not into partying will tend to feel out of place at a campus with a big party reputation, but another student might feel perfectly happy.

"I want to be a part of a program that is a more prestigious school in both academics and sports. I don't want to go to a school that when I tell someone where I go, they refer to it as a 'party school.'"

Previous Preparation

Many students enter college and find themselves well prepared by their previous educators. They can jump right in and are able to understand the material in most of their courses and perform at a satisfactory level. Other students find that their preparation is sorely lacking—they are missing important content or skills that their fellow classmates possess and often feel "behind" and have to work harder to perform well. According to the Your First College Year (YFCY) study, 26.6% of students said that they were "completely successful" at adjusting to the academic demands of college. However, 19% felt only "somewhat successful," and 3% felt "unsuccessful." The quality of a student's previous academic preparation can create a positive or negative transition to the university's academic environment.

"I felt my grades were adequate and I am up to the level of education needed to participate in the university setting."

"I was completely unprepared. It seemed like most of the students knew what the professor was talking about and I was totally lost. I didn't pass that class."

Pace of the Academic Term

This refers to the overall quantity and quality of work that are expected in the amount of time allowed. Most university students find that they often cover in one term what took a year to cover in their previous school. The pace of the student's workload is faster and more intense than they previously experienced, especially if the campus is on the quarter system. First-year students struggle the most with this as they are adjusting, but it eventually gets easier and more comfortable.

Academic Success Skills

As is mentioned in Chapter 2, there are several skills that students need to master to succeed at a research university. For example, critical thinking is a cornerstone of the research university. Some first-year students find that they do not have well-developed critical thinking skills and may struggle a bit in their classes while they are developing and honing them. This is especially challenging for freshmen who come from high schools where academic work was conducted in the lower levels of Bloom's hierarchy. In addition, time management, writing, and other important skills might also need developing.

Academic Performance

Many first-year students experience a drop in their GPA as compared to their previous school. It is quite common for freshmen to experience a 1.0 drop in their GPA from their high school GPA. This is obviously due to the transition to a more challenging academic environment and the lack of the success skills mentioned in Chapter 2. Most students learn from these experiences and are able to improve their skills and performance during the latter part of the first year and on through graduation. Transfer students can also experience a decline in their GPA if they do not adequately adjust to the new pace and performance standards of a research university.

Intellectual Self-Confidence

One negative consequence of the above-mentioned academic issues is that they often have the combined effect of undermining a student's academic self-esteem. Most university students come from schools where they were among the strongest students, and many take these initial challenges as an indication that they are not "university material." Students can doubt their abilities and often perceive themselves to be the only one struggling. According to the YFCY study, 72.5% of the students rated their academic ability as "above average" or in the "highest 10 percent" at the beginning of college, but this dropped to 65.6% at the end of the first year. Mathematic ability also showed a decline from 48.1% to 44.5%, while intellectual self-confidence rose slightly (1% gain).

> "I learned that I might not necessarily be a top student and that I have to accept that. I took an Anthropology class and was in the honors section. I really loved the class—it was great, and we had a terrific section. I had full understanding of the material, the book, etc., but for some reason, everyone who was in my study group for that class got A's on the paper and I got a D-minus. I talked to the professor but I didn't get any specifics on what I needed to change. He let me rewrite it, which I did, and then I got a C+. The experience really affected my perception. It gave me a more negative perception of my abilities but I guess it made me more realistic about myself."

It is important to note that a serious decline in a student's self-confidence can lead to the onset of depression. Symptoms of depression are quite common among college students and can be alleviated through assistance from campus student health or counseling professionals.

Academic Dishonesty

As a result of some of the issues discussed above, some students turn to cheating as a way to improve their performance or at least to keep from failing. As was mentioned in Chapter 1, research universities take academic integrity very seriously, so students might find themselves facing suspension or expulsion for cheating, even for a first-time offense. Even if the student is successful in cheating, she or he has shortchanged himself or herself in terms of the preparation that particular assignment or course provided for their future academic performance.

Contact with Faculty

This is often an area of complaint for students at larger universities, where classes may include several hundred students, compared to both high school and community college environments, where classes were smaller. Some courses might not even be taught by professors but rather by graduate students, and faculty often do not often hang around after class but head back to their research projects. While the YFCY study indicated that 50.5% of students were satisfied and 18.1% were very satisfied with their contact with faculty, some students find their interactions with faculty to be unsatisfactory.

"The classes are too big, and there is minimal communication between professors and students."

Approachability of Faculty

Many first-year students find that the approachability of their faculty is a very important factor in determining whether or not they seek help. Students comment on watching how an instructor treats other students in the classroom, and this becomes a primary basis for whether or not they would choose to seek help from that instructor. Faculty who seem distant or even mean to students are avoided, while faculty who are perceived to be caring and approachable are thought of highly. Sadly, many students will not seek help from faculty who seem unapproachable even if they are struggling in a class. According to the YFCY study, 31% of students frequently or occasionally felt intimidated by their professors. However, 48% felt they had been fairly or completely successful in getting to know faculty.

"I feel very welcomed and comfortable here. The professors and tutors have been very helpful."

"I tend to like TAs and professors who are more friendly because they don't seem like they are on a 'power trip' and then are more likely to explain things better. For example, my math professor treated everyone like a number and seemed to like to intimidate the students. I think most professors are not kind to students."

Use of Office Hours

Not surprisingly, students' use of office hours is often directly connected to how they perceive their instructor in terms of approachability and helpfulness. Many students who go to office hours find it extremely helpful and are able to improve their performance through seeking this additional support. The YFCY data indicate that while 41.4% of students attend faculty office hours one to two times per term and another 26.8% attend one to two times per month, 9.1% never attend faculty office hours, and 57.9% never attend their teaching assistants' office hours. Nearly one third of students (27.1%) never interact with faculty outside of class or office hours.

"I didn't interact with my faculty because I felt intimidated. I thought they would think I was asking stupid questions."

"Going to office hours was the best thing I did. My professor looked over the draft of my paper and I was able to use her comments to rework it and get an A."

Experiences with Specific Departments

Many students comment on experiences with certain departments, especially as first-year students are often required to take a number of courses from certain key departments such as math, chemistry, writing/English, and foreign language. On any particular campus, students can tell you whether those departments are "student friendly" or not, which often translates into how approachable the faculty are and whether or not students feel supported. This can be especially noted in the case of departments that offer required classes that are designed to weed out students. For example, if the campus cannot accommodate all those who wish to pursue biology or pre-med majors, the math and chemistry classes might be set at a difficult level to weed out many of those students. In these classes, students often do not feel that they were supported to do their best, which can be both discouraging and frustrating.

"In my calculus class, 75% of the students got less than a C on the midterm. I'm sorry, but that seems really unfair."

"My writing teacher was awesome. He spent a ton of time helping us work on our writing. He even let me change the assigned paper topic to another one that really interested me."

Use of Academic Services

Using academic services is often necessary for first-year students to achieve academic success. Many students find that utilizing the academic skills and tutoring services as well as assistance from instructors is what helps them to succeed, or at least not fail. Many students credit these experiences as crucial to their academic survival the first year, and it is clear that the most successful students actively chose to use them.

"I really liked my chemistry tutor at the Skills Center. I couldn't have survived Chem 1 without her. She really helped me improve my performance, which increased my confidence. I also used the writing lab and it was really great."

Majors and Programs Offered

This issue is directly related to whether or not a student thoroughly understood the nature of a research university before applying or accepting admission. Many students assume that all universities offer the same majors and may not explore if what they are looking for is offered at their particular institution. In addition, universities offer a range of academic programs that can enhance the intellectual engagement of its students.

"I would like to change my major to animal science but this campus does not have that major."

"The honors program catered to my academic needs and helped stimulate my intellectual growth, which I would not have gained otherwise."

Level of Students

Students attend a university amid thousands of their peers. Some find that they are in synch with those around them in terms of academic focus and abilities and some do not.

"I feel that I belong here because I'm surrounded by individuals who are hard working, intelligent, and motivated like me."

"I have been in several situations in which I take school/studying more seriously than the other students here seem to."

Level of Competitiveness

Every campus harbors a different atmosphere in terms of the competitiveness amongst its students. For some, a competitive environment is motivating and an indicator of intellectual stimulation whiles others find a less competitive environment to be more supportive of their college experience.

"Everyone here does not revolve their life around grades, which is something that fits me well. I cannot just be a student. I need other activities to have my mind be at peace and this campus offers those to me."

Social Issues

Within the social experience of college, there are several factors that can affect the overall nature of a student's experience. While these are not so often controlled or provided by the university specifically, they still have a very powerful effect on the overall quality of a student's experience.

Living Situation

Students' living situations have a strong impact on their university success because these situations affect the student every single day. If they live with others with whom they get along, and the overall living environment is conducive to their academic and personal goals, then students tend to have a positive experience. However, roommate conflicts or environments that are too noisy or too crowded can create a negative experience. Even in the best of circumstances, most college living situations require students to share small spaces with other people, which can be quite unnerving, especially since most students need some private and/or quiet time. The YFCY study indicates that 29.5% of students had difficulty getting along with roommates or housemates.

> "My roommate and I get along great. We talk about everything and do stuff together all the time."

> "My roommate was a challenging experience because he was not talkative and we had minimal communication. We didn't fight or anything and we worked out a 'live and let live' philosophy. It was basically a neutral situation but I'd hoped for a more positive experience. I ended up hanging out a lot in the hall since it was uncomfortable in our room."

> "I hated my residence hall. My roommate was Japanese and the two of us and our suitemates were really close because we were the only minorities in the whole building. Everyone on our floor was only into partying. We were close to each other but felt separated from the whole hall so we stuck to ourselves."

Social/Friend Networks

The quantity and quality of a student's friendships can greatly affect the overall social experience. The ability to create a satisfying network of friends often takes time and depends on the student being outgoing enough to seek out venues where she or he could meet others and being able to find others who share common goals, values, and experiences. Once friendships begin to form, time provides the truest test as people weather the ups and downs of the academic year together. Most friendship networks that are formed in the fall are rarely still intact by June because some kind of "drama" occurs that causes tension and distance among the group. For the student who had invested all of his or her energy into one network, this dissolution can be very stressful because he or she might now need to find new connections in the middle of the year. Students who have more than one network tend to fare the best. More than one third (37.3%) of the freshmen in the YFCY survey state that they worried about meeting new people, but 79.3% said that they interacted daily with close friends at their campus. Fifty-three percent felt "completely successful" developing close friendships with other students. Over time, students experienced an increase in their social self-confidence, with 46% rating themselves as "above average" or in the "highest 10 percent" at the beginning of college and rising to 52.7% at the end of the first year.

> "I started working at the campus radio station where I met a lot of people. I developed 8 to 10 solid friends from the station and that's mainly who I hung out with."

> "I am having trouble adjusting. I haven't made any good friends yet and my roommate situation is not a good one but I will stick it out through the year."

Activities Offered

This refers to the amount and type of cocurricular activities that are offered at the campus. Some students find that there is a good match between their interests and the school's offerings; other students experience a lack of options that meet their needs. This can affect a student's overall sense of social connection to the campus. Generally, students eventually find things they enjoy because universities tend to offer such a wide range of options. Over half (59.7%) of students in the YFCY study said that they participated in student clubs or groups, and 76.1% said that they were satisfied or very satisfied with the campus's recreational facilities.

Impact of Working and Other Commitments

Most students will work at some time during their undergraduate experience, whether it is a casual part-time job to earn some extra spending money, a pre-professional internship to prepare for a future career, or even near full-time hours to put themselves through school. Working, or any kind of involvement, up to twenty hours per week has been shown to have a positive impact on students because it improves their time management skills and provides another avenue for social connections. However, full-time students who have to work more than twenty hours per week usually find that this has a negative impact on both their academic performance and their social connections because they just do not have the time for studying or casual social interactions. This is also true for any nonacademic commitment, including clubs such as Greek organizations, athletic teams, and hobbies. The YFCY data show that 27.8% of students had a paying job on campus and 24.3% had an off-campus job. Twenty-two percent of students indicated that their job frequently or occasionally interfered with their coursework. This is discussed more in Chapter 7 because it tends to affect lower-income students the most.

> "The money strain is really putting the burden on my family and my school work is hard to juggle with my job where I work 35 hours a week."

Party/Social Scene

Socializing and partying are obviously a cornerstone of the college experience and a main component of the overall social experiences a student has at his or her university. Ideally, there is a match between the types of social events and parties offered and the student's personal interests. As was mentioned earlier, if the school has a reputation as a party school, the students who enjoy drinking and partying will probably feel comfortable with the focus on alcohol, but this can be quite a negative experience for students who are not interested in those activities. Students who feel a strong disconnection with the overall social atmosphere might choose to transfer to a different type of school. The YFCY study indicated that 27.5% of students partied six or more hours per week, and statistics indicate that this is a 5% increase over the partying the same students did in high school. The party scene is discussed in more depth in Chapter 5. Half of the students (49.2%) said that their social life frequently or occasionally interfered with their schoolwork.

"The atmosphere around here is boring, and there are no alternatives for people who don't like to get drunk."

Impact of Athletic Involvement

Student athletes often have extraordinary responsibilities and pressures compared to nonathletes at the same campus. Athletes have lengthy daily trainings that are rigorous and mandatory. The scheduling of these training sessions often prevents athletes from taking certain classes, which can even eliminate the possibilities of entire majors. In addition, athletes in their competitive season have to travel frequently, missing classes and exams while still needing to perform academically at a successful level. This can be quite stressful, and many first-year athletes are not able to maintain their grades and their athletic performance. As a result, some first-year athletes leave their team, and this creates additional negative experiences, as the team is most likely their primary social network. Furthermore, many student athletes have been doing their sport their whole lives, so they often experience an identity crisis of sorts as they lose one of their primary senses of self. The YFCY data indicate that 18.5% participated in intercollegiate athletics.

Being in the Minority

The term *minority* here does not necessarily refer to ethnicity, although that is certainly true on many campuses. It refers to any student who feels that she or he is in the minority compared to the overall student body. While this can be true for a whole host of issues, it is most prevalent for students who are in the minority in terms of a primary component of their identity such as race, economic class, political affiliation, sexual orientation, religion, and age. These students often face daily challenges in a place where they may not feel comfortable or even safe, and they certainly feel conspicuous and conscious of their identity because of being "the only one" in a classroom or a residence hall. Needless to say, this can have a negative impact on a student's social experience and create challenges that are not experienced by the students in the majority. We discuss this in much more detail in Chapter 7.

"This campus is not diverse—it's predominately White or upper class and I can't relate to the people here. Those who do not fall into these categories have to build their own cliques."

"I feel very comfortable here—I love the diversity of the campus—everyone fits in."

"My roommate and I were the only African Americans on our hall. It seemed like whenever we would come around, the only topics the White students would bring up would be about rap music, basketball, and women. There was never anything else. At first, I didn't see it at all but after a while it started to get repetitive. Sometimes, you know, I wanted to talk about how to do better on my chemistry test, and it would be turned back around to my music or whatever. Maybe they really did like rap music and basketball but it was the only conversations we had with them."

General Campus Environment

When a student goes to college, she or he spends a significant amount of time on the physical campus. This can also be a source of experiences that either positively or negatively affect a student's overall college experience.

Physical Environment

This refers to the actual physical environment of the campus and the surrounding community. If the environment is similar to the student's home community, then the student will often feel a sense of overall comfort in the environment. However, students who come from a different environment might feel overwhelmed and uncomfortable, maybe even unsafe, on their college campus. Some specific examples include students from a busy urban/city environment feeling uncomfortable on a quiet, rural campus and vice versa. Students usually adjust to this over time, but if the experience represents frequent challenges to the student in terms of overall comfort, as well as the availability of certain services and experiences, she or he might choose to transfer.

"I love being near the mountains, and surrounded by kids my own age. It's fun, but most of all I love the really beautiful atmosphere."

"I missed home and the big city. Being on campus all the time is very confining and I missed living in a huge city and community."

Emotional Environment

Most campuses have a certain kind of feel or "vibe" to them that is conveyed in the actions, words, and nonverbal communication of its students. Some campuses feel very competitive, while others are laid-back. Some campuses feel very progressively focused, and others are more conservative. It goes without saying that a good match between the student and the student body will lead to positive experiences, while a poor match will cause some level of disconnection and even tension. Seventy percent of the students in the YFCY study were satisfied or very satisfied with the overall sense of community among students at their campus.

Distance from Home

This refers to the physical distance the student's campus is from his or her community. Although this can certainly be measured in miles, most students refer to a more emotional factor of whether it is the "right amount" of distance from home. Students who are close to their families often want to visit home frequently, so the "right amount" of distance will be that which is convenient in terms of both time and modes of transportation. For students who seek more independence from their family or who do not wish to be surprised by unannounced visits, the "right amount" will tend to be farther—still close enough to visit a couple of times per term but not much more than that. Some students consider this distance factor when selecting their university; others discover its relevance after the term has begun. The students who have a match between their needs and the actual distance rate this as a positive factor; students who are either too close or too far for their tastes are sometimes frustrated. This is especially true for the students who find that they are too far from home; extreme homesickness can contribute to a choice to transfer to another college closer to home.

"I'm getting a good education. I got a car so that eliminated my problem of being too far away from home."

"I am from out of state and everyone I know, including all of my friends, family, and boyfriend, are there so I wanted to go home. I'll be transferring back at the end of the year."

Personal Issues

Students are more than young adults enrolled at a research university—they are people with personal lives and experiences that can contribute to, or detract from, their college experience. Personal issues, especially problems, often impede a student's academic success and sometimes social success as well. While there are many campus services and counselors available to help students address personal issues, students need to let people know they are struggling and seek out support. Some of the common personal issues that affect college students include the following:

Family Separation Process

The details of this complex process are discussed in Chapter 4. Needless to say, students who have a lot of frustrating experiences with family members who are not willing to either let go or support their choices report negative feelings and increased distance from their family. Students who are given appropriate levels of distance and support from their families report increasingly positive interactions and relationships with family members. These students often get closer to, and have better relationships with, family members than ever before.

"Before I left for college, it seemed like I was fighting with my folks all the time. But now we are closer than ever before. I think I needed to get away before I could really appreciate them and they could see me as more of an adult."

"When I came out to my parents, they freaked out and cut off all contact with me. I'm now putting myself through college and I'm pretty stressed out most of the time."

First-Generation Status

College students are considered "first generation" if they are the first in their family to either attend or complete college. First-generation students have family members who do not necessarily understand the college experience and therefore might not be able to provide the same kinds of suggestions or support that other students experience. In addition, first-generation students' families are often immigrants, so the family might not speak the language in which the university conducts its official business via orientation, forms, parent newsletters, and the like. The English-speaking students often find themselves not only taking care of all of their university business by themselves, but also having many responsibilities serving as the family's interpreter. Many students in this situation travel home frequently to carry out this role, and this can detract from their academic and social success.

Personal Crises

Many students experience personal crises throughout the year, which can seriously impede their success if they are not able to seek or secure the appropriate support. Some examples include a parent battling a serious illness or dying; a parent losing a job; the family's home or business being damaged in a fire; the student developing a serious illness such as cancer, depression, or an eating disorder; the student experiencing a physical debilitation such as a broken back and being unable to attend classes; and the student being the victim of crime such as sexual assault. Here are some examples of crises that students faced during their first year at college.

> One male student confided that his father had died two weeks prior to school beginning. He was completely overwhelmed and unable to study or focus but could not go home because his father told him to "stay in school" just prior to his death. However, this student did not inform anyone of his situation because he did not want to receive any "special treatment."

> A male student was a member of a gang and tried to maintain his membership throughout fall quarter. Midway through the fall, his cousin, who was 16 years old, was shot twelve times and killed in a gang shooting. Over winter break, the student negotiated with his gang and received "permission" to leave, but he found that home was not the same after that.

> One female student developed a severe eating disorder during fall quarter because of the pressure she felt on the campus to be attractive and thin (she had no prior history of eating disorders). This caused major difficulties with her roommate and her friends who tried to help her. Finally, she sought counseling (through student health) in the middle of winter quarter, which she found very helpful.

> A male student was incredibly shy and introverted. This caused problems with his roommate and others, so he felt more and more socially isolated. He had a series of very negative academic experiences, including winter quarter, when he registered for an upper-division biology class. He asked the professor whether he should leave, but the professor told him that he would be fine as long as he had taken chemistry in high school. The student proceeded to spend an inordinate amount of time on the course, to the detriment of all his other classes, and he ended up on academic probation. However, he could not tell

his parents because of the pressure from his father to follow in his footsteps as an engineer. These and some other negative experiences at college led him to feel suicidal.

Mental Health

Quite a few first-year students have been previously diagnosed with a mental illness that requires medication and the supervision of health care professionals. In addition, many students develop depression for the first time in college. The stresses of college life, such as erratic sleeping and eating patterns, and possible increased consumption of alcohol and other drugs can exacerbate a mental health illness beyond the effectiveness of the medication. Since most university students move away from home, they are no longer being regularly monitored by their parents, who know them well and can get them to their doctor when needed. Some students even stop taking their medications because they want to "be like the other students." Colleges across the country are dealing with drastic increases in students who exhibit behaviors such as self-mutilation (e.g., cutting), suicidal thoughts and/or behaviors, depression, anxiety/panic attacks, and even aggressive and violent actions toward others. A study at Kansas State University found that the number of depressed students had doubled over the past ten years and the number of students who had thought about suicide had tripled. In addition, students without mental health issues can be significantly affected by the mental health issues of their family and friends.

"During Fall, my younger brother developed schizophrenia. He was always running away from home so I went home every weekend to help out my parents. He was eventually put into a home for troubled teens. This has been really hard on me because I'm very close with my brother."

"I found my roommate cutting herself in the bathroom. It really scared me because she's always talking about how depressed she is. I know she's working with a therapist but it's really stressful living with her. I wish I could move to another apartment."

Money and Credit Management

Many students do not have well-developed money management skills when they move away from home. They might not know how to establish a reasonable monthly budget and then live within it. In addition, they might not be skilled at balancing their checking account or keeping track of bills and late fees. Needless to say, students can get in trouble financially if they have not learned these skills before college begins. Furthermore, a growing trend on college campuses across North America is for students to accrue unacceptable amounts of both loan and credit card debt. Nationally, 10–20% of college students have unacceptably high levels of credit card debt, some charging $10,000 or more. Students with debt of $3000–7000 rose 61% in 2001. Students who receive financial aid are especially susceptible if their aid amount does not cover their annual expenses. However, even financially secure students are in danger because of the ease with which they can qualify for credit cards. Students are turning to credit cards as a way to "solve" their money management problems instead of learning to create a budget and live within their means. Many students are unaware of how interest rates work and are lured by the temptation to "charge" their way out of a jam. In 2001, the Federal Educational Loan Program determined that 83% of undergraduate students had on average 4.25 credit cards with an average balance of $2,327. If a student with this balance stopped using the card and then paid the minimum monthly payment (at an APR of 18%), it would take more than 33 years to pay off the debt. In addition, the student would pay $5,912 in interest—that's more than twice the actual amount charged.

"I got hooked on internet gambling and just couldn't stop. They take credit cards and now my debt is so high that I can't tell my folks. I'm really in trouble and have no clue how I am going to get out of it."

Burnout

This seems to haunt first-year students and to diminish with each subsequent year. It refers to the student's ability to withstand the academic and social experiences for the length of the entire academic year. The increased pace and demand in the academic sphere paired with interactions with hundreds, if not thousands, of peers can be tiring, and students often report feeling "burned out" by spring. This burnout can often cause students to lose focus academically before they complete their courses. In addition, students often say that they are tired of the social scene on their campus and/or in their living environment and look forward to the summer break.

"I was looking forward to going home because I was tired of school, tired of partying, and tired of people always interrupting me and dragging me out to do something."

"Spring finals are the worst! I have a really hard time getting psyched, again, for that last batch of exams and papers. And with the great weather, well, just forget it."

What This Means to You

Ideally, after reading about the typical experiences that first-year students have, you realize two things. One, you are normal! There are lots of other students who are struggling with the same issues you are, and all of you can still be very successful in the university environment even if you are facing some big challenges. Two, the students around you might be having a really different experience from the one you are having. Many of the issues listed in this chapter might be affecting someone you know, and you might not know it unless they choose to tell you or you choose to ask. Not everyone will read this book, so you could prove to be invaluable to someone else's success by checking in with them and encouraging them to seek support.

> ## Might I Suggest...
>
> Go back to Table 6.1 and mark next to the list of various issues the ones that are currently affecting you and the ones that you suspect might affect you in the future. Rate each one on a scale of 1–5, with 1 being "not affecting me at all" and 5 being "seriously affecting my success" in college. Focus on the higher numbers first and seek out some assistance in addressing those issues. A general campus advisor or someone in the office of the Dean of Students can probably point you in the right direction. It's important to address any issues that are negatively affecting your experience early on so that you can have a good first year, both academically and socially.

Issues Unique to Transfer Students

Transfer students can and do experience many of the issues previously listed, especially if they were living at home and have now moved away to attend the new institution. In addition, there are some issues that are unique to transfer students. These days, there are many types of transfer students: the traditional transfer, who starts at a two-year school and transfers to a four-year institution; the reverse transfer, who starts at a four-year institution and transfers to a two-year one; the lateral transfer, who transfers from one institution to another of the same type; and even the "swirling" transfer, who is enrolled in more than one institution simultaneously. For the purposes of this book, we will focus on the traditional transfer student, since that is the most common type of transfer student found at research universities.

According to the American Association of Collegiate Registrars and Admissions Officers, there are over 1,200 two-year community colleges in the United States, and together, they enroll approximately 10 million students each year (although not all of these students are working toward a degree). Almost half (46%) of first-time college students begin at a two-year college, compared to 26% at four-year institutions. Community colleges are typically more diverse, with students of color making up 48% of their student population. Community college students are typically older as well: 30% are between the ages of 22 and 29, and 27% are over 30; many of these older students attend part-time while also working and having families.

Many students attend community colleges because these schools are much more affordable than universities. Tuition is approximately half that of four-year schools, and students can complete many of their requirements while keeping costs down. In addition, many students find that community colleges can be a gateway to a prestigious school to which they might not have been admitted after high school graduation. Students get a "second chance" and are often able to earn their bachelor's degree from a school for which they did not qualify earlier.

Following is a summary of issues that first-year transfer students often face, especially moving from a community college to a research university.

Academic Differences Between Institutions

Transfer students have already proven themselves to be quite successful in the college environment; otherwise, their GPA would not be sufficient to support their admission to a research university. This often leads transfer students to feel overconfident in their abilities and, as a result, not to take advantage of the services provided to assist their transition, such as orientation or academic advising. The truth is that transfer students often struggle during their first term or two until they become accustomed to the new pace (especially if are moving from the semester to the quarter system) and level of performance expected by the faculty. Even simple things such as where offices are located or procedures for filing forms can be new and confusing to the transfer student. This can cause a first-term transfer student not to perform as well as she or he hopes. A poor performance in the first term can be quite disheartening to transfer students and might lead them to doubt either their abilities or their choice of university.

Transferability of Previous Work

Unless a student transferred within campuses of the same university system, his or her previous work will need to be evaluated and deemed transferable by the new institution. Some transfer students receive excellent academic advising, and all courses transfer as they expected. However, every year, thousands of college transfers are surprised to learn that certain courses did not transfer as expected. This can be quite frustrating and might hurt the student's ability to complete his or her degree in two years. Students may have to utilize an appeal process to correct the situation. Usually, courses are only transferable if the current university the student is attending has a course that is nearly identical to the one from the previous institution. Vocational-prep courses that are commonly found at community colleges are rarely offered at research universities so transferability of these courses is very limited.

Transferability of GPA

Again, if the student is not transferring within the same system, it is possible that the previous GPA will not transfer to the new campus. While it will always be part of a student's overall academic record, the student might find that he or she is starting the first term with a 0.0 GPA. This puts pressure on a transfer student to do well the first term because an average to poor GPA can be difficult to raise in only two years.

Progress in Major

Depending on the situation, some students will find that they are on track for their major and can jump right into appropriate classes at the university and expect to complete the degree in two years. However, some universities admit transfer students on the basis of their academic performance and not necessarily their major. Every fall, many transfer students arrive at their new campus erroneously believing that all their previous work was approved by their new major department when that is not actually the case. Needless to say, this can create problems if the student has to make up certain courses, and this can affect the ability to graduate in two years. Even if everything transfers smoothly, the student might still need to adjust to the new course content and different new ways of teaching that are unique to every department on campuses across the country.

Nontraditional/Reentry Students

Nationally, the age of the average college student is 26, but many students are older and have professional jobs as well as families. This reflects a large population of older students who are earning their degree or returning to complete a

Might I Suggest...

The most important thing a transfer student can do is to take advantage of the services that are provided. Most transfer students could avoid problems by treating their new campus as a brand-new experience instead of approaching it with an attitude of "been there, done that." It is definitely worth your time to attend orientation, meet with advisors, and become quickly acclimated to your new university. Sure, some of it will be somewhat repetitive, but that is a small price to pay to ensure that you don't miss out on some crucial information.

If you find that your work did not transfer as you had planned, don't give up. Many institutions are not able to fully evaluate all the courses you took simply by looking at the course name and number on your transcript. If there is any doubt, the evaluator tends to deny credit first and leave it up to students to appeal. There are advisors who specialize in transfer issues, and they can help you sort things out. They can also help you with the appeal process if you feel that your previous work has not been adequately evaluated. Typically, the appeal process goes more smoothly when you can provide more detailed information, such as catalog descriptions, the actual syllabus from the course you took, and even the papers you wrote. You will want to provide as much information as you can to help the evaluators correctly assess your work.

Also, I strongly recommend that you get involved. It will be important for you to find a few social networks to join, though it might take a little effort to find ones that you connect with. Most universities have clubs and organizations that are affiliated with certain majors and careers, and there might even be a transfer student club. Join those right away. Also look for a way to meet students who share similar hobbies and interests because you won't want all of your social connections to be academically based. Take a swing dancing class, go on organized hikes or bike rides, attend film festivals—whatever it is that suits your interests.

Finally, if you are finding the transition particularly challenging, don't get discouraged. Even if you are experiencing the kind of problems that will delay graduation, remember that you will still be getting your degree from a research university, the most prestigious type of institution of higher learning in the country. But in the meantime, be sure to get support. The advisors who specialize in transfer students are aware of and sensitive to your experiences. You are paying for their services, so be sure to utilize them.

degree that was begun years ago. Although every research university has nontra-ditional/reentry students in its freshman population, they are much more commonly transfer students. This group of students is usually older than the typical college student for that campus and might even be older than many of their instructors. In addition, they often continue to hold jobs and might have a spouse or partner to support and/or children to care for. These students have extraordinary responsibilities that they must manage while also competing with the traditional student population in their courses.

Social Networks

Transfer students sometimes do not develop social networks at the new campus. This is usually attributed to two factors. First, some students feel that they are "only here two years" and so do not make much of an effort to meet students through the range of available venues. Second, the majority of the campus community has already been attending together since their freshman year, so many students have settled into well-established friendship networks. These networks might or might not be open to new members, a situation that can present a challenge to the newly arrived transfer student. More often than not, transfer students who leave a university do so for social rather than academic reasons.

Chapter Summary

In this chapter, the following topics were discussed:

- Theories of college student development
  - Chickering's seven vectors of college student development
  - Perry's nine positions of cognitive development
  - Tinto's model of institutional departure

- Overview of common themes in the first-year experience:
  - Academic issues
  - Social issues
  - General campus environment
  - Personal issues
  - Issues unique to the transfer student experience

Reflections and Exercises

1. Get Stats for Your University

This chapter provides you with many national trends and statistics. This exercise will have you gather similar information for your own campus that is current and relevant to your particular situation. Typically, the office that houses the Dean of

Students or the office that coordinates student life activities will be a good place to start. Another good place would be an office of institutional research; if your campus participated in the national Higher Education Research Institute (HERI) study, there will be a copy of the results that provide your campus's specific data as well as the national results. Go to these offices and ask for any current data on the issues you are most interested in or affected by. Even if statistical data are not available, counselors and advisors could most likely share with you their sense of the issue based on their daily work with students. They might be able to provide you with some insights that could be quite useful to your own transition.

2. Take Inventory of Own Experience

Using the theories of Chickering, Perry, and Tinto (each focuses on different things), assess your own development according to the tenets of each theory. Rate yourself in terms of your development along Chickering's seven vectors, Perry's nine stages, and Tinto's concepts of academic and social integration. Identify where your strengths lie and where you might be experiencing trouble spots. For each of the less strong areas, search for campus resources or personnel that could assist you in strengthening that area. Design an action plan to accomplish these goals (see Chapter 9 for more information on action plans). Meet with an advisor to discuss your plan and ask his or her advice for improving it. Implement your plan, seeking assistance whenever possible or necessary.

3. Interview Another Student

The goal of this activity is to help you become familiar with the experiences another student has had on your campus and to discover similarities with, and differences from, your own. Find a student who is at the same class level as you are and ask the following questions. Be sure to take good notes and ask questions if you need more information or clarification about what she or he is telling you. You might want to clarify what expectations she or he has about confidentiality and what you will do with this information (and your notes) after the interview is completed.

> As an interviewer, it is your goal to have this person share with you what his or her experience is *really* like. This means that you need to be open to hearing about experiences that might vary greatly from your own or that you would have interpreted differently. Be careful not to listen through the filter of your own experience but to really hear and capture the other person's experience as it occurred for him or her.

1. Why did you choose to attend this university?

2. When was your first visit to the campus? What were your impressions of our school?

3. Did you think you would fit in here? Why or why not? How did that compare to the reality of being here?

4. Did you move away from home to attend school here?   Yes   No
   What have been your family members' reactions to your attending this university?

5. If you moved away from home, what were your first impressions of your roommate? Describe that relationship over the course of the year. What impact has this had on you?

6. What were your first impressions of your classes?

7. Describe your academic experience in your first year. What impact has this had on you?

8. What were your first impressions of the social/party scene at our university?

9. Describe your social/party experience over the course of the year. What impact has this had on you?

10. How did your relationships with your family members change over the course of the year? What impact has this had on you?

11. How did your relationships with your friends back home change over the course of the year? What impact has this had on you?

12. Describe the first time you met someone at this university who was very different from you. How were they different? What impact has this had on you?

13. Given your experiences over the first year, what would you have done differently?

14. What advice would you give to an incoming student?

After you complete the interview, review your notes and notice the similarities and differences with your own experience during your first year. Do you have any thoughts or ideas about possible sources for these similarities and differences?

Were there any aspects of the other student's experience that were difficult for you to understand or relate to? If so, why?

What observations or conclusions can you make about the first-year experience at your university?

Community Development

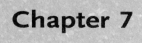

Chapter 7

The Diverse Campus Community

You might have noticed that some of the themes in the previous chapters deal with diversity and the experiences that students have in being part of, and interacting with, different groups. Most universities and colleges value diversity in all its forms. There is an inherent assumption at research universities that in order to discover new knowledge, you need to embrace diverse ways of thinking about a topic because multiple views and perspectives aid in the process of discovery. In addition, most university administrators and faculty believe that the educational process is enriched for all when a wide range of diversity is found in the students, faculty, and staff. A diverse community brings the strengths of all of its members and each can learn from interacting with the others. However, diversity also brings challenges. When people do not share an experience, belief, or value, they might not communicate effectively, or they might even experience conflict or tension. Also, people and institutions can value diversity in theory but their daily actions might not actually achieve that. In this chapter, we are going to specifically look at issues of diversity on university campuses and how they affect the community of scholars. Using current statistics and theoretical models of identity development, we will explore many aspects of human identity that shape the university experience.

Diversity of the University Community

In this chapter, you will find many references to two national studies done by UCLA's Higher Education Research Institute (HERI). Each year, HERI conducts a nationwide study of incoming college freshmen; in 2003, the study included 276,449 first-year students at 413 colleges and universities across the United States. This study has been done annually for 35 years and has become a central source of data on current freshmen as well as trends over time. In addition, HERI now conducts an annual study of college freshmen at the end of their first year of college, called Your First College Year (YFCY). This samples 24,824 college freshmen at 105 four-year institutions in the United States. Although not all of

Might I Suggest...

Before we get started, I want to address the importance of this chapter. By far the biggest obstacle to college success for many students is how they are treated by their peers with regard to aspects of their identity. Students of color, low-income students, lesbian, gay, bisexual, and transgender students, and students with disabilities not only experience additional challenges, but also often experience verbal and physical harassment. This issue is of great importance to institutions of higher education, and you will find that conversations about diversity issues are common on college campuses. In my experience, some first-year students, especially freshmen, are resistant to talking about diversity. They say things like "But I attended several diversity workshops in high school. I know about this stuff already." While they might have talked about diversity in some ways before, the truth is that dynamics on university campuses are far different from those in high school; the ways in which these issues can be discussed and addressed are very different as well. I encourage you to read this chapter with an open mind and to see how diversity issues might be different from what you already know or have experienced.

In addition, these discussions are an important part of your education and career preparation. Many employers now are acutely aware of the multicultural society and global community in which they must compete. Many are seeking to hire students who have developed *cultural competence,* which is an awareness of various ideas of diversity and how they might shape a person's experience and interactions within a community. Becoming culturally competent is an important skill for college students to master and the ideas discussed in this chapter can serve as the groundwork for that development.

the participating institutions are research universities, the data provide an overall picture of the current freshman experience in the United States.

Because research universities bring together so many unique populations (e.g., faculty, staff, administrators, undergraduate students, graduate students, alumni, parents, donors, surrounding community members) from around the world, the term *diversity* takes on a far greater meaning than just ethnic or racial diversity. The university community is unique in that it actually creates a microcosm of society that is not replicated in any other type of institution—people of all ages and backgrounds are living and working together year-round, and this creates opportunities for both wonderful and problematic interactions. Each group within the university community, and each member within each group, has their own needs and preferences, some of which might be at odds or in conflict with the needs of others. This chapter will explore some of these issues in more depth.

Diversity issues should be of importance to every college student. It is through the college experience that you can gain valuable experiences and information that will prepare you to work in a global economy and live in a multicultural society. Research universities create a unique and precious opportunity to live in a truly diverse community with some of the best minds from around the world working, living, and learning together. Many college students seem to understand the importance of this opportunity and embrace it. According to the YFCY survey, many students indicate an interest in social awareness issues and say that this interest grew over their first year in college. Students indicated the following as being either "essential" or "very important" in their life goals at college entry compared to the end of their first year:

Entry	End	
29.4%	45.3%	Helping to promote racial understanding
37.6%	59.5%	Influencing social values
32.5%	47.9%	Becoming a community leader
63.8%	77.2%	Helping others who are in difficulty

In addition, students indicated that they had grown (i.e., felt stronger or much stronger) in the following areas compared to when they entered college:

57.5%	Knowledge of people from different races/cultures
55.2%	Understanding of national issues
53.7%	Understanding of global issues
40.0%	Understanding of problems facing their community

Dimensions of Identity

In discussing "diversity," it is important to look at all of the different aspects of a person's identity. There are primary dimensions of our identity, which are the things that we are born with or cannot easily change about our physical being. These are gender, race, ethnicity, sexual orientation, age, and physical abilities/qualities. Then there are secondary dimensions of our identity—elements that still significantly shape who we are but that there is some degree of choice or ability to change. These include geographic location, education, political ideology, work experience/style, physical appearance, learning style, marital status, religious beliefs/spirituality, economic status, parental status, military experience, language/dialect, and personality. All of these factors interact in unique ways to create the identity of any one individual. Even a group of people who share a primary identity will find a huge range of differences based on their other primary and secondary dimensions. As is mentioned in Chapter 6, Chickering indicates that college students are going through several stages (i.e., vectors) of development, many of which are related to these primary and secondary dimensions of diversity. Students are learning about themselves and their own self-concept, and then they are interacting with a wide range of people and developing their interpersonal skills and relationship to tolerance.

As students go through these developmental processes, in relation to both their own personal identity and their abilities to interact with others, both positive and negative interactions can occur. As is mentioned in Chapter 6, many common themes of the first-year student experience revolve around these issues. This chapter will focus the dimensions that seem to be most closely connected with the university experience: age, gender, sexual orientation, race and ethnicity, economic class, spiritual identity, and political ideology. While other aspects of identity are certainly important, space prevents us from exploring more than just a few.

Age and Generational Issues

One aspect of the university community that makes it unique is that it contains members of all ages ranging from 0 (newborn babies of students, staff, and faculty) all the way up to the 90s (emeritus faculty who are still involved in campus business and even students who have chosen to attend college late in life). According to the 2003 HERI study, the age of freshmen students on Dec. 31, 2003 was as follows:

17 or younger: 1.8%
18: 68.2%
19: 28.7%
20–24: 1.3%
25 or older: 0.1%

Faculty age was assessed by HERI in its 2001 study on the American College Teacher, which found the following:

34 or younger: 8%
35–44: 22%
45–54: 35%
55–64: 30%
65 or older: 5%

This means that the university community facilitates interactions among all of the living generations in ways that are not seen in most neighborhood and work environments. Each generation is unique, and understanding the different needs and styles of each generation is useful for understanding the university community.

There are many researchers who look at the various generations of people within a society. A *generation* is defined as a societywide peer group who collectively have common values and attitudes. A generation is determined by birthrates, which tend to rise and fall in a classic bell-shaped curve; the lowest point of the curve marks the end of one generation and the beginning of the next. According to Neil Howe and William Strauss, authors of *Millennials Rising: The Next Great Generation* (2000), the current living generations are as follows:

G.I. Generation	Born 1901–1924
Silent Generation	Born 1925–1942
Baby Boomers	Born 1943–1960
Generation X	Born 1961–1981
Millennials	Born 1982–1999

Table 7.1 Comparison of the Living Generations at the University

Traditionalists (Combination of the G.I. and Silent Generations)

In university communities, they are in the higher leadership roles (e.g., presidents, deans, directors), senior faculty (emeriti and full professors), and occasionally older/reentry students.

Shaped by	Values and Attitudes
• World War I • Roaring 20s • Great Depression • New Deal • Pearl Harbor and World War II • Korean War • "American Dream"	This group is characterized as hardworking and patriotic. They are the epitome of loyalty and truly believe that the best way to accomplish something is to put aside individual needs and work together as a group for common goals. The Depression shaped their financial views, making them tend to be careful and thrifty—they have the highest saving rate of any generation. They are likely to look to institutions for help because of the role the government played in recovering from the Great Depression. They tend to be very hierarchical in their approach to management and expect the respect due their position.

Baby Boomers

They are the middle- to upper-level administrators, faculty (all levels), and some reentry students and graduate students.

Shaped by	Values and Attitudes
• Kennedy assassination • Beatles, Rolling Stones • First moon landing • Civil rights movement and Martin Luther King, Jr. • Woodstock, and counterculture • Women's liberation • Vietnam War • Watergate • Television and credit cards	Television greatly shaped this generation, through both the ability to see world events live and the power of TV shows and advertising as a way to define pop culture. Boomers are considered optimistic and competitive, and this led to more focus on individual and personal accomplishment—they are deeply defined by their work. They experienced economic growth that allowed them to have affluence in a way the Traditionalists never saw. Credit cards debuted during their lifetime, and as a result, Boomers have the lowest saving rate of any generation. This generation was more educated and idealistic than the Traditionalists were, which led to questioning the status quo and bringing about change in the United States. They are more likely to challenge authority and focus on change. They are the generation that fought for equality and justice for many marginalized groups. They tend to be more liberal in terms of political ideology.

Generation X

They are low- to middle-level administrators, entry- to middle-level faculty, and some reentry students and graduate students.

Shaped by	Values and Attitudes
• John Lennon's murder • Challenger explosion • Chernobyl • Fall of Berlin Wall • Operation Desert Storm • Latchkey children • Massive corporate layoffs	The Internet and other media inventions (e.g., computers, cell phones) greatly shaped this generation and made them information-focused multitaskers with not much patience. They grew up at a time when more mothers worked outside the home and divorce rates tripled, making them the generation with the most latchkey children. This forced them to become independent and highly self-sufficient. During their lifetime, every major American institution was called into question, causing them to distrust institutions and relationships—*skepticism* and *cynicism* are the terms that are most used to define Generation X. This has led Xers to become very independent, resourceful, and pragmatic.

Millennials

They are undergraduate students, some graduate students, and future college students who are still in the K–12 system.

Shaped by	Values and Attitudes
• War in Kosovo • Oklahoma City bombing • Princess Diana's death • Clinton impeachment • Columbine shootings • September 11, 2001, attacks and the war on terrorism • Most "wanted" generation in history (planned pregnancies) • Children in danger (Baby Jessica, Polly Klaus, etc.), which increased parent concern for safety • Greatest economic boom (until 2001)	Millennials were also greatly influenced by technological inventions but are much more comfortable with them than any previous generation. The Internet has made the world accessible from their homes. The apparent rise in school shootings and other threats to child safety has made this generation (and their parents) very safety conscious. This has caused the parents of Millennials (Boomers who do not trust authority) to become actively engaged in almost all aspects of their children's lives in an effort to protect them. Their optimistic, idealist Boomer parents also raised them to believe in their personal power to take action to fix things. As a result, Millennials are often more confident than their abilities justify. Millennials have maintained *optimism* as one of their key traits, but it is paired with realism. Another key trait is their appreciation of diversity, and they often do not see or recognize the injustices that others identify. Millennials have been included in most of the major family decisions, so traditional lines of authority are not particularly relevant to them—they are more likely to focus on collaboration and believe in their right to participate. This generation has also been very pressured to achieve, and performing poorly is often quite upsetting to a Millennial. Politically, this tends to be a more conservative generation.

Every generation is shaped by history and events, technology, economy, society, and culture. These events have the most impact during the so-called formative years (ages 8 to 13 years) and the coming-of-age years (ages 17 to 23), when they can significantly shape a person's attitudes and behaviors. Although not all people in a given generation are affected in the same way, researchers have been able to identity widely held shared values and attitudes. Table 7.1 is a chart of the events that have significantly shaped each generation and the common values and attitudes that members of that generation share (this information is adapted from *Millennials Rising* and *When Generations Collide: How to Solve the Generational Puzzle at Work* by Lancaster and Stillman, 2002).

It is clear from reading the descriptions in Table 7.1 that there are likely to be conflicts and tensions between the different generations because some of their

What This Means to You

Each generation is known for different traits, and these differences often create challenging interactions. For example, the tech-savvy Millennials are often frustrated by their Traditionalist faculty who lecture without using even the most basic of multimedia tools. Faculty who are Boomers and value civil rights and challenging authority are shocked by what they perceive to be apathy on the part of the Millennials regarding social justice issues. Gen X administrators who could not wait to move away from their parents cannot relate to the closeness the Millennials have with their parents and their parents' insistence on being involved with their student's life.

The first way that in which this issue will affect you will be how you are treated by older generations. Often, the Traditionalist, Boomer and X generations see the optimism of the Millennials as insincere and annoying; they grew up in times of stress and are likely to view the world with some skepticism or even cynicism. They also do not relate to being close with one's parents so are likely to see it as a sign of dependence and immaturity. You might find that you have to work a bit harder to have your ideas taken seriously when you are working with the older generations.

Another way in which this issue will affect you is in the fact that you have the opportunity to gain valuable insights and skills from these interactions. Each of the generations has unique qualities and characteristics, and your ability to understand and interact with a wide range of generations will serve you not only in college, but also in the work environment. There are entire businesses devoted to helping the various generations work together in the work environment—for example, the books *When Generations Collide* (Lancaster and Stillman, 2002) and *Managing by Defining Moments* (Meredith and Schewe, 2002) are both dedicated to helping businesses and managers understand these issues. If you are able to become savvy about the various generations, how they work, and what they value, you will be well positioned for future career opportunities, especially one that requires people skills or management expertise. This is just one aspect of developing your cultural competence.

primary values are in opposition. Lynne Lancaster and David Stillman, authors of *When Generations Collide: How to Solve the Generational Puzzle at Work,* argue that generational differences are at the forefront of current personnel issues across the country. The effects can be seen in matters ranging from poor communication and not understanding each group's lingo to serious issues such as resentment and poor teamwork. As a result, many companies now work to address generational issues in the workforce.

Race and Ethnicity

Both race and ethnicity play important roles on college campuses because of how they influence the experiences that students have, as well as how people interact with each other. Race and ethnicity are often thought of as interchangeable, but they are actually quite different. According to the United Nations, race "refers to physical differences of skin tone, hair texture, and facial features. Because people can be grouped by any number of physical differences (height, foot size, resistance to certain diseases), race is an artificial way to categorize people. Nonetheless, race remains an important concept because of the social and political issues that arise from it." By contrast, ethnicity "refers to membership in a culturally- and geographically-defined group that may share language, cultural practices, religion, or other aspects. Examples include Italian, Kurdish, and Bantu. People of the same race can be of different ethnicities. For example, Asians can be Japanese, Korean, Thai, or many other ethnicities."

While the United States is fairly diverse, college campuses are less so. Table 7.2 shows a comparison of national census data (from Ameristat.org) and data collected by the National Center for Education Statistics for four-year

Table 7.2   Comparison of Race and Ethnicity for U.S. Population and College Freshmen

Race/Ethnicity	U.S. Population	Freshmen	Your Campus
White/Caucasian	69.1%	71%	
Black/African American	12.1%	10.9%	
American Indian/Native Alaskan	0.7%	0.8%	
Asian/Asian American/ Pacific Islander	3.7%	6.7%	
Hispanic/Chicano/Latino/ Puerto Rican	12.5%	10.7%	
Other	0.2%	N/A	
Two or more races	1.6%	N/A*	

*NCES data did not include multiracial or biracial selections.

institutions. (Note: Some categories were merged to create equivalent comparisons, but exact matches were not possible.)

Some ethnic groups are overrepresented on college campuses, while others are underrepresented, but in general, Whites represent more than two thirds of college students in the United States, while students of color represent one third. As you might have noticed in Chapter 6, interactions between different ethnicities were mentioned as having an important influence on the experiences of first-year students. This is because of the types of interactions, both positive and negative, that each student has with others. As Chickering notes in his fifth vector, part of each person's developmental process includes gaining "a sense of self in social, historical, and cultural contexts," which includes an understanding of yourself in relation to the larger cultural group to which you belong. In the United States, this process is different for each of the races and ethnicities because each group has a unique experience within the larger society, especially since White culture is the dominant culture, both statistically and in terms of representation in the major institutions of the country, such as politics, media, medicine, and law. Unfortunately, people of color still experience discrimination and prejudice based on their racial and ethnic identities. Some of these experiences stem from a lack of information or knowledge about race and ethnicity or a certain group of people. And some are definitely intentional, with a goal of causing physical or emotional hurt, such as vandalizing someone's property or punching them. According to the National Institute Against Prejudice and Violence, 20–25% of minority students on college campuses are victimized annually by acts of hate, with lesbian, gay, bisexual, and transgender students experiencing the highest rate of hate crimes.

Given this context, it is no surprise that minority groups would go through a different process than those in the majority. There are two useful models for understanding how people gain a sense of their racial or ethnic identity over the course of their lifetimes; one for ethnic minorities and one for the ethnic majority. These models can easily be applied to university students, since all young adults will be at some stage of the process during their college experience.

Minority Identity Development Model

In 1998, Atkinson, Morton, and Sue created a model that describes the stages of identity development for ethnic minority groups and their relationship to the dominant culture, that is, White culture in the United States. Their model was based on previous research and models that were focused on one particular ethnicity, such as Black or Latino. They argue that ethnic minorities develop their identity amid negative stereotypes and oppression of all kinds and that this affects their sense of identity.

Conformity

In this stage, the person reflects the values of larger society; the dominant culture's values are preferred, and the dominant culture is idealized. The person's own ethnic group and other ethnic groups that are nondominant are devalued, although those that are most similar to the dominant culture are valued the most.

The person assimilates many aspects of the White culture and demonstrates few aspects of his or her own culture. This is not a conscious choice but rather a naïve acceptance of, and preference for, the dominant culture's values.

Dissonance

A person in this stage is starting to notice and question negative stereotypes about nondominant cultures, especially his or her own. Personal experiences provide a catalyst for realizing that not all things about the White culture are positive and not all things about their culture are negative. A person often experiences mixed feelings of appreciation and devaluation for both dominant and nondominant cultures, including self and others. This stage often initiates feelings of anger and conflict about race and society.

Resistance

In this stage, a person is self-reflective about having bought into White values and having devalued his or her own culture, family, community, or self. This can cause feelings of guilt, shame, and/or anger. A strong focus is placed on valuing all things about the nondominant culture and devaluing everything about White culture. A person can often feel empathy for other nondominant cultures in this stage, but the primary focus is on the person's own culture. This stage is almost a complete swing to the opposite of the first stage of conformity.

Introspection

A person in this stage is beginning to question the extreme and dichotomous views of the previous stage (i.e., "all about my culture is good, and all about White culture is bad"). Instead of reacting against negative stereotypes, a more authentic and positive self-identity is developed. In addition, a person is able to see and criticize aspects of his or her own culture without feeling bad. The person also is having positive experiences with some Whites and is no longer comfortable uniformly devaluing White culture.

Integrative Awareness

This final stage allows the person to experience a "true appreciation for one's own culture and selective appreciation of White culture." The person recognizes and believes that all cultures exhibit both positive and negative elements. There is true pride in one's own culture as well as critical acceptance of the dominant group. This stage is very different from the first stage because the person is committed to maintaining his or her own cultural identity and not assimilating into White culture.

White Racial Consciousness Development Model

Unlike ethnic minorities who develop their cultural identity in response to negative stereotypes, Whites in the United States do not experience this process. Because they are members of the dominant culture, Whites grow up with either lots of positive messages about their cultural heritage or an absence of negative messages. Some theorists believe that Whites engage in a different process that is more about their awareness of race consciousness, rather than their own racial identity. Rowe, Bennett, and Atkinson (1994) propose a model that explores this process. They state that there are essentially two main statuses of White racial consciousness, and there are several types within each status. This model is less linear in nature (i.e., it does not outline a series of stages that a person passes through), but people do switch types on the basis of their experiences. The two primary stages are unachieved racial consciousness and achieved racial consciousness, each resulting in different types of beliefs and attitudes about people of color and the issues of race and ethnicity. The statuses and types are as follows.

Unachieved Racial Consciousness

The types in this status reflect either a lack of exploration of, or commitment to, racial issues and concerns.

- *Avoidant type:* People of this type do not consider racial issues relevant and usually engage in avoiding, denying, or minimalizing racial issues or concerns. They are likely to think that people of color are being "too sensitive" or are misinterpreting their experiences.
- *Dependent type:* A person of this type has adopted some beliefs and attitudes about people of color without doing any personal exploration. In essence, she or he has adopted someone else's views (e.g., those of parents or the media), and regardless of whether the beliefs are negative or positive, the person has not explored *why* she or he holds those views.
- *Dissonant type:* People of this type are in some kind of transition. Usually, personal experiences have conflicted with beliefs they have held, so they have been moved into a more active exploration of racial issues but are not yet sure what they believe. People of this type often experience confusion. This type correlates with the value development process described in Chapter 4.

Achieved Racial Consciousness

The types in this status reflect an exploration of, and commitment to, racial issues and concerns.

- *Dominant type:* People of this type have strong views of White supremacy. They see minorities as truly inferior and therefore believe that any problems people of color experience are due to their own qualities and not any societal disadvantage.
- *Conflictive type:* Whites of this type believe in equality among all races. While they might support certain antidiscrimination legislation, they might not support other programs that appear to promote people of color at the expense of Whites, such as affirmative action. People of this type still find themselves more comfortable around their own race, although they are careful to not be racist in their own language and actions.
- *Reactive type:* People of this type have explored racial concerns and are committed to addressing them. In comparison to the dominant type, they

see *all* issues as involving oppression and minorities as innocent victims, no matter what the circumstances. They dismiss any personal responsibility on the part of people of color and are upset with White culture and those who are not committed to ending the status quo. They have often romanticized or overidentified with one particular minority group to which they are especially committed. "White guilt," which is feeling guilty or bad for receiving privileges that people of color are denied, is often affiliated with this type.

- *Integrative type:* Whites of this type have explored their own "whiteness" and have achieved comfort with it while also being committed to social change. They acknowledge and work to change societal forces that oppress people of color through contributing to or participating in organizations that work against oppression. Their commitment does not arise from emotional needs, such as anger at, or guilt about, whiteness, or from a need to oppress or idealize people of color.

Biracial and Multiracial Identity Development Model

In our society, many people are of two or more races. They may be children of parents from two different races, and are biracial, or their ancestry may include several races, and are multiracial. Research on the experiences of biracial and multiracial people is fairly new, so models in this area are still under development and there are several different models to choose from. One model, by Kerwin, Ponterotto, Jackson, and Harris (1993), is useful in exploring the identity development of bi- or multiracial college students as they look at identity formation over time, especially as it relates to experiences in the school system. They argue that there are six phases that shape a person's identity: preschool, entry to school, preadolescence, adolescence, college/young adulthood, and adulthood.

Preschool

In this stage, up to the age of five years, a child is becoming aware of race. This process is accelerated for bi- or multiracial children because they notice differences between their parents in terms of physical characteristics like skin tone and hair texture.

Entry to School

In this stage, children begin to interact with other children and bi- or multiracial children are frequently faced with the question "What are you?" In an attempt to answer this question, children begin to use terms and labels to classify themselves and/or their group. The recognition of different social categories begins to emerge.

Preadolescence

The categorization of differences expands beyond skin tone to include other factors such as other physical traits or languages spoken. Students begin to explore who they fit in with among their peers and are drawn to those with whom they fit in most. This stage may also include the child's first experiences of racism or segregation.

Adolescence

The theorists argue that this stage is the most difficult for bi- or multiracial youth because of the social pressures that teens of all backgrounds seem to experience. All students are trying to find their place among their peers and may change their behaviors to fit in with a particular group. Bi- or multiracial students often feel forced to choose between the different aspects of their identity—in other words, they choose one part of their racial identity with which to align and minimize or reject the other. This can cause problems in their family relationships as one parent might feel rejected. The choice is influenced by the makeup of the school and/or neighborhood community.

College/Young Adulthood

This phase is characterized by the deepening immersion in one racial identity resulting in the rejection of the other. The choice may be the same as was made in middle or high school or it might be a shift from that period to the other racial identity. Students in this group still do not feel comfortable embracing all aspects of their racial identity. In addition, the student's personal appearance might put them in situations where others do not realize his or her racial identity. In these cases, the student may hear derogatory remarks about an aspect of his or her heritage and, as a result, become more aware of the advantages and disadvantages of being bi- or multiracial.

Might I Suggest...

Utilize the previous models to assess where you might be in terms of your own racial identity development. What experiences contributed to your views? What experiences have you had with race and ethnicity in terms of others' identity? What have you learned from your family? From teachers? From the media? It's important to take a look at the messages we have received and to examine how these might shape our beliefs, attitudes, behaviors, and actions. When others talk about their race or ethnicity, listen! Listen not only to what they are saying but also to what stage they might currently be in. Ask questions, such as the ones listed above. Also, be willing to educate others. There might be times when someone you interact with does not understand your experience or even says something insensitive. Most likely, this person is doing it from a place of ignorance, not malice. If you feel able to, turn the experience into a "teachable moment." Saying something like "I'm sure you didn't mean to but what you just said was hurtful to me because _____." Most people will be quite sorry that they did something harmful and will appreciate being given the opportunity to fix it. If not, then at least you got to speak up for yourself, and that can be an empowering experience. At the end of this book, you will find a list of books and movies, some which focus on racial identity (see Appendix B). Read and watch as many as you can. It is another way to actively increase your understanding of these important issues.

What This Means to You

Every day, students interact with each other in both formal and informal settings. These interactions are affected by each student's own process of identity development. How they see themselves and others of their own racial and ethnic groups and how they see people from different backgrounds are influenced by the stages of their developmental process. This can create awkward and even tense interactions between students of different ethnicities. This is especially true when students of color are in the stages of dissonance or resistance and they interact with White students who are in stages of unachieved racial consciousness, or when bi- or multiracial students interact with others who do not recognize their multiple identities. Use these models to aid your empathy for yourself and others. You will experience your own development and the development of others in this arena throughout your college career. Learning about the impact that race and ethnicity have on both individuals and diverse communities is a very important part of your education. It's one aspect of developing your cultural competence.

Adulthood

This final stage lasts the rest of the person's adult life and is the continued exploration and integration of his or her racial identities. Many adults find a way to embrace all aspects of their racial heritage at some point. Certain events can create catalysts for further exploration such as entering in to a romantic relationship or having children.

Gender and Sexual Orientation

Gender and Biological Sex

In discussing the biological sex, gender, and sexual orientation of any person, including a college student, it is important to understand the complexity of this topic. Although the general public believes these issues to be simple, they are not. Sociologists and biologists have discovered that enormous complexity exists and that the categories are not as neat or exclusive as was previously thought.

Gender is often confused with biological sex. *Biological sex* is the scientific or biological determination that makes a human male or female. There are several indicators that medical doctors use to assign a person's biological sex; these include chromosomes, hormones, internal reproductive organs, external genitals, and secondary sex characteristics such as breasts and facial hair (secondary characteristics usually become prominent during puberty and so are not used in identifying the sex of a newborn baby). When all of these indicators align, it is easy for a doctor to declare a baby to be male or female. However, there are many people (1 in 2,000 births) who have one or more of these characteristics that don't line up with the others; in other words, they share biological indicators of both the male and female sexes. This group of people is called *intersex,* and they (or, more likely their parents and doctors) face a lot of societal pressure to choose a sex early on. When intersex people reach maturity, some discover that they don't "feel" like the gender they were assigned at birth. One to four percent of the U.S. population is intersex, however, most don't even know that they are, because of surgery done when they were infants. Most discover in adulthood when loss of feeling during sex prompts them to discover that they are/were intersex.

The term *gender* is often used to refer to someone's biological sex, but that is incorrect. Gender is the socially defined character traits that are prescribed for a particular sex within a given culture. These traits are what we typically think of when we think of "masculine" or "feminine." Within a culture, young people are socialized to act in "appropriate" ways for their sex—also known as *traditional gender roles.* For example, in the U.S. young boys are taught that it is not okay to play with dolls, and young girls are taught that they should want to be mothers someday. Because these are actions done by choice, sociologists and biologists often refer to this as gender expression, and while children's gender expression is often highly controlled and monitored by adults in their lives, there is more freedom for young adults and adults to make their own choices about adhering to or stepping out from these proscribed gender roles.

This is different from gender identity, which is someone's psychological sense of being male or female. Most people's gender identity matches their biological sex, and they do not experience any conflict between the two. However, for many people who are intersex or whose biological sex does not match their gender identity, this can create problems because of society's strong need for clear gender expression. The term *transgender* is used as an umbrella term to classify people who do not have a gender identity that is either clearly male or clearly female. This includes people whose biological sex assignment does not match their gender identity, people who feel that they don't neatly fit into one gender category, people who intentionally resist gender categories and gender roles, people who perform as the other gender (i.e., drag queens and kings), and people who are sexually aroused or emotionally gratified by wearing clothing associated with the other gender (i.e., transvestites). Table 7.3 provides a chart that illustrates the interplay between these various concepts.

According to the National Center for Education Statistics, males make up 45% of all students attending a four-year degree-granting institution, and females make up 55%. This ratio is true for college freshmen as well (HERI). No measures have been reported for gender identity, expression, or sexual orientation.

Sexual Orientation

Completely separate from one's biological sex, as well as one's gender identity and expression, is the concept of sexual orientation, which refers to whom a person is attracted to physically and emotionally. A person can be attracted to men, women, or both; it is pairing sexual attraction with a person's sex and gender that then determines whether one is attracted to the "same" or the "opposite" sex or both. Some people think of sexual orientation as a dichotomy, that someone

Table 7.3   Matrix of Various Identity Markers and Possible Options

Identity Marker	Possibilities		
Biological sex	Male	Intersex (aspects of both)	Female
Gender identity	Man	Transgender	Woman
Gender expression	Masculine	Androgynous (equally both)	Feminine
Sexual orientation	Attracted to women	Bisexual (attracted to both)	Attracted to men

is either heterosexual or homosexual. However, researchers have found that this is not the case. Alfred Kinsey discovered in his survey of thousands of people that sexual behavior exists on a continuum (see Table 7.4), the ends representing sexual encounters exclusively with the same or opposite sex and the middle of the continuum representing rare, occasional, or frequent encounters with the different sexes (Kinsey et al., 1948).

In this model, bisexuality is harder to define; some argue that it is represented by those in the middle of the continuum (number 3) because they have sex equally with both sexes. However, others would argue that any encounter with a member of the opposite sex is bisexuality (numbers 1–5).

Another researcher, Fritz Klein, found that sexual orientation is more complex than that (Klein et al., 1985). He believed that one's true sexual orientation is based not just on actual sexual encounters but on other things as well. He argued that a person's sexual orientation could change over time and was actually a reflection of seven factors. He created the model shown in Table 7.5 to articulate the complexity of sexual orientation. In addition, he said that one should examine not only a person's present experiences, but also the person's past ones as well as those that would be "ideal." Klein argued that this gives a more authentic and complete picture of a person's sexuality.

Again, not much data focus on the sexual orientation of college students, but various national studies indicate that anywhere from 2% to 15% of any population identify themselves as lesbian, gay, bisexual, and/or transgender. This is certainly true for university communities as well.

Table 7.4   Kinsey's Continuum of Sexuality

0	1	2	3	4	5	6
Sex exclusively with other sex			Sex equally with both sexes			Sex exclusively with same sex

Table 7.5   Klein's Matrix of Sexual Orientation

	Past	Present	Ideal
Sexual behavior (with whom you actually have sex)			
Sexual attraction (to whom you are sexually attracted)			
Sexual fantasy (about whom you have sexual fantasies)			
Emotional preference (for whom you feel love)			
Social preference (with whom you prefer to socialize)			
Lifestyle (in what "culture"—gay or straight—you spend the most time)			
Self-identification (how you see yourself)			

Lesbian/Gay Identity Development Model

Theorists McCarn and Fassinger (1996) created a model that looks at how lesbian women form a sense of their identity. They discovered that this process occurs with reference to two areas: the individual herself and her relationship to group membership. Although McCarn and Fassinger did not do research on gay males specifically, this model is still useful for understanding how sexual identity development occurs among nonheterosexuals. Table 7.6 lists the four main stages that occur within both of these contexts: awareness, exploration, deepening commitment, and internalization or synthesis.

This process usually leads to a person "coming out," which means that the person tells others of his or her identity as a lesbian, gay, bisexual, or transgender person. The coming-out process is truly that—a process—and not a single event. A person has to come out continually over the course of his or her life in different situations and with different people. Some people are "out" to a select few people in their life; others come out to everyone they meet. Coming out is necessitated by the assumption made by most heterosexual people that everyone is heterosexual, in other words, "straight until proven gay." Because of this assumption of heterosexuality, lesbian, gay, bisexual, and transgender (LGBT) people are put into uncomfortable or awkward situations regularly that force them to either come out or misrepresent their identity. For example, asking a woman whether she has a boyfriend or whether she has met any cute guys recently assumes heterosexuality and can put her in an awkward position if she is not heterosexual. The reason this is awkward is because she

Table 7.6   McCarn and Fassinger's Model of Lesbian/Gay Identity Development

Stage	Individual Sexual Identity	Group Membership Identity
Awareness . . .	. . . of feeling different than peers toward opposite and same sexes	. . . of the existence of different sexual orientations
Exploration . . .	. . . of strong erotic feelings for the same sex (either with one particular person or in general)	. . . of one's position to others as a group (i.e., gay men or lesbians)
Deepening commitment . . .	. . . to self-identity, includes fulfillment and crystallization of choices about sexuality	. . . to personal involvement with reference group, with awareness of oppression and other consequences of choices
Internalization/ synthesis . . .	. . . of love for same-sex people, sexual choices, and overall identity as lesbian/gay	. . . of identity as a member of a minority group across contexts

has to make a choice to either conceal her identity or come out, which is not always safe to do.

The murder of Matthew Sheppard, a college student in Wyoming on October 12, 1998, as well as the thousands of other hate crimes that are committed annually constantly remind LGBT students that it can be risky to come out to others. In 2003, the Policy Institute of the National Gay and Lesbian Task Force issued a report entitled *Campus Climate*. It was a national perspective on the experiences of LGBT people at U.S. colleges and universities, and it featured a national survey of students, faculty, and staff/administrators from across the United States. Results indicated that 36% of LGBT undergraduates had experienced harassment within the past year. Seventy-nine percent said that the harassment came from fellow students. Of all respondents (students, faculty, and staff), 20% feared for their physical safety because of their sexual orientation or gender identity, and 51% concealed their sexual orientation or gender identity to avoid intimidation. Nearly half (43%) rated the campus climate to be homophobic. On a positive note, 72% felt that their institution provided visible resources on LGBT issues and concerns.

Heterosexuality Identity Development Model

Another theorist, Jonathan Mohr (2002) explored how heterosexuals situate their identity in relation to others. Similar to the White identity model, Mohr believed that heterosexuals engage in a different process that is more about their awareness of sexuality consciousness rather than their own sexual orientation. He argued that there are essentially four types of heterosexuality identity and a person could switch from one to another on the basis of knowledge and experiences.

Democratic Heterosexuality

This type of person sees all people as the same and equal and does not consider sexual orientation an important factor—he or she sees sexual orientation as an inherent trait, similar to eye color. People of this type essentially believe that "people are people"and, as a result, do not consider that someone's sexual orientation might have an impact on his or her experience. Their own sexuality has not been examined.

Compulsory Heterosexuality

People of this type feel that heterosexuality is the only acceptable model, often for cultural or religious reasons. They believe that sexuality is a form of behavior, and therefore a choice. They idealize their own heterosexuality and denigrate the sexuality of others who may be different, viewing it as wrong or a sin.

Politicized Heterosexuality

A person of this type focuses on the sociopolitical ramifications of sexual orientation and is conscious of the oppression that lesbian, gay, bisexual, and transgender people experience. They often are angry at the privileges that heterosexuals receive in society and experience some guilt. They see others as either LGBT affirmative or as homophobic; they have little patience for those who do not accept LGBT people.

Integrative Heterosexuality

This person views sexual orientation as a complex construct with multiple variables and levels. They do not see any significant difference between heterosexuality and homosexuality (it's only one aspect of a person's identity) but acknowledge that privilege and oppression exist. They see that society is an oppressive system in which all people participate and that there are no good and bad people with regard to their stance on sexual orientation.

Interestingly, neither McCarn and Fassinger's model nor Mohr's model is inclusive of bisexuality, and neither addresses the variations in development that bisexuals experience. For example, the coming-out process is even more challenging for bisexuals because so many people see sexuality as a dichotomy—a person is either gay or straight—so bisexuals often face even more frustration when coming out because both gay and straight communities erroneously believe that these people just "haven't made up their mind yet." At this time, there is no model of bisexual identity development.

As is noted in Chapter 6, college is a time when young adults are establishing their identity separate from that of their family of origin and home communities.

What This Means to You

University campuses tend to be a focal point for discussions around issues of sex, gender, and sexual orientation. You will most likely find that there are many forums, workshops, and other educational programs about these topics and that your campus values tolerance and nondiscrimination around a wide range of identities, including sex, gender, and sexual orientation. Your campus might boast a center and staff that focus on these issues, and there will certainly be student groups that do. If you are questioning your own sexuality or identify as LGBT, you will most likely find many caring people and safe places to support your identity. If none exist on your campus, look to another campus in your area or on the Internet. Learning about the impact that sex, gender, and sexual orientation have on both individuals and diverse communities is a very important part of your education. It's one aspect of developing your cultural competence.

Might I Suggest...

Many students believe that they do not know anyone who is LGBT, or at least not any close friends or family. This is just not true. There are definitely LGBT people in every community of the university campus, from the students to the faculty to the staff and administrators. You probably actually know several people, but they just might not be "out" to you yet. Remember, coming out is a risky thing to do. Most LGBT people have been hurt, emotionally and physically, for their identity; nearly all have experienced verbal harassment, and quite a few have been physically assaulted. As a result, most LGBT people look for clear clues that a person is accepting of their sexuality and will not pose a threat to them. If you want more people to feel comfortable enough to come out to you, you need to make sure you are sending clear signals that you are safe. The first and most obvious is your language. Using more inclusive language that does not assume that someone is heterosexual is a great start. Saying things like "Are you dating someone?" or "Let me introduce you to my partner" (as opposed to boyfriend/girlfriend) sends a message that you are aware how heterosexist society is. Certainly, not saying derogatory things like "fag" or "That's so gay" can make people feel safer as well. You can choose to display LGBT-supportive images in your space, such as a rainbow flag or "safe zone" sticker. (Many university campuses have Safe Zones projects that allow people to indicate with a symbol that they are supportive and accepting of all sexualities; visit www .lgbtcampus.org/faq/safe_zone.html for more information). You can show your support of the LGBT community by attending programs, workshops, rallies, and events that address LGBT themes or support the rights of LGBT people. Of course, how you vote in campus, local, and national elections also makes a difference. All of these things show that you are an ally of the LGBT community— someone who is committed to fairness for all people and does not support discrimination of any kind.

This freedom allows students to explore aspects of their identity that they might not have previously considered or seriously explored. This is especially true for issues of gender, sex, and sexual orientation. College campuses nationwide are at the center of discussions of these issues because college students are at the forefront of this exploration.

Spiritual Identity

As students go off to college each year, they also take with them their spiritual or religious identities. Some students have deeply held spiritual values based on religions that they have practiced their entire lives, while others only celebrate their religions on one or two holidays per year, and even others do not believe in any kind of religion or spiritual practice. Religion and spirituality are different, although there certainly is overlap between them. The Merriam-Webster OnLine Dictionary clarifies that *religion* is "the service and worship of God or the supernatural; commitment or devotion to religious faith or observance; a personal set or institutionalized system of religious attitudes, beliefs, and practices," whereas *spiritual* is defined as "of, relating to, consisting of, or affecting the spirit; of or relating to sacred matters." These definitions are useful when we explore data on college freshmen, as students may differentiate between their spirituality and their identified religion.

The 2003 HERI study asked students to indicate their "religious preferences" and found that 17.6% did not identify a religious preference, while 82.4% did, as shown in Table 7.7.

In recent years, more and more students have indicated that their spirituality is an important factor in their lives. In 2000, HERI began a longitudinal study of the spiritual development of college students. The sample included 3,680 freshmen from across the United States who attended a wide range of colleges and universities. These students were surveyed again in their junior year in 2003. Results from the second survey indicated that 77% of the students believe that "we are all spiritual beings," and more than 58% placed a high value on "integrating spirituality into my life." Thirty-nine percent rated themselves as "above average" in terms of spirituality, and 40% are "seeking opportunities to grow spiritually." Unfortunately, 62% indicate that their professors never encourage classroom discussions of religion or spirituality. This might be why enrollment in the nation's 104 "Christ-centered" colleges has risen 27% since 1997.

Interestingly, a majority of students have found that their religious/spiritual beliefs have helped develop their identity (73%), given meaning/purpose to their life (67%), and provided them with strength, support, and guidance (74%), and they have gained strength from trusting in a higher power (71%). Quite a few of the students indicated religious practices, with 70% attending religious services in the past year and 77% indicating that they pray.

Because the study was begun in the freshman year, the results also provided some insight about changes over time. The first noticeable change had to do with attending church. In their first year, 52% of the students indicated that they

Table 7.7   Religious Preferences of College Students in the U.S.

Religion	Percent	Religion	Percent
Roman Catholic	29.7%	Hindu	0.7%
Baptist	11.1%	Eastern Orthodox	0.7%
Methodist	5.8%	Mormon (LDS)	0.6%
Lutheran	4.9%	Seventh-Day Adventist	0.3%
Presbyterian	4.1%	Unitarian Universalist	0.3%
Jewish	2.4%	Quaker	0.2%
Episcopal	1.8%	Other Christian	13.4%
United Church of Christ	1.5%	Other religion	2.7%
Buddhist	1.2%	None	17.6%
Islamic	0.8%		

attended frequently, whereas only 29% were still doing so three years later. The self-ratings of "above average" in terms of spirituality started at 47% for freshmen and dropped to 39% for the same students as juniors. However, more students were likely to indicate that integrating spirituality into their lives was "essential" or "very important"—58% for juniors compared to 51% just three years earlier.

One issue that became evident was that students experience challenges and struggles in the development of their religious/spiritual identities. The HERI study states:

> Two-thirds (65%) report that they question their religious/spiritual beliefs at least occasionally (18% frequently), and a similar number (68%) say that they are "feeling unsettled about spiritual and religious matters at least 'to some extent.' " Three-fourths (76%) of the students have "struggled to understand evil, suffering, and death" at least occasionally (21% frequently), and nearly half (46%) have at least occasionally "felt angry with God" (6% frequently)." One-third (38%) of the students reported feeling "disillusioned with my religious upbringing" at least "to some extent."

These last statistics reflect a common process for many students in college: questioning some of their values and beliefs. Although this general process is addressed in detail in Chapter 4, it is worth mentioning here because a unique, additional process shapes questioning one's religious/spiritual beliefs. Different researchers and theorists have explored spiritual development to ascertain the various processes that occur as a person develops and maintains a set of spiritual beliefs. One model that is useful is Fowler's Faith Development Theory.

Faith Development Model

James Fowler (1981) created the following six-stage model to articulate the faith development from infancy to full adulthood. It's important to note that many of these correlate with typical child development patterns, but Fowler has articulated how faith development is interwoven into the traditional developmental process.

Pre-stage: Primal

This phase sets up the six stages and occurs when a child is 0–2 years old. No faith development, per se, occurs in this pre-stage; rather, this is a time when the infant's environment teaches the infant about trust, hope, courage, and love, and about abandonment, inconsistencies, and deprivation. These experiences serve to establish the relationship the child has with his or her parents and caregivers. Whether a child has a healthy and happy environment or a threatening and scary one, these issues will eventually underlie or undermine later faith development.

Stage 1: Intuitive-Projective Faith

This occurs when a child is two to five years old. In this stage, a child is often permanently and strongly affected by the visible faith of primary caregivers (e.g., parents). Developmentally, children at this age have powerful imaginations and fantasies that are not inhibited by logical thought. This makes religious/ spiritual stories and images quite impactful and long-lasting if they are introduced at this time.

Stage 2: Mythic-Literal Faith

Children are around seven to nine years old in this stage. Developmentally, children at these ages are beginning to integrate the stories, beliefs, and observances of their family and community into their own sense of self, and their interpretations are often quite literal. The processes become more concrete, and there is a decrease in the use of imagination and fantasy. Stories become quite impactful and often become a primary way to give meaning to experiences, but the child is not able to step back and reflect or form conceptual meanings. In terms of spirituality and religion, symbolic and dramatic materials can affect a child powerfully and deeply; children can often describe things in endless detail but not be able to reflect on their meanings.

Stage 3: Synthetic-Conventional Faith

This often occurs during the teenage years when conformity is a primary focus. While teenagers might hold strong beliefs, these are largely unexamined. The person's identity has not been developed to a stage at which independent reflection is common. As a result, religious/spiritual values are often held simply because the family and/or community holds them. While the teenager's values might be deeply felt, they have not been independently or critically examined at a thorough level. This stage can extend into college and young adult years.

Stage 4: Individuative-Reflective Faith

This stage is less associated with a specific age but most likely occurs in young adulthood. However, this stage is highly correlated with the same ages of college attendance. Developmentally, the person begins to develop a sense of identity that is separate from family and community. The person begins to develop his or her own worldview, which may be different from, or in conflict with, those of important close friends and family. During this process, long-held beliefs and values are often tossed out en masse while the person sorts through what she or he believes versus what she or he was taught to believe. This obviously can include religious and spiritual beliefs, which can be a bit more difficult to reinforce and maintain owing to busy schedules and other challenges in the college environment. In addition, people in this stage often begin to notice contradictions in their faith or issues that their faith does not adequately address, and this can lead to increased questioning of faith.

Stage 5: Conjunctive Faith

This stage represents moving through some of the questions that were generated in the previous stage. A person is able to create a new sense of faith or spirituality that reflects his or her worldview and also accounts for paradoxes. This person might return to or re-embrace the faith in which she or he was raised or might find or create a new sense of faith through a different religion or spiritual practice or a combination of many. This person is also able to acknowledge and support the values of others and the various faiths they choose to embrace.

Stage 6: Universalizing Faith

Few people achieve this last stage, as it requires the person to take his or her faith and move it to a central role in his or her life. Often, this includes serving others in a faith-based way, and there are strong and deep ties to their faith that guide their actions. Most religious leaders, such as rabbis, priests, imams, and nuns, are at this stage. Mother Teresa is the perfect example of a person who achieved the epitome of all that this stage represents.

It is clear that Fowler's model shares some elements of Perry's nine positions of cognitive development (1981), as described in Chapter 6, as the person moves from seeing aspects of the world in very dualistic and clear-cut terms to seeing the complexity and pluralism of their faith and others'. This model also connects with several of Chickering's vectors (1993) and elements of integration as discussed by Tinto (1993).

What This Means to You

It is very likely that you will be moving through some of the stages that Fowler has articulated in your own personal development with regard to your faith. You will also most likely encounter other students who believe that spirituality is important to them in some way and are trying to find ways to express, maintain, or develop their faith while in college. If you are experiencing this yourself, you will find that you have many things in common with other students who are also on this journey. If this is not important to you, it's important to realize that it is a focus for many of your peers, and you might need to be sensitive to this aspect of campus diversity. Learning about the impact that faith, spirituality, and religion have on both individuals and diverse communities is a very important part of your education. It's one aspect of developing your cultural competence.

Might I Suggest...

College communities are often wonderful places to explore spirituality because many of the campus and local congregations are more focused on young adults than might be the case in your hometown. Churches, synagogues, mosques, temples, and other places of worship that are near college communities often offer services at times that work well for students' schedules. In addition, they might have an almost entirely student-age congregation as well as leaders who are close in age to college students. Many students find that there are avenues for their spiritual practice and expression that are age-appropriate and address the kinds of issues that college student often struggle with. With this in mind, I recommend seeking out and exploring religious/spiritual opportunities on or near your campus. It never hurts to check them out, and you might find that there are actually several to choose from. Explore them all until you find a good match between your own needs and interests and the services provided by the various organizations. In addition, I recommend intentionally learning about and exploring a wide variety of faiths, Even if you are very committed to your own, this will make you more knowledgeable about, and sensitive to, the experiences and values of different communities, and this will serve you in the future. You will also gain a better understanding of many global issues and conflicts that are rooted in religious beliefs.

The Impact of Economic Class on College Success

Across North America, high school students will find that their educational future is greatly affected by their parents' income and their socioeconomic status. Income is the amount of money their parents make each year, and socioeconomic status "refers to individual differences in wealth, income, economic power, or social position," according to the definition used by the United Nations. People often use terms such as *upper class, middle class,* and *working class,* which have sociopolitical ramifications. For the purpose of this chapter, we will focus primarily on parental income and its impact on a student's success.

According to the HERI study, the estimated parental income for 2003 freshmen ranges from less than $10,000 a year (3.1%) to more than $250,000 a year (5.5%). When grouped together, 30.6% of parents make less than $50,000 a year, another 38.2% make $50,000 to $99,999 a year, and 31.2% make more than $100,000 a year. Although students at a particular campus come from homes where their parents make from a little to a lot of money, they end up at the same university, taking the same classes, and competing with each other to do well, both academically and socially.

Long before many students set foot on a college campus, their future is shaped by their parents' income, and this affects their ability to apply for, be admitted to, and eventually attend and graduate from college. Students from middle- and higher-income families have far more resources and opportunities than do poorer students and therefore have a distinct advantage in college preparation and success. These advantages are separate from students' intellectual abilities and performance both in high school and on standardized tests.

Students from low-income households or communities find that they do not have access to the same educational opportunities as students from higher-income communities do. A primary difference has to do with the quality of the K–12 schools to which they have access. Not all junior high and high schools are equal in quality, nor do they receive the same resources. It is not uncommon for poorer public schools to lack current textbooks, honors and AP classes, computer labs, and adequately trained teachers and counselors, as well as other resources that help prepare students to be competitive when applying to colleges. Contrast this with public schools in higher-income neighborhoods, where you will find a plethora of qualified and certified teachers, plenty of current textbooks, many AP and honors courses, trained college advisors, up-to-date computer labs, and even classrooms with Internet access. Needless to say, students in one school will more likely to be prepared and competitive for admission to college than those just down the road at a poorer school.

In addition to the school's resources, each student's family resources play a role in college preparation. Low-income families tend to have one or both parents holding multiple jobs, which means that they might not be available to help the student with homework, drive him or her to practice, or attend college fairs.

The family might even need the student to work and contribute income to the household and this limits the student's opportunities to participate in cocurricular activities and to study adequately. The home might not have a computer or access to the Internet, a range of books, newspaper subscriptions, and other useful resources for academic work. A trip to the local library to access these resources might require use of public transportation if the family does not own a car, and libraries in low-income areas tend not to have as many resources and sometimes are not open as many hours as libraries in higher-income areas. Low-income students rarely can afford SAT preparation courses or private tutors, nor can they afford some of the costs associated with many popular extracurricular activities. Even basics such as medical and dental care might be scarce or nonexistent. Furthermore, poor communities tend to have higher crime rates, which can add stress and safety concerns to the equation. All of these things affect students' abilities to perform well and have the well-rounded experiences that make them competitive with their peers from higher-income families.

Even applying to college can be more challenging for the lower-income student. College choice often depends more on the cost of tuition and the availability of financial aid than on whether the campus is a good fit for the student academically and socially. In addition, attending a residential campus is far more expensive than living at home and commuting, so location may be a primary factor, especially if the student will need to continue working and sending money home while in college. The number of applications a student can submit can be affected by how many she or he can afford to file, regardless of grades. Even access to something as simple as a typewriter or computer to complete the application might require effort to locate and use. The HERI study found that 13% of college freshmen have major concerns about financing their college education and are not sure they will have enough funds to complete college, whereas 34.3% have no concerns at all because they have sufficient funds. And one third of college freshmen listed "was offered financial assistance" as a top reason for selecting the college they are currently attending.

Once the student is admitted to a university, the journey does not get easier. Most campuses provide some type of orientation program to help new students become adjusted to the college campus. Lower-income students might find the fees prohibitive or might not be able to afford to lose wages by taking off work to attend. It is more challenging to also afford the attendance of family members. Arriving at orientation might even require a bus or train ride. The wealthier students who can attend orientation gain important academic advising and even course selection priority over those who cannot attend.

For students who are able to attend a residential campus, economic disparity becomes very clear during the move-in process when some students are unpacking computers, stereos, lots of clothes, and mini-fridges. According to the HERI study, 77.4% of freshmen will live in a residence hall, and 16.4% will live with family or other relatives. Even things like splitting the phone bill can become an issue if one person wants lots of add-on features and the other can't afford them. Low-income students often begin to feel "different" at this stage and might feel somewhat disconnected socially from their wealthier peers. This can be aggravated if many social activities involve additional money, such as eating out, going to the movies, or dancing at nightclubs.

Higher-income students usually do not have to work to support themselves in school, so they have more time to focus on studying and getting involved in cocurricular activities. They also have more time in their schedules to utilize campus services such as advising, student health services, and educational workshops. If low-income students are working a lot (more than twenty hours per week), they often find that their academics suffer. Some even have work commitments at home with a family-owned business and might be traveling home every weekend. This obviously prevents the student from engaging in typical campus weekend activities such as studying and social events. If the working student is worried about money and faces difficulties in making ends meet, she or he might have to make hard choices about buying required textbooks or even eating three meals a day.

The 2001 report by the Advisory Committee on Student Financial Assistance found that low-income students attending four-year public institutions had an average unmet need of nearly $4,000: "even after financial aid has been awarded, low-income students need an average of $3,800 per year to meet the costs of college." More than half (51%) of low-income students who work at paid employment said that they could not afford a college education without doing so.

In 2002, the Higher Education Project of the States Public Interest Research Group (PIRG) published a report entitled *At What Cost? The Price That Working Students Pay for a College Education*. This national report found that 74% of all full-time college students also work while attending college. Of this group, 46% work twenty-five or more hours per week. The students who work the most, more than twenty-five hours per week, experience some difficulties: 42% of these students said that it negatively affected their grades, 53% said that working limited their class schedule, and 38% felt that it limited their choice of classes. Almost two thirds (63%) said that they could not afford college if they did not work full time.

What This Means to You

It is very rare to find a college campus that has a homogeneous student population in terms of income levels. Even the most expensive and elite private colleges admit low-income students and may provide financial support for their attendance. No matter what your own economic background is, you will find students who are both richer and poorer than you on your campus. As was stated above, economic disparity can create challenging interactions between students, and you will most likely experience some of these during your college experience. Learning about the impact that parental income and socioeconomic status have on both individuals and diverse communities is a very important part of your education. It's one aspect of developing your cultural competence.

Might I Suggest...

If you are a low-income student, you might want to prepare for interacting with other students who have more financial and material resources than you do. It can be frustrating at times to see others with more resources than you, especially if they take those resources for granted. You might have to work harder, and with less, than some of the students with whom you are competing in classes. This might feel unfair at times, and at times it is. These are normal feelings, but it is important not to let that get in the way of your success. When things get challenging, seek out support. There is most likely a service or department on our campus that serves low-income students (the educational opportunity program or the dean of students office might be a good place to start)—be sure you take advantage of the support that is available. The advisors in these programs are especially knowledgeable about campus resources that might be valuable to you. They can also advocate for you with financial aid and other campus departments.

Most universities provide access to important resources such as computer labs, transportation, and medical and dental care. Find out what resources are available to you and use them. If they are not open at the hours you need, speak to the director and make a request. Sometimes it takes a student speaking up for university administrators to realize that they could make some shifts that would make students' lives easier. Finally, form a network of friends who share your experiences. They can be a great support to you on difficult days, and you might even be able to pool your resources to assist in each other's success. It will also help you to deal with frustration you might feel with your wealthier peers who are most likely not aware of your financial situation.

If you are a middle- or high-income student, you might also face some challenges attending a campus that is economically diverse. First, you might experience some frustration if people assume that because you have financial resources, you have an easy college experience. This is absolutely not true—even high-income students struggle in college and have personal challenges that can interfere with their success. If you find that you are not being accurately understood, speak up for yourself. Also, don't feel guilty about what you have. It's a wonderful thing to have support and resources available to you, so enjoy them and appreciate them.

Second, you will probably be attending classes and perhaps living with low-income students. It is certainly not your responsibility to make their lives easier, but it can be helpful to be aware of, and sensitive to, some of the challenges that low-income students face. Being sensitive to someone's financial limitations and not putting them in awkward situations can be very helpful. This spares the low-income student the embarrassment of having to say that they cannot afford something or the loss of just not being able to participate. It's also supportive to honor someone's pride and not try to "help" them when they have not requested it. Most important, remember that good listening and communication skills can guide you in most interactions with students, regardless of the issue.

The quality of the high school environment also becomes evident in the first few weeks when higher-income students are finding that they are well prepared in their science, math, and writing classes. They will find that their instructors make references to information or books that they have either learned in high school or had access to in their home environments. This is often not the case for low-income students.

All of these issues add a layer of stress on the low-income student that higher-income students have the privilege not to experience. Low-income students not only carry the burden of making up for these lack of experiences and resources, but also must often do so alone (if they cannot access advising) and quietly, as many want to fit in with their student peers. Interestingly, research indicates that despite all these disadvantages, low-income students are more likely than their wealthier peers to make the most of their education (Flacks and Thomas, 1998). Students from disadvantaged backgrounds are more likely to value their education more than their privileged peers do as well as to utilize services more, interact with faculty more, volunteer more, and party/binge drink less.

Political Ideology

Another aspect of a student's identity is his or her political ideology. College students often arrive at campus having been socialized by the values of their family, neighborhood, school, community, spiritual center, and media. The degree to which college students are informed of, or care about, political matters has often been a function of their parents' views and activities as well as these other socializing entities. Political ideology is also influenced by a person's experiences. For example, membership in a marginalized group, such as an economic, ethnic, or sexual minority, brings about awareness of sociopolitical issues that members of the dominant group often cannot or do not see. In addition, a particular experience, such as being sexually assaulted or wrongly accused of theft, brings a painful awareness of the rights and experiences of people who have had a similar experience. These can lead to a greater awareness of, and commitment to, engaging in the political process on some level.

Not all students are particularly interested in or informed about political matters; other students are actively engaged in them. For some students, this interest is focused on the local campus community, where they participate in school government, while other students are more focused on state, national, or global matters and participate in activities that seek to bring about change. Either way, students will find most campuses to be hotbeds of political discussion on some level, as there are frequent forums, lectures, and informal conversations about all kinds of national and international matters.

Don Daves-Rougeaux, the Executive Director of Student Government at the University of California at Santa Barbara, has been involved in campus politics since his own student days in the 1980s. Now he mentors and advises the student government, including the elected student officers. He classifies students' political development on the following continuum:

- *Apathetic:* These students just don't care about politics of any sort.
- *Disillusioned:* These students are aware but don't believe that they can make a difference.
- *Actively uninformed:* These students actively choose to stay out of politics, often because they are too busy.
- *Aware but uninvolved:* These students are fairly aware of issues but choose to participate minimally, sometimes only through voting.
- *Conscious:* These students are aware of issues and participate on simple levels such as attending forums and rallies. They would probably get involved if approached but might not actively seek out involvement.
- *Active:* These students are keenly aware of issues and actively participate in a range of activities to bring about change; these are often the activists and are at the forefront of social change.

Any number of experiences can affect where someone is on the continuum, and movement on the continuum often coincides with college attendance, for a number of reasons. Since citizens in the United States cannot vote until the age of 18, the college years coincide with the student's first foray into participating in this country's political process. College students are an important voting entity to many parties and candidates, so students will find themselves subjected to many efforts to get them registered to vote and recruited to support certain issues or candidates.

In addition, each campus has a different kind of political climate. Universities have historically been places of political movements, especially movements that are counter to the status quo. University students have access to new ideas, cutting edge knowledge, and vast resources (access to computers, libraries, and free Internet access), as well as the time and energy (compared to working adults with families) to become informed and get involved. Students have often been the first to speak out and seem to be the most in tune with the changing moods of society. The protests against the Vietnam War began on college campuses, as did concern about apartheid in South Africa and the recent activities of the World Trade Organization. This is not just limited to campuses in the United States; the uprising in Tiananmen Square in China was the work of university students, including the brave soul who stood in front of the tanks while the world looked on. Students often see universities for what they are—institutions that are part of the bigger sociopolitical structure of the country—and change brought about at universities can have a ripple effect on the rest of society. If a campus is rife with political activism, the students who attend will be more likely to be exposed to, and possibly inspired by, their active peers.

A student's political ideology is often influenced by his or her personal commitment to being involved. Many students find that they do not have the time to be politically involved simply because of their academic and cocurricular commitments; other students prioritize their political involvement above their studies and participation in other campus activities. Activism inherently comes from dissatisfaction, so student activists are more likely affiliated with people who are marginalized in some way or who are aware of the marginalization of others.

Finally, university students are exposed to new aspects of political dialogue in the classroom. Most students at a liberal arts college will be required to take a course that focuses on some aspect of political issues, either domestic or foreign, that exposes them to new ideas, historical information, and multiple perspectives compared to those taught in high school. Some of these may come from the content of the course, and some may come from the personal views and life experiences of their faculty, who often have lived through some aspect of the history the course discusses.

A recent issue on many college campuses has stemmed from the perceived differences of political views between faculty and students. Students today, the Millennials, are more conservative politically than the previous generations who make up the faculty. According to the HERI study, college freshmen have become much more politically aware in the past thirty years, but political views and affiliations have also changed; many students have moved more to the center or right than previously (from 1970 to 2003). This can be compared to the political views of faculty, as shown in Table 7.8 (from a HERI study of college faculty done in 2001).

Students today are less liberal than their faculty, and this is creating a tension in classrooms across the United States. In 2003, when President Bush declared war on Iraq, many faculty expressed their displeasure in the classrooms and even staged "teach-ins" and "sit-ins"—the tactics that many of them used during their student days against the Vietnam War. Many students who did not share their faculty's views were frustrated by this activity and felt that it not only negatively affected their academic experience but was also an inappropriate use of the faculty's and institution's resources. Some students also have had faculty who made disparaging remarks about certain political leaders, ones for whom the students might have voted. This has led some students to feel uncomfortable in the classroom—afraid that if they disagree with the faculty member or put forth a different view, they might be treated differently than the other students. Others feel that their education is being shortchanged because they perceive a

Table 7.8   Political Views of Student and Faculty

Views	Students		Faculty
	1970	2003	2001
Far left	2.9%	2.8%	5.3%
Liberal	35.7%	24.2%	42.3%
Middle of road	43.4%	50.3%	34.3%
Conservative	17.3%	21.1%	17.7%
Far right	0.8%	1.6%	0.3%

What This Means to You

You will most likely find more political activities on your campus than you have seen before. You will be exposed to ideas and views that you might have never heard of before or are vehemently opposed to. Whether or not you choose to be politically active, you will still be surrounded by political discussions and debates, especially during election years. Learning about the impact that political ideology has on both individuals and diverse communities is a very important part of your education. It's one aspect of developing your cultural competence.

lack of intellectual diversity in which several different and opposing viewpoints can be explored.

As was discussed in Chapter 1, academic freedom is a cornerstone of the tenure system and the research university. Some faculty feel that this gives them the right to believe, say, and teach anything they desire in their classrooms as long as it does not cross any legal or ethical boundaries—an aspect of freedom of speech. Others feel that political and personal views belong in the classroom only if they are specifically relevant to the content of the course being taught. There has been a recent surge of activity nationwide around this issue. Many articles have appeared in the *Chronicle of Higher Education,* a weekly publication that discusses current issues in higher education. In addition, conservative speaker David Horowitz has created an "Academic Bill of Rights" that he claims is aimed at creating more balanced intellectual diversity in college classrooms (http://studentsforacademicfreedom.org/abor.html). Others feel that this bill is a hindrance to academic freedom and is an attempt to silence more liberal views. Regardless of where you stand on this issue, you will most likely hear it debated on your university campus and in the national media.

There are many more aspects of identity that clearly affect the student experience, and each is worthy of a chapter, if not an entire book. For the sake of space, this chapter focuses on the elements of identity that are most often mentioned in research on the first-year experience. However, it is important to know that the experiences of the following populations, and many others, are worthy of exploration and reflection: immigrant status, physical ability, physical appearance and size, language or dialect, marital and parental status, and military involvement. Your campus has courses, programs, and services that address these aspects, and it is important that you seek them out.

Building Community

Institutions of higher education tend to have a strong commitment to creating a diverse community. Research universities in particular have an impetus for being committed to building a diverse community because the creation of new

Might I Suggest...

College is a wonderful time to gain more information about current events and political issues locally, nationally, and abroad. You will find that most universities host internationally renowned speakers and authors, and students can attend for very low cost or even no cost. After graduation, you will not have the same kind of access to these forums and debates, so it's an excellent idea to take advantage of them. Campuses usually bring many famous speakers to campus, from biologists to historians to politicians. Usually, the speakers who are doing a speaking tour are in the news and represent some of the current views on a wide range of topics. Again, this is an excellent opportunity to open your mind to other thoughts, ideas, and views and to increase your cultural competence.

In addition, you will be able to actively participate in the political process through campus, local, state, and federal elections. You will be able to make decisions that affect your daily experiences as a student on your campus, as a member of your local town or county, as a resident of your state, and as a resident of this country. Your voice really does matter, and your vote really does count—so vote! But before you do, get informed. Whether you are voting on a campus referendum to build a new stadium or for the president of the United States, find and read information about the issue or candidate, go to public debates, and use the critical thinking skills you have developed.

knowledge is based on the premise that all views and perspectives should be explored. Without the ability to consider alternative ideas or solutions, true discovery would be seriously impeded. In addition, ideas and thoughts need to be able to be voiced, critiqued, and evaluated within a context of honest and respectful exploration. For these reasons, the community of scholars is committed to creating an environment for respectful discourse, even when its members are in vehement opposition to one another on certain ideas or beliefs.

In addition, since prejudice and discrimination (e.g., racism, classism, religious oppression, sexism, homophobia) still exist in society and in its institutions, including higher education, university communities are actively engaged in dialogue about these issues. You will find that many groups and individuals at your campus spend time and energy discussing matters of race, class, sexual orientation, political ideology, and the whole range of primary and secondary identities.

Together, these conditions form a strong motivation for universities to create *true* community among a diverse group of members, where all people are valued and respected. Diversity, without respectful relationships, would not be enough to build community because diversity, in and of itself, often breeds conflict as people have opposing views, beliefs, and experiences. In addition, individuals always bring their personal biases and prejudices, both conscious and unconscious, to their interactions.

As members of the diverse community of scholars, you will also be in a place to participate in community building on many levels. It's important for you to know that this is a large part of your university experience, and, more important, your education. Many students find the information presented in this chapter to be a bit eye-opening. This is normal—as humans, we have only our own personal experience in the world, and it is often not easy to think about how someone else's experience might differ from ours, especially in a place like a university community where people are sharing the same daily experiences in ways that most communities do not. College can create a unique sense of community among students simply because of the commonality of sharing large classes, late-night study sessions, boisterous sporting events, engaging instructors, and fun parties. Many students find a sense of camaraderie with others in sharing and surviving the trials of university life.

However, this camaraderie can often mask important differences that students feel affect their college experience. For example, a male student might feel perfectly safe on campus and never consider that his female friend does not—they share so many other experiences and feelings that this might not cross his mind. Likewise, a White student might always feel comfortable in the dining commons, not ever considering that her Latina roommate might feel suddenly self-conscious about being a "minority," especially if the campus is not particularly diverse in terms of ethnicity. Generally, being in the minority of a campus's population creates additional challenges and experiences to those experienced by the students in the majority. Regardless of which aspect you experience for the different parts of your identity, you will want to listen to, and learn about, the experiences and views of others.

The goal of this chapter is to give you information about the experiences that are affecting you and your peers, even if you do not see them or experience them directly yourself. The concept of building community requires people not only to embrace that which they do share, but also to become informed about, and sensitive to, those things that are *not* shared. The primary focus of getting an education is about learning those things that you did *not* previously know—in other words, becoming open-minded in the fullest sense of the word. This is true not only in terms of courses such as physics and anthropology, but also in terms of the human experience and the diversity that it represents. Building community is an active process that requires everyone to be open to learning in order to better the experience for all.

It is important to actively engage in this process, not only for the sake of your campus community but also for your own future. As was stated at the beginning of this chapter, many employers are now acutely aware of the multicultural country and global community in which they must prosper. Many are seeking to hire students who have developed what is termed *cultural competence,* which is an awareness of these various ideas of identity and how they might shape a person's experience. Your education will be enhanced if you actively seek to gain this cultural competence by exploring various aspects of identity and how they shape the human experience. Your campus probably has many services and programs that will expose you to these concepts, such as academic courses (e.g., history, ethnic studies, and sociology), discussions, films, lectures, readings, informational fairs, and performances. Take advantage of them! Enroll in courses, attend events, participate in forums, ask questions, listen to answers, and continue to expand your knowledge.

One of the best sources to help you expand your cultural competence is your fellow members of the campus community. They will have many different views, ideas, and experiences with these issues, and it's important to listen. By listening, you will gain something very precious: knowledge that is denied to you because of your own individual identities. If you are a male, you will *never* be able to have the experience of being female in this society—but you can learn about it by listening, asking questions, and, most importantly, believing what someone tells you. A White person can never know what it is like to experience racial discrimination and oppression on a regular basis, and a straight person cannot appreciate the fear that homophobic remarks generate. The same is true for every single one of the primary and secondary identities mentioned at the beginning of this chapter. Seek out experiences that will help you to grow in all areas of cultural competence. However, it's important to gain many different

Adam's Story

Growing up in downtown Sacramento and going to a very diverse high school, I went to college thinking that I was a very accepting person; someone who was very comfortable with all races, gender and sexuality. During my freshman year, my roommate was Black and we had many friends on my dorm floor that were minority students. At first, I thought that everything was fine and that we all got along great. As I started to pay attention to my surroundings more, I noticed that there were different "interest" floors in my residence hall, like the African American floor, the Chicano floor and so on. I felt that all these floors did was to segregate students into their different backgrounds and this made me mad because I believe that diversity is important. I even got into a discussion with my roommate about how uncomfortable I felt when I was on one of those floors. I felt that I stood out and that everyone was looking at me because I was different. However, my roommate told me that he felt this way most of the time. In fact, the only place he *didn't* feel out of place was on the African American floor or at predominately Black events. I had never realized this and I couldn't imagine how hard it would be to feel uncomfortable most of every day. After that discussion, I started to see the real makeup of our campus and that almost every class and event was predominately White. I had never noticed that before. It made me realize that I was very privileged in society and in the college realm, not only being White, but being male and straight. Since then, I have made an effort to learn more about diversity of all kinds and how it impacts people in our society. I have also come to accept that I have privileges that other people don't have and that I can either ignore that I do or I can do my part to make our society better.

views as well. It is generally not a good idea to ask one woman about an issue and think that you know how *all* women feel. Nor does it make sense to conclude that one person of color speaks for his or her entire group or for all minorities. Every identity has a vast range of diversity within it because of the complex interplay between the primary and secondary identities. Seek out many, many experiences to successfully gain a richer and therefore more accurate understanding.

Students, especially those in the minority, often find themselves cast in the role of spokesperson for their group and spend much of their time educating others. While many of these students want to help others learn, it can also be very tiring because it is an ongoing process. Within one week, a student might be asked several times to explain something about his or her culture, group, or experience. Even though many of these inquiries are genuine requests for education, they are still an additional responsibility on top of those of being a university student. For that reason, it is important to look at the many different ways in which you can educate yourself about the issues. This is especially useful because it empowers you to work on your own learning and not always need other people to teach you. Another great way to learn about the experiences of others is to read books and watch movies that focus on issues of identity. At the end of this book, you will find a list of books, films and websites (see Appendix B). Read and watch as many as you can. It is another way to actively increase your cultural competence.

The Dynamics of Oppression

Unfortunately, not everyone on a university campus is informed about, and sensitive to, the experiences of others, nor are they actively working to build community. Oppression exists on university campuses, just as it exists in all elements of our society. In addition to its presence on campuses, oppression has already affected many of the lives and experiences of it members, as seen in the various identity development models described earlier in this chapter. This directly affects relationships and interactions on campuses because past painful experiences have shaped how people view themselves and others. This ultimately affects communication, respect, and trust between individuals and groups.

Although you might be an open-minded and aware individual, it doesn't mean that your roommates and friends are. The truth is that students regularly experience ignorant comments and attitudes from their peers, which deny their real experiences, feelings, or both. In addition, some people (students, staff, and faculty) hold stereotypes of, or engage in prejudicial or discriminatory behavior against, other members of the campus community. Negative slurs, jokes, and comments are heard at parties, in classes, in living environments, and in neighborhoods. Some students even experience physical harassment, vandalism, and assault because of their identities. These words and actions can greatly harm the overall feelings of acceptance and even safety that a student feels in the university environment, thus destroying a sense of community.

Some of these phrases or words are recognized as offensive by everyone, so their use is usually intentional. with the purpose of degrading a person or group. Other words and phrases, such as "That's so gay," have become popular among young adults without people really understanding the negative impact they have on people. This concept of "intent versus impact" is a useful one to consider. In many cases, tension between individuals or groups around issues of identity often stem from confusion about the intent versus the impact of words and actions. One student might feel offended or hurt by the words or actions of another (the *impact*) while the other student didn't mean it that way (*intent*). These two people can end up arguing unless they are able to hear each other. The first person would need to believe that the intent was not negative, and the other person would need to acknowledge that the impact was indeed negative. If both parties can explore intent versus impact, many possibilities for understanding and reconciliation are created.

As a student, you might receive feedback that some of your own words or actions have impacts other than those you intended. You might learn that you said or did something that offended or hurt another member of the community. While it can be difficult to hear this feedback, the fact that the other person shared it with you is a sign that they see the possibility for more positive interactions with you and wish to build community. If you wish to build positive relationships with other individuals or groups, take this feedback and examine how you might incorporate it. Everyone is learning how to navigate diversity and build community, so mistakes are to be expected as part of this process. If the intent is positive, then words and actions can be adjusted to create the desired impact.

While many students are able to create tolerance and respect in their own words and actions, they are not always sure what to do when they see or hear others violating these standards. It can be difficult to overhear a racist joke or witness a homophobic act and not be sure how to respond. Many people wrongly assume that the person who was the target of the joke or act should speak up about it, but often that person is too stunned, hurt, or fearful to respond. Another situation that often occurs is that people say and do offensive things *only* when members of the target group are not around to see it or hear it—implying that there is some kind of unspoken agreement among the rest of the people that it's okay to do this. Unfortunately, you will probably find yourself in situations in which you see and hear things that offend your belief in tolerance and respect and are a threat to the sense of community.

To understand some of the concepts underlying these kinds of campus interactions, it is useful to explore some theories about societal groups and the dynamics of oppression. Adams, Bell, and Griffin (1997) argue that for every major identity in our society, there is a group that is in the majority and another that is in the minority, in terms of numbers and/or representation in power structures such as the government, legal system, education, and media. Because the minority group is not represented in the power structures, its members tend to be misunderstood by the rest of society. In addition, various events in U.S. history have contributed to negative connotations about the minority group for every primary identity. For example, Native Americans were feared as ruthless murderers during the expansion out west, Asian Americans were feared as enemies after Japan bombed Pearl Harbor during World War II, and some people have assumed all Muslims are terrorists since 9/11. As a result, the minority group is likely to suffer various forms of oppression, usually aimed at them by the majority group.

Stereotypes, prejudice, discrimination, and "isms," such as sexism or racism, are all part of oppression. Some occur at the individual level and then build to become systemic or societal. The National Conference for Community and Justice (www.nccj.org), which is dedicated to "promoting understanding and respect among all races, religions, and cultures through advocacy, conflict resolution, and education," discusses many of these topics in its workshops and retreats that are hosted nationally at high schools, colleges, and corporations. Jarrod Schwartz (2000), who expanded on the work of Kate Kirkham, created a model to explain the dynamics of oppression. According to Schwartz, stereotypes are fixed ideas about a group or person that are based on information gained from societal systems such as media, education, and interactions. Stereotypes live in individual's thoughts and can be positive or negative, but they do not tend to match reality. For example, Black men are often stereotyped as criminals, and Asian students are often seen as good at math.

Prejudice is "pre-judging" a person or a group, and the judgment is usually based on stereotypes. This leads to feelings of like or dislike, of fear or comfort, and also occurs on the individual level, as it is housed in feelings—for example, feeling fear or distrust around Black men or feeling jealous of an Asian student. Discrimination occurs when stereotypes and prejudice become expressed as actions or behaviors toward another person or group. This is when it leaves the internal world of an individual's thoughts or feelings and become expressed as visible words or actions—for example, not giving a Black man an application for a job or apartment or asking an Asian student for help with homework simply because he or she is Asian.

Finally, systemic oppression occurs when enough people share stereotypes, prejudice, and discrimination that these get woven in the policies, procedures, laws, and systems of the larger society and culture. For example, laws that allow for racial profiling and are used to target Blacks, or the difference between crack and cocaine laws when the substance is the same but the populations who use the two forms are different. Table 7.9 shows how these concepts are related.

These systems then feed or confirm the stereotypes, thus creating a cycle of socialization that affects the next generation in society. While this describes a broad pattern, the history of oppression for each minority group is unique. To learn more about a specific group, enroll in ethnic studies and history courses that explore these concepts in detail and can illuminate the specific historical events and societal factors that contributed to the oppression of that group.

Hardiman and Jackson (1997) argue that in most societies, the minority group experiences oppression of some kind while the majority group does not. The group that does not experience oppression is often referred to as the *nontarget group,* or the *group with privilege,* as they have the privilege of not experiencing

Table 7.9   Dynamics of Oppression

	Intrapersonal (Within Individuals)	Interpersonal (Between Individuals or Groups)	Systemic/ Institutional
Thoughts	Stereotype		
Feelings	Prejudice		
Behaviors		Discrimination	
Policies, Procedures, Practices, Structures, etc.			Systemic oppression

the negative actions and words that make up the various forms of oppression. The minority group is often called the *oppressed* or the *target group* because they are the targets of various forms of oppression. Hardiman and Jackson have explored the privilege and target groups for many of the primary identities discussed earlier, and they are illustrated in Table 7.10.

It is clear that any individual can be in both privileged groups and target groups for various aspects of his or her identity. For example, a disabled man would have privilege around gender but could experience oppression around

Table 7.10   Partial List of Privileged and Target Groups in the United States

Identity	Privileged Group	Target Group
Race and ethnicity	Whites	People of color
Gender	Men	Women
Age	Adult	Young, elderly
Religion	Christians	Jews, Muslims, Buddhists, etc.
Sexual orientation	Heterosexuals	Lesbian, gay, bisexual, transgender people
Economic class	Middle and upper class	Poor and working class
Disability (psychological, physical, developmental)	Able people	Disabled people

---

What This Means to You

Regardless of how you view issues of oppression or your personal experiences with them, you will find that they are frequently discussed and hotly debated on university campuses. The concepts of privilege, oppression, and stereotypes, are mentioned in many social science and humanities courses, as these disciplines seek to explore various aspects of society. You will also find them discussed in residence halls, student activities, public performances, and casual conversations. You will find many opportunities to learn more about these issues and to engage in both analytical and passionate discussions about them. In addition, you will witness many of these concepts at play in interactions among the members of your campus community. You will have many opportunities to explore your own relationship to these issues and to take responsibility for your words and actions as well as the opportunity to interact with others about these topics.

---

ability. A heterosexual would have privilege around sexual orientation but could be targeted if he or she is not Christian. And a White person would have race privilege but might be targeted for gender or economic class. This makes understanding these concepts incredibly complex because there is a multitude of layers, and people have a range of experiences. This also means that there are no "bad guys" or "good guys," since everyone experiences both sides of the privilege/oppression coin and many of the identity development models are the process by which individuals discover, react to and adjust their perceptions of their own group and other groups. The fact that every person in the United States shares the experience of privilege and oppression allows for diverse groups of people to connect, since they probably can identify with others around these experiences.

However, just because all people share the dynamics of oppression doesn't mean that they have no responsibility for changing these dynamics. Some theorists who study the dynamics of oppression believe that there are several players in any oppressive situation. There is the person or people who are engaging in the oppressive acts toward others, there are those who are experiencing the oppression, and then there are the bystanders. According to Griffin and Harro (1982), people's reactions to oppression fall along a continuum, with actions that either support oppression (in other words, colluding with it), and actions that confront oppression. Their model is illustrated in Figure 7.1.

Griffin and Harro argue that "actively participating" involves actions against people or groups (e.g., telling offensive jokes, insulting, avoiding, verbally or physically harassing) based on their identity. Some of these folks truly believe that another group is bad or inferior, but young adults sometimes participate in these activities just to be "cool" without really thinking about the true meaning of their actions or words. The next group are people who "deny or ignore" that oppression exists. When they hear someone describe an incident in which she or he felt

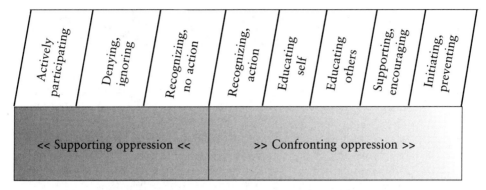

Figure 7.1 Action Continuum for Oppression

discriminated against, they are likely to say things like "You're being too sensi-tive" or "You took that the wrong way." This still supports oppression, even though they might not be actively oppressing others themselves. Similarly, peo-ple who recognize that oppression is occurring but still take no action are also supporting oppression. Often, this lack of action stems from confusion about what is happening, uncertainty about what actions to take, and fear.

Confronting oppression has various levels as well, each making an effort to end oppression. The first level of recognizing oppression and taking action in-volves both confronting others and changing one's own language and actions if they are oppressive in some way—in other words, honoring impact regardless of intent. At this stage, a person might interrupt a racist joke that is being told. The stage of "educating self" is about taking actions to learn more about op-pression and groups through the many ways already discussed in this chapter. Educating others moves beyond the self to engaging with others and discussing the issues. With regard to a racist joke, in addition to just stopping it, a person in this stage might initiative a discussion about why the joke is offensive. "Sup-porting and encouraging" is about connecting with others who are committed to confronting oppression by joining groups and organizations and supporting others who are speaking out against it. Finally, "initiating and preventing" moves to working on dismantling oppression in the larger context of systems, policies, and institutions. This might involve planning educational programs, working for passing relevant legislation, and ensuring the full inclusion of op-pressed groups in organizations. Many student activists are working at this stage of the continuum, although they might be doing it for only one or two groups.

This concept of confronting oppression is known by another phrase—it is called *being an ally,* and you will hear this phrase on many campuses across the country. An *ally* is someone who is not experiencing oppression of a certain type

Might I Suggest...

Seriously consider the topics of discrimination and oppression and also the roles that you currently play in the dynamics of oppression, both as a member of some privileged groups and as a member of some target groups. If you are interested in becoming an ally to others, consider the following:

1. Assume that you have the perfect right to be concerned about other people's oppression and that it is in your best interest to do so and to be an ally.
2. Think about the privileged and target groups you belong to—recognize privilege where you have it and oppression where you experience it.
3. Believe that people from oppressed groups are the experts on their own experience and that, as an ally, you have much to learn from them.
4. Recognize that membership in one or more oppressed groups does not absolve you of the responsibility of being an ally to members of an oppressed group to which you do not belong.
5. Take responsibility for learning about oppressed groups' history of struggle and resistance, as well as the history of how allies have engaged in struggles involving the rights of oppressed groups. Learn as much as you can about issues affecting oppressed groups. Seek out information sources (e.g., books, magazines, films, courses, other media) that are authored by people from that group. Create opportunities for learning about these issues and histories for members of your own group through invited speakers, films, forums, book clubs, and the like.
6. Begin to act as an ally now, as best you know how, but be open to feedback, criticism, and learning. Do not let the fact that you "do not know enough" be an excuse. Everyone always has more to learn, and everyone is learning.
7. Start where you are. Being an ally can take many different forms, and all contribute to ending oppression. Review Figure 7.1, and start by taking actions where you are and then take more. There is no ranking of "fair-good-excellent" allies, so focus on making a difference in your own sphere and honor your comfort zone. Also, you might find that certain identities are easier for you to connect with. Maybe it's easier to start with race or class. That's fine. Focus on learning in those areas and using some of the strategies listed here. Then, down the road, review the list of identities and choose the next identity issue to explore and take action on.
8. Recognize that as a member of a privileged group, you know best how to use your privilege to interrupt oppressive attitudes and behaviors among members of your own group. Recognize that as an ally, you have the responsibility to work to improve your ability to do this and develop other allies by sharing strategies that have worked for you. You can certainly learn

more about being an ally through the Internet, various books, and workshops on campus.

9. Assume that other people in your group also want to be allies to people in minority or oppressed groups. You are not the exception to the rule. Assume that you will always have something to learn about how to be a more effective ally. Have confidence in your ability to be an effective ally and to help others be more effective as well.

10. Realize that members of the oppressed group can spot "oppressor socialization" (behavior that perpetuates privilege and oppression). Realize that as a member of a privileged group, you often do not. Do not try to "convince" them that this conditioning did not happen to you—it happened to everyone who was raised in the United States.

11. Unlearning oppressive behavior is one step toward building a stronger, more inclusive movement for ending oppression; it allows us to communicate and work together better so that we may collectively fight oppression better. It is *not* so that you can learn to be less personally or overtly prejudiced or to assuage the guilt you might feel as a member of a privileged group.

12. Assume that people in the oppressed group want you and members of your group as allies but that their experience of oppression and previous experiences with members of your group might make them reluctant to accept you as such. Recognize that considering the history of mistreatment and mistrust between some groups, actions often speak louder than words.

13. Do not expect gratitude from members of the oppressed group. Remember, being an ally is a matter of choice for you, being oppressed is not. If you are committed to social justice, being an ally is a responsibility.

14. Be a 100% ally, with no strings attached. For example, do not allow yourself to think, "I'll oppose your oppression if you oppose mine." Everyone's oppression needs to be opposed unconditionally. Nobody wins a competition of oppressions, so resist thinking of oppression in a hierarchical way.

15. Being an ally is an action, not a status. You must be *doing something* to "be" an ally.

16. Remember that we are never done. Fighting oppression is a lifelong process. Pace yourself and don't expect ever to "arrive." You will certainly see your own growth, and you will participate in changes that are visible on your campus or in our society, but as long as there are majority and minority groups, there will be a need for allies.

Adapted from a handout entitled "Strategies for Allies," author unknown.

but who takes a stand against the oppression of another. Any person can be an ally to another, but this concept is most often applied when talking about the primary identities that were mentioned at the beginning of this chapter. In essence, being an ally is often about using the privileges you have to fight oppression and bring about social change for others.

As was noted above, there are several primary and secondary identities, and each has a privileged and target group. An ally is a person of the privileged group (e.g., men, Whites, heterosexuals) who takes a stand against social injustice directed at people in the target groups. For example, an ally would be a White person who confronts a racist joke, a man who fights for equal wages for women, a wealthy person who votes for laws that benefit poor people, or a Christian who speaks out against vandalism of Jewish or Muslim sanctuaries. An ally works to be an agent of social change rather than supporting oppression. Members of the target groups can also be allies to other communities, for example, an African American who confronts homophobia or a young person who protests budget cuts to Medicare for the elderly. This means that people can be allies to several communities simultaneously.

Chapter Summary

In this chapter, the following topics were discussed:

- Diversity of the university community

- Age and generational issues

- Race and ethnic identity
  - Minority identity development model
  - White racial consciousness development model
  - Biracial and multiracial identity development model

- Gender and sexual orientation
  - Gender and biological sex
  - Sexual orientation
  - Lesbian/gay identity development model
  - Heterosexual identity development model

- Spiritual identity
  - Faith development model

- Impact of economic class on college success

- Political ideology in the campus community

- Building community
  - Dynamics of oppression

Reflections and Exercises

1. Reflecting on Diversity

This exercise, developed by The Dialogue Consultants with assistance from Dawn Bond, is best done by limiting your focus to the following primary dimensions of identity: race/ethnicity, sex/gender, sexual orientation, political ideology, religion/spirituality, immigrant status, and physical/learning disability. Keeping this list in mind, answer the following questions:

Which aspect of your identity most emphasized while you were growing up? How?

Which aspect of your identity least emphasized while you were growing up? How?

Which aspect of your identity are you most reminded of day to day on campus? What do you experience?

Which aspect of your identity are you the most proud of? Why?

If you could ask others to be an ally to an aspect of your identity, which aspect would you choose? What would you want them to do or say?

2. Observing Oppression

Choose one or two identities that you know are in the minority on your campus but that you are not a member of. For one week, keep a log of your observations of how members of those groups are treated. Consider the following questions, ascertaining intent versus impact when possible:

What identities did you choose to observe?

What interactions between people did you observe?

How are members of these identity groups represented on campus? What percentage of the student population do they make up? The staff population? The faculty population?

How, if at all, are members of these groups portrayed in campus publications? The local media? National media?

What did you notice over the week?

How did these aspects of identity shape the interactions you observed?

How were members of the identity groups you chose discussed when their members were present?

How about when no members of that group were present?

Describe the interactions you observed in which the intent was not the same as the impact. How could these interactions have been made better for the parties involved?

What did you learn from doing this activity?

3. If You Haven't Lived It, Learn about It!

One way to learn about people who are different from yourself is to explore the vast array of human experiences through books, films, and videos. Select a group or population for which you would like to become more knowledgeable about their experiences. Use Appendix B to select two or three books on that population and read them; you can also use films.

What were the majors themes represented in the books or films you chose?

How did these themes relate to the concepts presented in this chapter?

What similarities existed between the books or films?

What were the differences?

How do you think the themes presented relate the college experience in general?

How do they relate to the experiences of students on your campus?

Chapter 8

Leadership Development and Involvement Opportunities

In addition to completing degree requirements, many university students wish to gain leadership experience in order to make a difference on their campus and to prepare themselves for future careers. Even the most focused student scholars find that their education is enriched by engaging in cocurricular activities. Whether you are interested in getting involved just to have a little break from your studies, you wish to bring about change on your campus or in the larger community, or you want to seriously develop your leadership skills, you will find a host of options available to you. This chapter will cover the importance of leadership development, review two theoretical models of leadership, and provide an overview of opportunities for getting involved on university campuses.

The Importance of Involvement and Leadership as Part of Higher Education

A successful university education is not measured just by completed requirements and exemplary grades. It is also about how a student matures and develops as a person and a future leader. It is a widely held assumption that the next generation of local, national, and world leaders are cultivated at university campuses where the brightest minds gather to be educated. As a result, universities tend to offer a plethora of opportunities for leadership development as a way to provide a training ground for future leaders. These opportunities reflect a wide range of options from the curricular to cocurricular and even many that are off-campus. These different kinds of involvement can provide significant experiential training for both graduate school and future careers. Thousands of students graduate each year with a degree from a research university, but far fewer also have a well-developed resume built on involvement and leadership. The students who do are highly sought after by graduate programs and employers because they have already demonstrated high levels of maturity and leadership.

Another consideration is that getting involved in some aspect of campus life directly contributes to a student's university success. First, getting involved can positively affect both academic and social integration, as described by Tinto (1993) in Chapter 6. Curricular and cocurricular opportunities allow students to develop their scholarship and leadership skills while also connecting with other members of the campus community.

Furthermore, getting involved and holding leadership positions are ways in which undergraduate students can play an active role in affecting their campus community, an aspect of citizenship. Faculty, administrators, and staff come to campus each day for their jobs and might not always accurately see the current state of the student experience. These people are often older than undergraduate students and have different needs and considerations. As a result, it is often the leadership and commitment of the students that brings about important changes to campus. Many student leaders believe that it is a responsibility to do so. How else can we ensure that our universities change and grow in ways that are appropriate for the education of future generations?

Separate from affecting the university community, many people argue that leadership roles in college prepare young adults for leadership roles with the larger state, national, and global community. In fact, many argue that the real purpose of a college education is to create leaders who make a difference in the world.

The Purpose and Power of a College Education

Dr. Claudine Michel has some wonderful thoughts about the purpose and power of a college education. She has a Ph.D. in international education and has been on the faculty of the University of California at Santa Barbara for nineteen years. She is adored by students—her classes are always filled to overflowing, and students line up at her office hours, more often just to talk with her than to review an assignment. She talks about education as not a tangible thing that you can buy, but a process, a lifelong process that opens our minds and opens doors for us. She often recounts the life of the famous slave, Frederick Douglass, to make her point. Douglass was being taught to read by his mistress, and one day, his master discovered them and was very angry. Douglass recounts hearing the master say, "Do you realize that if you educate him, you will forever make him unfit to be a slave?" It was at that moment that Douglass realized that education was the pathway to freedom, literally. He eventually escaped and became a famous orator.

Dr. Michel goes on to say that when you really educate someone, you open all kinds of doors and opportunities for that person, and you literally change his or her life forever. Education is a process that develops important abilities, plays a role in socializing people to fit in a society, is the key to many important opportunities, and develops not only a person's mind, but also his or her heart and character. To deny someone an education is to deny him or her the opportunity to learn and develop critical faculties that are necessary to take charge of one's life and to make contributions to the world.

The importance of education in the global context is underscored by examining how it is utilized in countries around the world. Many governments have used the power of education—more accurately, the power of denying people access to education—to stay in power and control the people. A recent documentary film entitled *Tibet: Cry of the Snow Lion* details the plight of people in Tibet. The government of China, which does not wish to acknowledge Tibet as a free country, has done many things to control the people of Tibet, including destroying Buddhist monasteries, murdering dissidents, and closing down all the schools so that Tibetan children can no longer get an education. The parents of small children in Tibet, desperate for them to have access to education, send the children on dangerous treks across the Himalayan mountains to escape. They take this journey to reach a school outside of Tibet that is run by Tibetan monks. There, they can live with the monks and complete their schooling. Many children, as young as 3 and 4 years old, die on these trips as they travel through freezing mountain passes wearing little but cotton clothing. Even if they do survive, most never see their families again. The story of these people clearly illustrates the power of education and that people will risk death to have access to it. Education creates freedom, and it gives people the power to change the world.

Dr. Michel argues that education should do three things: inform, form, and transform. Informing, of course, is the process of taking people from one level of knowledge to another level by providing them with facts, information, perspectives, and interpretations. This process is closely linked with Bloom's hierarchy of knowledge described in Chapter 1. Forming is about the process by which people take new knowledge and form new values and beliefs. At this point, people take ownership for what they think, what they are about, and how they will live their lives on the basis of what they have learned. The final process of transforming is about using your education to transform—to better yourself, your family, your community, your country, and your planet.

In that context, Dr. Michel quotes Hymon Johnson, who said, "Education without responsible use is of no use." The power of education needs to be taken seriously and honored for the privileges it provides. It should not be used for frivolous goals but to bring about change in the world. Dr. Michel argues that this is especially true for students at a research university. Research universities are the top educational institutions in the world, with a cadre of brilliant minds brought together in the community of scholars. The best and brightest are admitted to research universities, giving these students even more responsibility for using their education for the common good, especially if those institutions are publicly funded, because taxpayers are funding their education in order to develop future leaders. Only 28% of adults in the United States have a college degree, and far fewer attended research universities. Some research universities, such as the University of California, admit a limited top percentage of the state's high school graduates (12.5%); this model is echoed at campuses across the country. Dr. Michel argues that this 12.5% of students have a responsibility to the other 87.5% to use their education to be leaders and make the state, country, and world a better place in which to live. She believes that you have a responsibility to use this amazing privilege (attending a research university) to better not only your own life, but also the lives of others. Every student should ask himself or herself, "How can I use my education to be the voice of others who are not here? How can I improve their experience?"

Examples of Outstanding Student Leaders

To give you an idea of the kind of leadership that students demonstrate during their years at a research university, here are the stories of some of the winners of the highest leadership awards given at research universities in the United States. These descriptions are excerpted from the 2004 awards programs.

Brian Still Smoking, Montana State University, Bozeman

Brian Still Smoking of Browning is the winner of the Outstanding Graduate Achievement Award for a Master's Student. Still Smoking maintained a 3.97 grade point average while earning a master's degree in architecture. Still Smoking is a leader in the School of Architecture's Community Design Center. The Browning native's instinctual understanding of urban communities resulted in a plan for the MSU Urban Design Studio that was praised by professors from Columbia University for its clarity of understanding and insightfulness. Still Smoking is working with Daniel Glenn, architecture professor, in the design and development of the Seven Buffalo Lodge on the Crow Reservation. He has been active as a leader in the Arts Link Program for high school students and helped form the Native American Students in Arts and Architecture Mentorship Program. Still Smoking is a recipient of the Phyllis Berger and Third Row scholarships for academic achievement.

JonJoseph Aranas Gatchalian, University of California, Santa Barbara

JonJoseph is one of the recipients of the 2004 University Award of Distinction. J.J. made important contributions to the quality of life for disabled individuals at UCSB through his participation in a research project that evaluated campus accessibility for people with disabilities, his advocacy for educational mainstreaming, and his work on music literacy for musicians with visual impairments. His contributions are all the more remarkable because he has been blind from birth and was diagnosed with Hodgkin's lymphoma in his freshman year. Despite these challenges, J.J. persevered and did outstanding scholarship in his major while working to benefit future students with disabilities.

Jennifer Garlich, University of Missouri, Columbia

Jennifer Garlich is the winner of the 2004 Community Service Leadership Award. Jennifer helped construct a service organization from an idea to reality. She had a dream of building an organization in which students who want to serve, but who cannot commit to it on a regular basis, can have the opportunity to play a vital role in bettering their community. Along with a few others last year, Jennifer helped develop Service on Saturdays, an organization that has given nearly 200 hours of service to the Columbia community this year alone. She herself has given countless hours performing the service and helping plan the events, while empowering others to employ their ideas and visions for Service on Saturdays' future. Upon graduation, Jennifer continued her spirit of service as she traveled to Boston to serve in Americorps, helping young children in impoverished communities learn how to read and write. I think it is best summed up in what one of her nominators said about her: It is more than that she leads, but that she fosters leadership in others. More than that she volunteers, but that she inspires and develops outlets for others to volunteer. Our university and our community are better off for her having been here.

Langston Dugger, Brown University, Rhode Island

Langston Dugger is one of the recipients for the 2004 Joslin Award. Langston served as the Co-chair of the Organization of United African People, Co-editor in chief of the *African Sun,* Chair of the Brotherhood, Third World Center Staffer and a founder of the Five Brother Initiative. He was also a member of the Varsity

Might I Suggest...

One way to think of your development is to look at three areas: scholarship, leadership, and citizenship. These three contribute to a rich and engaging college experience and also position you for wonderful opportunities after graduation. You are at an amazing place, where the best and brightest minds in the country come together to discover new knowledge. You are now part of this community of scholars, and it is a true privilege to be so. You owe it to yourself and to the millions who cannot be in your place to take your education seriously. Don't just passively go through the motions of checking off your requirements and getting that piece of paper at graduation. Engage! Milk everything you can out of your education. Meet those world-renowned professors and find out what you can learn from them. Build your repertoire of skills—not only those for academic success, but also those for your success as a future leader. Get computer savvy, learn to be a strong public speaker, and become culturally competent.

This larger picture of the power and purpose of a college education is important to keep in mind while you reflect on your first year and set goals for the remainder of your college experience (discussed in Chapter 9). How can you use the resources that are available to you to not only move toward earning your degree, but also to prepare you to be an important and effective leader in the future? How can you get involved on your campus in ways that support your development as a scholar, a leader, and a citizen? What leadership positions are available to you and how might you step into them? Are there ways to begin using your education now, while you are still in college, to be the voice of others or to improve the experience of others?

Remember, education at a research university is not a right, but a privilege. How will you make the most of yours?

Track and Field team and served as Chair of the Undergraduate Finance Board, Vice president of Brown Student Agencies and assisted many organizations in designing their websites. Langston will receive his degree in Economics.

Greg Aitchison, University of Saint Thomas, Minnesota

Greg Aitchison was selected the 2004 Tommy Award winner by a vote of students, staff and faculty. He is majoring in theology, with a minor in Catholic studies, and has been involved with many volunteer activities on campus and in the community, including mission work in Honduras and on the Mohawk Indian Reservation in New York. This summer he will be a coordinator at Camp Shalom, a Christian camp in eastern Iowa where he has been a counselor for two previous summers. In the fall he plans to enter a Catholic seminary to further discern a vocation to the priesthood. If he does not become a priest, he would like to teach theology in high school. Among the most fulfilling activities during his years at St. Thomas were his work as a resident adviser in Ireland Hall, and his work with the university's VISION volunteer program.

Theories of Leadership

The concept of leadership has been researched over the years as people have tried to ascertain the qualities that make a good leader and the kinds of behaviors that strong leaders perform. There are many theories on different leadership styles and strategies, some of which are based on empirical studies and others that stem from business practices in the corporate world. Two that are useful to college students are Kouzes and Posner's (1995) Five Practices of Exemplary Leadership and Hersey and Blanchard's (1993) Situational Leadership Theory.

Kouzes and Posner's Five Practices of Exemplary Leadership

This model ties closely to Dr. Claudine Michel's thoughts about the responsibility leaders have to others. Kouzes and Posner's Five Practices grew out of the Transformational Leadership Model, which looks at leaders in terms of the influence that they have on followers. Transformational leaders share a variety of qualities, including the ability to create and promote desirable visions of the organization, generate creative solutions to problems, facilitate the emergence of other leaders within organizations, and are concerned with "doing the right thing."

Kouzes and Posner further developed this model after they interviewed thousands of managers. They discovered that strong leaders consistently utilized five practices, which they described in their book *The Leadership Challenge*. They later did research on student leaders and found that student leaders also utilized these five practices. In 1998, they developed the *Student Leadership Practices Inventory*, which allows students to assess their skills in the five practices, and they identified some strategies that students can use to develop their skills. The Five Practices are as follows:

Challenging the Process

This practice has to do with "thinking outside the box." Kouzes and Posner found that good leaders are pioneers who are willing to take risks and experiment to create better solutions. Leaders who utilize this practice actively seek out possibilities for change and view mistakes as opportunities for growth. Some student strategies include the following:

- Make lists of tasks you perform and identify ways in which they can be significantly improved.
- Read about people who were pioneers in their field to learn what you can about their experience. Don't forget your faculty as possibilities.
- Sign up for an outdoor adventure program or a creative problem-solving class.

Inspiring a Shared Vision

This practice is about how the leader looks to the future. Strong leaders dream about what *could* be and have a long-term vision for the development of the organization. Leaders are able to involve others in the organization in both creating the vision and bringing it into reality. This vision ultimately gives direction and purpose to all the members. Some student strategies include the following:

- Change your everyday language to be positive; for example, say, "will" instead of "try."
- Read about or interview people who inspire you.
- Create a motto, logo, or slogan for your values and vision.

Enabling Others to Act

Kouzes and Posner found that strong leaders realize that they cannot do it alone and therefore work from a belief of cooperation and collaboration. They are able to create an atmosphere of mutual trust and respect within their organization by designing opportunities for others to do work that matters to the organization. This also helps members to grow and develop as future leaders. Some strategies are the following:

- Take a class or workshop on team building or effective communication skills.

What This Means to You

Whether or not you serve in a formal leadership position, your college experience will provide you with many opportunities to utilize the Five Practices of Exemplary Leadership. These are excellent skills to develop for your future after college as well. Review your abilities in each of the five practices and identify areas for growth. Utilize campus services and involvement opportunities to further hone your skills.

- Ask for volunteers to take on tasks and give people choices about what they are assigned to do.
- Study a social movement and find out how the leaders motivated others to get involved.

Modeling the Way

This practice has to do with "walking your talk" and reflects the consistency between the leader's words and actions. Strong leaders are guided by a personal set of standards and values to which they adhere and role model for others. Strong leaders also help others to see what is possible, thus creating opportunities for success.

- Visit a store or business that has been complimented for its customer service. Observe what employees do to create their reputation.
- Develop a personal mission statement about your values and principles.
- Allow less experienced members to "shadow" you for a day so that they can observe how you do your work.

Encouraging the Heart

This final practice is about encouraging others to contribute. Leaders accomplish this by having high expectations for themselves and others and then giving clear directions, providing strong encouragement and personal attention, and giving meaningful feedback to help others grow. Good leaders also express their pride in what individuals and the team accomplish.

- Celebrate your organization's accomplishments and acknowledge people's contributions.
- Find someone who you believe is good at encouraging the heart. Interview this person and ask for advice or coaching to improve your own skills.
- Ask everyone in your organization how they like to be recognized. Make a list of the information and make sure everyone gets a copy.

Hersey and Blanchard's Situational Leadership Theory

Another useful leadership theory is Hersey and Blanchard's Situational Leadership Theory (1993). They argue that there is no one best style of leadership but rather that "Successful leaders are those who can adapt their behavior to meet the demands of their own unique situation." This means that leaders can make effective and ineffective choices in any given situation.

Their theory identifies three primary factors in any situation that a leader must assess in order to make good choices. The first is task behavior, which is information the leader needs to provide the followers in order for them to know how to accomplish their tasks. This is often achieved through one-way communication and includes information on where, when, and how the followers are to do the specific tasks. The second factor is relationship behavior and is about how the leader interacts with the followers through two-way communication. This focuses on the leader providing socioemotional support to the followers, which creates positive relationships and good feelings about the organization. Leaders provide support, engage in active listening, and help the followers to have a positive experience.

Hersey and Blanchard argue that leaders are always engaging in both the task and relationship behaviors, but the amount of each changes depending on the situation. They have identified four possible combinations: high task and low relationship, high task and high relationship, low task and high relationship, and low task and low relationship.

The correct combination depends on the third factor: the readiness level of the followers. Readiness, in this instance, refers to the followers' capacity to set high but attainable goals, their willingness and ability to take responsibility, and their education and/or experience for the task at hand. In other words, assessing whether the followers are willing, able, and confident to perform the required tasks. Hersey and Blanchard believe that the leader's choices of task and relationship behavior should be based on assessing the readiness of the followers.

When followers are new, the leader should engage in more task behavior to provide instructions and supervise performance. This is also known as the *telling phase*. As the level of readiness increases, the leader should maintain high task behavior and increase relationship behavior by explaining decisions and allowing the group to ask questions—also known as *selling*. Next, the leader would maintain high relationship behavior but decrease task behavior as the group becomes more skilled and needs less instruction. The leader shares ideas and includes the group in decision making. This stage is called *participating*. Finally, when the group is very ready, the leader moves to both low task and low relationship behavior because the group is essentially capable of performing without the leader's guidance. The leader turns over responsibility to the group in the phase known as *delegating*. This model is illustrated in Figure 8.1.

Hersey and Blanchard believe that good leaders are able to develop both their task and relationship behaviors and then use them accurately to guide the group to the highest level of performance and cohesion. A strong leader is skilled in assessing the readiness of the group and adjusting his or her behaviors to that particular situation.

What This Means to You

Later in this chapter, you will find a discussion of specific skills and abilities that student leaders often need in their roles with organizations. You will discover that they relate in some way to either task or relationship behavior. A strong leader is able to do both as they adjust to the readiness of the followers. This can be especially challenging for leaders of student organizations because members are constantly coming into and leaving the organization. This means that members are rarely all at the same stage of readiness, as new members will need more task behavior than more advanced members. Student leaders have to make decisions in this very complex environment, perhaps adapting their behaviors to meet the needs of subgroups of followers instead of using the same strategies with the entire group.

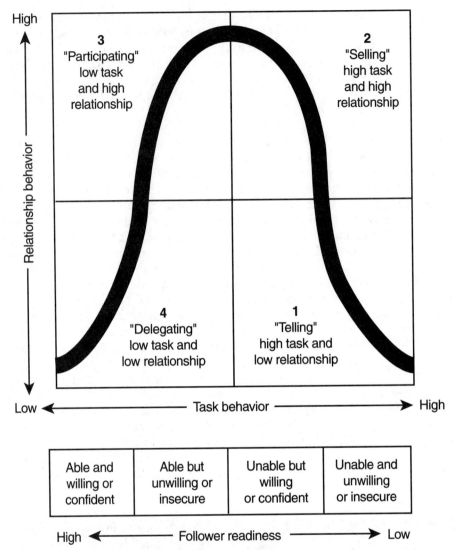

Figure 8.1 Diagram of Hersey and Blanchard's Situational Theory (1993)

Opportunities for Involvement

The best way to begin this process of developing yourself as scholar, leader, and citizen is to get involved in a few areas. You don't want to take on too much at first; devote some of your energy to mastering other transition issues mentioned in this book. However, it is fine to pick one or two involvements your first year and then build from there. Many students know that they want to get

> ## Might I Suggest...
>
> Developing your leadership skills can only enhance your educational experience and future opportunities. I strongly recommend giving attention to your leadership development and utilizing your campus's resources to help you. If there are courses on leadership theories or skills, definitely enroll in them. Likewise, you will see many workshops and presentations on your campus about a variety of leadership skills—attend them. Your campus will also host many special engagements for current leaders in politics, medicine, economy, arts, science, and world affairs. Even if they cost money to attend, they will be well worth your time, and you might find that a special event has been arranged for students to interact with the speaker. Don't miss these! Your campus might also have a leadership conference or retreat where you can gain valuable skills. To find out about your options, visit the office of student/campus life or student activities and make plans to participate in as many events and programs as possible.

involved in some way but are not sure how to begin. The most important thing you need is simply to have the desire. There are literally hundreds of opportunities on campus, and they are there for those who want the experience. Next, you'll want to become familiar with the options available to you. Your university probably has an office of student activities or student/campus life, and this is a great place to start; the staff there will be able to provide you with more specific information about how and where to go to pursue your interests.

In this section you will find an overview of both academic and cocurricular options that are commonly found on university campuses. Read through them and mark all the ones that interest you. It is fine to pursue many options—you have two to four years to do so, and you can either pursue a wide range of involvements or pick one or two and become more deeply involved over a long period of time. If you are still figuring out what interests you, start by exploring several interests and narrow them down as you get more clear about what you enjoy and what you are good at. Some opportunities will be open to all students all year round, so it will be easy to participate; for example, most clubs and organizations take new students throughout the year. Others may have specific times for getting involved, such as Greek life, which has a formal period of recruitment, or athletic opportunities that begin and end around competition seasons. In addition, some opportunities may be more like jobs with an application and selection process. It's always a good idea to call about options that might interest you and write down their typical cycle so that you can plan out your future involvement. You would be surprised at how early university departments begin working on things. For example, at some universities, applications for the highly coveted positions with summer orientation staff are due as early as January. There might be a lengthy selection process that takes weeks or months.

Might I Suggest...

Once you find a few (or twenty!) possibilities that interest you, make contact. Find the phone number or email address of a person who is responsible for, or affiliated with, your interest and contact that person. Simply introduce yourself, express your interest, and request the information you need or the response you would like. For example, you might want to write a note like this:

"Dear fill in name here,

My name is Sabrina Burton, and I am writing you about fill in opportunity here. I would really like to participate. Please contact me with more information about how I can get involved. You can reach me at fill in your contact information here. I would love to hear from you by fill in date here, as I am making plans for next term and this information is important to me.

Thank you,
Sabrina Burton"

This method works for all kinds of opportunities. If the deadline you stated comes and goes, don't give up. Sometimes people are very busy and lose track of things to which they are supposed to respond. Also, you might not have sent it to the right person, so if possible, double-check the name and contact information you used. If it still seems valid, then send another note along the following lines:

"My name is Sabrina Burton, and I contacted you a few weeks ago about fill in opportunity here. I realize you are very busy, but I would really like to participate. I would appreciate it very much if you could please contact me with more information about how I can get involved. You can reach me at fill in your contact information here. If you are not the correct person, or if there is another way I should be seeking this information, please write me back

Those who are selected most likely spend spring term getting trained so that they are ready to help new students and their families in summer. Students who call in the spring miss out on this great opportunity until the following year.

Overview of Academic and Curricular Opportunities

Within the academic, or curricular, aspect of a university education, there are many ways to get involved, and research universities offer a range that is not seen at other campuses. These are especially important to explore for the students who are considering graduate school or a career in higher education in the academic and let me know. I would love to hear from you by <u>fill in date here</u>, as I am making plans for next term and this information is important to me.

Thank you,
Sabrina Burton"

Many universities have some kind of club day or activities fair early in the fall term. This event usually brings together many, if not all, of the campus clubs and organizations and other involvement opportunities. It makes it very easy for a student to peruse all the options, meet folks, and learn about the different possibilities. It's usually possible to join or sign up right on the spot. If your campus has a day like this, be sure to write the date on your planner and attend.

Another great way to find out about opportunities is to become an avid reader of all the fliers and posters you see around campus. You would be surprised just how many things are going on at a university at any one time. Some of them might be events, such as lectures or movies, and some might be meetings. Attending events like these will help you to find out what you enjoy and put you in contact with the students and groups that are hosting them. Your campus may have a centralized location for learning about campus events, such as an on-line event calendar or a central place where fliers are posted. Get in the habit of checking it out every couple of days. If you find something you like, write it in your planner. Students often fail to attend something and miss out simply because they forgot. The best way to ensure that you don't miss something is to write it in your planner, and be sure to also note the time and location so that you won't end up wandering around trying to find it.

Finally, don't be shy. If you see something happening on campus that interests you, stop in and check it out. Most campus events and activities are open to everyone or are clearly marked if they are not. So if you see or hear something that intrigues you, just walk up and check it out. You might stumble across the perfect opportunity for you.

arena. The options that are purely academic and involve additional coursework and assignments or projects will be excellent preparation for further studies beyond the bachelor's degree. In fact, they may provide the base for a student's research or teaching career and usually culminate in some kind of final project that could be presented or published in a variety of venues. Each university is organized differently, so it is difficult to give concrete information on where you would find information about these options. However, most academic advisors in major departments and college offices should be able to point you in the right direction. In addition, you might want to look at your general catalog or campus website for information. Some opportunities are preprofessional in nature and provide the student with an opportunity to explore various career options while gaining valuable work experience. Many of these options are treated more like jobs and often have an application and interview process. The following chart and descriptions provide an overview of the academic and curricular opportunities available to students at research universities.

Independent Study and Directed Readings

Students who wish to gain exposure to a discipline that is not available through current course offerings can approach faculty members to sponsor them in independent study projects or directed readings. These are usually arranged between a student and a faculty member on a case-by-case basis, and the student often initiates the process. Directed readings allow the student to earn credit for doing more in-depth reading or exploration of a topic. The sponsoring faculty member assigns readings and books that are customized to the student's needs. Independent study projects can take a wide variety of forms and are often codesigned by the student and faculty member. Both of these options are often most utilized by juniors and seniors.

Table 8.1   Overview of Curricular Opportunities

Opportunity	Possible Requirements	Interests You
Independent study and directed readings	Major, GPA, faculty sponsor, credits	
Academic conferences	Fee	
Colloquiums and seminars	Fee	
Faculty research projects	Major, GPA, credits	
Senior thesis projects	Major, GPA, senior standing	
Graduate level courses	Major, faculty sponsor, credits	
Studying abroad	GPA, language, credits, application	
Academic peer advisors	Major, GPA, selection	
Curricular and career clubs	—	
Professional organizations	Fee	
Honors societies	Major, GPA	
Honors programs	Major or college, GPA	
Honors at graduation	GPA, credits	

Academic Conferences

National and international academic conferences are held at university campuses around the world. Your campus will probably host several of these during your undergraduate experience. These conferences tend to bring together the top minds in that particular discipline to share ideas and findings. Students often can attend free of charge or might be able to volunteer for certain portions of the conference. This is excellent way to learn more about a discipline and to network with faculty (especially useful if you are thinking about graduate school).

Colloquiums and Seminars

Every term, individual academic departments often organize a series of seminars or presentations on a variety of topics termed colloquiums. Sometimes the speakers are the resident faculty, who share their recent findings or ideas on a particular topic. Sometimes guest speakers are invited who are doing interesting or groundbreaking work in the field. These events are usually open to the campus community and are free. Students can attend to find out more about a particular topic or to interact more closely with faculty.

Faculty Research Projects

As was stated in Chapter 1, the primary mission of a research university is to conduct research. Faculty often use undergraduate assistants in their research projects, doing tasks that can range from simple duties to high levels of responsibility and involvement. While these opportunities may have qualities similar to those of jobs or internships (i.e., a set number of hours per week, established compensation), they also provide students with a unique opportunity to participate firsthand in research. This experience is quite impressive to graduate programs because it indicates that a student has familiarity with the research process and desires to pursue it further.

Senior Thesis Projects

These are usually sponsored by an academic major for its advanced students. A senior thesis or research project is a student research project in which the student (as opposed to the faculty member) is the primary investigator. These research projects are often smaller in scale than a faculty member's project and are designed to be finished within an academic year. The topic and research methods would be in alignment with the student's major or discipline and so would be unique to each individual student. A student in the social or hard sciences might identify a problem, conduct a study or experiment, and write up the final results in a senior thesis. A student in the arts might create an original piece such as a dance or music composition. Some universities recognize completion of a senior thesis by awarding some type of special distinction in the major upon graduation.

Graduate-Level Courses

In some circumstances, faculty members can approve an undergraduate student's request to take a graduate seminar in the department. Usually, the student is a senior with an interest in graduate school, and the seminar matches his or

What This Means to You

You can significantly improve your chance of graduate school admission by participating in a research project as an undergraduate, for either a faculty member's project or your own. This involvement sets you apart from the thousands of students who apply to graduate programs because they believe that an advanced degree will get them higher-paying jobs. While this might be true, faculty at research universities are interested in training future researchers who are serious about careers in academia. The majority of the degree will be designed to train a future researcher, and this might not be the experience a naïve applicant was seeking. If you participate in a research project as an undergraduate, your application will be taken more seriously because it is assumed that you know what the general process of research is about and therefore will make the most of your advanced degree education. This does not mean that you have to pursue a career in research, but it means that you will be perceived as less likely to experience disappointment or to drop out of a research-focused program compared to the other applicants.

In addition, you will most likely be able to include a letter of recommendation from a faculty member who can attest to your research skills and potential as a graduate student. This will also set you apart from the majority of your peers. If you choose to not pursue graduate school, your faculty supervisor can still write an excellent letter of recommendation about your skills and abilities that will make you a strong candidate for a variety of professional jobs.

her scholarly interests. Graduate seminars are usually very small (two to ten students), and the undergraduate is expected to participate fully in readings, discussions, and assignments.

Studying Abroad

Most universities offer some type of study abroad program in which a university student can live and study in a foreign country for one term or up to one year. This is an amazing, life-changing experience, and one that is not to be missed if you can do it. The best types of programs are officially connected to, or sponsored by, your university, because they can guarantee that the credits and coursework you complete abroad will transfer and count toward your degree and/or major. Often, you continue to pay the same tuition as you otherwise would and to receive financial aid, as the program is administered through your campus. In addition, there will most likely be a formal model of mentorship and assistance in place in the foreign location such as a faculty member who lives in that country and oversees the program. You would be amazed by the range of opportunities that are available, including programs that are specific to certain majors. For example, my campus offers a six-week summer program for biology majors working in the rain forests of Costa Rica, one of the most biologically diverse places on the planet. Many of these programs have language requirements, so you will want to find out about them early in your college career so that you can plan accordingly. Most students travel abroad as juniors or seniors, but there are some sophomore programs too, and transfer students can also participate during their senior year. There are also many opportunities to study abroad that may not be officially affiliated with your university. These are also worth exploring, although they might require more work on your part, and the credit might or may not transfer. Check out the Internet for these opportunities.

Academic Peer Advising

These are usually paid positions in which a student holds a job with academic advising duties for either the major department or college. These students are trained in the relevant requirements and policies and can provide general advising to students on an appointment or walk-in basis. Usually, these positions require the student to be in good academic standing and to be a member of that department or program.

Curricular and Career Clubs

These are usually student-run clubs or organizations that are composed of students pursuing a certain major or career. For example, there may be an Economics Club or a Pre-Med Association. The student members determine the focus of the club and work together to create meetings, events, and opportunities that are beneficial to the current members. Often, these clubs are designed to help prepare students for future opportunities, such as graduate schools and professional careers, so activities might include guest speakers, workshops on various topics, and the like.

Student Chapters of Professional Organizations

Most academic disciplines have professional organizations of which the faculty are members. For example, most faculty who research or teach in psychology or related fields are members of the American Psychological Association, and most mechanical engineers are members of Pi Tau Sigma. National and international associations like these provide a series of benefits for members (in exchange for annual dues) such as national and regional conferences, monthly publications like newsletters or journals, and networking opportunities. Many of these professional organizations offer membership to students at very low rates. Membership in such organizations can provide students, especially juniors and seniors, with wonderful opportunities including internships, scholarships, and networking. Most academic departments can provide a list of related professional organizations as well as information on local student chapters.

Finally, there are usually several involvement opportunities that are available to students who have achieved a certain level of outstanding academic performance. There are usually certain criteria that must be met for admission, which might be by invitation only.

Honors Societies

These can be campus, regional, or national groups and usually require a certain GPA for admission. Depending on the sponsoring group, information would be available at a campus department or a national office. Honors societies can also be focused on a certain population, such as freshmen or seniors, or they might be open to students in a certain discipline, such as environmental studies or a foreign language. Some honors societies, such as Phi Beta Kappa, are nationally recognized. Often, honors societies have some kind of induction ceremony as well as annual fees or dues. Benefits include access to conferences, publications, and networking opportunities for alumni.

Honors Programs

These are usually academic programs run by a college or major department and require a certain level of participation and excellence in order to participate. Often, certain benefits are offered such as priority enrollment, special events, and higher levels of access to university resources such as the library or computer labs. Some programs are designed to be an acknowledgement for achievement, and participants receive admission and benefits based on maintaining a certain GPA. Other programs are designed to be an additional experience and may have requirements for completion of certain courses or a certain number honors sections to "complete" the program on graduation.

Honors at Graduation

This is an academic acknowledgment bestowed by the university and is based on the performance of the senior class. There are usually three levels that reflect placement in the highest percentages (based on GPA) of the senior class as a whole:

- Honors, also known as cum laude
- High honors, also known as magna cum laude
- Highest honors, also known summa cum laude

Students do not apply for these honors but rather receive them from the university at graduation. These levels are usually indicated on the diploma and may be noted in commencement programs or by special regalia to be worn by students during commencement. Since this honor is based on an individual student's placement in comparison to the senior class, exact GPAs for qualification cannot be determined, since these change with each group of students. However, a university usually keeps records of the results each year, so a student could learn the general level of accomplishment that will be required. It is important to note that participation in honors programs and societies is usually unrelated to honors at graduation, although there will be a certain overlap among the students who qualify for them. Many students who completed an honors program are confused and disappointed that this did not earn them honors at graduation. Major departments can also award special honors to graduating seniors in various forms. There may be prestigious awards presented to students as well as departmental honors based on academic performance. These vary by department; an academic advisor can usually provide more information.

Overview of Cocurricular Opportunities

In addition to the academic, or curricular, aspect of a university education, there are ways to get involved in cocurricular opportunities. While these are outside of the academic arena, they can provide a plethora of opportunities to gain valuable experience and skills that can prepare students for postgraduation possibilities. Most graduate schools and employers are looking for students who have developed more than just their transcripts—who have experience working with others, possess good communication and leadership skills, and conduct themselves in mature and professional ways. Cocurricular opportunities can provide opportunities to develop all of these and also can help to prepare students for a wide range of future careers, especially those not affiliated with research and academia. Each of these options may be housed in, or affiliated with, a different campus program, so you might want to consult your campus website or student handbook for information. Also, most universities have an office of student life or campus activities, which would be a natural place to begin your search for cocurricular opportunities. Table 8.2 provides an overview of common cocurricular opportunities and possible requirements for participation. You can check off those that interest you.

Student Government

Most universities have some form of student government in which students get elected to represent their peers in campus issues. There may be many more positions to which a student can be elected than students experienced in high school. In addition to elected positions, many student governments provide a range of other opportunities, such as serving on boards and committees that work on certain issues (e.g., environment, use of student fees, gender/ethnic equality, social programming) as well as student services that are run by students for students. Depending on the position, these opportunities can prepare you for political and policy-making careers as well as careers that focus on specific issues, such as the environment. In addition, there may be other forms of student government, such as within a residence hall or campus facility, in which students govern programming and use of student fees.

Table 8.2   Overview of Cocurricular Opportunities

Opportunity	Possible Requirements	Interests You
Student government	Application, election	
Clubs and organizations	Fee	
Greek life	Rush, selection, fee	
Athletics and recreation	Tryouts, selection, fee	
Religious groups	Service, fee	
Performing groups	Audition, selection	
Peer advisors	Selection	
Committee appointments	Appointment	
Volunteering	—	

Clubs and Organizations

According to the national Your First College Year (YFCY) study on freshmen, 60% of students participate in student clubs or groups. Most clubs and organizations are created and run by students, which allows for the organizations to change and evolve as students' needs change and evolve. It is usually easy to start a new club or organization, so students are empowered to create the involvement opportunities that interest them most. These can run the gamut from academic and career-focused to hobbies and personal interest to ethnic and religious identity. Following is a sample of the types of clubs or organizations you might find on a typical university campus:

- *Academic:* Environmental Studies Students Association, Communications Association, Los Ingenieros
- *Career focus:* Pre-Med Association, Accounting Association, Society of Women Engineers
- *Community service:* Habitat for Humanity, Blood Drive Group, Best Buddies
- *Cultural:* Chinese Student Union, Hermanos Unidos, Israeli Club, Irish Students Association, Gay and Lesbian Student Alliance
- *Ethnic:* Black Student Union, Korean Student Association
- *Health:* Students Against Drunk Drivers, Safer Sex Peer Educators
- *Hobbies:* Chess Club, Japanese Anime Association, Mask and Scroll, Reggae Club
- *Honorary:* Alpha Lambda Delta, Mortar Board, Mensa Society
- *Ideological/political:* Campus Democrats, College Republicans, El Congreso, National Organization of Women
- *Recreational:* Synchronized Swimming Club, Billiard Club, Swing and Ballroom Dance Club, Water Ski Club Team, Mountain Bike Club
- *Religious:* Asian American Christian Fellowship, Muslim Student Association, Campus Crusade for Christ, Hillel, Catholic Student Organization, Zen Sitting Group, Nichiren Buddhists, United Methodist Student Movement, Real Life
- *Social:* Friday Night Film Fanciers, Hip Hop Club
- *Special interest:* Rainforest Alliance, Future Leaders of America, Disabled Students Advocacy Union, Club Britain

Greek Life

There are many forms of Greek life on campus these days, and they are becoming less and less like the "animal house" stereotype of years past. Risk management has forced universities and national organizations to crack down on excessive drinking and hazing, which have been the negative and dangerous sides of the Greek community. In addition, many campuses have a wide range of involvement opportunities, so Greek life is no longer the only, or most popular, option for students, and this has contributed to major reforms as well. There are many benefits to Greek life, such as the opportunity to meet people through shared interests and experiences, the opportunity to hold leadership positions, and the experience of performing community service. There are still the traditional sorority and fraternities that have national organizations and in which a group of men or women live together in a "house." These often have a social focus and host many parties and gatherings, although many of these are "dry" because of stricter alcohol regulations. In addition, there are many local and regional Greek organizations that offer a wider range of options in terms of a particular focus. There are Greek organizations for different academic and career fields as well as ones that focus on certain cultural or spiritual heritages. With all of these options available, it is important to explore the ones that best suit your needs. There are certain times of the year that students can apply to join a Greek organization, known as recruitment or "rush"; consult with your campus office of Greek affairs to learn more. According to the national YFCY study on freshmen, 11.6% of students joined a sorority or fraternity.

Athletic and Recreational Events

There are usually many opportunities to get involved in athletic and recreational events at a university campus. Talented and motivated athletes can usually pursue competitive opportunities through university-sponsored teams and club sports. University-sponsored teams play in division and national leagues and are supported financially by the university. Club sports are not officially sponsored or supported by the university but also compete at divisional and national levels. "Walk-on" spots are often available to talented individuals who were not recruited, but auditions might be required. It's important to note that collegiate competitive sports require a lot of practice and training time, which can affect a student's academic performance. For the less serious athlete, intramural sports can be a great way to get involved. There are usually different levels of competitiveness, so this can be an option for the beginner as well as the expert (although they would never compete in the same league). Intramural teams are usually organized each term to play for one term, and the sports change with the season. Students usually have the option to form a team with friends or join an open team. In addition, there may be opportunities to take classes, from beginner to expert levels, in a variety of sports and recreational activities. Finally, if a campus has a popular athletic team, such as football or basketball, there will be opportunities to get involved with the pep squad, marching band, and cheer or dance squad. Consult your campus gym or recreational facility for more information.

Religious and Spiritual Groups

In any community where humans gather, there will be ways to express religious and spiritual beliefs. This is certainly true in a university community as well. Many students choose to join a place of worship in the local community surrounding their campus; these can be found by looking in a local telephone directory. However, sometimes students' schedules prevent them from taking part in regularly scheduled services and events, or they might find that a congregation's needs are different from their own. As a result, many students choose to participate in religious/spiritual student organizations or groups that focus more on the needs and experiences of young adults in college. These often are registered as campus clubs and provide opportunities for learning, worshiping in community, addressing the challenges of maintaining spirituality in college, and performing community service. The office that coordinates student clubs and activities should-be able to provide you with a list of options at or near your campus.

Performing Groups

Many college students have a developed interest for, or talent in, one of the performing arts, such as music, dance, drama, and art. While serious performers will most likely choose to pursue one of these fields as a major, there are many more who perform just for fun. Most campuses have opportunities for students to fulfill this interest through informal and formal performance groups. There might be already established ensembles and groups that students can audition to join, and there are most likely opportunities that are open to all who are interested, such as student choirs and swing dance clubs. These opportunities are most likely affiliated with the academic departments in the arts, but you can also check the student clubs as well as general fliers posted around the campus and local community.

Peer Advising for Nonacademic Departments

Many nonacademic departments and services utilize undergraduate students in peer advising positions. These are a wonderful way to get involved around a particular issue and also gain valuable training and preprofessional experience, as most provide extensive training in important skills. In addition to academic peer advisors mentioned earlier, there are many peer positions on campus that can focus on topics such as stress management, peer health topics such as sexual health or body image/eating disorders, athletics, career advising, diversity issues such as ethnicity and sexual orientation, leadership training, and summer orientation. In addition, if your campus has university-owned living environments, there will be resident assistant or coordinator positions, which are great opportunities to explore whether a career in counseling or higher education would be for you.

Campus Committee Appointments

As is mentioned in Chapter 3, campus committees that include faculty, staff, and student members address many important campus issues. These committees meet regularly to discuss and provide recommendations on a particular issue. There are usually one or two student spots on these committees, and they are excellent ways for students to get involved. Student members participate in the actual workings of a university and gain valuable experience working in a team environment with a wide range of people. In addition, they become very familiar with the committee's topic so students usually choose one that interests them or might be relevant to their future career. Most academic departments and college offices would be able to point you to the office in which these committees are coordinated.

Volunteering

According to the national YFCY study on freshmen, 63% of students participated in volunteer or community service. Volunteerism is very important and is highly valued by future employers and graduate programs. It is also a way in which the campus community, particularly students, can give back to the local community. Students can contact local organizations directly to find out whether there is a need for volunteers, or there might be an office on your campus that coordinates such efforts. The office that works with campus clubs and organizations would be a good place to start if you do not find information on your campus website. Some campuses require students to participate in service learning programs as part of their degree requirements. You can ask your academic advisor if this is true at your campus or if other programs exist that provide or promote service learning.

Other Exciting Options

Most of the activities listed above occur during the academic year and are based on or near your campus. However, there are also several exciting opportunities that exist off your campus that you might find very valuable.

Summer Opportunities

Many universities have exciting summer opportunities for students, both on the campus and in the students' home communities. Most universities host summer conferences for national and international organizations, and there are often student positions available with these programs. Your university might also host a summer academic program for high school students in which positions are available. Of course, there will be some kind of orientation for new students and their families that requires the assistance of current students. There might also be an alumni vacation program that utilizes students to coordinate and host activities for alumni and their children. The campus activities or student life office can most likely help you find information about all of these options. Finally, most universities can help you find an exciting summer internship in your home community and even internationally. These internships can be great ways to build your preprofessional skills as well as a way to earn some money. Contact the career advisors to learn more about summer internships.

Internships in the Nation's or State Capital

Our nation's capital has a long history of utilizing college students as interns in every kind of office from the White House to the Smithsonian Institution to national nonprofit organizations. Students, usually juniors and seniors, from all over the United States can spend a term in Washington, D.C., interning at an office. Many universities even offer academic credit for this experience and host students in group living environments with local mentors for guidance and support. A similar internship program might be available in your state's capital.

These internships provide truly exciting opportunities and help students to prepare for their future careers. In fact, some students have even been offered permanent jobs with the same organization.

Semester at Sea

This unique program is run out of the University of Pittsburgh; your university might or might not have a formal relationship with it. The program conducts a university term on a cruise ship that travels the world. Students live and study on the ship, taking regular classes while the ship is at sea. When the ship docks in a port, the students, faculty, and staff have a few days to disembark and travel in the country on either prearranged trips or ones of their own planning. There is a spring and a fall voyage, each lasting approximately 3.5 months, and a shorter summer voyage lasting two months. The fall voyage leaves from the West Coast and travels to Japan, China, Vietnam, Thailand, India, Tanzania, South Africa, Brazil, and Cuba, ending on the East Coast. The spring voyage leaves from the East Coast and repeats the trip in the other direction with a few changes in destinations to include Korea and Kenya. The summer voyage often travels through the Mediterranean and European countries. Even if not all of the classes transfer, this amazing experience is not to be missed. Most students utilize their tuition and rent savings to afford the program and financial aid is also available. To learn more, check out the website at www. semesteratsea.com.

Serving in a Leadership Role

Once you find opportunities you enjoy and you have participated for a while, you can begin to explore how you might move into a leadership role in that organization. Serving in leadership roles is very important because these roles allow you to gain very valuable leadership skills that will make you more desirable for both graduate programs and employers. There are many kinds of leadership roles, both formal and informal. Formal roles will have some kind of official title or set of responsibilities, such as vice president of an organization, chair of recruitment for a sorority, captain of an athletic team, resident assistant, or coleader for a freshman seminar. Some of these positions are highly competitive and require some type of selection or election process and some just require the interest of a committed person who is willing to serve. Informal roles do not have a specific title or set of responsibilities yet play a vital part in the successful running of the group or organization. These are often a reflection of the individual person's leadership skills and abilities, and people in informal roles sometimes lead more effectively than those in formal ones do.

This highlights the importance of leadership skills. It is really the development of genuine leadership skills, not a title or position, that make a person an effective leader. Although you will certainly want to apply for and hold leadership positions, it is more important to focus on developing leadership skills and serving as an effective leader.

Tricia's Story

Upon entering college, campus involvement was the furthest thing from my mind. I spent the first half of my freshman year adjusting to residence hall life, memorizing the campus map, and learning how to balance classes and a part-time job. However, I soon began to feel that something was missing. I felt a sense of disconnection from my university and a desire to connect with my peers on a more personal level. The answer to my dilemma came through my eventual role as a student leader.

My journey towards student leadership began with my attendance at a leadership retreat sponsored by the university's Office of Student Life. At the retreat, I found myself surrounded by students who both recognized themselves as leaders and wished to develop the skills and abilities they brought to the clubs and organizations to which they belonged. We were there for a common purpose and each brought unique examples of involvement in the campus community. I saw the relationship they had with the campus through their involvement and knew that was what I was seeking as well. When the retreat came to an end, I not only felt I had grown in my understanding of what student leadership was but was eager to begin my campus involvement.

The next three years were a time of incredible growth and personal development. I applied for and was selected for the student Summer Orientation Staff. The next year, I was promoted to the Coordinator position and I hired, trained, and supervised the student staff along with my co-coordinator. As an orientation leader and student coordinator I developed skills in diplomacy, professional conduct and organization. I worked with a large group of incredible student leaders who all had an appreciation for their school and wished to help new students develop the same feeling.

That same year, I applied for the Capps Leadership Intern position with the Office of Student Life and helped to coordinate our campus' leadership program. The year I spent in this position introduced me to event planning, public speaking, and communication with a variety of groups (students, faculty, and staff). Involvement that I had with the student government gave me a better understanding of the power students have over their education and the importance of the student voice. My senior year, I was able to work in the Office of the Vice Chancellor for Student Affairs. Not only was I developing close relationships with peers and mentors through my involvement, but I was learning lessons that I knew would be beneficial in my professional career.

All of these positions taught me that I wanted to continue working in higher education where I plan to play an active role in encouraging student involvement and helping students to recognize the leaders within themselves. I am now pursuing a Master's degree in Higher Education and Student Affairs at the University of Vermont. When I graduated from my university, I left with feelings of pride and accomplishment. My experience would not have been the same if I had failed to pursue campus involvement or to believe in my ability to be a leader. Through these experiences I formed long-lasting friendships and found mentors who continue to serve as role models in my life today.

Developing Important Leadership Skills

A search on the Internet will lead you to hundreds of websites about leadership skills. Leadership skills are often very specific to a certain position or context; for example, the skills that are necessary to be successful as a leader in the U.S. Air Force might be different from those needed to be an entrepreneur or an elementary school teacher. For this reason, this chapter will focus on the leadership skills that are most often needed by college students, although many of these will certainly translate to other settings. Please note that leadership skills are in addition to the skills for academic success discussed in Chapter 2. It is important to maintain your status as a successful scholar while adding leadership roles to your university experience. You will need to find a balance and not forsake one for the other.

Some of these leadership skills will come through experience, but all of them can be learned and sharpened with some focused effort. There will probably be opportunities on your campus to take classes or workshops on these skills/topics. In addition, the community surrounding your campus will most likely have similar programs available for local businesses and organizations. Finally, there are hundreds of books and websites on these topics. The point is that any person who is serious about developing leadership skills will take the time to study, learn, practice, and improve their skills as often as possible. If you are lucky enough to have a leadership development program on your campus, take advantage of its resources as early in your college career as possible. All of the skills below refer to the needs of a "group" or "members" as well as an "organization"—no matter what kind of leadership position you hold, most likely your position will influence the actions and behaviors of others. Table 8.3 provides an overview of student leadership skills.

Time Management

This is a mandatory skill for leaders to master, as their success will depend on their ability to balance their academic and cocurricular involvements, as well as meet their obligations on time. This skill is discussed in more detail in Chapter 2, but will get more intense as more deadlines and responsibilities are added to the student's schedule. As a result, most leaders need to fine-tune their time management skills to make them as effective and efficient as possible. Student leaders often take on too many commitments, which results in either a poor performance or sacrificing their personal well-being by losing sleep or skipping meals to meet a deadline. Strong leaders are able to meet their commitments at a high level of performance while also maintaining a calm and well-balanced personal life. This also includes the ability to say no when appropriate.

Delegation

This skill goes hand in hand with time management. Delegation requires the leader to be, first, willing to let go of some duties and responsibilities and, second, able to pass those duties on to another in a way that is not bossy or dictatorial. Delegation requires the leader to share the workload with others so that

Table 8.3   Overview of Student Leadership Skills

Fill out this table by ranking yourself for your level of competence in that particular area. Use a scale of 1–5, 1 being "no experience" and 5 being "extremely competent." Also, do some research about what is available on your campus to help you develop these skills.

Skill/Area	Your Rating	Campus Support Available
Time management		
Delegation		
Teaching and training		
Communication		
Public speaking		
Interpersonal skills		
Collaboration		
Conflict management		
Motivating and inspiring others		
Organizational skills		
New member recruiting		
Event planning		
Marketing and advertising		
Securing funding		

she or he is not too overwhelmed with work and to allow other members to learn and grow.

Teaching and Training

Connected to time management and delegation is a leader's ability to teach and train others. In the process of delegating, the leader might need to provide information and/or skills to others so that they can perform the duties successfully. This also requires the foresight to realize that the future of any organization depends on its leader's ability to train future leaders. This is especially relevant for student leaders, since student organizations often have high turnover each year when students graduate. A strong leader makes sure that she or he is training and developing the next generation of leaders by giving them opportunities to learn and develop leadership skills.

Communication

Every leader needs strong communication skills, written, verbal, and nonverbal. Communication is the primary way in which a leader leads. There are different communication styles, and a strong leader can adjust his or her style to the needs of the group and when interacting with different individuals. In addition, a leader needs to be able to ascertain when to utilize passive, assertive, and aggressive communication skills as needed for the situation.

Public Speaking

While not every leadership role requires a person to give speeches in front of large audiences, most leaders do find that they are required to speak at various gatherings pretty frequently. A leader is often seen as the primary representative of a group, so it is not uncommon for a student leader to be asked to speak at a meeting, event, or assembly. In addition, leaders will find that they have to speak in front of their group often and also might need to speak in public in the process of recruiting new members. Public speaking is a skill that can be improved with practice, especially since the biggest challenge for most people is dealing with nerves. Public speaking classes and organizations such as Toastmasters are great ways to work on this important skill.

Interpersonal Skills

This has to do with how well a person can interact with a wide range of people who may differ in terms of personality, age, gender, ethnicity, spirituality, political ideology, sexual orientation, physical disability, and other dimensions. It is important for a leader to have the ability to listen, as that will be a primary way to learn how best to connect with others. Furthermore, a leader might need to gain competence with understanding various aspects of diversity as discussed in Chapter 7. Most universities provide classes, programs, and workshops that focus on diversity issues.

Collaboration

This skill focuses on being able to work well with others. Obviously leaders are going to encourage collaboration among the members of their group, but it is also important to collaborate with other groups. Nowadays, most student groups can accomplish more when they collaborate with other campus entities, such as the administration, various departments or services, and other student groups. Within the group, collaboration is the epitome of teamwork. A strong leader can help members to collaborate with each other by helping them to see and appreciate each person's strengths (as opposed to competing with each other). In addition, a good leader maximizes the effectiveness of the group by matching each member's strengths to a need of the organization in terms of roles and responsibilities. Many student organizations utilize a form of collaboration called *coalition building*. Coalitions are formed when several groups have an interest in a certain outcome but cannot achieve that outcome single-handedly. This might take the form of lobbying together for a certain campus change, cosponsoring events in ways that create a bigger event than could be achieved by a single group, or sharing resources in a way that serves all of them better.

Conflict Management

All groups experience conflict, which is one of the natural stages of group development. A good leader recognizes this and is not afraid of conflict. In addition, strong leaders are able to assist the group in moving through the conflict smoothly in ways that strengthen, rather than splinter, the group. Training in mediation or conflict resolution is especially helpful to most leaders.

Motivating and Inspiring Others

This skill speaks to the leader's ability to work well with followers. When the leader can work with members to cocreate a vision and/or a mission statement, then followers are more likely to take ownership of the success of the group and not leave it to the leader to make this happen. Leaders who are able to motivate and inspire others have an easier time delegating and dealing with conflict in the group.

Organizational Skills

This skill has to do with keeping clear and organized records. Student leaders are often responsible for a wide range of information and activities. It is important for leaders to keep detailed records of all information related to the position, from memos and conversation notes to receipts and meeting agendas. This is especially true when money is involved. Students are held to high standards of fiscal responsibility, and accurate record keeping is a must. Keeping an organized file or notebook allows leaders to be more effective and efficient in performing their duties, as it provides a central location in which to find all relevant information. In addition, these documents can be shared with others and passed on to the next generation of leaders.

New Member Recruiting

On a more practical level, many student organizations need to be able to keep their organization running so that it continues to exist and function in the future. This includes being able to recruit new members so that there are future leaders who can take over when the current leaders graduate. This will obviously build on a number of the skills discussed above, such as interpersonal skills, public speaking, and motivating and inspiring members. New member recruitment also requires a leader to be able to identify potential new members and communicate with them in a way that encourages interest in, and eventual commitment to, the group. With students being as busy as they are, recruitment can be challenging and requires a leader who is able to make connections between the group's mission and the potential member's personal goals and aspirations.

Event Planning

In addition, many student groups organize events as a way to fulfill their group's mission. If a group holds events occasionally, whether they are rallies, dances, performances, or blood drives, someone will need to be strong in event planning. Event planning first requires strong organizational skills, as there will be many records to keep. A crucial tool for event planners is an accurate and detailed timeline of what needs to be accomplished by when. In addition, the leader will need to know how to reserve various campus facilities, order services such as sound and public address systems, tables and chairs, and refreshments. There might also be a need for security guards and ticket sellers.

Marketing and Advertising

For the activities of a group to be successful, people need to know about them. The ability to craft and disseminate announcements will require a knowledge of desktop publishing and writing skills as well as knowledge of campus policies regarding posting, and avenues for advertising (both paid and free) through campus and local media.

Securing Funding

Many organizations have to operate within a budget, and money is getting tighter and tighter on college campuses. Student leaders should learn about various sources of funding and the methods for applying for them. There might also be a need to engage in fundraising by hosting events, selling products, or seeking individual sponsors. In addition, collaboration and coalition-building skills come in handy when there is a need to bring together a wide range of people and resources to make the most of the funding at hand.

All of these skills are very helpful to the success of any organization, and your office of campus activities might offer training or information on these topics. It would be a challenge for any one student leader to be strong in all of the areas discussed above, yet every one of them is needed for the overall success of an organization, whether student or professional. In any organization, there will most

What This Means to You

Most universities provide for the leadership development of their students through a range of support services. First will be the various ways in which students can get involved on their campus or hold a leadership position, as mentioned in this chapter. Get started early on joining so that there will be time for you to move into leadership positions. Second, you will find educational workshops, talks, and even classes that focus on leadership skills. You can piece these together to create your own curriculum for leadership development. Don't forget options that are not affiliated with campus. Many communities have workshops and seminars on leadership topics for local business owners and leaders of organizations. Contact the Chamber of Commerce in the town in which you attend college to find out more. Third, you might even have a formal campus leadership program that includes classes, retreats, conferences, workshops, and mandatory service in a leadership role. If such a program exists, enroll early and participate often.

Might I Suggest...

Consider the development of your leadership skills to be as important as the requirements for your bachelor's degree. While you can certainly graduate without leadership skills, your future opportunities are expanded considerably if you have paid attention to developing them. Intentionally take advantage of campus resources to help you develop as many of these skills as possible during your college experience. You want to gain some experience with many and then focus on excelling in areas that are the best matches with your natural talents and future interests. Also, don't be intimidated. You don't have to be the outgoing person who enjoys speaking in public to be an amazing leader. Leadership takes all forms, and you will want to find your own special style.

likely be a group of leaders, each of whom has different levels of these skills, who come together to ensure a group's success. Whether they hold formal or informal positions, each person will serve in an important leadership role. Over time, they can learn from one another through observation and experience. Ideally, they will be able to cross-train and gain skills in each of the areas.

Awards and Other Forms of Recognition

Most universities seek to acknowledge outstanding student leaders with formal awards. Some of these are scholastic in nature; others are focused on cocurricular involvements. Scholastic awards can be given by a department, program, college, or university, and are based on the student's academic performance. This may be based on overall GPA or may reflect outstanding research or writing in a particular area. Cocurricular awards usually focus on the contributions a student has made to his or her organization or campus. Some have minimum GPA requirements, and some do not. While all universities will have awards for graduating seniors, many also have class-based awards for every year as well as awards for student groups. In addition, there are annual national competitions and awards for which students can enter or be nominated. Table 8.4 lists some awards that are granted to graduating seniors at various research universities around the United States.

Needless to say, any student's record is improved by the achievement of an award or honor. It is in your best interest to learn about opportunities for which you might qualify. It is important to find out what awards exist on your campus and how they are determined. By gathering this information early in your university career, you can make informed choices about how to ensure that you will qualify for consideration. It is always disappointing when a student leader just narrowly misses qualifying for an award when a small change could have corrected the situation. It is perfectly appropriate for a student to ensure that she or he is considered for awards.

Might I Suggest...

Although it is always nice to have someone recognize your talents and nominate you, this doesn't always happen. I saw a truly deserving student not be considered for an award because no one in a group of staff submitted his name—each of us thought that someone else was nominating him. We were all very upset to learn about this, but it was too late to fix it. Depending on the type of award it is, there are different strategies that are appropriate for you to utilize.

Some awards are based on rigid criteria, and the students who meet those criteria are automatically considered. For example, at my campus, we have the Mortar Board Award, which is given to the graduating senior with the highest GPA. Every spring, the records of all the graduating seniors with a 4.0 GPA are reviewed (you would be surprised by how many there are!). Most never even know that they are under consideration. The award is given to the student with the most A-pluses on his or her transcript, and she or he is notified a couple of weeks before commencement. Students cannot apply for this award, although any student who really wanted to receive it could have learned about it as a first-year student and worked hard to earn only A's and A-pluses.

Other awards have an application process that is advertised to students. Students apply by the deadline and are considered along with the other applicants. Students can increase their chances of receiving these awards by learning about the awards early in their career. This will allow students to make choices that can make them more eligible or more competitive depending on the criteria for the award. In addition, the student who marks the deadline on his or her calendar and takes ample time to submit a professional application will have better chances than those who submit a mediocre application or who miss the deadline entirely.

There are also a host of awards that have a nomination process. If self-nominations are allowed, then obviously, a student can nominate himself or herself, but I recommend finding out whether self-nominations are given the same credence as others. In some cases, they are; in other cases, they are not. If not, then you will want to find someone to nominate you. Some awards might allow for students to nominate other students. In this case, you can probably ask a friend and even nominate each other. Just be sure that this person knows enough about you to describe your qualifications accurately.

Some awards, usually the most prestigious ones, allow nominations only from faculty and staff. While faculty and staff try very hard to nominate all the students who qualify, this doesn't always happen. If you find an award for which you believe you qualify, I strongly recommend that you bring it to the attention of a faculty or staff member whom you have gotten to know. I suggest approaching this in the following way (this can be done either in writing, including email, or in person). Print out the award information and the nomination form. Give it to the person along with a note that says something like the following:

Dear <u>fill in name here</u>,

I recently came across information for the <u>fill in title here</u> award. I believe I may qualify, for it but I wanted your opinion. Could you please read the attached information and let me know whether or not you think I might qualify. I would love to hear back from you by <u>fill in date here</u>, since the deadline is <u>fill in date here</u>.

Thank you so much for your time.

Sincerely,
Brendan Ewing,

<u>fill in email and phone here</u>

If the person does not believe that you qualify, she or he will probably tell you why. Sometimes there are certain stipulations that might not be clear in the materials, or the person might be able to give you a better sense of how competitive the award is and how strong your chances might be. If the person does think you qualify, you might get a response like "Yes, I agree with you. It sounds like you meet the criteria for consideration." This will allow you to write back and ask whether she or he will nominate you. Or you might get a response such as "Yes, you do. I was already planning on nominating you and will get the form in by the deadline. I hope that you get it."

I am never offended if a student approaches me in this way. In fact, I am grateful! I always want to nominate my deserving students for awards, but frankly, there are so many different awards that I cannot always keep track. I would rather a student approach me than find out later that I missed an important deadline.

Table 8.4   Sample of Awards from Research Universities

Universities	Awards
University of Alabama, Birmingham	Thompson T. Abercrombie Distinguished Graduate Award Respiratory Therapy Program Clinical Excellence Award The Dean's Leadership and Service Award
University of Maine	Francis J. Hovey Award in Physics Wofford Gardner Award in Communication Young Women's Social Justice Award
New Mexico State University, Main Campus	American Indian Program Outstanding Senior Award URC Research Award Emerson Award in English
Texas A&M University	Charles Gordone Writing Award Stanley Kaplan Achievement Award Texas Academy of Science Award
Virginia Commonwealth University	Presidential Award for Community Multicultural Enrichment William H. Duvall Award for Student Activities and Involvement The Glenn B. Hamm Academic Achievement Recognition in Art Education

Chapter Summary

In this chapter, the following topics were discussed:

- The importance of involvement and leadership as part of higher education
  - The purpose and power of a college education
  - Examples of outstanding student leaders

- Theories of leadership
  - Kouzes and Posner's five practices of exemplary leadership
  - Hersey and Blanchard's situational leadership theory

- Opportunities for involvement
  - Overview of academic and curricular opportunities
  - Overview of cocurricular opportunities
  - Other exciting options

- Serving in a leadership role
  - Developing important leadership skills

- Awards and other forms of recognition

Reflections and Exercises

1. Get Involved!

Visit your campus's office that supports student clubs and organizations (often the office of student life or student activities center). Look through the listing of students clubs and organizations and identity at least five that sound interesting to you. Try to find some for different aspects of your life like your major, career interest, cultural/spiritual identity, social issues, and hobbies. Next, find the contact information for an officer or advisor for that club or organization. If possible, find the mission of that club or organization along with when and where the next meeting will be held. (You might have to contact the officer or campus life office to do this.)

Club	Contact	Mission	Meeting

At your earliest convenience, attend the meetings of all five organizations. With any luck, you found at least one that you really like. If so, then join it! If not, redo this process until you find at least one or two that you would like to become a member of and do so.

2. Research Opportunities for Research

Ask your academic advisor in your major or college about how undergraduates can become involved in faculty research projects. If there is a resource such as a book or a website, look through the options and identify at least two that sound interesting to you. Next, explore what qualifications you might need and how you would apply to work on that project. If it interests you, follow up and apply. If there is no such resource, ask two or three of your faculty members or teaching assistants whether they know of any research projects that utilize undergraduate students. Follow the leads until you find one that you might want to work on.

3. Assess Your Leadership Style

If your campus has a leadership program, it will most likely offer some assessments and trainings in leadership styles and skills. Another great source is MySkillsPro-file.com, which offers a battery of online assessments that are excellent. (Note: Some of these have a moderate fee of less than $10.) Check them out at http://etesting.modwest.com/.

How did the assessment you took classify you?

Does that seem accurate to you? Why or why not?

What does this information tell you about yourself as a student leader?

How might this information guide your future career choices?

Are there any specific skills or experiences that would aid in your leadership development? How might you take action about this at your campus?

4. Exploring Honors and Awards

Go to your campus website and utilize the search mode to learn about student awards. Use search terms such as "awards," "achievement," and "honors," and see what is available.

Write down at least three academic awards and cocurricular involvement awards that interest you.

What are the criteria for these awards and how are students considered?

Start a file of awards that you might like to earn or for which you might qualify. Include the results from this activity and redo this search each year so that you are aware of the most current information. You can also do this process on the Internet to learn about national awards for college students attending any campus.

Chapter 9

Planning for the Future

This book has focused on many of the experiences first-year students have during their enrollment at a research university. I hope you have found it informative and illuminating. The goal of this chapter is to help you take what you learned to improve your remaining educational experiences, both for your college degree and beyond. While this chapter certainly fits in Section II of this book (Personal Development), it is placed here because I want to encourage you to reflect on your experiences during your first year as a freshman or transfer student. On the basis of this reflection, you will be invited to set specific objectives for the next years of your university attendance through graduation. You will also be provided with tips and strategies to set goals that support your academic, social, and personal success.

The Importance of Reflection

As you go through and eventually finish your first year at a research university, it is important to reflect on your experiences. Each experience you have, academic and social, provides you with valuable information that can allow you to improve your future experiences. Positive experiences can lead you to repeat certain actions and behaviors, and negative ones can assist you in making changes to avoid repeating the same experiences. You will be gaining valuable lessons in two areas. One is the university itself and all it entails, including expectations of faculty, policies, departments and services, overall climate, the study body in general, and so on. In addition, you will learn many things about yourself: your values, your preferences, your skills and abilities, and your strengths and weaknesses. Together, these can inform your future choices so that you can navigate the university environment with ease and success.

One way in which you can ensure that you learn from your experiences is to review what has happened during your first term or first year of university life. An in-depth review of your academic and social experiences can provide you with valuable insight for shaping your future goals. Take some time to reflect on the following questions. You can also do this with a partner.

1. What have you learned about the academic environment of the campus?
2. What have you learned about the social environment of the campus?
3. What have you learned about your academic strengths? And weaknesses?
4. What have you learned about your social strengths? And weaknesses?
5. What were the things that contributed to your academic successes?
6. What were the things that hindered your academic successes?
7. What were the things that contributed to your social successes?
8. What were the things that hindered your social successes?
9. What things from your first term or first year should you definitely try to continue or repeat in the future?
10. What things from your first term or first year should you definitely try to change or avoid in the future?
11. Are there any other questions you should ask yourself?

After engaging in this reflection, you will want to use these insights to set concrete goals for the remainder of your college experience. While these are not set in stone and will likely change over the years as you learn more, it is good to start with a clear set of goals and then review every term and adjust accordingly. The following sections will help you to create more specific and measurable goals that will guide you during the remainder of your college experience.

Developmental Goals for Sophomores, Juniors, and Seniors

As is mentioned in Chapter 6, there are many theories that explore the development of young adults through the college years. There are different stages of development in many different areas, but all lead to a more mature and functioning adult who is ready to step into the world in many roles, such as a leader, an employee, a community member, or a parent. Here at the University of California at Santa Barbara, our academic, career, and personal counselors got together and outlined a general set of guidelines for development during each of the four years of college, with attention to the areas of academics, personal, social, and career development. It has been edited to be appropriate for almost any college or university experience. You will want to explore this plan of action and see how and where your own insights from the prior exercise might fit in.

A Plan of Action

Each year of your career in college will be marked by challenges and opportunities as you learn more about yourself and make choices about your future. The keys to success are planning ahead, using your time well, taking advantage of campus and community resources, and being proactive. Every student's experience is different, but the plan of action in Table 9.1 should help you make your way toward the person you would like to be in four years.

Table 9.1 Overview of Appropriate Goals by Class Level

Freshmen (Exploring)	Sophomore (Defining)	Junior (Researching)	Senior (Implementing)
Academics **Explore the University** • Read the general catalog and other campus materials • See an academic advisor • Meet many professors and go to office hours • Attend workshops on study skills, test taking, time management, etc. • Develop and hone your academic success skills • Explore general education requirements and electives to explore your interests • Enroll in freshman seminars • Explore the honors programs	*Academics* **Gain Specific Information** • Seek academic advice from teaching assistants, professors, and advisors • Talk to many professors about academic and career goals • Establish a personal GPA goal • Choose a major and talk with people in your major • See a career advisor • Develop an academic plan with an academic advisor • Explore study abroad programs to become eligible • Explore summer school and summer internships	*Academics* **Make Initial Choices** • Take mock GRE, MCAT, or LSAT exams • Attend seminars/conferences that relate to major • Request a junior progress report from your college • Find an academic mentor • Participate in a faculty research project • Apply for internships • Participate in study abroad or Washington, D.C., internship programs • Explore summer school and summer internships	*Academics* **Long-Term Decisions** • Prepare grad school applications • Apply for awards • Present at scholarly meetings • Do a senior thesis project • Develop an independent study project or a directed reading with a professor • Request a senior progress check • Investigate senior honors program or seminars • Take a graduate course • Attend a national conference in your field
Personal **Self-Understanding** • Develop a group of friends • Take a personality test (e.g., Myers-Briggs) • Do values clarification exercises • Explore individual counseling • Identify fears of college life • Redefine your relationship with family	*Personal* **Explore New Roles** • Learn about cultural diversity through events; join a counseling growth group • Find a mentor who can offer support	*Personal* **Risk Personal Openness** • Seek out sources of support • Help others with their problems • Continue discussions with a mentor • Test ideas through discussion groups • Disagree with an authority	*Personal* **Make Commitments** • Prepare for your chosen lifestyle • Attend stress workshops • Talk about your first year out of school • Make a list of your firm decisions • Write down three life goals

Social
Initiate Relationships
- Join residence hall government or committees
- Join an activity, club, or organization
- Make summer travel plans; nurture hobbies
- Develop a peer group
- Seek out volunteer opportunities

Social
Increase Involvement
- Work on a project for a club/organization
- Serve on student committees
- Volunteer in the community
- Join intramural sports teams
- Attend campus events (e.g., films, lectures, performances)

Social
Exercise New Skills
- Start a small business
- Get involved in student government
- Apply for a peer advisor position with the residence halls, colleges, or other campus departments
- Volunteer in the community
- Mentor younger students

Social
Leadership
- Lead a group or club
- Supervise a few student projects
- Join a professional organization
- Tutor high school students
- Take leadership classes and workshops
- Join a public speaking club

Career
Explore Career Areas
- Attend a Choosing a Major workshop
- Talk with parents, friends, professors, and career advisors
- Do career testing by trying out jobs through volunteering
- Identify the following: past accomplishments, skills and abilities, hobbies, personality style, career values
- Explore summer internships

Career
Collect More Information
- Read about careers
- Talk with professionals in several careers (do an information interview)
- Make short-term goals
- Look for a summer internship
- Volunteer to "shadow" a professional for a day
- Talk with career advisors; explore career resources such as workshops, Internet sites
- Attend career workshops

Career
Increase Experience
- Find interesting internships
- Make tentative career choices
- Attend grad school or career fairs
- Attend resume writing workshops
- Do more information interviews
- Develop awareness of career options in many areas
- Talk with a career advisor
- Take career preparation courses or workshops

Career
First Career Choice
- Attend workshops on: job searches, interviewing, recruiting, mock interviews, resume writing, applying to grad school, etc.
- Establish life goals
- Develop a contact list
- Interview for jobs
- Develop a budget for job or grad school
- Check job listings

> ## Might I Suggest...
>
> Review Table 9.1 often and use it to guide you during each of your years at the university. Highlight areas in which you feel you need to focus and set specific goals for doing so. Seek advice from advisors and counselors when you have questions or need support and to help you customize this plan for your campus.

Creating and Achieving Goals

Most people would agree that setting and achieving goals is a way to create success. Goal setting is a way for a person to clearly state what she or he hopes to achieve; it creates a point toward which to head and inevitably guides thoughts, actions, and behaviors. However, goal setting can be a bit more complex than some people might think. It is easy to say, "I'll have a 4.0 GPA," but this statement lacks many things that are essential to good goal setting and the ultimate success of achieving them.

SMART Goals

One technique that is espoused by many is known as the SMART goal technique. According to Dr. Cherie Carter-Scott (2000) from her book *If Success Is a Game, These Are the Rules,* the SMART technique states that goals should have the following five qualities: Specific, Measurable, Action-oriented, Realistic, and Timely.

Specific

The goal needs to be very specific so that it is clearly defined and achievable. For example, "I'll have a 4.0 GPA" is a bit general. The goal "I will earn straight A's in the four classes I am taking spring term" is much more specific. Another general goal might be phrased as "I'll be thinner by summer." Again, this is too general—what does thinner mean? When, exactly, is summer? A specific goal would be "I will lose a half-inch each from my waist, hips, and thighs by the end of finals week." Another example of a general goal might be "I will get involved on campus my sophomore year." A better goal would be "During the fall term, I will attend three club meetings and join the one I like the most." This is much more specific, and it will be easier to recognize whether you are on track. Try to include information on who, what, where, how, and why.

Measurable

This quality also has to do with specificity and reflects how you would know whether you had achieved the goal or not. The goal "I will feel better about school" is not measurable. By what criteria can you measure that? You need to set goals that have some kind of measurable benchmark. These might be inherently available in the goal (e.g., GPA points, pounds, inches), or you might have to create a benchmark, such as a scale of 1 to 10. For example, "On a scale of 1 to 10, I'm currently at a 3 in terms of liking my college experience. I would like to increase that to at least a 6 by June."

Action-Oriented

This is the quality that empowers you to be in control. You will want to set goals that allow you to take some specific actions to achieve them. The goal "I want to be liked by more people" is not action-oriented; it is based on the actions of others. However, the goal "I will meet at least ten new people by the end of the term" is action-oriented, as is the goal "I will ask roommates how I could be a better person to live with." You want your goals to have some action in them so that you can be proactive in achieving them. This is especially important to remember in relationships. You cannot control the behavior of others, so having a goal of getting more flowers from your boyfriend is not a good idea. You certainly can set a goal for telling him that flowers are important to you and for requesting that he give you flowers more often. You can even have a goal regarding how you will handle the situation if he does not honor your request. These are all the things for which you can control the action.

Realistic

It's very important that goals be realistic; otherwise, you set yourself up for failure. While you might wish to lose twenty pounds in two weeks, this is not a realistic goal. Neither is earning straight A's the next term if you are currently flunking your classes. You can certainly improve and bring your GPA up, but it may not be realistic to expect perfect grades if you have not mastered average grades yet. You have to be able to envision yourself accomplishing the goal and believing that you can—otherwise, you won't.

Timely

Each goal needs to have a target date for completion; otherwise, it is too easy to put it off. It's important to get specific about when you will accomplish something because this holds you accountable for taking action. However, it's important to be realistic about the time frame too—too far away will not be very motivating, and too close can be discouraging.

Once you have a clear goal that has all of the SMART qualities, you will want to break each goal into smaller steps that will lead to the achievement of that goal. Each smaller step should also have a specific deadline, and they should lead to accomplishing the SMART goal by its stated time frame. Table 9.2 shows examples of smaller steps for some of the goals stated above.

Obstacles to Success

Setting goals can be fairly easy, but achieving them can be another matter. If achieving goals were easy, then everyone would have exactly what they want. People could set goals and then just achieve them—there would be no disappointments or unhappy students on campuses. Unfortunately, the best intentions

Table 9.2 Sample of Goals Written as SMART Goals with Specific Steps

General Goal:
To be more involved

SMART Goal:
During my second year, I will attend three club meetings and join the club I like the most.

Specific Steps:
- I will get a list of all of the clubs and organizations at the university. By Oct. 1.
- I will review the list and select five that sound interesting to me. By Oct. 15.
- I will contact officers for those five clubs and find out more about the organization, including when they meet. By Nov. 1.
- I will select the three that sound the most interesting and attend their next meeting. By Dec. 1.
- If I need to, I will attend a second meeting. By Feb. 1 (earlier if finals and break do not interfere).
- I will officially join the organization of my choice and make a commitment to attend at least two meetings per month. By Feb. 15.

General Goal:
To do better academically

SMART Goal:
I will earn straight A's in the four classes I am taking spring term.

Specific Steps:
- I will review my previous term's grades and assignments so that I can see what I did wrong last term. By Jan. 10.
- I will meet with an academic skills advisor to create a plan for improvement. By Jan. 15.
- Every other week, I will attend office hours for each of my classes to ensure that I am on track. By Jan. 15, Feb. 1, Feb. 15, Mar. 1, Mar. 15, April 1.
- Each week, I will use the scheduling grid and assignment planner to ensure that I have made accurate time to finish all of my studying. Will review every Sunday.
- I will start each paper as soon as it is given to me and do no fewer than three drafts before handing them in. TBA.
- If I am struggling, I will hire a tutor to work with me until I feel more confident. As needed.

General Goal:
To get along better with roommates

SMART Goal:
This term, I will improve my relationship with roommates so that my enjoyment of my living situation goes from a 3 to at least a 7 (on a scale of 1–10).

Specific Steps:
- I will read over the roommate handbook provided by our housing department. By Sept. 15.
- I will meet with my resident advisor to get suggestions about how to improve our living situation. By Sept. 15.
- I will go to lunch with each of my roommates (one-on-one) and ask them how they think we can make our situation better. I will also share my request to have them not eat my food without asking and to use earphones for music after 11 P.M. on weeknights. By Oct. 15.
- On the basis of the previous meetings, I will set specific goals to improve in the areas determined. By Nov. 1.
- I will do at least one social thing with my roommates every week.
- I will meet with my roommates again to see how things are coming along. By Jan. 1 and adjust accordingly.

are not always carried out easily. Most students who are doing poorly genuinely want to earn better grades, and they may set SMART goals to help them do better. However, sometimes, in trying to achieve your goals, you might find that you have some obstacles in your way. These might be unforeseen challenges, such as becoming sick with mononucleosis or discovering that you have no talent for physics. If you are knocked off track by an unforeseen situation, such as becoming ill, you might have to adjust your timeline accordingly. You want to be reasonable with yourself and know when flexibility is appropriate.

In the case of not being good at physics, that might not be something you can change. There are certain things you can control, such as how much time you devote to studying and using resources like office hours and tutoring groups. But if after your best effort, physics continues to be a challenge, you might need to rethink your dream of being an astrophysicist. All the goals in the world cannot always solve a situation, and it's prudent to know when to move on and set different goals.

Other obstacles might be more emotional, such as realizing that you are majoring in something only to please your parents but that you have no real interest in it. Another common problem is setting a goal of a certain career because it is pays well. Often, if we set goals to please others in some way, we might not have the personal motivation to succeed. People often set goals because they feel that they should—the "shoulds" frequently undermine people's success because, without the personal motivation, the difficult or challenging circumstances can stop someone's forward movement. If you discover that you are not making progress on a goal, look at whether it is something *you* really want in your heart of hearts. If not, look at why you think you should have that goal. Has someone made a specific request of you, such as parents who have told that you must

Tasha's Story

Tasha is a junior who wanted to lose weight to be thinner but then found herself unmotivated to accomplish this no matter how many goals she set. She beat herself up emotionally and then set new goals, which she did not accomplish. This went on for months, and finally, Tasha decided to work with a counselor about it. Over a few sessions, she discovered that growing up, she had overheard her brother and his friends talking about how great certain women's bodies were and that they wanted to have sex with these women. She realized that part of her didn't want to lose weight because she didn't want guys to just want to have sex with her and not care about her for herself. Meanwhile, another part really did want to lose the weight because she knew it was healthier and that she would feel better. So there were two parts of her that were in conflict about the goal, and this prevented her from achieving it. She was able to work through this, and then she was able to lose weight and get in shape with confidence.

major in the sciences? Or have you assumed that you should for some reason, such as thinking you will be happier if you have a job that would allow you to afford a sporty car. If you can identity why you set that goal in the first place, it can help you to evaluate whether or not you want to keep the goal. If you decide to keep it, you will need to find your own personal reasons for wanting that goal so that you have the motivation to succeed.

You might even discover some hidden obstacle that you didn't know was there, such as an internal emotional conflict that you were not aware existed. Sometimes we discover that we have more complex emotions at work underneath the experiences, ones that might have to do with our past and might require meeting with a professional counselor to work through.

Using Resources and Seeking Support

To overcome these obstacles, it is important to utilize all the campus resources available to you. You are already paying for them in your tuition, and they are there for your benefit. As was mentioned earlier, many of the staff and faculty on your campus have years of training and experience in helping students be successful. While you can certainly go it alone, that's not the necessarily the best use of your time and energy, not to mention your tuition. You don't win any prizes for suffering through challenges alone—the prize comes in achieving the goal, whether you needed support or not. So use your resources with abandon. These resources include workshops, educational programs, one-on-one advising, courses, and websites. If you don't find exactly what you need, don't hesitate to look beyond your specific campus to another nearby or other businesses and services, both local and web-based. There are also many great books available on topics that affect college students. Check out your campus bookstore regularly for possibilities, as well as local and web-based bookstores.

Think about it this way: Everyone has the ability to cut their own hair—all they need is a pair of scissors, and they can snip away. But most people recognize that there is more to a good haircut than simply cutting hair with scissors. With this is mind, they hire a professional, someone who is trained in cutting hair and who knows how hair lies and how best to cut different types of hair. Think of the services on your campus as a "success salon" and the staff and faculty as trained professionals who know useful tricks and strategies to turn your college experience into the vision of which you have dreamed.

In addition to utilizing the services provided at your campus, it's always a good idea to also have a support team in place. The purpose of a support team is to help you achieve your goals, especially when you hit an obstacle. They are people who either can give you specific assistance or are there to encourage you when the going gets a little rough. These should be people whom you can count on and whom you trust. Sometimes people are automatically on your support team; for example, most academic advisors can be counted on for giving you sound and accurate advice that would lead you to successful completion of your college degree. Others might need to be asked or informed that you would like them on your team. It's always a good idea to tell someone what kind of support you would like from him or her; this gives you can a much better chance of getting exactly what you need when you need it. Your request might go something like this: "I'm calling because you have always been really helpful to me in the past. Right now, I am working on a specific goal, and I'd like your help. The goal is (<u>fill in here</u>), and what I'd like from you is (<u>fill in here</u>)." Then ask for what you would like, whether it is specific advice, to listen to you vent when something is hard, to remind you of your strengths and that you can do it, to give you brutally honest feedback, and so on. A good support team for a college student would include family members, friends (both at home and at school), counselors, advisors, mentors, and allies.

Mentors and allies are very important. A *mentor* is someone who has a bit more experience than you in the particular area on which you are focusing. She or he should have achieved some level of success that you are hoping to emulate. This mentor will share his or her own story with you and can provide you with advice about how to achieve your goal. You can have different mentors for different parts of your life, and they should change with time as you achieve a certain level of success and need a new mentor for the next level you wish to achieve. Look for people who could serve as mentors to you and then approach them. Most people are quite flattered to be told that they are looked up to and to be asked to mentor someone. If they do not have the time to serve as a mentor, they might be able to connect you other people who might be available.

Allies are different from mentors in that allies do not need to have achieved anything in the area in which you have set goals. The only thing they need to do is to care about you and believe in your ability to achieve your goals. Allies are like cheerleaders—when the going gets rough, they enthusiastically remind you that you said you wanted this goal and that you absolutely can achieve it. You can never have too many allies, but be sure that they are on board for believing in you for that particular goal. A person who is a strong ally in supporting your goal to get good grades might not be the best ally for career planning if this person really doesn't want you to move across the country. His or her personal preferences might get in the way of supporting you completely. So choose you allies carefully, be explicit about what you want them to support you on, and even give them guidance about how best to support you when the going gets rough.

What This Means to You

It is ultimately *your* responsibility to make the most of your university experience. You need to ensure that you are not only making progress toward your degree, but also preparing for your life after college. There is no prescription for how this should look, which gives you a lot of freedom for designing your college years in ways that you both enjoy and get the most from. Be actively engaged in the process. Seek advice from faculty and staff, use campus resources and services, learn from your mistakes, set goals, and meet them.

Might I Suggest...

Attending a premier research university in the United States is an amazing opportunity. You are one of a small group of lucky individuals who get to live and learn in this special environment. Your college degree can, and should, be more than satisfying your requirements and being handed your diploma. It's a time to discover who you are, what you value, and what you are meant to contribute to this world. These answers might come easily for some of you, but most of you will need to explore and experiment to gain more clarity. As you progress through college, you will learn and grow in ways that will shape your sense of yourself and your future. Be open to this process and embrace it fully. Set goals and make plans, but also be flexible enough to change them as new experiences influence your path. Finally, be proactive about making your university years all that you had hoped for and more.

Chapter Summary

In this chapter, the following topics were discussed:

- The importance of reflection

- Developmental goals for sophomores, juniors, and seniors
  - A plan of action

- Creating and achieving goals
  - SMART goals
  - Obstacles to success
  - Using resources and seeking support

Reflections and Exercises

1. Making SMART Goals

Using the SMART technique described in this chapter, set some goals for your next term or next year of college. Make sure they have all of the SMART elements and then add in the smaller steps that will help you accomplish each one. Some areas to consider include the following:

- Academic performance
- Interacting with faculty
- Selecting a major
- Utilizing campus services
- Exploring career options

- Getting involved
- Becoming healthy and fit
- Building positive friendships
- Increasing independence from family
- Developing a spiritual practice
- Developing cultural competence

General Goal:	General Goal:	General Goal:
SMART Goal:	SMART Goal:	SMART Goal:
Specific Steps:	Specific Steps:	Specific Steps:

2. Making the Most of Your Education

Take a few moments to answer the following questions:

If you could make a difference in the world, what would you like to do?

What issues or values are most important to you?

How can you take what you just wrote and incorporate it into your college education?

Are there ways in which you can begin to work on these dreams now?

In addition to earning your degree, how would you like to your education to serve your family?

How would you like your education to serve your community?

How would you like your education to serve your state, your country, and your planet?

If you have ideas but are not sure how to make them possible, take this list and discuss it with a career advisor. She or he can most likely help you find creative ways to begin working on these dreams now.

Appendix A

Carnegie Classification of Universities and AAU Membership

In the United States, the Carnegie Foundation classifies all institutions of higher education for the Advancement of Teaching. They use size, the amount of federal funding received, and the number of doctoral degrees awarded per year to classify all universities as public or private, and "intensive" versus "extensive." All private universities are not-for-profit institutions unless otherwise specified. The list below represents their classifications of universities in 2000. For a more current listing, visit their website at www.carnegiefoundation.org.

Universities that are members of the Association of American Universities (AAU) are marked with an asterisk (*). A current listing of members in the Association of American Universities is available on-line at www.aau.edu.

State	Public	Private	Extensive	Intensive
ALABAMA				
Alabama Agricultural and Mechanical University	X			X
Auburn University	X		X	
University of Alabama	X		X	
University of Alabama at Birmingham	X		X	
University of Alabama in Huntsville	X			X
University of South Alabama	X			X
ALASKA				
University of Alaska at Fairbanks	X			X
ARIZONA				
Arizona State University, Main Campus	X		X	

State	Public	Private	Extensive	Intensive
ARIZONA (continued)				
Northern Arizona University	X			X
University of Arizona*	X		X	
ARKANSAS				
University of Arkansas, Main Campus	X		X	
University of Arkansas at Little Rock	X			X
CALIFORNIA				
Biola University		X		X
California Institute of Technology*		X	X	
Claremont Graduate University		X	X	
Loma Linda University		X		X
Pepperdine University		X		X
San Diego State University	X			X
Stanford University*		X	X	
United States International University		X		X
University of California at Berkeley*	X		X	
University of California at Davis*	X		X	
University of California at Irvine*	X		X	
University of California at Los Angeles*	X		X	
University of California at Riverside	X		X	
University of California at San Diego*	X		X	
University of California at San Francisco	X			X
University of California at Santa Barbara*	X		X	
University of California at Santa Cruz	X		X	
University of Southern California*		X	X	
University of La Verne		X		X
University of San Diego		X		X
University of San Francisco		X		X
University of the Pacific		X		X
COLORADO				
Colorado State University	X		X	
University of Colorado at Boulder*	X		X	
University of Colorado at Denver	X			X

State	Public	Private	Extensive	Intensive
COLORADO (continued)				
University of Denver		X	X	
University of Northern Colorado	X			X
CONNECTICUT				
University of Bridgeport		X		X
University of Connecticut	X		X	
University of Hartford		X		X
Yale University*		X	X	
DELAWARE				
University of Delaware	X		X	
Wilmington College		X		X
DISTRICT OF COLUMBIA				
American University		X	X	
Catholic University of America		X	X	
George Washington University		X	X	
Georgetown University		X	X	
Howard University		X	X	
FLORIDA				
Florida Atlantic University	X			X
Florida Institute of Technology		X		X
Florida International University	X		X	
Florida State University	X		X	
Nova Southeastern University		X		X
University of Central Florida	X			X
University of Florida*	X		X	
University of Miami		X	X	
University of Sarasota (for profit)		X		X
University of South Florida	X		X	
GEORGIA				
Clark Atlanta University		X		X
Emory University*		X	X	

State	Public	Private	Extensive	Intensive
GEORGIA (continued)				
Georgia Institute of Technology	X		X	
Georgia State University	X		X	
University of Georgia	X		X	
HAWAII				
University of Hawaii at Manoa	X		X	
IDAHO				
Idaho State University	X			X
University of Idaho	X		X	
ILLINOIS				
DePaul University		X		X
Illinois Institute of Technology		X		X
Illinois State University	X			X
Loyola University of Chicago		X	X	
National-Louis University		X		X
Northern Illinois University	X		X	
Northwestern University*		X	X	
Southern Illinois University at Carbondale	X		X	
University of Chicago*		X	X	
University of Illinois at Chicago	X		X	
University of Illinois at Urbana-Champaign*	X		X	
INDIANA				
Ball State University	X			X
Indiana State University	X			X
Indiana University at Bloomington*	X		X	
Indiana University-Purdue University Indianapolis	X			X
Purdue University, Main Campus*	X		X	
University of Notre Dame		X	X	
IOWA				
Iowa State University*	X		X	
University of Iowa*	X		X	

State	Public	Private	Extensive	Intensive
KANSAS				
Kansas State University	X		X	
University of Kansas, Main Campus*	X		X	
Wichita State University	X			X
KENTUCKY				
University of Kentucky	X		X	
University of Louisville	X		X	
LOUISIANA				
Louisiana State University and Agricultural and Mechanical College	X		X	
Louisiana Tech University	X			X
Tulane University*		X	X	
University of Louisiana at Lafayette	X			X
University of New Orleans	X			X
MAINE				
University of Maine	X		X	
MARYLAND				
John Hopkins University*		X	X	
University of Maryland at Baltimore	X			X
University of Maryland Baltimore County	X		X	
University of Maryland at College Park*	X		X	
MASSACHUSETTS				
Boston College		X	X	
Boston University		X	X	
Brandeis University*		X	X	
Clark University		X		X
Harvard University*		X	X	
Massachusetts Institute of Technology*		X	X	
Northeastern University		X	X	

State	Public	Private	Extensive	Intensive
MASSACHUSETTS (continued)				
Tufts University		X	X	
University of Massachusetts	X		X	
University of Massachusetts at Boston	X			X
University of Massachusetts at Lowell	X			X
Worcester Polytechnic Institute		X		X
MICHIGAN				
Andrews University		X		X
Central Michigan University	X			X
Michigan State University*	X		X	
Michigan Technological University	X			X
Oakland University	X			X
University of Michigan at Ann Arbor*	X		X	
Wayne State University	X		X	
Western Michigan University	X		X	
MINNESOTA				
Mayo Foundation-Mayo Graduate School		X		X
University of Minnesota at Twin Cities*	X		X	
University of Saint Thomas		X		X
Walden University (for profit)		X		X
MISSISSIPPI				
Jackson State University	X			X
Mississippi State University	X		X	
University of Mississippi	X		X	
University of Southern Mississippi	X		X	
MISSOURI				
Saint Louis University		X	X	
University of Missouri at Columbia*	X		X	
University of Missouri at Kansas City	X			X
University of Missouri at Rolla	X			X
University of Missouri at Saint Louis	X			X
Washington University*		X	X	

State	Public	Private	Extensive	Intensive
MONTANA				
Montana State University at Bozeman	X			X
University of Montana	X			X
NEBRASKA				
University of Nebraska at Lincoln*	X		X	
NEVADA				
University of Nevada at Las Vegas	X			X
University of Nevada at Reno	X		X	
NEW HAMPSHIRE				
Antioch New England Graduate School		X		X
Dartmouth College		X		X
University of New Hampshire	X		X	
NEW JERSEY				
New Jersey Institute of Technology	X			X
Princeton University*		X	X	
Rutgers (State University of New Jersey at New Brunswick)*	X		X	
Rutgers (State University of New Jersey at Newark)	X			X
Seton Hall University		X		X
Stevens Institute of Technology		X		X
NEW MEXICO				
New Mexico Institute of Mining and Technology	X			X
New Mexico State University, Main Campus	X		X	
University of New Mexico, Main Campus	X		X	
NEW YORK				
Adelphi University		X		X
City University of New York Graduate Center	X		X	
Clarkson University		X		X

State	Public	Private	Extensive	Intensive
NEW YORK (continued)				
Columbia University in the City of New York*		X	X	
Cornell University*		X	X	
Fordham University		X	X	
Hofstra University		X		X
New School University		X		X
New York University*		X	X	
Pace University New York Campus		X		X
Polytechnic University		X		X
Rensselaer Polytechnic Institute		X	X	
Rockefeller University		X		X
Saint John's University		X		X
State University of New York at Albany	X		X	
State University of New York at Binghamton	X		X	
State University of New York at Buffalo*	X		X	
State University of New York College of Environmental Science and Forestry	X			X
State University of New York at Stony Brook*	X		X	
Syracuse University*		X	X	
Teachers College, Columbia University		X	X	
University of Rochester*		X	X	
Yeshiva University		X	X	
NORTH CAROLINA				
Duke University*		X	X	
East Carolina University	X			X
North Carolina State University	X		X	
University of North Carolina at Chapel Hill*	X		X	
University of North Carolina at Greensboro	X			X
Wake Forest University		X		X
NORTH DAKOTA				
North Dakota State University, Main Campus	X			X
University of North Dakota, Main Campus	X			X

State	Public	Private	Extensive	Intensive
OHIO				
Bowling Green State University	X			X
Case Western Reserve University*		X		X
Cleveland State University	X		X	
Kent State University, Main Campus	X		X	
Miami University	X			X
Ohio State University, Main Campus*	X		X	
Ohio University, Main Campus	X		X	
Union Institute		X		X
University of Akron, Main Campus	X			X
University of Cincinnati, Main Campus	X		X	
University of Dayton		X		X
University of Toledo	X		X	
Wright State University, Main Campus	X			X
OKLAHOMA				
Oklahoma State University, Main Campus	X		X	
University of Oklahoma, Norman Campus	X		X	
University of Tulsa		X		X
OREGON				
Oregon State University	X		X	
Portland State University	X			X
University of Oregon*	X		X	
PENNSYLVANIA				
Carnegie Mellon University*		X	X	
Drexel University		X		X
Duquesne University		X		X
Indiana University of Pennsylvania	X			X
Lehigh University		X	X	
MCP Hahnemann University		X		X
Pennsylvania State University at University Park*	X		X	

State	Public	Private	Extensive	Intensive
PENNSYLVANIA (continued)				
Temple University	X		X	
University of Pennsylvania*		X	X	
University of Pittsburgh, Pittsburgh Campus*	X		X	
Widener University		X		X
RHODE ISLAND				
Brown University*		X	X	
University of Rhode Island	X		X	
SOUTH CAROLINA				
Clemson University	X		X	
University of South Carolina at Columbia	X		X	
South Carolina State University	X			X
SOUTH DAKOTA				
South Dakota State University	X			X
University of South Dakota	X			X
TENNESSEE				
East Tennessee State University	X			X
Middle Tennessee State University	X			X
Tennessee State University	X			X
University of Memphis	X		X	
University of Tennessee at Knoxville	X		X	
Vanderbilt University*		X	X	
TEXAS				
Baylor University		X		X
Rice University*		X	X	
Southern Methodist University		X	X	
Texas A&M University*	X		X	
Texas A&M University at Commerce	X			X
Texas A&M University at Kingsville	X			X

State	Public	Private	Extensive	Intensive
TEXAS (continued)				
Texas Christian University		X		X
Texas Southern University	X			X
Texas Tech University	X		X	
Texas Woman's University	X			X
University of Houston	X		X	
University of North Texas	X		X	
University of Texas at Arlington	X		X	
University of Texas at Austin	X		X	
University of Texas at Dallas	X			X
University of Texas at El Paso	X			X
UTAH				
Brigham Young University		X	X	
University of Utah	X		X	
Utah State University	X		X	
VERMONT				
University of Vermont	X		X	
VIRGINIA				
College of William and Mary	X			X
George Mason University	X			X
Old Dominion University	X		X	
University of Virginia	X		X	
Virginia Commonwealth University	X		X	
Virginia Polytechnic Institute and State University	X		X	
WASHINGTON				
University of Washington	X		X	
Washington State University	X		X	
WEST VIRGINIA				
West Virginia University	X		X	

State	Public	Private	Extensive	Intensive
WISCONSIN				
Marquette University		X	X	
University of Wisconsin at Madison	X		X	
University of Wisconsin at Milwaukee	X		X	
WYOMING				
University of Wyoming	X		X	
PUERTO RICO				
University of Puerto Rico, Rio Piedras Campus	X			X
CANADA				
McGill University*	These universities are not classified by the Carnegie Foundation but are members of the AAU.			
University of Toronto*				

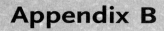

Books and Films on Topics of Diversity

If You Haven't Lived It, Learn about It!

One way to learn about people who are different from yourself is to explore the vast array of human experiences through books, films, and websites as a way to increase your cultural competence. Visit http://success.wadsworth.com/andreatta for an extensive and updated list of books and films on the following experiences:

Books and Films

- African American Experience
- Asian American/Pacific Islander Experience
- Chicano/Latino Experience
- Multicultural and Cross-Cultural Experience
- Native American Experience
- Experiences With Religion and Spirituality
- Women's Experience
- Men's Experience
- Caucasian Experience

Websites

The Internet is an amazing source of information about diversity issues. Check out the following websites to learn more.

- Association of American Colleges and Universities (www.diversityweb.org)
- Anti-Defamation League (www.adl.org)
- Social Justice Resources Center at Virginia Tech (http://edpsychserver.ed.vt.edu/diversity/)
- The Dialogue Consultants (www.dialogue-consultants.com)
- Center for the Study of White American Culture (www.euroamerican.org)
- MultiCultural Education Pavilion (www.edchange.org/multicultural/index.html)
- The National Conference for Community and Justice (www.nccj.org)

- Teaching Tolerance: Pioneering Anti-Bias Education (www.splcenter.org/center/tt/teach.jsp)
- Diversity Resources at Wright State University (www.ed.wright.edu/diversity/)
- Our Common Ground at the University of Vermont (www.uvm.edu/ourcommonground/resource.htm)
- Intergroup Relations Center at Arizona State University (www.asu.edu/provost/intergroup/)
- XY: Men, Masculinities, and Gender Politics (http://www.xyonline.net/index.shtml)

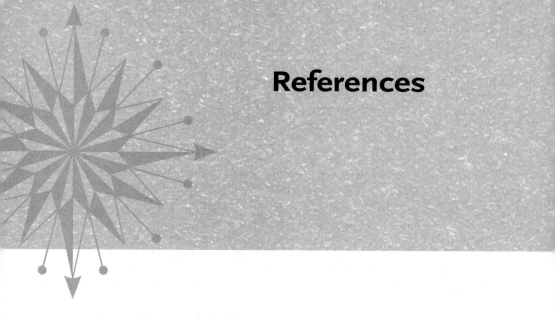

References

Adams, M., Bell, L. A., & Griffin, P. (1997). *Teaching for diversity and social justice: A sourcebook*. New York: Routledge.

American Association of Collegiate Registrars and Admissions Counselors (2004). *The college transfer student in America: The forgotten student*. Washington, DC: Author.

American Psychological Association (2001). *Publication manual of the American Psychological Association* (5th ed.). Washington, DC: Author.

American Psychological Association (2004). Retrieved November, 8, 2004, from http://www.apa.org/

American Sociological Association (2004). *Careers in sociology*, (5th ed.). Washington, DC: Author.

Anderson, L. (1990). *The revised Bloom's taxonomy*. Retrieved June 30, 2004, from http://rite.ed.qut.edu.au/oz-teachernet/index.php?module=ContentExpress&func=display&ceid=29

Andreatta, B. J. (1998). The effects of social and academic integration on the retention of first year university students: A quantitative and qualitative study. (Doctoral dissertation, University of California at Santa Barbara, 1998). *Dissertation Abstracts International, 59*(07), 2375.

Association of American Universities (2004). *AAU membership: Public and private*. Retrieved May 4, 2004, from: http://www.aau.edu/aau/pubprivate.html

Astin, A. W., & Astin, H. S. (2003). *Spirituality in college students: Preliminary findings from a national study*. Los Angeles: Higher Education Research Institute.

Atkinson, D. R., Morton, G., & Sue, D. W. (1998). *Counseling American minorities*. Boston: McGraw-Hill.

Bloom, B. S. (Ed.) (1956). *Taxonomy of educational objectives: The classification of educational goals: Handbook I, cognitive domain*. New York: Longmans, Green.

Bloom, M.V. (1980). *Adolescent-parental separation*. New York: Gardner Press.

Brody, J. (2003, August 26). Hello to college joys: Keep stress off campus. *The New York Times*, p. F7.

Budke, K. (2003). *The effects of alcohol*. Retrieved March 15, 2004, from University of Iowa, Student Health website: http://www.uiowa.edu/~shs/substance.htm

Carnegie Foundation for the Advancement of Teaching (2000). *Carnegie classification of institutions of higher education*. Retrieved January 21, 2004, from http://www.carnegiefoundation.org/Classification/index.htm

Carter-Scott, C. (2000). *If success is a game, these are the rules: Ten rules for a fulfilling life*. New York: Random House.

Centers for Disease Control (1995). *National college health risk behavior survey*. Retrieved January 18, 2004, from: http://www.cdc.gov/HealthyYouth/YRBS/previous_results/college1997.htm

Chickering, A. W. & Reiser, L. (1993). *Education and identity*. San Francisco: Jossey-Bass.

Compton, H. T. & Tait, F. E. (1994). The liberal arts and critical thinking. In J. Gardner & A. Jewler (Eds.). *Your college experience: Strategies for success* (1st ed.). Belmont, CA: Wadsworth.

Core Institute (2003). *Core alcohol and drug survey*. Carbondale, IL: Southern Illinois University.

Cornell Advocates for Rape Education (2004). *What to do if you are sexually assaulted*. Retrieved November 7, 2004, from Cornell University, Cornell Advocates for Rape Education website: http://www.care.cornell.edu/help.html

Daves-Rougeaux, D. (2004, January 29). *The political development of college students*. Lecture presented at Interdisciplinary 20, University of California, Santa Barbara.

Facts on Tap (2004). *Blood alcohol and you: Behavior by the numbers*. Retrieved November 7, 2004, from: http://www.factsontap.org/yourbody/Yourbody.htm

Family Educational Rights and Privacy Act (1974). Retrieved October 19, 2004, from http://www.ed.gov/policy/gen/guid/fpco/ferpa/index.html

Felder, R. M., & Silverman, L. K. (1988). Learning and teaching styles in engineering education. *Engineering Education* 78(7), 674-681.

Felder, R. M., & Soloman, B. A. (2004). *Index of learning styles questionnaire*. Retrieved August 10, 2004, from North Carolina State University website: http://ncsu.edu/felder-public/ILSdir/styles.htm

Flacks, R., & Thomas, S. (1998, November 27). Among affluent students, a culture of disengagement. *The Chronicle of Higher Education, 45*(14), A48.

Florio, M., Mudd, D., Peosay, T., Peosay, S. (Producers), & Peosay, T. (Director). (2002). *Tibet: Cry of the snow lion* [Motion Picture]. (Available from New Yorker Films, 85 Fifth Avenue, 11th Floor, New York, NY 10003).

Fowler, J. (1981). *Stages of faith: the psychology of human development and the quest for meaning*. New York: Harper & Row.

Frezza, M., di Padova, C., Pozzato, G., Terpin, M., Baraona, E. & Lieber, C. S. et al. (1990). High blood alcohol levels in women: The role of decreased gastric alcohol dehydrogenase activity and first-pass metabolism. *New England Journal of Medicine, 322,* 95-99.

Glenn, C., Miller, R. K., Webb, S. S., Gray, L., & Hodges, J. C. (2004). *Hodges' Harbrace handbook* (15th ed.). Boston: Thomson Wadsworth.

Grasha, A. (2004). *Teaching styles.* Retrieved December 29, 2004, from Indiana State University, Center for Teaching & Learning website: http://web.indstate.edu/ctl/styles/tstyle.html

Griffin, P., & Harro, B. (1982). Action continuum. In M. Adams, L. Bell, & P. Griffin (Eds.). *Teaching for diversity and social justice: A sourcebook* (Appendix 6C). New York: Routledge.

Hardiman, R., & Jackson, B. W. (1997). Conceptual foundations for social justice courses. In M. Adams, L. A. Bell, & P. Griffin (Eds.). *Teaching for diversity and social justice: A sourcebook* (pp. 20-23). New York: Routledge.

Harvard School of Public Health (2004). *About CAS.* Retrieved November 8, 2004, from Harvard School of Public Health, College Alcohol Study website: http://www.hsph.harvard.edu/cas/About

Hawking, S. (2004). *A brief history of mine.* Retrieved October 10, 2003, from http://www.hawking.org.uk/home/hindex.html

Hersey, P., & Blanchard, K. (1993). *Management of organizational behavior: Utilizing human resources* (6th ed.). Englewood Cliffs, NJ: Prentice-Hall.

Higher Education Center for Alcohol and Other Drug Prevention (2004). *What campuses and communities are doing.* Retrieved February 3, 2004 from http://www.edc.org/hec/framework/

Hingson, R. H., Zakocs, R., Kopstein, A., & Wechsler, H. (2002). Magnitude of alcohol-related morbidity, mortality, and alcohol dependence among U.S. college students age 18-24. *Journal of Studies on Alcohol, 63*(2), 136-144.

Horowitz, D. (n.d.). *Academic bill of rights.* Retrieved March 30, 2004, from http://www.studentsforacademicfreedom.org/

Howe, N., & Strauss, W. (2000). *Millennials rising: The next great generation.* New York: Random House.

Huth, E. J. (1994). *Scientific style and format: The Council of Biology manual for writers, editors, and publishers* (6th ed.). Cambridge, United Kingdom: Cambridge University Press.

Kerwin, C., Ponterotto, J. G., Jackson, B. L., & Harris, A. (1993). Racial identity in biracial children: A qualitative investigation. *Journal of Counseling Psychology, 40,* 221-231.

King, T., & Bannon, E. (2002). *At what cost? The price that working students pay for a college education.* Washington, DC: Higher Education Project of the States Public Interest Research Group.

Kinsey, A. C., Pomery, W. B., & Martin C. E. (1948). *Sexual behavior in the human male.* Philadelphia: Saunders.

Klein, F., Sepekoff, B., & Wolf, T. J. (1985). Sexual orientation: A multi-variable dynamic process. *Journal of Homosexuality, 11,* 1-2.

Kouzes, J. M., & Posner, B. Z. (1995). *The leadership challenge* (2nd ed.). San Francisco: Jossey-Bass.

Kouzes, J. M., & Posner, B. Z. (1995). *Student leadership practices inventory: Student workbook*. San Francisco: Jossey-Bass.

Lancaster, L., & Stillman, D. (2002). *When generations collide: How to solve the generational puzzle at work*. New York: Harper Collins.

Lindholm, J. A., Astin, A. W., Sax, L. S., & Korn, W. S. (2002). *The American college teacher: National norms for the 2001-2002 HERI faculty study*. Los Angeles: Higher Education Research Institute.

Marlatt, A. (1999). *Brief alcohol screening and intervention for college students*. New York: Guilford Press.

McCarn, S., & Fassinger, R. (1996). Revisioning sexual minority identity formation: A new model of lesbian identity and its implications for counseling and research. *The Counseling Psychologist, 24* (3), 508-534.

Meredith, G. E, & Schewe, C. D. (2002). *Managing by defining moments: America's seven generational cohorts, their workplace values, and why managers should care*. Indianapolis, IN: Hungry Minds.

Merriam-Webster OnLine Dictionary (2004). Retrieved January 21, 2004, from http://www.m-w.com/

Michel, C. (2004, March 11). *Making the most of your college experience*. Lecture presented at Interdisciplinary 20, University of California, Santa Barbara.

Mohr, J. (2002). An identity perspective on sexual orientation dynamics in psychotherapy. *The Counseling Psychologist, 30*(4), 532-566.

Narcanon (2004). *Cocaine and cocaine addiction information*. Retrieved on November 4, 2004, from http://www.stopaddiction.com/narconon_drugs_cocaine.html

National Center for Education Statistics (2004). *Digest of education statistics, 2002*. Retrieved March 6, 2004, from the United States Department of Education website: http://nces.ed.gov/programs/digest/d02/ch_3.asp

National Institute Against Prejudice and Violence (2004). *The Prejudice Institute factsheets*. Retrieved March 6, 2004, from http://www.prejudiceinstitute.org/factsheets.html

National Institute on Alcohol Abuse and Alcoholism (1995). *Alcohol alert, 29*. Retrieved January 11, 2004 from http://www.niaaa.nih.gov/publications/aa29.htm

National Institute on Alcohol Abuse and Alcoholism (1995). *High-risk drinking in college: What we know and what we need to learn*. Retrieved January 15, 2004, from http://www.collegedrinkingprevention.gov/Reports/Panel01/ExecSum_00.aspx

National Institute on Drug Abuse (2004). *InfoFacts*. Retrieved February 9, 2004, from http://www.nida.nih.gov/Infofax/Infofaxindex.html

Nellie Mae (2001). *2001 credit card usage analysis* Retrieved October 19, 2004, from http://www.nelliemae.com/library/research_9.html

Painter, K. (2004, March 2). Colleges throw a lifeline to students. *USA Today* [Electronic version]. Retrieved March 4, 2004, from http://www.usatoday.com/news/health/2004-03-02-college-mental-health_xhtm.

Pennsylvania State University (2004). *Helping someone who has been raped: A guide for family and friends.* Retrieved November 7, 2004, from Pennsylvania State University, Center for Women Students website: www.sa.psu.edu/cws/images/helping.html

Perry, W. (1970). *Forms of intellectual and ethical development in the college years: A scheme.* New York: Holt, Rinehart, & Winston.

Perry, W. (1981). Cognitive and ethical growth. In A. Chickering & Associates (Eds.). *The modern American college: Responding to the new realities of diverse students and a changing society.* San Francisco: Jossey-Bass.

Pi Tau Sigma (2004). Retrieved November 8, 2004, from http://www.pitausigma.net/

Rankin, S. (1998). *Campus climate for gay, lesbian, bisexual, and transgender people: A national perspective.* New York: The Policy Institute of the National Gay and Lesbian Task Force.

Rowe, W., Bennett, S. K., & Atkinson, D. R. (1994). White racial identity models: A critique and alternative proposal. *Counseling Psychologist 22*(1), 129-146.

Sax, L. J., Keup, J. R., Gilmartin, S. K., Stolzenberg, E. B., & Harper, C. (2002). *Findings from the 2002 administration of Your First College Year (YFCY): National aggregates.* Los Angeles: Higher Education Research Institute.

Schwartz, J., & Kirkham, K. (2000). *Dynamics of oppression* [Handout]. Santa Barbara, CA: National Conference on Community & Justice.

Semester at Sea (2004). Retrieved November 1, 2004, from www.semesteratsea.com

Tinto, V. (1993). *Leaving college: Rethinking the causes and cures of student attrition* (2nd ed.). Chicago: The University of Chicago Press.

Staff of UCSB Counseling & Career Services (2004). A plan of action for UCSB students. In the *2004-06 UCSB Kiosk student handbook.* Retrieved October 19, 2004, from University of California at Santa Barbara, Orientation Programs website: www.kiosk.ucsb.edu

Steptoe/Ridgewood, S. (2003, October 27). Ready, set, relax! *Time,* p. 17.

United Nations (2004). *Cyberschoolbus.* Retrieved October 14, 2004, from http://cyberschoolbus.un.org/discrim/ethnicity1.asp

United States Surgeon General (2004). *HIV/AIDS and adolescents.* Retrieved November 8, 2004, from http://www.surgeongeneral.gov/AIDS/factsheets/adolescents.html

University of Chicago Press (2003). *The Chicago manual of style: The essential guide for writers, editors, and publishers* (15th ed.). Chicago: Author.

University of Colorado at Boulder (2004). *Support for sexual assault victims.* Retrieved July 9, 2004, from the University of Colorado at Boulder, Student Health website: www.colorado.edu/healthcenter/studenthealth/victim/support.html

University of Connecticut (2004). *Alcohol impairment charts for men and women.* Retrieved July 8, 2004, from the University of Connecticut, Party Smart website: www.partysmart.uconn.edu/bac.html

University of Miami (2004). *Helping family or friends with substance abuse problems* Retrieved November 9, 2004, from the University of Miami, PIER 21 website: www.miami.edu/UMH/CDA/UMH_Main/ 0,1770,2406-1; 9485-2;1298-3,00.html

U.S. Population: The basics (2002). Retrieved January 30, 2004, from: www.Ameristat.org/Content/NavigationMenu/Ameristat/Topics1/ Estimates_Projections

The Vaults of Erowid (2004). *Plants and drugs.* Retrieved March 26, 2004, from www.Erowid.org

Winters/Azusa, R. (2004, February 2). Higher learning. *Time,* p. 58.

Worthington, R., Savoy, H., Dillon, F., & Vernaglia, E. (2002). Heterosexual identity development: A multidimensional model of individual and social identity. *The Counseling Psychologist, 30*(4), 496-531.

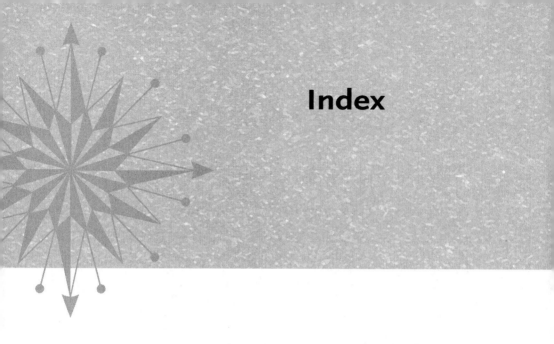

Index